Law and Disorder in the Postcolony

1 (

Edited by **Jean Comaroff and John L. Comaroff**

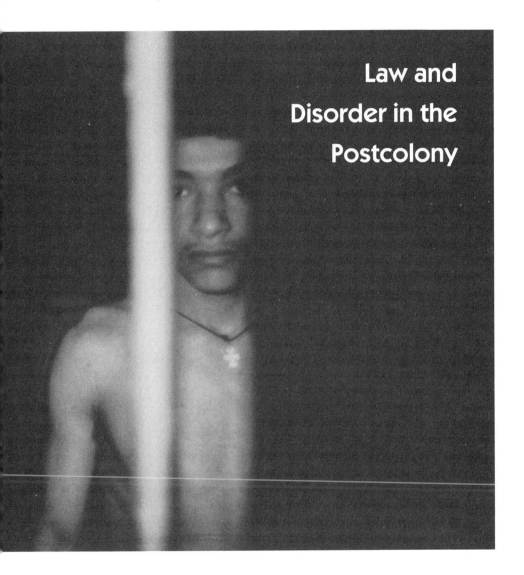

Law and
Disorder in the
Postcolony

The University of Chicago Press

Chicago and London

Jean Comaroff is the Bernard E. and Ellen C. Sunny Distinguished
Service Professor of Anthropology at the University of Chicago and
Honorary Professor at the University of Cape Town. John L.
Comaroff is the Harold H. Swift Distinguished Service Professor of
Anthropology at the University of Chicago, a Senior Research
Fellow at the American Bar Foundation, and Honorary Professor
at the University of Cape Town.

The University of Chicago Press, Chicago 60637
The University of Chicago Press, Ltd., London
© 2006 by The University of Chicago
All rights reserved. Published 2006
Printed in the United States of America

15 14 13 12 11 10 09 08 07 06   5 4 3 2 1

ISBN-13 (cloth): 978-0-226-11408-8
ISBN-10 (cloth): 0-226-11408-2
ISBN-13 (paper): 978-0-226-11409-5
ISBN-10 (paper): 0-226-11409-0

Library of Congress Cataloging-in-Publication Data

Law and disorder in the postcolony / edited by Jean Comaroff
and John L. Comaroff.
     p. cm.
  Includes bibliographical references and index.
  ISBN 0-226-11408-2 (cloth : alk. paper) —
  ISBN 0-226-11409-0 (pbk. : alk. paper)
   1. Developing countries—Social conditions.
 2. Crime—Developing countries. 3. Violence—Developing
countries. 4. Democratization—Developing countries.
5. Postcolonialism. I. Comaroff, Jean. II. Comaroff,
John L., 1945–
HN980.L36 2006
364.9712′4—dc22
                            2006006541

♾ The paper used in this publication meets the
minimum requirements of the American National
Standard for Information Sciences—Permanence of
Paper for Printed Library Materials,
ANSI Z39.48-1992.

Contents

Preface

A PROBLEM, A PRESUMPTION, AND A PARADOX. In that order.

First, the problem. Are postcolonies in Africa, Asia, Europe, and Latin America haunted more by unregulated violence, un/civil warfare, and random terror than are other twenty-first-century nation-states? Are they sinking ever more deeply into maelstroms of disorder? Or does the imagining that they might be doing so mock reality? Is there, in short, anything distinctive about their contemporary predicament, about the kinds of criminality, coercion, corruption, conflict, even chaos often attributed to them? Does the implicit hyphenation on which they are erected—the dis/articulation, that is, between the post and coloniality—refer to a passing condition, an epochal transition, a Rabelaisian liminality? Or does it signal something more permanent: a *longue durée* unfolding, in which the modernist states put in place with "decolonization"—themselves a Weberian ideal type always more idealized than typical, always more the object of aspiration than accomplished fact, even in Europe—can no longer hold in the face of gathering lawlessness, of the privatization of almost everything, of creeping anarchy? The reflex answer to this brace of questions, supplied alike by critical scholars, conservative public intellectuals, and the popular media of the world—which is where the presumption comes in—is yes. Yes, postcolonies are especially, excessively, distinctively violent and disorderly. Yes, they are sinking ever further into a mire of conflict, coercion, and chaos. Yes, this does seem to be a chronic, not a temporary, state of being. The evidence is taken to be, well, self-evident; so much so that little heed has been paid to the possibility that something deeper may be at issue here, something inherent in the unfolding conjuncture everywhere of violence, sovereignty, il/legality, modernity. Of which more in chapter 1.

At the same time, and here is where the paradox appears to lie, many of these very same postcolonies seem to make a fetish of the rule of law, of its language and its practices, its ways and means. Even where they are mocked and mimicked, suspended or sequestered, those ways and means are often central to the politics of everyday engagement, to discourses of authority and citizenship, to the interaction of states and subjects, to the enactments, displacements, and usurpations of power. New constitutions are repeatedly written, appeals to rights repeatedly made, procedural democracies repeatedly reinvented, claims of material and moral inequity repeatedly litigated. And governments, ethnic groups, and coalitions of interest and identity go repeatedly to the judiciary, sometimes against "the market" and sometimes against each other, to settle differences. As we shall see, even the great narratives and epics of the past—colonialism itself, for one—are reargued before bewigged judges in the often tortured argot of torts. All this in spite of the fact that more and more rulers show themselves ready to suspend the rule of law in the name of emergency or exception, to undermine its autonomy, to ignore its sovereignty, to franchise it out, to bend it to their will.

Do these two putative tendencies—the excessive disorderliness of post-colonies on the one hand and their fetishism of the law on the other—describe a concrete reality? Or are they merely figments of fevered, stereotypic imaginations? To the degree that they have empirical valence, are they something new or merely a continuation of things past? And are they, in fact, two sides of a paradox? Or just different aspects of one phenomenon? What, in this respect, may we draw from Walter Benjamin's thesis—recently reworked, in various ways, by the likes of Derrida and Agamben—that violence and the law, the lethal and the legal, are constitutive of one another?[1]

It is this conundrum that brought a diverse coterie of scholars to the Radcliffe Institute for Advanced Study, Harvard University, in May 2003. Their specialist knowledge covered Africa, Latin America, the Middle East, and South and Southeast Asia. But, more important perhaps, their common and convergent interests lay in, among other concerns, theorizing "the" postcolony, that disparate class of polities so often reduced to a definite article by discursive fiat. How *are* we to make sense of, to distinguish, the forms of violence and dis/order commonly said to saturate those polities, plural? Why *does* the law appear to be so widely fetishized in them? And what might either or both of these things, and the relationship between them, have to do with broader, world-historical processes, not least the epochal rise of neoliberalism? Phrased thus, in the interrogative, law and disorder in the postcolony seemed, to this transdisciplinary assortment of academics, eminently worthy of critical attention—and critical to the yet more fundamental task of arriving at an understanding of what "the postcolony" actually *is*. With hindsight, it seems even more crucial.

The conference was facilitated by Katherine Newman, then dean of the Social Sciences at Radcliffe, who invited us to determine its content and to assemble its participants; it was funded by the good graces of the Radcliffe Institute for Advanced Study. The event itself consisted of a number of thematic sessions, at which papers were presented and subjected to the detailed attention of discussants. Those discussants were also the primary voices in a culminating roundtable conversation. Since their insights are echoed in our introduction (chapter 1 below) and in the chapters that follow, we should like to mention them by name: Arjun Appadurai, Homi Bhabha, J. Lorand Matory, Sally Merry, Ann Stoler, and Lisa Wedeen. Adam Ashforth, Fernando Coronil, Sally Falk Moore, Susan Slymovics, Mary Steedley, and Lucie White presented papers and also took an active part in the proceedings. For one or another reason, unfortunately, their essays could not be included here. To all of these people we express our warm appreciation. We also owe a considerable debt of gratitude to Maureen Anderson, our long-term, ever-resourceful research assistant. Apart from everything else she did to abet the realization of this project, she translated Achille Mbembe's chapter from its original French.

We began with a problem, a presumption, and a paradox. Let us close with an assertion. Or, more properly, a provocation.

Postcolonies have become especially critical sites for the production of social theory; social theory sui generis, that is, not merely anthropological theory addressed to the lives and times of those worlds formerly known as "third" or "second." This is why, for the contributors to the present volume, they are such eminently worthy objects of inquiry. This is not just for the obvious liberal humanist reason: that billions of human beings live their lives, and suffer their deaths, deep in the interiors of these polities, at a refractory angle to our television screens and the screaming front pages of the global press. Nor is it merely because their predicaments and ours are much more densely interwoven, much less extricable, than we typically imagine; indeed, the comfortable cleavage between "ours" and "theirs" has a habit of vanishing under scrutiny, notwithstanding the *cordons sanitaire* that histories of violence have forced between different parts of the planet. Neither is it because postcolonies are, with apologies to Agamben, often portrayed as the most exceptional of states. No. The reason that they are indispensable sites for theory production lies in the fact that many of the great historical tsunamis of the twenty-first century appear to be breaking first on their shores—or, if not first, then in their most palpable, most hyperextended form—thence to reverberate around the Northern Hemispheric cosmopoles. Thus, for example, the recession of the managerial, bureaucratic state into governance-by-franchise, and into an institutional nexus for the distribution of public assets into private hands, has proceeded at its most unmediated and unmitigated in many former colonies. So, too, expedited by one or other Washington consensus, have the radical privatization of the means of coercion, from policing and terror through incarceration to war and revolution; the displacement of the political into the realm of the legal, most notably into the interstices between rights and torts; the distillation of social policy, under the aegis of both government and nongovernmental organizations, into discourses of technical necessity; the increasing reduction of culture to intellectual property; the supersession of the Age of Ideology by the Age of ID-ology, in which identity-driven interest—identity defined by culture, confessional or congregational affiliation, race, gender, generation, sexual orientation, whatever—becomes the motor of most collection action. And much else besides.

It is from the perspective of "the" postcolony, then, that understanding the twenty-first century, tout court, might best begin. Decentered estrangement is, finally, the objective of this book. And of the historical anthropology of the present, to which it seeks to make a modest contribution.

Note

1. See Walter Benjamin, "Critique of Violence," in his *Reflections: Essays, Aphorisms, Autobiographical Writings,* ed. Peter Demetz, trans. Edmund Jephcott (New York: Schocken Books, 1978); Jacques Derrida, "Force of Law," in *Acts of Religion,* ed. Gil Anidjar (New York: Routledge, 2002); and Giorgio Agamben, *Homo Sacer: Sovereign Power and Bare Life,* trans. Daniel Heller-Roazen (Stanford, CA: Stanford University Press, 1998).

Law and Disorder in the Postcolony
An Introduction

John L. Comaroff and Jean Comaroff

Notes from the Front

CRIME VS. . . .

Who're the criminals, the gangs or the government?
Did the Capital just happen to have the power to punish men?
MonoPolice manipulate majorities to run with them
So whats the police force but a resource to reinforce the plans of the
    dominant?

I'm haunted by questions, spending time behind bars
Statistics on TV, that concede we're sadistic, deceive me
'cause murder and thievery thrives on all sides of the lines that
    divide class.
I take pepper-spray with a pinch a'ssault and battery and I'm charged to
    step 'n say:
"yo honour, go bother the office of your bosses where the crime starts."

And I ask, while cleaning dirty white collars for a living,
why law suites the raw brutes in board rooms that horde loot?
They set the precedent then send the president to assure you,
his lady, Justice, is blind. But she's got contacts that say too!
The colonists, the capitalists and wordy bright scholars make a killing.
    MARLON BURGESS, hip-hop verses, Cape Town, 15 September 2004

AMONG ALL THE THINGS that have been said about the spread of democracy since the end of the Cold War—and a great deal has been said about it, in every conceivable voice—one thing stands out. It is the claim that democratization has been accompanied, almost everywhere, by a sharp rise in crime and violence (see, e.g., Karstedt, forthcoming; Caldeira 2000: 1): that the latter-day coming of more or less elected, more or less representative political regimes—founded, more or less, on the rule of law—has, ironically, brought with it a rising tide of lawlessness. Or, put another way, that political liberation in postcolonial, posttotalitarian worlds, and the economic liberalization on which it has floated, have both implied, as their dark underside, an ipso facto deregulation of monopolies over the means of legitimate force, of moral orders, of the protection of persons and property. And an unraveling of the fabric of law and order. This may not be all that easy to demonstrate empirically; it depends in large part on how democracy and criminality, past and present, are measured.[1] But, as popular perception and party platforms across the planet focus ever more on escalating crime, and on the "problem" of dis/order, the co-incidence certainly *seems* to be beyond coincidence.

It has long been argued that social disorder, expressed in elevated rates of criminality, is in the nature of transition itself, that it inevitably follows epochal changes in the order of things. Our times, like many before, are commonly described in the language of historical disjuncture, whether by appeal to retrospection and renaissance (neoliberalism, neomedievalism), to ironic aftereffect (the postmodern, posthuman, post-Fordist, f-utilitarian),[2] or to the portentous dawning of New Eras (of Empire, Exception). Little wonder, then, that the ruptures of the ongoing present, real or imagined, are often associated, in collective consciousness as well as in social theory, with transgression, liminality, and lawlessness. As Hannah Arendt reminds us, Marx long ago saw a *generic* connection between transformation and violence, which, he insisted, "is the midwife of every old society pregnant with a new one"; even more, of "all change in history and politics."[3] Foreshadowings here of Fanon (1968) and other theorists of decolonization. To be sure, modern history *has* seen some very bloody transitions to populist rule. And it *has* born witness to regimes that, under the alibi of liberal democracy, have sanctified and sustained criminally brutal modes of domination, some of them highly rationalized, highly technicized, highly sanitized. Indeed, the relative ease with which autocracies have made the transition to constitutional democracy points toward the possibility that they—autocracy and liberal democracy, that is—share more mechanisms of governance than has conventionally been recognized, not least their grounding in a rule of law, an Iron Cage of Legality itself predicated, more or less visibly, on sovereign violence (cf. Agamben 1998: 10; Foucault 1978). Whether or not there is a necessary relationship between the lethal and the legal, as Walter Benjamin (1978) and his intellectual progeny would have it,[4] their historical affinity seems beyond dispute.

The coincidence of democratization and criminal violence has been most visible in, and most volubly remarked of, postcolonies: that is, nation-states, including those of the former USSR, once governed by, for, and from an elsewhere; nation-states in which representative government and the rule of law, in their conventional Euro-modernist sense, were previously "underdeveloped"; nation-states in which the "normalization" of organized crime and brutal banditry, themselves the product of a complex play of forces (see below), has been a central motif of the chapter in their history that began, at fin de siècle, with the end of the Cold War and the triumphal spread of neoliberal capitalism. With a new Age of Empire, the Age of US and Them.[5] This age has its mythic *fons et origo* in 1989, the year that history was supposed to end (Fukuyama 1992) with the *political* birth of a Brave Neo World.[6] The "neo" here refers to a reanimation—or, more precisely, to the fetishizing anew—of old panaceas from the history of liberalism: two in particular.

One dates back to the second half of the eighteenth century, to a time when political authority, social order, citizenship, and economy were also urgently in question (see, e.g., Becker 1994). It is the idea, often associated with Adam Ferguson (1995), that a measure of control over arbitrary governmental power, especially over the power of autocratic potentates, ought to be vested in, and exercised by, a citizenry.[7] This idea has come to be subsumed, loosely, in the term "civil society" which, in its neo guise, stands for many things, among them: (1) "society against the state," itself a highly ambiguous aphorism; (2) "the" market, often glossed as "the private sector," utopically envisaged as a technically efficient mechanism for producing the common good; and (3) "the community," a vague abstraction posited, somewhat mystically, as an appropriate site for, and agent of, collective action—and, more cynically, as the end point of the devolution of the costs and responsibilities of governance (J. L. Comaroff and J. Comaroff 1999).[8] But above all, since the late 1980s, "civil society" has connoted a teleological reversal: a move from increasingly rationalized, increasingly bureaucratized, increasingly elaborated regimes of rule toward ever more outsourced, dispersed, deinstitutionalized, constitutionally ordained governance—from political evolution, classically conceived, to political devolution. In theory, at least.

The other panacea is the ballot box: an appeal to the classic apparatus of mass participatory democracy. In its postcolonial neo-life, however, this has often proven, in practice, to involve a very "thin" distillation of the concept: a minimalist, procedural version that, notwithstanding the claims made for it by some political scientists (see, e.g., Przeworski et al. 2000; and, for a critique, Wedeen 2004 and forthcoming), equates freedom with the occasional exercise of choice among competing, often indistinguishable alternatives. Which, as we have said elsewhere (J. L. Comaroff and J. Comaroff 1997), renders the franchise to *homo politicus* what shopping has long been to *homo economicus:* a beatified, cosmic fusion of free will, human satisfaction, and ethical righteousness. This is historically apt: it is a version of democracy that shadows closely the neoliberal apotheosis of the market, the displacement of *homo faber* by the consumer-citizen, and the reduction of collective action to the pursuit of "enlightened" interest. It is also the version of representative government—a "small idea," Malcolm Bradbury (1992: 276) once wrote in a postmodern fiction, which "promises hope, and gives you Fried Chicken"—that is currently being thrust upon the world at large. Often it is imposed as a condition of financial aid, foreign investment, and moral salvation by an unadornedly coercive Western consensus led by the United States (see, e.g., Young 1993: 299–300)[9] and abetted by such instruments of the new global economy as the World Bank and the International Monetary Fund (Stiglitz 2002). Indeed, this is the translucent veil behind which has closed the iron fist of structural adjustment, with its demands on postcolonies to cleave to market principles and to deregulate in ways that privilege the private sector over the state. It hardly bears repeating any longer that these demands have had unintended, highly destabilizing effects on the fragile political and economic arrangements—on the ecologies of patronage, redistribution, and survival—that developed in many nation-states across the global south with the end of the high age of colonialism. Of which more in due course.

As this implies, civil society and the ballot box, as they have come popularly to be understood at the dawn of the twenty-first century, are not just panaceas for the contemporary predicament of postcolonies. More significantly, they have taken on the substantive forms of the Brave Neo World of which they are part. This, in turn, raises an obvious, and obviously loaded, question: To the degree that there *has* been an epidemic of criminal violence in these polities in recent times—to the degree, also, that they have seen the emergence of criminal "phantom-states" in their midst (Derrida 1994: 83) or even "the criminalization of the state" tout court (Bayart, Ellis, and Hibou 1999; see below)—does it really have anything at all to do with democratization? Or, *pace* the commonplace with which we began, does electoral democracy, itself long an object of critique outside the West (see, e.g., Mamdani 1990, 1992; Makinda 1996; Karlstrom 1996),[10] veil the causes and determinations of rising lawlessness, just as the material realities of the Brave Neo World disappear behind the ballot box?

The answers are *not* as straightforward as they may seem. Why not? Because rising criminality in postcolonies is not simply a reflex, antisocial response to poverty or joblessness, scarcity, or other effects of structural adjustment, important though these things are. Neither is it merely the working of unchecked power, clothed in the trappings of state—or of bandit quasi states[11]—serving itself by monopolizing the means of extracting value and doling out death (cf. Bataille 1991; Hansen and Stepputat 2005: 13–14). Nor even is it the consequence of normative slippage occasioned by the radical transitions of the recent past. It is part of a much more troubled dialectic: a dialectic of law and dis/order, framed by neoliberal mechanisms of deregulation and new modes of mediating human transactions at once politico-economic and cultural, moral, and mortal. Under such conditions—and this is our key point—criminal violence does not so much repudiate the rule of law or the licit operations of the market as appropriate their forms—and recommission their substance. Its perpetrators create parallel modes of production and profiteering, sometimes even of governance and taxation, thereby establishing simulacra of social order. In so doing, they refigure the pas de deux in which norm and transgression, regulation and exception, redefine each other both within and beyond national polities. In the process, the means and ends of the liberal democratic state are refracted, deflected, and dispersed into the murkier reaches of the private sector, sometimes in ways unimagined by even the most enterprising of capitalists, sometimes without appearing to be doing very much at all to disturb the established order of things.

Just as, according to Charles Tilly (1985: 170–71), many modern "governments operate in essentially the same ways as racketeers"—especially in the "provision of protection"—so, in many postcolonies, violent crime increasingly counterfeits government, not least in providing fee-for-service security, and social order (J. Comaroff and J. L. Comaroff, forthcoming: chap. 1). With market fundamentalism has come a gradual erasure of received lines between the informal and the illegal, regulation and irregularity, order and organized lawlessness. It is not merely that criminal economies are often the most perfect expressions of the unfettered principle of supply and demand, nor only that great profit is to be made in the interstices between legitimate and illegitimate commerce, between the formal and underground vectors of global trade, from differences in the costs and risks of production, north and south (see Mbembe 2001: 73). Vastly lucrative returns also inhere in actively sustaining zones of ambiguity between the presence and absence of the law: returns made from controlling uncertainty, terror, even life itself; from privatizing public contracts and resources; from "discretionary" policing and "laundering" of various kinds. From amassing value, that is, by exploiting the new aporias of jurisdiction opened up under neoliberal conditions.

Or so we shall argue.

But how particular is all this to postcolonial societies? After all, the co-existence of neoliberalization with the proliferating problem of lawlessness would appear to be an ever more global phenomenon; although whether there is more crime (Gray 1998: 32), more of an obsession with it (Baumann 1998: 47), or a greater readiness under current conditions to criminalize dystopic social phenomena, among them poverty and race (Wacquant 2001), remains a fraught question—especially if, as is likely, all are true, but in indeterminate proportions. That there *is* an empirical connection, though, is rarely in doubt these days. Thus, for example, the director of Europol, the European police agency, declared in 2001 that transnational crime posed a mounting threat to domestic security in Europe: its governments, he said, should "examine whether the resources that had previously been spent on military defense would be better invested . . . in domestic security."[12] And this was before 9/11, before established distinctions between criminality and terror, lawlessness and war, private enterprise and privateering, governance and vengeance, were seriously undermined, making palpable the immanent threat of disorder everywhere. Might it be that, in this as in other respects, the world at large is looking ever more "postcolonial"? And what might that mean?

We shall return to these large questions in due course. Let us begin, however, by interrogating the forms of criminal violence, the lawlessness and dis/order, typically taken to be symptomatic of *the* postcolony.

Inside the Postcolony: Geographies of Violence, Cartographies of Crime

Lawlessness and criminal violence have become integral to depictions of postcolonial societies, adding a brutal edge to older stereotypes of underdevelopment, abjection, and sectarian strife. "LATIN AMERICA: Graft Threatens New Democracies," "AFRICA: Corruption Is Crippling Growth," screamed twin, internationally syndicated headlines in August 2005, under a picture of tropically shaded hands passing banknotes.[13] Mounting images—of Colombian druglords and Somali warlords, Caribbean pirates and Nigerian gangsters, Afghani poppies and Sierra Leonean blood diamonds—add up to a vision of global enterprise run amok: a Hobbesian nightmare of dissipated government, suspended law, and the routine resort to violence as means of production. More disturbing still are allegations that the line between the political and the criminal is fast eroding. In Africa, the epitome of post/colonial misrule in European eyes, metaphors of malfeasance—kleptocracy, neopatrimonialism, clientalism, prebendalism[14]—have long been the accepted terms, popular and scholarly alike, for indigenous modes of governance. But in the late twentieth century, these conventional images began to assume an even more sinister cast: in 1995, the French Ministry of Foreign Affairs issued a report on the radical "criminalization of politics" south of the Sahara, claiming that popular reformist movements were being resisted in many places, while links between the ruling regimes and organized crime were growing apace (Bayart, Ellis, and Hibou 1999: xiii). Elsewhere, vectors of state repression and sectarian conflict—their logic hitherto relatively transparent—appeared ever more chaotic and opaque as access to the means of force proliferated and crass utility reigned supreme. In fact, the "criminalization of politics" came to signify a new epoch in the sorry history of incivility in the global south: Bayart, Ellis, and Hibou (1999: 1), among the most acute observers of the African scene, went so far as to suggest that we are witnessing a move, there, from "Kleptocracy to the Felonious State."

For many, this merely confirms that the non-Western world remains inhospitable to representative government. But, argues Mbembe (2000, 2001, 2002), the new patterns of lawlessness are less obstacles to democracy than the consequence of what it has come to mean in places like Africa. In "the fuss over transitions to . . . multi-partyism," he notes (2001: 66), something far more significant has gone unremarked: the rise of "private indirect government," a caricature of liberalization in which the norms of redistribution once associated with clientalist rule have fragmented in the face of the displacement of sovereignty into more concentrated forms of power and accumulation, rooted in brute control over life and death. This shift has been accompanied by a transformation in the manner in which Africa is linked to the global market system: the continent, he claims, has not so much been marginalized as entangled in a parallel, pariah economy of international scale (2001: 66). The process has analogues elsewhere: in parts of the former Soviet Union, like the Balkans, a fairly predictable culture of state-centered corruption appears to have given way to a "free-for-all," making crime "the biggest single industry of the region";[15] likewise, in Latin America, where "epidemic" lawlessness is said to have accompanied the "democratic wave," linking local to transnational criminal networks and turning poor urban neighborhoods in Colombia, Brazil, and Mexico into battlefields (Pinzón 2003; Caldeira 2000: 373).[16] "Democratic Brazil," writes Scheper-Hughes (see chapter 4 below), has "the demographic profile of a nation at war, which in a sense it [is]." Criminality with violence, it seems, has become endemic to the postcolonial condition.

What makes the characterization of "private indirect government" so persuasive is its resonance with popular pessimism about the malaise and mayhem that continue to bedevil former colonies. Here, Africa retains pole position, having been excised from the map of global futures by such print media as the *Economist,*[17] by the daily grind of television reportage, and by any number of conservative public intellectuals.[18] These depictions have provoked criticism, of course: efforts to break into the definite article, *the* postcolony, and to deconstruct "its" archetypical representation; also to argue that conditions on the continent are less apocalyptic than they are made out to be, less extraordinary by contemporary planetary standards, more "business as usual."[19] And very good business at that. A recent World Bank report shows foreign direct investment south of the Sahara to have "yielded the highest returns in the world in 2002."[20] Not only have fresh infusions of capital come from the Middle East and Asia, but a "new scramble for Africa" is discernible among the nation-states of the Northern Hemisphere in pursuit of diamonds, oil, and the like.[21] These neo-colonial quests, which have reaped huge returns at the intersection of out-sourced and outlaw economies, blur the line between profit and plunder. While not strictly part of the "parallel" global economy, they interfere with indigenous means of producing wealth, recruiting local functionaries, brokers, even warlords, to facilitate their enterprises, often by extremely questionable means. As we write, investigators in the United States and Nigeria are looking into allegations that a number of international companies, including a Halliburton subsidiary—paid hefty bribes to secure the contract to build a $4 billion liquified-natural-gas plant on the oil-rich West African coast.[22] All of this exacerbates the unrest associated with many parts of the postcolonial world and renders murky the geographies of crime and violence that configure popular perceptions of that world. Lawlessness often turns out to be a complex north-south collaboration.

For now, suffice it to note that, as Cold War geopolitics has given way to a global order greased by transnational commerce, accounts of post-colonial disorder elsewhere have come to echo Africanist stereotypes: whether in Latin America or Indonesia, Eastern Europe or India, autocratic government is said to have mutated into a less stable species of politics in which personnel and institutions of state collaborate with enterprises deemed illegal by Euro-American norms. In fact, efforts on the part of the World Bank, the World Trade Organization, and governments of the north to democratize patrimonial systems—thus to eliminate the "politics of the belly" (Bayart 1993), *caudillismo,* communalism, and their cognates[23]—have only exacerbated their unruliness. Those calls to reform, it hardly needs noting, set great store by liberalization, both economic and political, the latter centered squarely on the panaceas mentioned earlier: on multiparty politics and the cultivation of civil society. And on unrestrained privatization. But such measures, as the *Report on the World Social Situation, 2005* (United Nations 2005) reiterates yet again, have widened inequalities within and across nation-states,[24] abetting the accumulation of wealth and power by elites, both licit *and* illicit. As Larry Rohter and Juan Forero, commenting on Latin America, point out, "With once-closed economies having been opened up and corporate profits at record levels, the opportunities for graft and bribes are larger than ever."[25]

Clearly, liberalization and democracy have done little to reduce violence. Quite the opposite. Not only have those excluded from the spoils tended to resort, ever more prosaically, to militant techniques to survive or profit (Bayart 1993: xiii; Olivier de Sardan 1999a; Caldeira 2000), but many ruling regimes have ceded their monopoly over coercion to private contractors, who plunder and enforce at their behest. In some African, Asian, and Latin American contexts, banditry shades into low-level warfare as a mode of accumulating wealth and political allegiance (see chapters 4, 5, and 9 below), yielding new cartographies of dis/order: postnational terrains on which spaces of relative privilege are linked to one another by slender, vulnerable corridors that stretch across zones of strife, uncertainty, and minimal governance. Here the reach of the state is uneven and the landscape is a palimpsest of contested sovereignties, codes, and jurisdictions—a complex choreography of police and paramilitaries, private and community enforcement, gangs and vigilantes, highwaymen and outlaw armies. Here, too, no genre of communication is authoritative: "dark circuits" of rumor and popular media alike flash signs of inchoate danger lurking beneath the banal surface of things, danger made real by sudden, graphic assaults on persons and property. What is more, capricious violence often sediments into distressingly predictable, repeated patterns of wounding as those most vulnerable—but sometimes also, Patricia Spyer (see chapter 5 below) notes of Indonesia, those precisely in "one's own image"—become the bodies on which mastery is acted out (see Gore and Pratten 2003). Thus it is that sexual violence in postapartheid South Africa, the execution of young "marginals" in Northeast Brazil, and the reciprocal slaughter of Christians and Muslims in Indonesia are the lethal labor that authorizes stark inequalities (see chapters 2, 4, and 5 below). Zones of deregulation are also spaces of opportunity, of vibrant, desperate inventiveness and unrestrained profiteering.

At the same time, patently, deregulation and democratization have *not* eliminated older-style autocrats or oligarchs. They have merely altered the sorts of resources and rhetoric at their command. Now organs of civil society and humanitarian aid, alike local and transnational, exist alongside the Mugabes of this world, who seize incoming assets and feed their clients in the name of majority rights, redistribution, and anti-imperialism. Kleptocrats may no longer draw succor from superpowers with geostrategic anxieties. But they do very well out of donor aid and no-questions-asked global commerce. "Dictator's Son on City Spending Spree" blared the *Cape Times* of 20 July 2005, detailing the millions spent in Cape Town on cars, hotels, and entertainment by the ruling dynasty of oil-rich Equatorial Guinea,[26] the latter having recently staved off a coup funded by European corporate bandits of the "neo-criminal classes"[27]—like Mark Thatcher, himself a beneficiary of state kickbacks, British style. Again we glimpse the entanglements that tie postcolonial graft to the metropolitan scramble for tropical spoils.

Globalization, Crooked and Straight

Postcolonial societies, most of them rooted in historically extractive economies, with small bourgeois sectors, low levels of formal skill, and modest civil administrations, have shown varying capacities to profit from mainstream global enterprise.[28] While a few have prospered, many fill a classic neocolonial niche: they are providers of raw materials and cheap labor. But the very qualities that constrain their participation in the world of corporate endeavor—that have rendered them, as one African statesman put it, "appendages of metropolitan powers" in the global trading regime[29]—have made postcolonies ready and able players in the twilight markets fostered by liberalization. Thus, in the face of the subsidies and trade tariffs that have sped the onslaught of agribusiness, non-Western producers find a competitive edge in contraband cultivation. Notoriously extensive regional economies, as vibrant as they are violent, flourish in the Golden Crescent of Afghanistan-Iran-Pakistan and in Colombia-Peru-Bolivia around crops like opium poppies or coca.[30] As with mainstream enterprise, the value added, and the profit reaped, increase as these products move further away from the sites of their primary production. Nature also yields other illegal niche markets based on the canny commodification of the "inalienable" qualities widely associated with "third-world" peoples: endangered species and ancient artifacts, sex workers and undocumented migrants, human infants and organs. There is, as well, the lucrative, often bloody trade in illicitly extracted raw materials that are in especially high demand, most notably gemstones and coltan.[31]

Crooked economies, like their straight equivalents, show a massive recent expansion in their service sectors. Here again, postcolonial workforces find employment where formal opportunities are few. Some national treasuries now rest almost entirely on conveying contraband: former entrepôts like Gambia, Togo, Benin, and Somalia, for example, have morphed into "smuggling states" (Bayart, Ellis, and Hibou 1999: 20). While a proportion of their traffic in pirated goods, stolen cars, and drugs finds local markets, most valuable cargo makes its way to merchants and customers in the north, some slipping seamlessly into respectable, aboveground commerce.[32] It has also been widely noted that the business of transporting narcotics—centered in Nigeria, Senegal, Ghana, Togo, Cape Verde, and South Africa but shifting in response to local opportunity and patterns of policing—links African, Latin American, and central Asian producers to consumers in Europe and North America (Bayart, Ellis, and Hibou 1999: 9ff.).[33] Suave couriers traverse the planet, swelling the population of migrants to Europe, where "Nigerian" almost invariably qualifies "drug dealer" and "illegal alien," and to North America, where "Mexican" has similar connotations (Ajibade n.d.).[34] Anxieties about immigration and terror are not far behind, feeding fears about the link between organized crime and underground cells and fueling the racialization of lawlessness.[35] As a result, profiles of criminality become more explicitly xenophobic: "Illegal Aliens' Unstoppable Third World Crime Wave in US" runs one exasperated headline.[36] "Immigrants 'Behind Crime Wave'" trumpets Britain's *Observer,* sparking yet another asylum row.[37]

These instances remind us, if a reminder is needed, how politics and crime, legitimate and illegitimate agency, endlessly redefine each other. The line between them is a frontier in the struggle to assert sovereignty or to disrupt it, to expand or contract the limits of the il/licit, to sanction or outlaw violence. Most postcolonies, as we suggested above, bear the historical traces of overrule that either suspended legalities or deployed them to authorize predation and criminalize opposition. A decade after the end of apartheid in South Africa, the poor and the marginal still look skeptically upon statutes protecting the rich: a large proportion of them see crime as an acceptable means of redistribution (Sissener 2001), even vengeance. Nigerian tricksters think similarly about defrauding gullible Europeans. As privatization and enclosure create new forms of property, they simultaneously define new forms of theft, from piracy and poaching to cloning and hacking. Such practices are not always deemed illegitimate across social and national divides. Hence the disregard for copyright shown by producers of generic pharmaceuticals in Thailand, India, and

Brazil. And the attacks by "cyberpunks" on the "Patent Absurdity" of proprietary computer software (Coleman 2005).

The species of property that have emerged out of the digital revolution have had an especially profound effect on the means of producing and controlling value—and on definitions of the licit and illicit. While most postcolonials lack the wherewithal to navigate the fast lanes of the knowledge economy or the electronic commons, they have again found profitable niche markets by making a virtue of their situation. A massive increase in outsourcing Western technological services and telemarketing to India, for instance, has led to the dispersal of personal information across space, priming a thriving business in cybercrime and data theft.[38] Likewise, factories—often small family firms—have sprung up in Asia to supply cloned credit cards, complete with holograms and embossing, to those who perpetrate "plastic fraud" across the planet (Levi 1998: 427). The former third world, it appears, has cornered the market in the manufacture of counterfeit documents, faux IDs, and fakes of every conceivable kind.

At one level, this growing specialization is no mystery. A volatile mix of economic exclusion, technological enablement, and lax policing here meet an almost insatiable planetary demand for instruments of personal authentication. In an age of heightened mobility and government-at-a-distance, human identities congeal along borders in paper and plastic; certification, ultimately, controls the capacity of people and objects to cross frontiers and to enhance their value. This is particularly so for those who traverse the routes that separate peripheries from centers of prosperity and relative security, both within and between national spaces. Where aspiration, even survival, is tied closely to the capacity to migrate (see chapter 9 below), official "papers" take on a magic of their own. And the techniques of their manufacture command a compelling power and fascination, rendering forgery a form of creativity that transcends easy definitions of legality (Siegel 1998: 58). Thus, a huge industry has evolved, especially outside the West, for the fabrication of false credentials, from marriage and divorce certificates to passports and university degrees; entire bureaucratic biographies and family archives are expertly counterfeited by means that wrest control over the production of the insignia of civic personhood from the state. It is an industry astonishingly in step with the latest techniques of authentication; so much so that the Fifth International Conference on Fraudulent Documents, held in Amsterdam in 2002, drew scientific experts from all the major countries of Europe and North America in pursuit of new methods, from laser procedures to biometrics, to keep abreast of the inspired captains of fakery to the east and the south.[39]

Fakery has also been expedited by ever more effective, affordable, personalized machinery. With the advent of highly-quality desktop reproduction, the arts of counterfeiting, of literally "making money," have expanded rapidly in the non-Western world.[40] It has been estimated that as much as a third of all currency now in circulation is false—although paranoia in this respect, most of all in the United States, multiplies with advances in technology and with a sense of threat to national sovereignty. Suspicion comes to rest on familiar foes, on "highly-skilled counterfeiters backed by Iran and Syria," held to have produced as much as $1 billion in old US hundred-dollar bills; North Korea, believed to be engaged in similar mass printings of "Superdollars"; the Philippines, where a raid is said to have discovered some $50 billion in bogus cash and Treasury notes; or Colombia, thought guilty of manufacturing more than a third of the forged notes seized in the United States in 1999.[41]

Counterfeit Modernities

All of this points to something much larger: to the fact that post-colonies are quite literally associated with a counterfeit modernity, a modernity of counterfeit. With fictitious documents, fake brand names, pirated drugs and movies, and a range of other sorts of appropriated intellectual property. With *palsu*, as Indonesians term it—the word derives from the English "false"—which, according to James Siegel (1998: 52), is more a matter of the "almost authentic" than the bogus. Mimesis has classically been an attribute projected onto Europe's others, of course, marking the distance between civilization and its apprentices, those perpetually deemed "almost, but not quite," the real thing (Bhabha 1994: 91). Times, though, have changed. In the postcolonial era, copies declare independence as commodities and circulate autonomously. The electronic revolution has abetted this by democratizing the means of mechanical reproduction. It has demystified proprietary goods, whose aura can be mass-produced and flogged at a discount. These brazen simulacra, like counterfeit money, expose a conceit at the core of the culture of Western capitalism: that its signifiers can be fixed, that its editions can be limited, that it can franchise the platonic essence of its mass-produced modernity. Branding, the assertion of a monopoly over a named species of value, invites cloning; this because something of the exclusive cachet of the "authentic article" is congealed in the copy. Thus it is that a recent Internet ad from Malaysia offers "high quality" Rolexes, complete with logos, at 40 percent the cost of other *un*licensed replicas.[42] As this implies, fakes also circulate in a sphere of their own. Common in South Africa and elsewhere is the idea of the "genuine fake," which, ironically, underscores the

uniqueness of the original, with which it exists in a reciprocally reinforcing relationship. The zest and ingenuity with which such "quality" counterfeits are fabricated make it plain that this kind of artifice is a legitimate
practice, almost an aesthetic form, for many of those who fashion and
consume them (Sissener 2001; chapter 7 below). Producers of faux commodities seem less concerned to pretend that their goods are the real thing
than to take hold of the very mystique of the first-world "label" and flagrantly, joyously, appropriate the means of its replication. The genuine
fake gives South African or East Asian teenagers access to things they
could not otherwise have, filling the gap between globally tweaked desires
and local scarcities. The admiration at work here, Siegel (1998: 57) insists,
is not about defying authority. It is about "creating a sort of authority for
oneself."

The enterprise that drives cultures of counterfeit recalls an observation
made by Béatrice Hibou (1999: 105) with regard to fakery in contemporary Africa—from the fabrication of faux currency, reports, and statistics
to the production of bogus fertilizer, pharmaceuticals,[43] and salt. These
practices, she says, should be understood less as "a tendency to criminalization *per se* than in terms of the widespread use of deception and 'dirty
tricks,' represented by games of chance, pyramid schemes and other adventures" (see also Niger-Thomas 2001); they are much in the spirit, too,
of "casino capitalism," the ethos of neoliberalism that favors speculation,
play, and gambling over virtuous labor as a source of wealth (J. Comaroff and J. L. Comaroff 2000; chapter 6 below). The resort to deception is
tangible, as well, in the notorious, irrepressible Nigerian 419, an inspired
postcolonial pastiche of its American original, the Francis Drake scam of
the Depression years.[44] The ruse is initiated by a letter, nowadays mostly
an e-mail, that reproduces, more or less effectively, the verisimilitude of
para-statal communication. It offers the Western "investor" huge profits
for allowing her or his bank account to be used in the transfer abroad of
an otherwise-inaccessible estate, often that of a deceased adventurer like
Jonas Savimbi and Lauren Kabila. In its beguiling invocation of intestate
dictators, ill-gotten gains, and the secret transfer of vast fortunes, the hoax
exploits common stereotypes of African corruption as the key to its plau-
sibility (Apter 1999: 274). Another scam does the opposite, taking the
moral high ground to work its tricks: a bogus Nigerian "Nelson Mandela
Foundation" recently solicited dot.com donations for the indigent, payable into a Cypriot bank account (O'Toole 2005: 54). Apter (1999: 270)
notes that "419" has come to refer, broadly, to a mode of production based
on impersonation and forgery, itself a major, often government-backed

industry in Nigeria. It is estimated to be second only to oil and narcotics in generating foreign currency.

Some of its perpetrators may regard 419 as righteous reparation, reversing the flow that, since the age of slavery, has diverted African assets into European hands (see chapter 7 below). But the scam pervades the Nigerian social fabric, not discriminating among those whom it rips off. It capitalizes on a "crisis of value" precipitated by the boom-and-bust oil economy of the Babangida years—a crisis also discernible in other postcolonies that have suffered structural adjustment, hyperinflation, drastic currency devaluations, and excessive violence (Apter 1999: 298). In disrupting received relations between media and the value they represent, these convulsions unsettle accepted indices of truth (Blunt 2004; chapter 5 below). They open an uncertain space between signifiers, be they omens or banknotes, and what it is they signify: a space of mystery, magic, and uncanny productivity wherein witches, Satan, and prosperity prophets ply an avid trade (see chapter 6 below). Under such conditions, signs take on an occult life of their own, appearing capable of generating great riches. Under such conditions, too, there is little practical difference between real and faux currency.

Forgery also begets forgery, in an infinite regress: witness a fantastic meta-419, in which fake cops "double-dipped" victims by posing as government agents investigating past scams—and by promising, for a fee, to restore their lost funds.[45] Crime *itself* is frequently the object of criminal mimesis. Counterfeit kidnappings, hijack hoaxes, and bogus burglaries are everywhere an expanding source of profit, to the extent that, in the Cape Province of South Africa, where simulated claims are becoming epidemic, a Zero Tolerance Task Group has been created to put a stop to them.[46] Hibou (1999: 102ff.) adds that, in countries hospitable to the "economics of dirty tricks," many "official" investigations and initiatives are themselves false, generating a spiral of double-speak in which agents of enforcement, international observers, and donors all become implicated. In the absence of robust political institutions, an intricate tissue of gifts, favors, services, commissions, and rents knits outsiders to insiders in what is sometimes called the "development state"—but is better described as a state of endemic expropriation. Efforts to make foreign aid accountable by introducing tight auditing regimes have offered fresh formulae for fabrication, rendering even more inchoate the line between the forged and the far-fetched, the spirit and the letter of the counterfeit. The fetish and the fake. Each, finally, fades into the other.

Thus, argues Andrew Apter (1999: 300), in Nigeria fetishism has come to saturate the state itself, yielding a politics of illusion that, more than just front the appropriation of resources by ruling elites, has erected an edifice of "simulated government": government that concocts false censuses and development schemes, even holds fictitious elections. Bogus bureaucracy, in fact, has surfaced as a pervasive theme in analyses of postcolonial politics. Reno (1995, 2000), for example, speaks of "the shadow state" in Sierra Leone and beyond, in which a realpolitik of thuggery and profiteering is conducted behind a facade of formal administrative respectability; similarly, Bayart, Ellis, and Hibou (1999: 20ff.) stress that, in the "felonious" state, hidden power brokers, doppelgangers of a legitimate civil service, control political and economic life, often ostensibly under the sway of partisan spiritual forces. Shades here again of Derrida's (1994: 83) "phantom-states," in which organized crime performs for citizens the functions once provided by government. In these circumstances, the official edifice becomes the counterfeit, predation the reality. Indeed, as James Ferguson (2006: 15) remarks, there is "an abundance of shadows" in recent accounts of African political economy. But not only there. Saddam Hussein's "shadow state" was said to "defy democracy" in Iraq;[47] nocturnal "shadow players" are alleged to thrive where offshore banking meets illegal money laundering in Belize (Duffy 2000); "shadow" business is blamed for thwarting economic growth in Peru.[48] Conversely, the fragile peace that currently prevails in Ambon, Spyer (chapter 5 below) says, was made "in the shadow of the law." Ferguson (2006: 16f.) insists, correctly, that there is more at work here than old colonial archetypes: the trope conveys a *contemporary* sense of inscrutability. And also a doubling, the existence of parallel worlds of clandestine government, irregular soldiers, and occult economies that revives long-standing talk about "dark" vestiges of the modernist idyll. But shadows, he reminds us, are less dim copies than likenesses, others who are also selves. After all, many have insisted that the vaunted European state is itself as much a chimera as a reality (Miliband 1969: 49; Abrams 1988: 76).

The Shadow and the Thing Itself

The resonance between shadow and counterfeit realities also captures something of the effects of neoliberal deregulation on governance, something evident worldwide but most marked in postcolonies: the unsettling counterpoint between the outsourcing of the state and the usurpation of sovereignty, not least in the realm of policing and warfare. Government, as it disperses itself, becomes less and less an ensemble of bureaucratic institutions, more and more a licensing-and-franchising authority. This, in turn, provides fresh opportunities, at all levels, for capitalizing both on the assets of the state and on its imprimatur. Kickbacks have become a sine qua non of office in many places, countries with sustained cultures of corruption heading the list. In India, for one, bribes are said to be routine in securing contracts, loans, and handouts, although, as Akhil Gupta (1995: 384) notes, high-level functionaries raise large sums from relatively few clients, while their humbler counterparts collect small amounts from larger constituencies—and hence are more visibly "corrupt."[49] Nothing new, this, for those familiar with politics in cities like Chicago. But in South Asia, Africa, and Latin America, these practices are often disarmingly explicit and unpoliced. To wit, police and customs personnel, especially where their pay is low or unreliable, frequently take part in modes of extraction in which insignias of public position are deployed to raise rents (Blundo and Olivier de Sardan 2001; Roitman 2005: 186). Reports of cops who turn checkpoints into private tollbooths are legion; an *Economist* team driving in 2002 from Douala, Cameroon, to a town less than five hundred kilometers to the southeast encountered more than forty-seven roadblocks.[50] Revenues are also routinely raised by impersonating the state: by putting on counterfeit uniforms, bearing phony identity documents, and deploying other fake accouterments of authority.[51] In like vein, as sovereignty splinters, agents of a motley array of statelike entities, from quasi-corporate religious organizations to militias, find ways of demanding recognition and tribute.

The readiness of ordinary people to exploit the interstices between official and backstage realities, and to seize insignias of authority, may be symptomatic of the tendency under market fundamentalism everywhere to blur the lines separating licit from illicit business. Heightened pressure to make profit, to undercut competition and reduce costs, has spawned ever more complex articulations of "formal" and "informal" production. As a recent account of the construction industry in Miami makes plain, convoluted chains of subcontracting now tie the most reputable firms to traffickers in illegal immigrant labor, building criminality into the very heart of the "American dream business."[52] In the murky world of outsourcing, the informal shades into the illicit, whether it be in hiring undocumented workers, greasing palms, or moving contraband. This reinforces our earlier observation about the dangerous liaisons between north and south, about the ways in which "respectable" metropolitan trade gains by deflecting the risks and moral taint of outlaw commerce "beyond the border." An increasing proportion of postcolonial enterprise may appear shady and brutal, but it is integral to the workings of the global scheme of things.

The labyrinthine entanglements of these worlds of light and shade come through clearly in a recent survey conducted by Gallup International. It concluded that there has been a sharp rise in the efforts of multinational corporations to secure valuable contracts—especially in arms and defense, public works and construction—by paying off officials in "emerging economies"; Western media sometimes gloss this, disingenuously, by noting that companies setting up shop in the south must deal with local "cultures of business," informal "start-up costs," "import duties," and the like.[53] The Gallup Bribe-Payers Index was commissioned by fifteen countries (among them, South Africa, Nigeria, and Argentina) to counter a prior study, undertaken for Transparency International, that had targeted only bribe-takers, not bribe-givers, and had stressed the prevalence of payoffs in "developing" countries. While Gallup found that firms in a few developing countries *do* engage in a great deal of bribery, they were followed closely by Russia, China, France, the United States, Japan, and Italy, all of whom were among the top ten. African commentators noted that, as members of the G8 alliance, these nations were supposed to be committed to "kick-starting prosperity" on the continent by boosting trade and uprooting malpractice. But kick-backs negate kick-starts: their proceeds tend to end up in offshore bank accounts in the north, further draining resources from the resource poor.[54]

The symbiosis revealed by the Gallup Bribe-Payers Index between overt and covert deals, bribe-givers and bribe-takers, involves chains of transaction that diffuse accountability as they cross social, national, and moral frontiers, chains built on a complicity between legal and illegal practice. It is tempting to see in all this a neocolonial map of unequal interdependence between northern profit, probity, and security and southern poverty, plunder, and risk. This geography is not so simple, however. As Étienne Balibar (2004: 14) remarks, "the line of demarcation between 'North' and 'South,' between zones of prosperity and power and zones of 'development of underdevelopment,' is not actually drawn in a stable way." The north, these days, contains much south. And many others from the south hope to follow. Brazil and South Africa complicate the picture, having substantial, vibrant economies, although they too permit Western capital to profit from cheap labor, raw materials, and lax enforcement. Because they are highly polarized societies, however, they exemplify postcolonial landscapes in which domains of prosperity and order feed off, and perpetuate, zones of scarcity and violence.

Take, again, South Africa: a recent study of the Cape Flats[55] in Greater Cape Town (Standing 2005) reports that the outlaw economy there, which embraces a very large population, is not easily separated from lawful, mainstream commerce. What is more, argues André Standing (2005: 1), in impoverished areas, where the legacy of apartheid has been exacerbated by a withdrawal of capital and the state, organized crime may be a "rational" strategy of social survival. While the white bourgeoisie of the city lives a protected, cosmopolitan existence, its underclasses of color must fend for themselves in an environment in which steady incomes are scarce, in which unemployment rates hover around 46 percent, in which 61 percent of those under thirty have no work. Here the illegal sale of drugs, guns, sex, and stolen goods represents a major sector of the market, much of it controlled by an elaborate underworld of gangs and criminal elites that links street to prison populations and reaches deep into the fabric of community life (Steinberg 2004; chapter 4 below). The violent fallout of its enterprise, and its mythic imperviousness to policing, have provoked spates of local vigilantism. But its insouciant druglords, apotheoses of consumption-without-constraint, also enjoy frank admiration. Like the bosses of Brazilian *favelas* and the big guns of "Cities of God" across the world, they disburse flamboyant philanthropy (Standing 2005: 9). At the same time, "Gangland (Pty) Ltd," aka Gangland Inc., is a sophisticated, multimillion-dollar business.[56] Supporting a workforce of tens of thousands, its upper levels operate like multinational corporations while its street outlets are said to be run "like 7-Eleven franchises."[57] Reminiscent of the bush economies of the Chad Basin, its ways and means are treated by those whom it serves as legitimate, as acceptable, that is, in a context in which "transgression [is] the norm" (chapter 7 below). Its organizations, which are known to employ accountants and consultants, invest in legitimate businesses, from hotels and nightclubs to taxis and fisheries—which is how they extend into the aboveground economy and local governance. Said to trade regularly with Chinese triads and other "mobs" across the globe, they are showing signs, too, of becoming transnational, although they are not as much so yet as, say, Salvadoran youth gangs, notably Mara Salvatrucha (MS-13), which have become a major presence in the cities of the United States (Richter 2005: 8).

The Law, Again

Neoliberalism may have intensified the presence of organized crime in the social and moral fabric of postcolonies. But these polities are by no means "lawless." On the contrary, as we have suggested and will return to show in some detail, their politics and popular cultures, even their outlaw cultures, are infused with the spirit of the law, a spirit as much the product of the moment as is new-wave criminality. Hence the dialectic of law and disorder that runs through the essays below. A pertinent example of this is the impact on the Babangida regime in Nigeria, itself the apotheosis of malfeasance, of the heroic exploits of the elusive bandit Lawrence Anini, aka Jack the Ripper, Robin Hood, and, most tellingly, "The Law": "The Government itself had become increasingly concerned about 'The Law.' It saw Anini not just as a threat to law and order, a common criminal terrorizing people, but as the 'hit-man' of an organized conspiracy by powerful groups to undermine the military regime's legitimacy, and to show it as incapable of protecting order, law, and the people" (Marenin 1987: 261). So much so that Babangida felt moved to announce increased support for "enforcement agencies" to ensure the safety of "law-abiding citizens," although it was less public security that was put at risk by Anini than the sovereign authority of the state.

Why this anxiety about "The Law" and why the public fascination with a figure iconic of the very law that he so flagrantly violates[58] when, as Marenin (1987: 261) emphasizes, large numbers of criminals operate in Nigeria all the time, little hindered by the police? Both the anxiety and the fascination point to a very general preoccupation in the postcolonial world with "the law" and the citizen as *legal* subject (see chapter 2 below), a preoccupation growing in counterpoint to, and deeply entailed in, the rise of the felonious state, private indirect government, and endemic cultures of illegality. That counterpoint, so easily read off the schizophrenic landscapes of many postcolonies, has come to feature prominently in popular discourses almost everywhere. As governance disperses itself and monopolies over coercion fragment, crime and policing provide a rich repertoire of idioms and allegories with which to address, imaginatively, the nature of sovereignty, justice, and social order: thus the lyrics of underworld hip-hop in São Paulo, verses—as in "Crime vs. . . . ," to recall Marlon Burgess, with whom we began—that give voice to "attitude" in the face of terrifying violence, much of it meted out by the cops (see chapter 3 below); or the action movies of Nollywood,[59] Nigeria's $45 million straight-to-video film industry, in which forces of justice joust with outlaws, both human and supernatural; or the immensely appealing Hong Kong gangster genre, whose plotlines offer the assurance that brutality can be brutally overcome; or the vibrant home-grown television shows in South Africa, in which, night after night, fictional detectives apprehend felons like those on the loose in real life, iterating an order that remains distinctly fragile by day. Compromised rulers, too, under pressure to act authoritatively in the face of civil unrest, stage police dramas in

which they are seen to "crack down" on mythic felons, thereby enacting
the very possibility of governance in the face of rampant lawlessness
(chapter 8 below; see also Siegel 1998). Mass mediation gives law and disorder a "communicative force" that permits it to "traverse the social
field," to use Rosalind Morris's terms, appearing to deliver its publics,
again and again, from "the "primal confusion between law and lawlessness" on which "all states are founded" (see chapter 2 below).

Law and lawlessness, we repeat, are conditions of each other's possibility. As a motorcycle-taximan in Cameroon told Janet Roitman (chapter 7):
"So that the system can continue to function properly, it's important
that there are people in violation." Conversely, criminal profits require that
there are rules to be broken: without some modicum of border control,
there can be no smuggling, just as the legalization of drugs would inevitably reduce their market value. Also, twenty-first-century kleptocrats
commit grand larceny as much by deploying legalities—by enacting legislation in order to authorize acts of expropriation—as by evading them (see
below). Money, as we have said, is also to be made in the aporias of regulation, perhaps the best examples being the "flex organizations" of the former Soviet bloc, which mobilize shadowy networks that are neither illicit
nor licensed and exploit gaps in the penal code to redirect public resources
into private hands;[60] or a range of questionable new cyberoperations that
accumulate wealth in the lee of the law, compelling the United Nations to
take a lead in subjecting them to international convention.[61]

But the fact that crime demands rules to break, evade, or circumvent in
order to be profitable, or that "the system," à la Durkheim, demands "vio-
lators" to sustain itself, or that kleptocrats mobilize legalities to their own
nefarious ends, or that money is to be made in the interstices of regulation,
only scratches the surface of the dialectic of law and disorder in the postcolony. So, too, does the fact that, when the state tries to deal with perceived threats to public order by judicial means, as Geschiere (chapter 6)
shows of witchcraft in Cameroon and South Africa, it merely intensifies
fears of disorder. Questions remain: *Why* has a preoccupation with legalities, and with the legal subject, come to be so salient a dimension of postcolonial dis/order and its mass-mediated representation? What is the evidence that it is as ubiquitous as we have asserted? And *is* it particular to
postcolonies? Most importantly, how might all this be related to the rise of
a neoliberalism that—in restructuring relations among governance, production, the market, violence—seems to have abetted criminal economies
everywhere? To address this clutch of questions, to move beyond the surfaces of the dialectic, let us turn our attention to the fetishism of the law.

**The Fetishism of the Law: Sovereignty, Violence,
Lawfare, and the Displacements of Politics**

The modernist nation-state, it hardly needs saying, has always been
erected on a scaffolding of legalities. Nor only the modernist nation-state.
In classical Greece, too, Hannah Arendt (1998: 194–95) observes, "the
laws [were] like the wall around the city": "Before men began to act, a definite space had to be secured and a structure built where all subsequent
actions could take place, the space being the public realm of the *polis* and
its structure the law." The metaphorical link here between the architectural and the jural is noteworthy. Thomas Hobbes (1995: 109), whose
specter hovers close to the disorderly surfaces of life in the postcolony, was
even more explicit: "Laws [are] the walls of government, and nations."
Since the dismantling of the wall that marked the end of the Cold War—
and, with it perhaps, the ideological monopoly over the political exercised
by the modernist nation-state—law has been further fetishized, even as, in
most postcolonies, higher and higher walls are built to protect the propertied from lawlessness, even as the language of legality insinuates itself
deeper and deeper into the realm of the illicit. "The Law," uppercase again
but not now as a Nigerian criminal alias, has become the medium in which
politics are played out, in which conflicts are dealt with across otherwise-
incommensurable axes of difference, in which the workings of the "free"
market are assured,[62] in which social order is ostensibly erected and the
substance of citizenship made manifest (see chapter 2 below). "Lawfulness," argues Roger Berkowitz (2005: ii), "has replaced justice as the measure of ethical action" in the world. Indeed, as the measure of a great deal
of action beyond the ethical as well.

*On Constitutions, Criminality, and
Cultures of Legality*

Striking, in this regard, is the number of national constitutions (re)writ-
ten since 1989: roughly one hundred and five, the vast majority of them
in postcolonies (Klug 2000).[63] Also striking is the almost salvific belief in
their capacity to conjure up equitable, just, ethically founded, pacific polities; this in the midst of the lawlessness that has accompanied laissez faire
in so many places. There are now forty-four constitutional courts, the ultimate arbiters of the law and executive propriety, functioning across the
planet, from Uganda to the Ukraine, from Chile through Croatia to the
Central African Republic, Madagascar to Mongolia, Slovenia to South
Africa. Many of them have had to deal with moral panics arising from
crime waves, imagined or real, and from the "popular punitiveness" of the

age (Bottoms 1995; Haggerty 2001: 197)—not least in respect of capital punishment, for some the ultimate signifier of sovereignty. Many enjoy a great deal of authority: in India, for instance, the highest tribunal in the land became so powerful in the mid-1990s that, according to the *Wall Street Journal,* it was the effective hub of governance (see below).[64] As Bruce Ackerman (1997: 2, 5) puts it, "faith in written constitutions is sweeping the world," largely because, in many places, their promulgation marks a "new beginning," a radical break, at once symbolic and substantive, with the past. And with its embarrassments, its nightmares, its torments. What is more, the "constitutional patriotism" that often accompanies such new beginnings, Paul Blokker (2005: 387) notes in a discussion of Eastern Europe,[65] envisages a democratic "political culture" erected on "popular sovereignty, individual rights, and association in civil society."[66] Civil society little troubled in its imaginings, we might add, by the criminal violence within its walls.

Even more important than the number of new constitutions drafted over the past two decades is a not-so-subtle change in their content, especially in former colonies. It is a change, David Schneiderman (2000) argues—using Colombia, often said to be the "murder capital of the world," as a case in point—owed to a global shift in "constitutional design." The move from a state capitalist model to a neoliberal one is, for him, largely the product of an epochal transformation in the relationship between the economics and politics of market capitalism. Thus, whereas the constitutions promulgated in the decades of "decolonization" after World War II gave little autonomy to the law, stressing instead parliamentary sovereignty, executive discretion, and bureaucratic authority, the ones to emerge over the past twenty years have tended, if unevenly,[67] to emphasize the rule of law and the primacy of rights, even when both the spirit and the letter of that law are violated, offended, distended, purloined.

Take the case of Togo, for instance, whose late president, Eyadéma Gnassingbé, came to office in 1963 in a coup. During his reign, in 1992, a new democratic constitution was approved by referendum. Togo also became a member of the Human Rights Commission, in spite of its dubious record in this respect. Although two national elections were held in the 1990s, both were heavily tainted with accusations of fraud and violence. Then, on 5 February 2005, Eyadéma suffered a fatal heart attack. The army—which, along with his "clan," had underpinned his power— replaced him with his son, Faure; the law had been changed in 2002 to admit this possibility, reducing the eligible age of the presidency to thirty-five. Nonetheless, the installation was unconstitutional. The speaker of parliament ought to have become temporary ruler and elections called within sixty days. But the generals exploited the fact that the man in question, Mbaré Outtara Natchaba, was out of the country—and they made sure he stayed away by sealing the borders. In the circumstances, they could easily have staged a putsch. Instead, the legislature was instructed to dismiss Natchaba and elect Faure in his place, thereby making his accession lawful. The military also insisted that the Constitution be amended to remove the clause requiring elections within two months, which, de jure, made the younger Gnassingbé acting president until the end of his father's term. It also provided legal language with which to reply to the surrounding West African states that demanded adherence to the Constitution. Faure ruled for twenty days. Still under pressure from neighboring countries, he then resigned and a ballot was scheduled for April. In the midst of this flurry of events, Parliament reversed its constitutional changes, though Faure was not required to stand down. He won the election, ignoring allegations of fraud, and was sworn in on 4 May. Togo, governed by an extended family firm, military strong-arm, and a strangely refracted conception of the Spirit of Law, continues to cloth itself in constitutionality.[68]

This case is interesting not just because Africa has produced so many variants of it, most dramatically, of late, the Mugabe regime in Zimbabwe, which demonstrates ready fluency in the *langue* of legality—it regularly enacts into law the whims of the president and ruling party—while playing havoc with its *parole* (see below).[69] The Togo story is also telling because, by comparison to post-Soviet Europe and other postcolonial theaters, African nations are commonly said *not* to show as great a commitment to constitutionalism (see Mbaku 2000: passim; Oloka-Onyango 2001), even as thirty-six of them have produced new constitutions since 1989.[70] But that is not our only, or our primary, point here. There are two others.

One, to reiterate, is that the fetishism of constitutionality may be as evident in the breach—in acts of suspension, exception, violation—as it is in contexts in which the Spirit and the Letter of the Law appear to pervade social, moral, and political being. The other is that "constitutional patriotism" also manifests itself, albeit variably, at levels "beneath" that of the state, beyond the horizons of political and legal institutions, across the ordinary axes of civil society. In South Africa, the Constitution—both its content and the found object itself, as aura-infused in its little red-book reproductions as in the original—is *the* populist icon of nationhood (J. Comaroff and J. L. Comaroff 2003). Possibly because of the particular history of national liberation and rebirth there, citizens, even in the remote reaches of the countryside, even in penitentiaries, have come to speak its text as a lingua franca; this at the same time as they bemoan the criminal violence that imprisons them in their homes and mocks the freedoms conferred by the new democracy (cf., on Brazil, Caldeira 2000; chapter 3 below).

But there is more to the fetishism of the law than merely an enchanted faith in constitutions. As the essays below make plain, a "culture of legality" seems to be infusing the capillaries of everyday life, becoming part and parcel of the metaphysics of disorder that haunts all postcolonies (see chapter 6), if in variable measure. In rural north India, to take one instance, villagers discuss the penal code in agonizing detail as they argue over the legality of the behavior of local officials who routinely "circumvent" normal procedures (Gupta 1995: 375). The term itself—"culture of legality"—appears in a recent initiative of the Mexican Ministry of Education as the cornerstone of its new "citizenship education program."[71] It is also the rationale behind a game for children and teachers in Sicily, mythic home of northern banditry. Called, yes, Legalopoli, its object is to promote "the diffusion of [a] culture of legality."[72] Even Vatican scholars have been intoning the phrase: in February 1998, *Jubilaeum* carried, as its opening contribution, an essay with the title "A Strong Moral Conscience for a Culture of Legality" (Torre 1998). A new chapter in the "judicial experience has been opened," it declared, one we might "call the 'rights of [individual] desires.' . . . [T]he emancipation of rights is a phenomenon in expansion, easily seen by anyone."

Whether this is true or not, there has certainly been an explosion of law-oriented nongovernmental organizations in the postcolonial world: lawyers for human rights, both within and without frontiers; legal resource centers and aid clinics; voluntary associations dedicated to litigating against historical injury, for social and jural recognition, for human dignity, and for material entitlements of one kind or another. Situated at the intersection of the public and the private, nongovernmental organizations of this sort are now commonly regarded as the civilizing missions of the twenty-first century. They are asserting their presence over ever wider horizons, encouraging citizens to deal with their problems by legal means. The upshot, it seems, is that people, even those who break the law, appear to be ever more litigious, sometimes with unforeseen consequences for states and ruling regimes. In South Africa, as we write, a plumber convicted of drunk driving is demanding $167,000 in damages from three cabinet ministers and the commissioner of Correctional Services for holding him in custody when, he says, by rights they should have had him in rehabilitation.[73] And two well-known alumni of the liberation struggle, the national chair and the secretary of the Umkhonto weSizwe Military Veterans Association (MKMVA), announced in 2005 that they would seek a high-court interdict against two others who had claimed to be elected officials of the organization and had entered financial deals, fraudulently, in its name. In times past, this kind of conflict among the African National Congress elect would have been fought out by more conventional political means, less by using the law and its breach as their weapons of combat. But then, in times past, the MKMVA would not have been a thoroughly neoliberal organization, as much an investment holding company for its members as a commons for ex-guerilla heroes.[74]

The global impact of legal nongovermental organizations on postcolonial consciousness is such that it is not uncommon nowadays to hear the language of jurisprudence in the Amazon or Aboriginal Australia, in the Kalahari or the New Guinea highlands, or among the homeless of Mumbai, Mexico City, Cape Town, and Trench Town. Spyer (chapter 5) notes for Ambon that, even where all means of enforcement are absent, there may be "a genuine regard for the law" and "repeated appeal to the judiciary" to restore order. Postcolonies, in sum, are saturated with self-imaginings and identities grounded in the jural, even in places in which trafficking outside it is as common as trafficking within it—presuming, of course, that the distinction can be made at all. In Nigeria, for instance, where the fetishism of the legal has very different parameters than in constitution-obsessed South Africa, the tax code requires that adult citizens must swear to having children and aged dependents to obtain family deductions. Everyone, it is said, claims the *maximum* number, whether they have them or not. And every bureaucrat, it appears, is aware that they do so. The infraction goes unprosecuted and nobody is self-abnegating enough not to take advantage of the fact. But the legal fiction, indeed a whole plethora of legal fictions, is sustained as though a perfectly ordinary judicial order exists;[75] faint traces here of 419, which also mimics, distends, and mocks the form and substance of fiscal law.

The Judicialization of Politics:
From Liability to Lawfare

It is not just self-imaginings, interests, identities, rights, and injuries that have become saturated with the culture of legality. Politics itself is migrating to the courts—or to their popular, even criminal, replicas. Conflicts once joined in parliaments, by means of street protests, mass demonstrations, and media campaigns, through labor strikes, boycotts, blockades, and other instruments of assertion, tend more and more—if not only,

or in just the same way everywhere—to find their way to the judiciary.
Class struggles seem to have metamorphosed into class actions (J. Comaroff and J. L. Comaroff 2003); people drawn together by social or material predicament, culture, race, sexual preference, residential proximity,
faith, and habits of consumption become legal persons as their common
plaints turn them into plaintiffs with communal identities—against an-
tagonists who, allegedly, have acted *illegally* against them. Citizens, subjects, governments, and corporations litigate against one another, often at
the intersections of tort law, human rights law, and the criminal law, in an
ever mutating kaleidoscope of coalitions and cleavages. For example, in
the wake of the Bhopal disaster, the Indian government, having passed
legislation to make itself the sole guardian of the *legal* interests of its citizens, sued Union Carbide in 1986, first in New York and then back
home,[76] eventually yielding a $470 million settlement—only to see the vic-
tims initiate their own action in 1999, in part to "take back control" of
the litigation itself.[77] Even democracy has been judicialized: in the Argen-
tinian national elections of 2002, amid floods of accusations of improper
and illegal conduct, the bench was asked to decide "hundreds" of disputes
involving primaries—echoes here of the United States, to which we shall
return—and even to set the day on which ballot boxes should be ready for
the polls.[78] By such pathways are quite ordinary political processes held
hostage to the dialectic of law and disorder.

For their part, states find themselves having to defend against public
actions in unprecedented numbers, for unprecedented sorts of things,
against unprecedented kinds of plaintiff. In 2000, the Brazilian federal appeals court found the government of Brazil, along with Fundação Nacional do Índio, guilty of the death and suffering of Panará Indians since
the time of "first contact" and ordered that compensation be paid. A year
earlier, the Nicaraguan regime was held to account by the Inter-American
Court on Human Rights for violating the territory of a community of
Awas Tingni by illicitly granting a logging concession to a Korean timber
company (Hale 2005: 14–15).[79] As this instance also indicates, the global
map of jurisdictions is changing—a fact attested to, famously, by the trials
and tribulations of Augusto Pinochet—as courts reconsider the spectrum
of complainants and the species of suit, many of them profoundly political in the old-fashioned sense of the term, that they are prepared to entertain. Which, in turn, has added both quantitatively and substantively to
the judicialization of politics and to its conduct as a practice of law and
order. Or, rather, law and disorder.

Thus the well-known chain of events involving HIV/AIDS drugs in the south, the politics of health being among the most significant issues of mass public concern across much of the postcolonial world (Robins 2004; J. Comaroff, forthcoming). In a single year it involved, among a bewildering free fall of suits, threatened suits, lawmaking, lawbreaking, and challenges to the global intellectual property regime: (1) litigation initiated—and aborted under pressure—by the Pharmaceutical Manufacturers' Association of South Africa, representing subsidiaries of thirty-nine multinational corporations, against the South African government over its Medicines and Related Substances Control Amendment Act 90 of 1997, which set aside the complainants' patents; (2) the intervention in that suit, via an *amicus* ("friend of the court") brief, of the Treatment Action Campaign (TAC), which, along with trade unions, OXFAM, Médecins sans Frontières, and others, pronounced the outcome a major *political* victory over the market; (3) mock murder trials—an especially provocative genre of street theater in the circumstances—held by advocacy groups in front of the US headquarters of GlaxoSmithKline (GSK) and Bristol-Myers Squibb; (4) formal complaints made, and later dropped, by the United States to the World Trade Organization against Brazil, which had used its patent and trade laws first to manufacture its own drugs and then to pressure Roche to reduce the price of Nelfinavir by 40 percent;[80] (5) threats of legal action on the part of GSK against Cipla Ltd., the Indian generic drug producer, for selling an inexpensive version of Combivir in Africa; (6) a successful court action by TAC against the South African government, whom it had supported earlier against the pharmas, to enforce the "roll-out" of anti-retrovirals; and (7) a campaign by the Affordable Medicines and Treatment Campaign in India to enshrine access to medicines as a fundamental human right in the constitution. Even before all this, the TAC leadership had flagrantly smuggled generics into South Africa, challenging the state to prosecute it, thus to open up a site of confrontation over the politics of "bare life" and the entitlements of citizenship. Throughout the entire chain of events, conventional politics was limited to threats by the US administration, which colluded with the drug companies, and protests by advocacy groups under the "Lilliput Strategy"—itself orchestrated by the World Social Forum, which is dedicated to "globalization from below" to resist the planetary expansion of neoliberalism.[81] Both interventions, though, were intended to influence the *legal* proceedings in play: the law was the instrument connecting political means to political ends on all sides.

The history of AIDS drugs notwithstanding, the judicialization of politics has been mobilized effectively by corporate capitalism to create a deregulated environment conducive to its workings—and, at times, to protect some of its more equivocal operations from scrutiny. But, as we have already intimated, it has also been deployed at the nether end of the political spectrum: by the "little" peoples and marginal populations of the world. Some of those deployments have been intended to stop harmful intrusions into their lives. Others have sought restitution for damages arising out of egregious acts of violence against them: witness Nancy Scheper-Hughes's (chapter 4) account of the efforts of ordinary people and activists in the Northeast Brazilian interior to take a stand against death squads by invoking constitutional and human rights;[82] or the civil proceeding against Pluspetrol in 2002 by the Inter-ethnic Association for Development of the Peruvian Amazon to demand the cleanup of, and compensation for, an oil spill in the Marañon River; or the class actions filed by 16,000 or so alumni of Indian boarding schools in Canada against the Anglican, Presbyterian, Roman Catholic, and United Churches, alleging physical, sexual, and cultural abuse.[83] While most such suits arise out of an originary act of criminal violation, not all of them are directed primarily at reparation. The effort in 2001 by relatives of those killed by the Israelis at Shatila to indict Ariel Sharon for war crimes was intended as a volley fired in the struggle against Zionism, itself seen by its opponents as a crime against humanity. Many, although not all, such cases have failed. The Ogoni, for one, lost a landmark claim brought in the United States under the Alien Tort Claims Act[84] against Shell for its activities in Nigeria, in particular for its complicity in the execution by the Babangida regime of those politically opposed to the operations of the oil company. The law often comes down on the side of bandit capital, especially when the latter dons the mask of respectable business.[85]

It is not just the politics of the present that is being judicialized. The past, too, is increasingly caught up in the dialectic of law and disorder: hence the mobilization of legalities to fight anti-imperialist battles anew, which has compelled the British government to answer under oath for having committed acts of unspeakable atrocity in its African "possessions" (D. Anderson 2005; Elkins 2005), for having killed local leaders at whim, and for having unlawfully alienated territory from one African people to another. By these means is colonialism, tout court, rendered criminal. Hauled before a judge, history is made to break its silences, to speak in tongues hitherto unheard and untranslated, to submit itself to the scales of justice at the behest of those who suffered it, of its most abject subjects—and to be reduced to a cash equivalent, payable as the official tender of damage, dispossession, loss, trauma. In the process, too, it becomes clear that what imperialism is being indicted for, above all, is its commission of *lawfare:* its use of its own rules—of its duly enacted penal codes, its administrative law, its states of emergency, its charters and mandates and warrants, its norms of engagement—to impose a sense of order upon its subordinates by means of violence rendered legible, legal, and legitimate by its own sovereign word. And also to commit its own ever-so-civilized, patronizing, high-minded forms of kleptocracy.

Lawfare—the resort to legal instruments, to the violence inherent in the law, to commit acts of political coercion, even erasure (J. L. Comaroff 2001)—is equally marked in postcolonies, of course. As a species of political displacement, it becomes most readily visible when those who act in the name of the state conjure with legalities to act against some or all of its citizens. Any number of examples present themselves, but the most infamously contemporary is, again, to be found in Zimbabwe. The Mugabe regime has consistently passed laws in parliament intended to silence its critics and then has proceeded to take violent action against them; the media regulations put in place just after the presidential election of 2002 are a case in point. Operation Murambatsvina ("Drive out Trash"), which has razed informal settlements and markets, forced people out of urban areas, and caused a great deal of hardship, ill-health, and death under the banner of "slum clearance," has recently taken this practice to unprecedented heights—or depths. The most persuasive explanation for the operation, says Allister Sparks,[86] is that it is, first, an act of vengeance against urban Zimbabweans who voted overwhelmingly for the opposition Movement for Democratic Change in the national election of March 2005; second, an attempt to preempt uprisings on the part of a largely out-of-work population desperately short of food and fuel; and, third, a strike against the black market that has arisen in the informal sector to trade in the foreign currency sent back by citizens laboring abroad. Murambatsvina, according to the Mugabe regime, is merely an application of the law of the land: it is a righteous effort to demolish "illegal structures." For critics, on the other hand, it is not that at all. As one Caribbean journalist put it, in a phrase especially apt here, it is "political criminality."[87] Note, in this respect, how the Zimbabwean embassy in Jakarta responded to a censorious piece in an Indonesian newspaper:

> The rapid development of illegal informal small-scale industries, trading centers and outbuildings in all the cities and towns had destroyed the status of these urban centers and outstretched the capacity of the municipalities to provide adequate services. The inability of the urban local authorities to levy

most of the illegal vendors created an untenable situation that victimized everybody, including the licenced traders. Many illegal activities such as the hoarding of basic commodities and dealing in gold and foreign currency were thriving in the illegal informal sector. Over 22,000 people have been arrested for various offenses during the ongoing exercise. . . . The court also ruled that most of the structures were illegal as the owners did not follow the set approval channels with the respective local authorities.[88]

The word "illegal" appears five times in this passage.

Lawfare can be limited or it can reduce people to "bare life"; in some postcolonies, it has mutated into a deadly necropolitics with a rising body count (see chapter 9). But it always seeks to launder brute power in a wash of legitimacy, ethics, propriety. Sometimes it is put to work, as it was in many colonial contexts, to make new sorts of human subjects; sometimes it is the vehicle by which oligarchs seize the sinews of state to further their economic ends; sometimes it is a weapon of the weak, turning authority back on itself by commissioning the sanction of the court to make claims for resources, recognition, voice, integrity, sovereignty.[89] But ultimately, it is neither the weak nor the meek nor the marginal who predominate in such things. It is those equipped to play most potently inside the dialectic of law and disorder. This, to close a circle opened in the preface, returns us to Derrida, Agamben, and Benjamin: to the notion that the law originates in violence and lives by violent means, the notion, in other words, that the legal and the lethal animate and inhabit one another. Whatever the truth of the matter, politics at large, and the politics of coercion in particular, appear ever more to be turning into lawfare.

But this still does not lay to rest the questions that lurk beneath our narrative, although it does gesture toward some answers: Again, *why* the fetishism of legalities? What are its implications for the play of law and dis/order in the postcolony? And what, if anything, makes postcolonies different in this respect from other nation-states?

Of Heterodoxy, Commensuration, Cameras Obscura, and Horizontal Sovereignties

At one level the answer to the first question looks to be self-evident. The turn to law, like the popular punitiveness of the present moment (see above), would seem to arise directly out of a growing anxiety about lawlessness; although, as we have already noted, more law, far from resolving the problem of disorder, draws attention back to rising criminality, further compounding public insecurities. But none of this explains the displacement of the political into the legal, the ready turn to civil proceedings to resolve an ever greater range of private wrongs, and so on. To be sure, the fetishism of the law runs far deeper than purely a concern with crime. It has to do with the very constitution of the postcolonial polity. And its history-in-the-making. The modernist nation-state appears to be undergoing an epochal move *away* from the ideal of an imagined community founded on the fiction, often violently sustained, of cultural homogeneity (B. Anderson 1983), *toward* a nervous, xenophobically tainted sense of heterogeneity and heterodoxy. The rise of neoliberalism has heightened all this, with its impact on population movements, on the migration of work and workers, on the dispersion of cultural practices, on the return of the colonial oppressed to haunt the cosmopoles that once ruled them and wrote their histories, on the geographical re/distribution of sites of accumulation. These effects are felt especially in former colonies, which were erected from the first on difference, itself owed to the indifference of empires that paid scant attention to the organic sociologies of the "countries" they casually called into being. In the event, as is increasingly the case everywhere, postcolonials are citizens for whom polymorphous, labile identities coexist in uneasy ensembles of political subjectivity. In many postcolonies, the "vast majority . . . principally think of themselves" as members of "an ethnic, cultural, language, religious, or some other group" and "attach their personal fate" to it, rather than to the nation, although this does *not* necessarily imply that most of them "reject their national identity" per se (Gibson 2004: chap. 2).[90] Indeed, so-called communal loyalties are frequently blamed for the kinds of violence, nepotism, and corruption said to saturate these societies, as if cultures of heterodoxy bear within them the seeds of criminality, difference, disorder.

But an awareness of difference itself also points the way to more law. Why? Because, with the growing heterodoxy of the twenty-first-century polity, legal instruments *appear* to offer a ready means of commensuration (J. Comaroff and J. L. Comaroff 2000): a repertoire of more or less standardized terms and practices that permit the negotiation of values, beliefs, ideals, and interests across otherwise-impermeable lines of cleavage. Hence the displacement of so much politics into jurisprudence. Hence the flight into constitutionalism, which, in its postcolonial guise, embraces heterogeneity within the language of universal rights—thus dissolving *groups* of people with distinctive identities into *aggregates* of person who may enjoy the same entitlements and enact their difference under the sovereignty of a shared Bill of Rights. Furthermore, because social, spiritual, and cultural identities tend increasingly to *cross* frontiers, resort to the jural as a means of commensuration also transects nation-states, which is why there is so much talk nowadays of *global* legal regimes. Meanwhile, the effort to make human rights into an ever more universal discourse, and to ascribe ever more authority to it, gives impetus to the remapping of the cartography of jurisdictions.

While the growing salience of heterodoxy has been partly responsible for the fetishism of the law, another consideration is every bit as critical. It arises from a well-recognized corollary of the neoliberal turn, one spelled out earlier: the outsourcing by states of many of the conventional operations of governance, including those, like health services, incarceration, policing, and the conduct of war, integral to the management of "bare life." Bureaucracies do retain some of their old functions, of course, most notably the transfer of public wealth into private hands. But progressively (or, depending on ideological orientation, retrogressively), twenty-first-century governments have attenuated their administrative reach, leaving more and more routine political action—be it social projects, the quest for redress, or the search for (anything other than national) security—to citizens as individuals, as communities of one kind or another, as classes of actor, social or legal. Under these conditions, in which the threat of disorder seems everywhere immanent, everywhere proportional to the retraction of the state, civil law presents itself as a more or less effective weapon of the weak, the strong, and everyone in between. This, in turn, exacerbates the resort to lawfare. The court has become a utopic institutional site to which human agency may turn for a medium in which to achieve its ends—albeit sometimes in vain, given the disproportion everywhere between populist expectations of legal remedy and, law-oriented nongovernmental organizations notwithstanding, access to its means. This is all the more so in postcolonies, where bureaucratic apparatuses and bourgeoisies were not elaborate to begin with; where the executive was typically unapproachable; in which heterogeneity was undeniable from the start, often without the requisite instruments; in which state control over the means of violence was never that firm; in which foreclosed access to power makes Lilliputian crusades into foreign jurisdictions *very* appealing.

Put all of these things together and the fetishism of the law seems overdetermined. So, too, do its implications. The distillation of postcolonial citizens into legal subjects, and postcolonial politics into lawfare, charts the road from the past to the future, albeit less sharply in some places than in others. Not only are government and public affairs becoming more legalistic, but so are "communities" within the nation-state—cultural communities, religious communities, corporate communities, residential communities, communities of interest, outlaw communities—in regulating their own internal affairs and in dealing with others (see chapter 6). Everything, it seems, including the metaphysics of disorder, exists here in the shadow of the law (see chapter 5), which also makes it unsurprising that a "culture of legality" should saturate not just civil order but *also* its criminal undersides, its camera obscura, and the ambiguous, gray, alegal zones that infuse both, drawing them together into an intricate weave of practices, relations, and mediations (see chapter 7).

In a previous section, we spoke of the ways in which criminality appropriates, recommissions, and counterfeits the means and ends of polite society, of the state, of the market. Recall Gangland (Pty) Ltd. on the Cape Flats: organized crime there is not just a mirror image of the business world, a *lumpen* stand-in for those excluded from the service economy. For its consumers and customers, it also takes on some of the *positive* functions of government, not least the safety and security of its taxed client communities. Illicit corporations of this sort across the postcolonial world—loosely dubbed "mafias" and "gangs" but frequently much more complex, flexible structures than these terms suggest—often appoint shadow judicial personnel, duplicate legal rituals and processes, and convene courts to try offenders against the persons, property, and social order over which they exert sovereignty. Even in prison. Observe, in this regard, Steinberg's (2004) extraordinary account of the elaborate mock judiciary and its even more elaborate proceedings, which extend to capital punishment, among the Numbers gangs in South Africa. Many outlawed "vigilante" groups have developed quite complicated simulacra of the law as well. Some even have . . . constitutions and, significantly, are said to offer "alternative citizenship" to their members.[91]

It will be self-evident that the counterfeiting of a culture of legality by the criminal underworld—and by those who occupy the spaces between it and the realm of the licit—feeds the dialectic of law and disorder. After all, once government begins seriously to outsource its services and to franchise force, and once extralegal organizations begin to mimic the state and the market by providing protection and dispensing justice, social order itself becomes like a hall of mirrors: at once there and not there, at once all too real and a palimpsest of images, at once visible, opaque, and translucent. What is more, this doubling, this copresence of law and disorder, has its own geography, a geography of discontinuous, overlapping sovereignties.

We stated a moment ago that, with the proliferation of a culture of legality and the burgeoning resort to lawfare, "communities" of all kinds have become ever more legalistic in regulating their internal lives and in dealing with others; it is often in the process of so doing, in fact, that they become communities at all, the act of judicialization being also an act of objectification. Herein lies their will to sovereignty. Without joining the conversation occasioned by the revivification of interest in the work of Carl Schmitt on the topic, we take the term "sovereignty" to connote the more or less effective claim on the part of any agent, community, cadre, or collectivity to exercise autonomous, exclusive control over the lives, deaths, and conditions of existence of those who fall within a given purview, and to extend over them the jurisdiction of some kind of law (see Hansen and Stepputat 2005). Sovereignty, *pace* Agamben (2005), is as much a matter of investing a world with regulations as being able to suspend them, as much a matter of establishing the normative as determining states of exception. Any sovereignty, even if it is a criminal counterfeit, depends also on the institution of an order of rules in order to rule. "Lawmaking," argues Benjamin (1978: 295), "is power making, and, to that extent, an immediate manifestation of violence." But "power [is] the principle of all mythical lawmaking." In sum, to transcend itself, to transform itself into sovereign authority, power demands at the very least a minimal architecture of legalities—or, once again, their simulacra.

Because of their historical predicaments, postcolonies tend *not* to be organized under a single, vertically integrated sovereignty sustained by a highly centralized state. Rather, they consist in a horizontally woven tapestry of partial sovereignties: sovereignties over terrains and their inhabitants, over aggregates of people conjoined in faith or culture, over transactional spheres, over networks of relations, regimes of property, domains of practice, and, quite often, over various combinations of these things; sovereignties longer or shorter lived, protected to a greater or lesser degree by the capacity to exercise compulsion, always incomplete. Note, in this respect, Arendt's (1998: 234) observation that "sovereignty, the ideal of uncompromising self-sufficiency and mastership, is contradictory to the very condition of plurality"—plurality, patently, being the *endemic* condition of the postcolony. It is also why so many postcolonial polities appear to be composed of zones of civility joined by fragile corridors of safety in environments otherwise presumed to be, literally, out of control. Those zones and corridors are, to return to Thomas Hobbes, the "walled" spaces of sovereign legality, *mondo juralis,* in the patchwork geography that maps out the dialectic of law and order in the postcolony, the patchwork that makes human life habitable in a universe represented, archetypically, as at once ordered and unruly. And always just one step away from implosion.

Postcolonies in Perspective:
Taking Exception to Exceptionalism

Which brings us, finally, to the question of exceptionalism. Is the criminal violence archetypically attributed to "the" postcolony all that singular these days? Is the fetishism of the law in the south any different from
that found in the north? And what of the dialectic of law and disorder? Is
it confined purely to the postcolonial world? Geschiere (chapter 6), who
thinks not, suggests that the point of posing the question is not just to
understand postcolonies better but to subject to critical scrutiny tendencies otherwise taken for granted "in the supposedly modern countries" of
the global north. His point is well taken.

One way to answer the question is to turn to the empirical for counter
examples. There is plenty of evidence that the countries of Africa, for example, are more similar to than different from, say, Russia. In 1999 the
Economist anointed that country, *not* Nigeria, the "world's leading kleptocracy." Crime there, it went on, "is not at the margin of society, it is at
its very centre."[92] Consider the reported facts: the Russian underworld
controls 40 percent of the economy and half of the nation's banks and is
famous for its export of the arts of assassination; corruption and money
laundering flourish largely unchecked, to the extent that 78 percent of all
enterprises report that they regularly pay bribes;[93] state personnel, especially the likes of customs officers, are constantly on the take; many thugs
don fake uniforms to become counterfeit security personnel; "new organized crime," increasingly advanced in its business practices, preys on the
private sector—and when the state will not help collect debts, secure businesses, or provide public services, it offers those very services at a competitive price. At the same time, while vast amounts of wealth flow
through a "shadowy netherworld," the "structures and values of legality
are in place," and "even the most corrupt politicians pay lip service" to
them.[94] Sound familiar? There is one difference, though. If the *Economist*
is to be believed, the United States, quick to point to corruption in Africa
when loans and aid do not reach their intended recipients, has long turned
a blind eye to similar things in Russia, typically for political reasons.

Or, if Russia is set aside as itself postcolonial, which is implausible
given that it was until recently the imperium of the second world, Germany offers a salutary alternative. Often vaunted as the very epitome of
corporate respectability, that country has been rocked by revelations of a
"virus of corruption—not only in officially protected niches or in the
profit-crazy milieu of stock exchange brokers, but everywhere."[95] Echoes
here of Enron and epidemic corporate malfeasance in the United States.

This, of course, is not to suggest that Russia is just like Rwanda or Germany just like Guatemala or the United States just like the Ukraine. But it *does* point to the fact that, across the planet and often in the most unlikely places (Sweden, the Netherlands, Japan, England, and Canada, among others), there is growing anxiety, even moral panic, over rising malpractice, crime, and disorder—which has led to calls for more law, harsher enforcement, longer sentences, even citizen militias, and, in turn, especially as media attention focuses on these things, to yet more fear. Nor is that fear altogether groundless. Conservative theorist John Gray (1998) and others have argued that the downside of neoliberalism *is* an escalation in global incidences of lawlessness, due in part to the retraction of the state, in part to opportunities for outlaw activity arising out of deregulation and new business practices, in part to the ready market for the means of violence. All of which conduces, as in postcolonies, to a widening populist impression that the line between order and disorder is very fine indeed. This impression was given prima facie support in the United States during the late summer of 2005 by the looting and shooting in New Orleans that followed Hurricane Katrina, much of it perpetrated by victims left resourceless, unsaved, and unserviced by a regime whose president's first reaction, as the wealthy fled in their luxury vehicles, was to urge the poor to "take responsibility" for their situation. Having little alternative, many of them did. The repeatedly televised scenes, underscored by the slow reaction of the state, left embarrassed Americans gazing upon Louisiana in incredulity, confessing that what came to mind amid the scenes of destitution and violence were familiar pictures of . . . Africa. Complete with what were quickly called "refugees." The United States had come face to face with the reality that it, too, looks more than a little postcolonial: that it has its own "south," a racialized world of the poor, excluded and criminalized. In a striking reversal, South Africans likened "apocalyptic, devastated, benighted" New Orleans to Rwanda—and admonished themselves not to become "like that."[96]

But might this not be an exceptional event? Is Gray correct in claiming that there *is* more lawlessness everywhere? According to Barclay and Tavares (2003: 2), whose statistics come from the British Home Office, both robbery and crimes of violence *did* increase sharply across the world between 1997 and 2001: the former by 24 percent in Europe and a whopping 128 percent in Japan, the latter by 22 percent in Europe (50 percent in France, 35 percent in the Netherlands, and 26 percent in England and Wales) and 79 percent in Japan; and this does *not* include Internet criminality, which, according to a widely disseminated study done at Carnegie

Mellon University, is effecting a "profound change" in the nature and proportions of lawlessness as "cyberextortion" is added to the "digital Mafia's bag of tricks."[97] But here is the thing: in the United Nations' "grand total of recorded crime" for 2000,[98] which includes both violent and nonviolent offences, the ten leaders were New Zealand (at 11,152 felonies per 100,000 head of population), Dominica (10,763.01), Finland (10,242.8), England and Wales (9,766.73), Denmark (9,449.78), Chile (9,275.91), the United States (8,517.19),[99] the Netherlands (8,211.54), Canada (8,040.65),[100] and South Africa (7,997.06). While these counts have to be read skeptically (many nations do not submit figures and the reliability of those that are submitted are hardly beyond question), seven of the most crime-ridden reporting countries are *not* postcolonies, conventionally speaking. Moreover, in all of these nation-states, organized crime also appears to be extending its compass, reaching deeper and deeper into the inner cities of the United States and Europe (see Venkatesh 2000), becoming ever more sophisticated in its commercial practices, consolidating its spectral forms of governance in the mediated image of the rule of law— and doing ever more business with licit corporations and political cadres.

Given these facts and figures, it is not hard to conclude, as so many around the world have done, that the likes of the United States and the nations of Europe are themselves rife with corruption, even if they are more skilled than their postcolonial counterparts at hiding their questionable practices in a skein of lawfulness. After all, the first election of the current US president, determined *not* by popular franchise but by a nepotistic intervention and an ideologically stacked Supreme Court, was far from the epitome of political propriety; and his subsequent conduct of domestic and foreign policy to the express benefit of American capital—indeed, of cronies and corporations closely associated with his power base—appears to legalize by sovereign fiat precisely what is dubbed "corrupt" elsewhere. Thus is exception compounded of deception and extraction; not surprisingly, in Africa, where might does not always deceive as successfully, joking analogies are often drawn between Mr. Bush and Mr. Mugabe. Similarly in England, the Conservative governments of Margaret Thatcher and John Major were rocked by serial scandals, not least as they sold off public assets to wealthy Britons for a song and as one parliamentarian after another was revealed to have broken the law; the Labour government that followed has been shown less than honest in taking the country to war. As David Hall (1999) notes, speaking of the "more mature systems" of corruption in Europe: "recent years have seen leading politicians prosecuted and convicted of corruption in many Western European countries, including Austria, Belgium, France, Germany, Italy, Spain and the UK. In 1999, the entire European Commission, the highest political authority in the EU, resigned over corruption allegations. . . . According to a BBC radio program,[101] bribery is so routine that UK companies employ agents to recover bribes which have failed to produce the desired result."

It is hardly unexpected, then, that statespeople and politicians the world over, *not* just in postcolonies, have become figures of ill-repute, suspected or proven, that multinational companies are widely presumed to be complicit in their webs of deceit, that the line between licit business and the practices of organized crime are often difficult to tell apart; or that, just as the former bleeds into the latter, the latter tends more and more to counterfeit the former. In the final analysis, it is impossible to know whether or not there is as much bribery, violent crime, and organized lawlessness in the north as there is in the south. Apart from all else, official statistics of corruption, especially when they serve authority, often hide as much as they disclose. And, in any case, many things taken to be signs of graft in postcolonies—like massive "contributions" to politicians paid by interested businesses and individuals, or the blatant distribution of the spoils of warfare and power among political elites—are "lawful" activities in the north, where they are covered by the chaste clothing of an accountancy culture. But, as we have seen, the south often takes the rap for shady collaborations: a bribe there is often a "commission," a "finder's fee," or a "consultation fee" in "the supposedly modern countries of the West." The point? That many of the practices quintessentially associated with postcolonies are not confined to them. They are discernible elsewhere as well, if not perhaps as acutely or as vividly—or living under a legal alias.

This is true, too, of the other side of the dialectic of law and order, the culture of legality and the judicialization of politics. The *non*-postcolonial world, under the impact of neoliberalism, also appears more litigious than ever before; the United States, which used to be far ahead of everyone else in this respect, is becoming increasingly average. The readiness of Europeans to act first and foremost as legal subjects and to engage in lawfare is being exacerbated by the kind of market fundamentalism that makes the consuming citizen the guardian of her or his own well-being. But there is another consideration here, too. The growing heterodoxy of most nation-states, not only of postcolonies, has encouraged peoples of difference everywhere to protect their rights and entitlements by appeal to the one institution designed to deal with those rights: the courts. As we have noted, many of them are demanding to regulate their own affairs, frequently by recourse to their own tribunals under their own authorities. The struggle over Muslim headscarves in France, the effort of religious Jews in Manchester to constitute a Pale, and the growing assertions of autonomy by First Peoples in Canada and the United States are tokens of an even more familiar type. In the north, where the centralization of authority in the state has a longer and more elaborate history, a single, vertically integrated sovereignty may still continue to hold sway, preventing the politics of recognition from giving way to the sedimentation of horizontal, partial sovereignties—except in criminal enclaves and in inner cities, over which policing has as little purchase as it does in any postcolonial context. Yet the pressure to spin off into horizontal sovereignties, as Russia knows from its experience in Chechnya, seems to be becoming more and more insistent, particularly at the behest of religious and ethnonationalist movements, organized crime, multinational corporations, nongovernmental organizations, and other disparate forces in the world that seek the greatest possible independence in a deregulated universe. It is as if the south, again reversing the taken-for-granted telos of modernity, is the direction to which point the signposts of history unfolding.

The dispersal of politics into the law is also readily discernible in the north. The US case is legend. Perhaps its most flagrant instance is the appointment of justices to the Supreme Court: in spite of right-wing rhetoric *against* judicial activism, the Republican Party has, since the Reagan years, sought to stack the Court in order to have the bench institutionalize conservative ideology in such a way as to put it beyond the reach of formal politics, which is the most effective political act of all. The GOP has also turned to the legislature, most notoriously in the Terry Schiavo "right-to-die" case in 2005, in efforts to force the judiciary to do its bidding, not least in matters of faith. Such things, patently, are not confined to America. Most Italians, for example, have long believed that Sergio Berlusconi has used "his iron majority in Parliament to pass custom-made laws to resolve legal problems related to his business empire."[102] But, as in the postcolony, the law is also a site and an instrument of politics from the bottom up. Take, in the United States again, labor and welfare: with the weakening of labor associations and social services, the global market in cheap, unregulated work, and other effects of laissez faire, there has been a huge growth of suits against government agencies arising out of employment conditions and welfare provision, so much so that the state of Washington, for one, finds it difficult to purchase liability insurance anymore.[103]

There are many other sites of political contestation through litigation "from below." One concerns the place of religion in society, the object of numerous legal actions. A couple of years back, to take an unusual instance, George W. Bush was sued in a Texas court by a certain Douglas C. Welsch, a prison inmate, who alleged that, as state governor, he had violated the constitution by turning the pastoral care of the penitentiary over to the Prison Fellowship Ministry, thereby deliberately advancing evangelical Christianity over other faiths or no faith at all;[104] the dialectic of law and disorder has its own moments of divine irony. Gender equality, rights to sexual freedom and gay marriage, abortion, environmental protection, capital punishment, and the politics of race have also had many days in the courts of the north, all the more so since the public contexts in which they may be effectively fought out seem constantly to recede.

In sum, the similarities between the postcolony and the world beyond it are unmistakable. Everywhere these days, criminal violence has become an imaginative vehicle, a hieroglyph almost, for thinking about the nightmares that threaten the nation and for posing "more law and order" as the appropriate means of dealing with them. And everywhere the discourse of crime displaces attention away from the material and social effects of neoliberalism, blaming its darker undersides on the evils of the underworld. But the differences are also palpable. There is no question that the dialectic of law and disorder appears inflated, and more dramatically visible, in postcolonial contexts. In those contexts, the dispersal of state authority into patchworks of partial, horizontal sovereignties is far more advanced, although the devolution of governance is beginning to become more palpable in the north as well. Partly because of their colonial history, partly because they inherited political institutions ill-suited to their contemporary predicament (see Davidson 1992), partly because of the unequal effects of structural adjustment (see Hansen and Stepputat 2005), disorder seems more threatening, more immanent, more all-encompassing in them.

As this suggests, postcolonies are hyperextended versions of the history of the contemporary world order running slightly ahead of itself (J. Comaroff and J. L. Comaroff 2003). It is the so-called margins, after all, that often experience tectonic shifts in the order of things first, most visibly, most horrifically—and most energetically, creatively, ambiguously. Nor are we speaking here of a period of transition, a passing moment in the life and times of the postcolony, a moment suspended uneasily somewhere between the past and the future. This is the ongoing present. It is history-in-the-making. Which is why the "problem" of lawlessness, itself just one-half of the dialectic of law and disorder, is so much more than merely a corollary of democratization, whose own recent renaissance seems suspiciously correlated with the migration of politics away from conventional political institutions. And why, as we said in the preface, "the" postcolony has become such a crucial site for theory construction, sui generis. To the extent that they are harbingers of a global future, of the rising neoliberal age at its most assertive, these polities are also where the limits of social knowledge demand to be engaged.

Notes

We would like to thank Lisa Wedeen and Jeremy Jones for their astute feedback on this chapter.

1. Gross comparative statistics for the past few years—to be *very* skeptically regarded, of course—point to substantial increases across the world in both property crimes and crimes of violence (see J. Comaroff and J. L. Comaroff 2006), a matter to which we return below.

2. The term "f-utilitarian" is our own (J. Comaroff and J. L. Comaroff 1999). It is meant to capture the odd mix of postmodern pessimism and utilitarianism that followed the neoliberal turn wherever the promise of post–Cold War plenty—to be delivered by the triumph of the free market—gave way to growing poverty at the hands of so-called structural adjustment.

3. Arendt's (1998: 228 n. 70) citation is to the Modern Library edition of *Capital* (Marx 1936: 824).

4. See preface; also below. We have in mind here Derrida 2002 and Agamben 1998.

5. For discussion of the periodization of postcolonial history after World War II, see Bhabha and Comaroff 2002.

6. "Brave Neo World" is a term that we have used elsewhere in respect to postcolonial South Africa (J. L. Comaroff and J. Comaroff 2004) and revisit in the subtitle of a book currently in preparation (forthcoming).

7. Note, in this respect, Bayart's (1986: 111) conception of civil society less as a thing than as a process whose object is to "counteract the 'totalisation' unleashed by the state."

8. For wide-ranging discussion of the quest for "civil society" in what were then still called the "second" and "third" worlds, see, e.g., Woods 1992; Bayart 1993; Blaney and Pasha 1993; Fatton 1995; Monga 1996; Owusu 1997; Haynes 1997; Harbeson et al. 1994; Chabal 1986; Kasfir 1998; Hann and Dunn 1996. Hall and Trentmann's (2004) recent compendium also offers a broad spectrum of conceptual writings on the topic.

9. The United States is not the only state to exercise coercion of this kind. James Copnall (2005: 26) reminds us that, in 1990, the move toward democracy in Francophone Africa was "encouraged" by France when, at a summit at La Baule, President Mitterand told assembled leaders that "only those who opened their countries up to multiparty politics would continue to receive lavish aid packages."

10. When *Tel Quel* magazine and the US-funded National Institute for Democracy explored public attitudes to democracy in Morocco recently, not a single respondent associated it with elections; most linked it to the right to be pro-

tected from the police and other authorities (Harter 2005: 22). This is telling: in many parts of the world, *pace* Przeworski et al. (2000; and see above), the concept, at its most minimalist, has little to do with ballots and everything to do with rights.

11. See Navaro-Yashin 2005, although she uses the term in a somewhat different sense than we do here.

12. See Johannes Leithäuser, "Crime Groups Become an Increasing Security Threat, Officials Assert," *Frankfurter Allgemeine Zeitung*, 22 May 2001, English edition, p. 2.

13. Larry Rohter and Juan Forero, "Latin America: Graft Threatens New Democracies," and Sharon La Franiere, "Africa: Corruption Is Crippling Growth," *New York Times*, articles selected for *Sunday Times* (Johannesburg), 15 August 2005, pp. 1, 2.

14. The term "prebendalism" may be unfamiliar to general readers. Derived from Weberian historical sociology, it refers to a political order in which the wealth that accrues to any office may be appropriated by its holder for his or her personal benefit and that of his or her kin, constituents, or followers. In Africa, it has been applied especially to Nigeria (see, e.g., Joseph 1987; Lewis 1996). The reduction of African political systems—and their so-called corruption complex (Olivier de Sardan 1999b)—to such terms invokes a comparative political-science literature too large to annotate here. However, a volume entitled *Corruption: A Selected and Annotated Bibliography*, published online by the Norwegian Agency for Development Cooperation (NORAD), provides a useful point of departure; see www.norad.no/default.asp?V_ITEM_ID=1663, chapter 2 (accessed 12 July 2005).

15. David Binder, "Dimensions of Organized Crime in the Balkans" (paper presented at the conference "The Dark Side of Globalization: Trafficking and Transborder Crime to, through, and from Eastern Europe," UCLA Center for European and Eurasian Studies, 14 May 2004), http://www.isop.ucla.edu/article.asp?parentid=11513 (accessed 27 July 2005).

16. See also Paulo de Mesquita Neto, "Crime, Violence and Democracy in Latin America" (paper presented at the conference "Integration in the Americas," University of New Mexico, 2 April 2002), http://laii.unm.edu/conference/mesquita.php (accessed 27 July 2005); Andrew Gumbel, "Druglords Turn Mexican Town into Bullet-Scarred Battlefield," *Sunday Independent*, 7 August 2005, p. 16.

17. See, e.g., its notorious leader, "Hopeless Africa," *Economist*, 13 May 2000, p. 17, which was followed by a longer article, "Africa: The Heart of the Matter," pp. 22–24; see also "Economic Focus: The African Exception," *Economist*, 30 March 2002, p. 68.

18. Most famously, Robert Kaplan 1994, but for another egregious example, see Richburg 1997.

19. Or, as a recent *New York Times* headline put it, describing pervasive corruption in Russia, "Just . . . Business"; see Steven Lee Myers, "Pervasive Bribery in Russia Today 'Is Just Called Business,'" *New York Times*, articles selected for *Sunday Times* (Johannesburg), 28 August 2005, p. 3.

20. A synopsis of the report is to be found on the Global Policy Forum Web site; see "Africa 'Best for Investment,'" http://www.globalpolicy.org/socecon/develop/

africa/2003/0408fdi.htm (accessed 1 May 2005). This raises unnerving parallels with earlier moments of colonial extraction, given the reluctance of Western corporations to see the continent as a site of autonomous economic development.

21. David Leigh and David Pallister, "Revealed: The New Scramble for Africa," *Guardian,* 1 June 2005, p. 1.

22. Steve Inskeep, "Corruption Clouds Nigeria's Growing Gas Business," *NPR,* 26 August 2005, morning edition, http://www.npr.org/templates/storey/story.php?storyId=4797944 (accessed 31 August 2005).

23. Luis Vega, "A Plague on Latin America," *GO Inside,* 10 September 2004, http://goinside.com/04/9/plague.html (accessed 27 July 2005); Utkarsh Kansal, "Why Is Corruption so Common in India?" *India Information Initiative,* 2001, http://www.india-reform.org/articles/corruption.html (accessed 27 July 2005).

24. Consistent with what we said above, the Executive Summary of the *Report on the World Social Situation, 2005,* whose subtitle is *The Inequality Predicament,* begins by stating that the "global commitment to overcoming inequality . . . is fading," as a result of which many "communities, countries and regions remain vulnerable to social, political and economic upheaval" (United Nations 2005).

25. Rohter and Forero add that postauthoritarian governments across Latin America, with the exception of Chile and Uruguay, have all seen increased corruption; Larry Rohter and Juan Forero, "Latin America: Graft Threatens New Democracies," *New York Times,* articles selected for *Sunday Times* (Johannesburg), 15 August 2005, pp. 1, 2.

26. Karen Breytenbach, "Dictator's Son on City Spending Spree," *Cape Times,* 20 July 2005, p. 1.

27. See Mark Hollingsworth, "Wizard Jape That Cost Mummy R3 Million," *Sunday Independent,* 11 September 2005, p. 16.

28. Thus, Brazil is among the world's top ten economies, a matter to which we shall return. India has attracted a good deal of outsourcing in fields like electronic communications, while Mexico's *maquiladora* borderland prospered until undercut by sweatshops in East and Southeast Asia. Africa, on the other hand, while rich in primary resources, has benefited little from the global dispersal of industrial work. All of which raises questions, neither for the first nor for the last time, about the meaningfulness in this respect of the category "postcolonial."

29. The remark was made by Benjamin Mkapa, president of Tanzania; see Anthony Mitchell, "Globalization Like Slavery—Mkapa," *Cape Times,* 1 September 2005, p. 28.

30. "Field Listing—Illicit Drugs," *World Factbook 2002,* http://www.faqs.org/docs/factbook/fields/2086.html (accessed 1 August 2004).

31. See n. 32.

32. It is estimated that a proportion of so-called blood diamonds from Sierra Leone, Angola, and Liberia has found its way into the hands of De Beers, although an international outcry has led to the imposition of tougher regulations on the trade; see Dick Durham, "De Beers Sees Threat of Blood Diamonds," 18 January 2001, http://cnnstudentnews.cnn.com/2001/WORLD/africa/01/18/diamonds.debeers/ (accessed 15 July 2005). Most of the coltan (i.e., columbite tantalite, a vital component of cell phones and computer chips) illegally extracted in Zaire is thought to make its way, via secretive chains of exchange, into the stock of main-

stream high-tech companies in Europe, Japan, and North America; see Kristi Essick, "Guns, Money and Cell Phones," *Industry Standard Magazine,* 11 June 2001, http://www.globalissues.org/Geopolitics/Africa/Articles/TheStandardColtan .asp (accessed 1 July 2005).

33. See also "Cartels Shipping Drugs via Africa," *Mercury,* 29 July 2005, http://www.themercury.co.za/index.php?fSectionId=284&fArticleId=2644688 (accessed 28 July 2005).

34. See also "Mexican Drug Commandos Expand Ops in 6 U.S. States: Feds Say Violent, Elite Paramilitary Units Establish Narcotics Routes North of Border," *World Net Daily,* 21 July 2005, http://www.worldnetdaily.com/news/article.asp ?ARTICLE_ID=44899 (accessed 28 July 2005).

35. "U.N.: Drug Cartels Using African Connections," *World,* 27 July 2005, http://www.cnn.com/2005/WORLD/americas/07/27/cartels.reut/ (accessed 1 August 2005).

36. Frosty Wooldridge, "Illegal Aliens' Unstoppable Third World Crime Wave in US," 1 February 2004, http://www.rense.com/general48/comp.htm (accessed 28 July 2005).

37. Kamal Ahmed, "Immigrants 'Behind Crime Wave'—Police Claim by Britain's Most Senior Officer Sparks New Asylum Row," *Observer,* 18 May 2003, http://observer.guardian.co.uk/politics/story/0,6903,958380,00.html (accessed 15 August 2005). For a sensitive treatment of the subject—one that makes clear how these "criminals" are often themselves victims of organized crime—see Ian Rankin's *Fleshmarket Close* (2004, especially at p. 391), a work in the genre of detective fiction.

38. "India Cyber Crime," *VoIP Blog—Rich Tehrani,* 5 July 2005, http:// voip-blog.tmcnet.com/blog/rich-tehrani/voip/india-cyber-crime.html (accessed 15 July 2005).

39. Fifth International Conference on Fraudulent Documents, Amsterdam, 10 April 2002, http://www.vehicle-documents.it/convegni_corsi/1.pdf (accessed 2 August 2005).

40. It is estimated that some 43 percent of counterfeit money is now produced by inexpensive desktop publishing systems with the graphics necessary for printing plausible notes, rather than by cumbersome and expensive printing and engraving machines. One company, Eurovisions, actually used a scan of the microprinting on the new hundred-dollar bill to advertise the fact that "no other scanner can . . . capture the hidden detail as well as ours"; http://www.sniggle.net/counterfeit.php (accessed 2 August 2005).

41. "Counterfeiting," *Sniggle.nett,* http://www.sniggle.net/counterfeit.php (accessed 2 August 2005).

42. "Replica for You," from Cora Wong, corawong@pc.jaring.my, received 29 August 2005.

43. An estimated $30 billion international trade in bogus pharmaceuticals is prompting corporations like Pfizer and Lilly to develop a high-tech system that will equip medications with a radio chip tracking device. Fake drugs are thought to be concentrated in India, Africa, and Southeast Asia: 60 percent of all court cases involving counterfeit medicines are said to occur in developing countries. Given low production costs and levels of risk, some narcotics dealers appear to be shifting

their trade to fake medications; see Ben Hirschler, "Fake Drugs a Bitter Pill for Manufacturers: Increase in Lifestyle Medicines Has Created a Demand on the Illicit Supply Chain," *Cape Times,* 3 August 2005, p. 9.

44. During the late 1920s and 1930s, two American tricksters defrauded scores of their countrymen by convincing them that, for a fee, they could acquire shares in Drake's hitherto-untapped estate (Rayner 2002). The Nigerian fraud is named for the article of the British colonial penal code that it flouts (Apter 1999).

45. "Fake Nigerian Cops Help Victims Recover Losses," Loss Prevention Concepts Ltd., 2 November 2001, http://www.lpconline.com/Nigerian_fake_cops.html (accessed 8 August 2005).

46. For just two media reports, see "Lying about Crime," editorial, *Cape Argus,* 10 January 2002, p. 13, and Helen Bamford, "Probe into Arrests Based on False Charges," *Weekend Argus,* 7 August 2004, p. 8. The phenomenon is discussed further in Comaroff and Comaroff, forthcoming.

47. "Saddam's 'Shadow State' Defies Democracy," *Oxford Analytica,* 15 May 2003, http://www.oxanstore.com/displayfree.php?NewsItemID=91576 (accessed 4 August 2005).

48. Larry Muffin, "Slaying Latin American Corruption Dragon," *United Press International,* 3 March 2005, http://www.Washtimes.com/upi-breaking/20050303-045537-8073r.htm (accessed 27 July 2005).

49. See also Utkarsh Kansal, "Why Is Corruption so Common in India?" *India Reform Initiative,* 2001, http://www.inida-reform.org/articles/corruption.html (accessed 4 August 2005).

50. At one of the stops, a "robber-cop" declared: "I have a gun, so I know the rules"; see "The Road to Hell Is Unpaved: Trucking in Cameroon," *Economist,* 19 December 2002, print edition, http://www.economist.com/displaystory.cfm?story_id=1487583 (accessed 8 August 2005). Also see Steve Inskeep, *NPR,* "Navigating Nigeria's Muddy Landscape," 24 August 2005, http://www.npr.org/templates/story/story.php?storyId=4797950 (accessed 30 August 2005).

51. See, e. g., "Four Fake 'Cops' Hijack Truck on N12 near Delmas," KN News Desk, 15 July 2005, http://www.keralanext.com/news/index.asp?id=272150 (accessed 8 August 2005); "Fake Cops' Affair Earns Them Jail," *Times of India News Network,* 29 June 2005, http://timesofindia.indiatimes.com/articleshow/1156155.cms (accessed 8 August 2005); "Fake Cops—Beware," *Channels,* http://www.channels.nl.knowledge/26122.html (accessed 27 July 2005).

52. Alpen Suresh Sheth, "Under Construction: The Informality of Labor in Miami's Construction Industry," BA Honors paper, University of Chicago, 2005. As this study makes clear, illegal laborers—and those most directly responsible for recruiting them—are associated with various Latino ethnonational identities.

53. Ben Cratner, "South American Start-up," *Duke Magazine* 89(4) (May–June 2003), http://www.dukemagazine.duke.edu/dukemag/issues/050603/startup-shop1.html (accessed 8 August 2005).

54. See, e. g., Anthony Stoppard, "Corporate Bribery on the Rise Worldwide," *Inter Press Service,* 14 May 2002, http://www.globalpolicy.org/nations/corrupt/2002/0514rise.htm (accessed 8 August 2005).

55. The Cape Flats is a large sandy plain that forms the hinterland of the peninsula south of Cape Town, contrasting with the salubrious, white areas at the base

of Table Mountain. It has historically been the home of peoples of color (many settled there through forced removals during the apartheid era) and is characterized by relatively low levels of capital investment and high levels of poverty and violence.

56. Michael Morris, "Gangland (Pty) Ltd," *Cape Argus,* 4 August 2003, p. 1.

57. Michael Morris and Ashley Smith, "Gangland's Drug Franchises: Police Tactics on Gangs Blasted by New Report," *Cape Argus,* 18 August 2005, p. 1.

58. As he does so, Anini evokes with particular vividness Walter Benjamin's portrayal of the "great criminal"; see chapter 8 below.

59. Neely Tucker, "Nollywood, in a Starring Role: Nigeria's Thriving Film Industry Gets a Showcase at AFI Silver," *Washington Post,* 5 February 2005, p. C04.

60. See Wedel 2003: 230 on postcommunist Europe and Kaminski 1997 on Poland.

61. "UN Suggests International Cybercrime Convention," http://www .out-law.com/page-1649 (accessed 10 August 2005). The commission noted that cybercrime was increasingly becoming a problem in developing countries.

62. For a recent critique of the contradictory relationship between contemporary capitalism and the law, pointedly titled *Unjust Legality,* see Marsh 2001.

63. This number is based on the latest figures in the *World Fact Book,* 14 July 2005, http://www.odci.gov/cia/publications/factbook/fields/2063.html (accessed 27 July 2005). It includes only countries that have either enacted entirely new constitutions (ninety-two) or heavily revised existing ones (thirteen). Included are the nations of the former Soviet Union; see *Wikipedia,* the online encyclopedia, http:// en.wikipedia.org/wiki/List_of_constitutional_courts, for an almost complete list (accessed 26 July 2005).

64. Peter Waldman, "Jurists' Prudence: India's Supreme Court Makes Rule of Law a Way of Governing," *Wall Street Journal,* 6 May 1996, http://law.gsu.edu/ ccunningham/fall03/WallStreetJournal-India'sSupremeCourt.htm (accessed 5 May 2005). India does not have a constitutional court, but like many other nation-states, its supreme court enjoys judicial authority in matters pertaining to the constitution. Its extensive powers are based largely on two articles of that constitution: 142, which authorizes the court to pass any decree "necessary for doing complete justice," and 144, which commands the cooperation with it of *all* other authorities.

65. Central and Eastern Europe have been the focus of much concern with, and debate about, constitutionalism; they have yielded a substantial scholarly literature, not to mention a journal dedicated to the topic, *East European Constitutional Review.*

66. Blokker (2005), among others, also notes—of Eastern Europe in particular—that civic nationalism, constitutional patriotism, and deliberative democracy are not without their critics. But that is a topic beyond our scope here.

67. In a summary sketch of constitutional changes in Latin America, for example, Pinzón (2003) notes that, while some new constitutions (notably those of Colombia and Chile) emphasize basic freedoms and individual rights, others (e.g., Brazil and Venezuela) still favor the executive and "presidentialism." If Schneiderman (2000) is right, though, the trend in this region is toward the "neoliberal model."

68. A useful summary of these events is to be found in *Wikipedia,* http://en.wikipedia.org/wiki/Faure_Gnassingb%C3%A9 (accessed 25 July 2005).

69. A recent report of the International Bar Association speaks of a "crisis of the rule of law in Zimbabwe," while making it clear that the state often takes pains to discriminate lawful from unlawful acts—and, indeed, has consented to court orders, which it has then violated. In short, the Mugabe regime makes extensive use of the legislative process and sustains the principle that there ought to be an effective judiciary, as long as it does the bidding of the president in the putative national interest. For the executive summary of the report, see http://www.ibanet.org/ humanrights/Zimbabwe_report.cfm (accessed 18 August 2005).

70. *World Fact Book,* 14 July 2005, http://www.odci.gov/cia/publications/ factbook/fields/2063.html.

71. See   http://bibliotecadigital.conevyt.org.mx/transparencia/Formacion _ciudadana_Gto071103. pdf (accessed 1 August 2005). A somewhat similar initiative, directed at democracy and the rights of citizenship, has also been introduced for young children in Brazilian schools; see Veloso 2003.

72. Legalopoli: The Game of Legality has its own Web site: www.legalopoli.it. We came across it at http://www.cmecent.org/Legalopoli.htm (accessed 1 August 2005).

73. See, e.g., Fatima Schroeder, "Drunk Driver Sues over Being Kept in Jail instead of Rehab," *Cape Times,* 8 August 2005, p. 7.

74. See Wiseman Khuzwayo, "MK Veterans' Row Heads for Court," *Sunday Independent,* 14 August, 2005, Business Report, p. 1. The story made it clear that MKMVA has a complex corporate life: the men against whom the interdict was to be sought were referred to as "directors" of MKMVA Investment Holdings (which represents 60,000 members and their dependents) and of its financial arm, the Mabutho Investment Company (which serves 46,000); the former, moreover, has a 5 percent holding in Mediro Clidet 517, a consortium, with large stakes in six major corporations and several other business interests.

75. We are grateful to Harry Garuba, of the University of Cape Town, for alerting us to this case; it forms part of an essay of his in progress.

76. For an especially informative contemporary account, see "Indian Government Files Lawsuit against Union Carbide," *Houston Chronicle,* 6 June 1986, section 1, p. 19.

77. See "Bhopal Victims File Lawsuit against Union Carbide," on the Democracy Now Web site, 17 November 1999, http://www.democracynow.org/article.pl ?sid=03/04/07/0413230 (accessed 8 July 2005).

78. See *Kroll Argentine Risk Monitor,* 4 October 2002, p. 7, http://www .krollworldwide.com/library/arm/arm_041003.pdf (accessed 7 August 2005). Kroll, Inc. is a risk consulting company.

79. See also *Amazon Update,* no. 63 (November 2000), published by the Amazon Alliance for Indigenous and Traditional Peoples of the Amazon Basin, http://www.amazonalliance.ord/upd_nov00_en.html (accessed 15 July 2005).

80. On negotiations between Brazil and Roche, see, e.g., http://www .globaltreatmentaccess.org/content/press_releases/a01/090101_BG_HGAP_Brazil _efa.html. On the US complaint and its withdrawal, see, e.g., http://www.hsph .harvard.edu/bioethics/archives/200102/msg00000.html and http://news.bbc.co .uk/1/hi/business/1407472.stm (all accessed on 7 September 2005).

81. See Jeremy Brecher and Tim Costello, "Global Self-Organization from Below," http://countercurrents.org/organisationfrombelow.htm (accessed 1 June 2005).

82. Some of the cases mentioned here are summarized in M. A. Shaikh, "Lawsuits by 'Third World' Claimants a New Weapon against Multinationals," *Crescent International,* 1–15 July 2001, http://www.muslimedia.com/archives/features01/lawsuits.htm (accessed 9 August 2005). It should be noted that in suits filed in foreign courts, especially in the United States, it is often difficult actually to collect damages.

83. An informative popular account of these suits, which ended in the payment of major sums of money to the plaintiffs—most of whom had been forced into the schools—can be found in James Booke, "Indian Lawsuits Threaten Canadian Churches," *Incite Newsletter,* May 2001, http://www.incite-national.org/news/lawsuits.html (accessed 9 August 2005).

84. This act, which has a very long history, allows American courts to exercise supraterritorial jurisdiction over a range of claims, including some human rights violations. Significantly, it seems to be invoked more and more nowadays.

85. Interestingly, a federal court in New York *did* rule that relatives of political opponents killed in the run-up to the 2000 elections in Zimbabwe could file a $400 million suit against the Zanu PF; the defendants, however, did not respond, simply denying the existence of the case. The court also ruled that Robert Mugabe could not be sued because of the immunity granted to heads of state under the law. But it added, ambiguously, that, as Zanu PF's first secretary, he *could* be served with the legal complaint. For one account, see the archives of the Zimbabwe Information Centre, 4 November 2001, http://www.zic.com.au/updates/2001/4november2001.htm (accessed 3 August 2005).

86. Allister Sparks, "Now It's a Crime against Humanity: A Million Zimbabweans Left Homeless," *Cape Times,* 29 June 2005, online edition, http://www.capetimes.co.za/index.php?fSectionId=332&fArticleId=2604095 (accessed 4 July 2005).

87. Rickey Singh, "The Corruption of Absolute Power," *Trinidad Express,* 29 June 2005, reprinted online, http://www.zimbabwersituation.com/jun29a_2005.html (accessed 10 August 2005).

88. This letter to the *Jakarta Post* is also to be found at http://www.zimbabwesituation.com/jun29a_2005.html (accessed 10 August 2005).

89. The term "lawfare" has, of late, been applied by the Bush administration to describe the "strategy of using or misusing law as a substitute for traditional military means to achieve military objectives"; see Phillip Carter, "Legal Combat: Are Enemies Waging War in Our Courts?" *Slate,* 4 April 2005, online edition, http://slate.msn.com/id/2116169 (accessed 20 May 2005). "Lawfare," Carter adds, citing the National Defense Strategy published by the Pentagon in March 2005, is a weapon "of the weak using international fora, judicial processes, and terrorism" to undermine America. We are grateful to Omar Kutty, a graduate student at the University of Chicago, for pointing this out to us. In our own first use of the term, it connoted the systematic effort to exert control over and/or to coerce political subjects by recourse to the violence inherent in legal instruments.

90. Gibson (2004) is speaking of South Africa, although his findings resonate elsewhere. The citations here are from an insightful analysis of his study; see Jan

Hofmeyr, "Our Racially Divided City Can Ill Afford Another Fear-Based Election Campaign," *Cape Times,* 3 August 2005, p. 11.

91. For an excellent account of Mapogo a Mathamaga, South Africa's best-known (and much documented) "vigilante" organization—the scare quotes are meant to denote the fact that its leader repudiates the term—see Oomen 2004.

92. "Crime without Punishment," *Economist* 352(8134) (1999): 17–20.

93. This figure is from a recent World Bank survey. It is reported in Steven Lee Myers, "Pervasive Bribery in Russia Today 'Is Just Called Business,'" *New York Times,* articles selected for *Sunday Times* (Johannesburg), 28 August 2005, p. 3.

94. Ibid.

95. The quote is from an editorial in *Die Zeit.* It is cited in Jeffrey Fleishman, "Virus of Corporate Corruption Contaminates Germany," *Sunday Independent* (Johannesburg), 28 August 2005, p. 14.

96. See, e.g., Tony Weaver, "Get Tough On Tik or Scenes Like Those from New Orleans May Not Be So Far from Home," *Cape Times,* 9 September 2005, p. 11.

97. See Timothy L. O'Brien, "Tracking the Crimes of the Digital Thugs," *New York Times,*" articles selected for *Sunday Times* (Johannesburg), 28 August 2005, p. 8.

98. These figures are contained in the Seventh United Nations Survey on Crime Trends and the Operations of Criminal Justice Systems (1998–2000), http://www.unodc.org/pdf/crime/seventh_survey/7sc.pdf (accessed 13 July 2003).

99. The US figure is for 1999, but there is no evidence of a major drop between 1999 and 2000.

100. There is a discrepancy here: Statistics Canada puts the rate for all crimes at 8,404.7 for 2000. See http://www.statcan.ca/english/Pgdb/legal02.htm.

101. The program, *Bribes,* was broadcast by BBC Radio 4 on 28 April 1996.

102. Daniel Williams, "With Italy's New Laws, an Anti-corruption Era Wanes," *Washington Post,* 11 November 2002; see http://www.globalpolicy.org/nations/corrupt/governmt/2002/1111berlusconi.htm (accessed 12 August 2005).

103. See, e.g., Jason Mercier and Amanda Jarrett, "Tort Suits: State Treats Symptoms, Not Problems," Evergreen Freedom Foundation, *Policy Highlighter* 11(8), (10 October 2001), http://www.effwa.orf/highlighters/v11_n28.php (accessed 9 August 2005).

104. "Lawsuits against Prisons: Texas Prisoners' Religious Rights Violated," *North Coast Xpress,* http://www.sonic.net/~doretk/Issues/01-03/lawsuits.html (accessed 9 August 2005).

References

Abrams, Philip. 1988. "Notes on the Difficulty of Studying the State. *Journal of Historical Sociology* 1(1):58–89. (Originally published 1977.)

Ackerman, Bruce. 1997. "The Rise of World Constitutionalism." *Yale Law School Occasional Papers,* 2d ser., no. 3.

Agamben, Giorgio. 1998. *Homo Sacer: Sovereign Power and Bare Life.* Trans. Daniel Heller-Roazen. Stanford, CA: Stanford University Press.

———. 2005. *States of Exception.* Trans. Kevin Attell. Chicago: University of Chicago Press.

Ajibade, Babson. n.d. "Nigerian Igbo Youths in the Fragile European Diaspora: Re-mediating

Identities Ruptured by the Bakassi Boys." Unpublished paper produced in partial fulfill-
ment of the MA, University of Basel.

Anderson, Benedict. 1983. *Imagined Communities: Reflections on the Origin and Spread of Nationalism.* London: Verso.

Anderson, David. 2005. *Histories of the Hanged: The Dirty War in Kenya and the End of Empire.* London and New York: W. W. Norton.

Apter, Andrew. 1999. "IRB=419: Nigerian Democracy and the Politics of Illusion." In *Civil Society and the Political Imagination in Africa: Critical Perspectives, Problems, Paradoxes,* ed. John L. Comaroff and Jean Comaroff. Chicago: University of Chicago Press.

Arendt, Hanna. 1998. *The Human Condition.* 2d ed. Chicago: University of Chicago Press. (1st ed., 1958.)

Balibar, Étienne. 2004. *We, the People of Europe? Reflections on Transnational Citizenship.* Trans. James Swenson. Princeton, NJ: Princeton University Press.

Barclay, Gordon, and Cynthia Tavares. 2003. "International Comparisons of Criminal Justice Statistics, 2001." London: RDS Communications and Development Unit, Home Office, Government of the United Kingdom. http://www.homeoffice.gov.uk/rds/pdfs2/hosb1203.pdf (last accessed 1 September 2003).

Bataille, Georges. 1991. *The Accursed Share: An Essay on General Economy.* Vols. 3 and 4. Trans. Robert Hurley. New York: Zone Books.

Baumann, Zygmunt. 1998. *Globalization: The Human Consequences.* New York: Columbia University Press.

Bayart, Jean-François. 1986. "Civil Society in Africa." In *Political Domination in Africa: Reflections on the Limits of Power,* ed. Patrick Chabal. Cambridge: Cambridge University Press.

———. 1993. *The State in Africa: Politics of the Belly.* New York: Longman.

Bayart, Jean-François, Stephen Ellis, and Béatrice Hibou, eds. 1999. *The Criminalization of the State in Africa.* Bloomington: Indiana University Press; Oxford: James Currey in association with the International African Institute.

Becker, Marvin B. 1994. *The Emergence of Civil Society in the Eighteenth Century: A Privileged Moment in the History of England, Scotland, and France.* Bloomington: Indiana University Press.

Benjamin, Walter. 1978. "Critique of Violence." In *Reflections: Essays, Aphorisms, Autobiographical Writings,* ed. Peter Demetz, trans. Edmund Jephcott. New York: Schocken Books.

Berkowitz, Roger. 2005. *The Gift of Science: Leibniz and the Modern Legal Tradition.* Cambridge, MA: Harvard University Press.

Bhabha, Homi J. 1994. *The Location of Culture.* New York: Routledge.

Bhabha, Homi J., and John L. Comaroff. 2002. "Speaking of Postcoloniality, in the Continuous Present: A Conversation between Homi Bhabha and John Comaroff." In *Relocating Postcolonialism,* ed. David Theo Goldberg and Ato Quayson. Oxford: Basil Blackwell.

Blaney, David L., and Mustapha Kamal Pasha. 1993. "Civil Society and Democracy in the Third World: Ambiguities and Historical Possibilities." *Studies in Comparative International Development* 28(1):3–24.

Blokker, Paul. 2005. "Populist Nationalism, Anti-Europeanism, Post-nationalism, and the East-West Distinction." *German Law Journal* 6(2):371–89.

Blundo, Giorgio, and Jean-Pierre Olivier de Sardan. 2001. "La corruption quotidienne en Afrique de l'Ouest." *Politique Africaine* 83:8–37.

Blunt, Robert. 2004. "'Satan Is an Imitator': Kenya's Recent Cosmology of Corruption." In *Producing African Futures: Ritual and Reproduction in a Neoliberal Age,* ed. Brad Weiss. Leiden and Boston: Brill.

Bottoms, Anthony E. 1995. "The Philosophy and Politics of Punishment and Sentencing." In *The Politics of Sentencing Reform,* ed. C. M. V. Clarkson and R. Morgan. Oxford: Clarendon Press.

Bradbury, Malcolm. 1992. *Doctor Criminale.* New York: Penguin Books.

Caldeira, Teresa P. R. 2000. *City of Walls: Crime, Segregation, and Citizenship in São Paulo.* Berkeley and Los Angeles: University of California Press.

Chabal, Patrick, ed. 1986. *Political Domination in Africa: Reflections on the Limits of Power.* Cambridge: Cambridge University Press.

Coleman, Enid G. 2005. "The Social Construction of Freedom in Free and Open Source Software: Hackers, Ethics, and the Liberal Tradition." PhD diss., University of Chicago.

Comaroff, Jean. Forthcoming. "Beyond the Politics of Bare Life: AIDS and the Global Order." In *AIDS and the Moral Order,* ed. Ute Luig.

Comaroff, Jean, and John L. Comaroff. 1999. "Occult Economies and the Violence of Abstraction: Notes from the South African Postcolony." *American Ethnologist* 26(3): 279–301.

———. 2000. "Millennial Capitalism: First Thoughts on a Second Coming." *Public Culture* 12(2):291–343.

———. 2003. "Reflections on Liberalism, Policulturalism, and ID-ology: Citizenship and Difference in South Africa." *Social Identities* 9(4):445–74.

———. 2006. "Figuring Crime: Quantifacts and the Production of the Unreal." *Public Culture* 18(1):209–46.

———. Forthcoming. *The Metaphysics of Disorder: Crime, Policing, and the State in a Brave Neo World.*

Comaroff, John L. 2001. "Law, Culture, and Colonialism: A Foreword." *Law and Social Inquiry* 26(2):101–10.

Comaroff, John L., and Jean Comaroff. 1997. "Postcolonial Politics and Discourses of Democracy in Southern Africa: An Anthropological Reflection on African Political Modernities." *Journal of Anthropological Research* 53(2):123–46.

———. 1999. Introduction to *Civil Society and the Political Imagination in Africa: Critical Perspectives, Problems, Paradoxes,* ed. John L. Comaroff and Jean Comaroff. Chicago: University of Chicago Press.

———. 2004. "Criminal Justice, Cultural Justice: The Limits of Liberalism and the Pragmatics of Difference in the New South Africa." *American Ethnologist* 31(2):188–204.

Copnall, James. 2005. "France in Africa: No Smoke without Fire." *BBC Focus on Africa* 16(3):26–27.

Davidson, Basil. 1992. *The Black Man's Burden: Africa and the Curse of the Nation-State.* New York: Three Rivers Press.

Derrida, Jacques. 1994. *Specters of Marx: The State of Debt, the Work of Mourning, and the New International.* Trans. Peggy Kamuf. New York: Routledge.

———. 2002. "Force of Law." In *Acts of Religion,* ed. Gil Anidjar. New York: Routledge.

Duffy, Rosaleen. 2000. "Shadow Players, Ecotourism Development and Corruption in State Politics in Belize." *Third World Quarterly* 21(3):549–65.

Elkins, Caroline. 2005. *Imperial Reckoning: The Untold Story of Britain's Gulag in Kenya.* New York: Henry Holt.

Fanon, Franz. 1968. *The Wretched of the Earth.* Trans. C. Farrington. New York: Grove Press.

Fatton, Robert, Jr. 1995. "Africa in the Age of Democratization: The Civic Limitations of Civil Society." *African Studies Review* 38:67–100.

Ferguson, Adam. 1995. *An Essay on the History of Civil Society.* Ed. Fania Oz-Salzberger. Cambridge: Cambridge University Press. (1st ed., 1767.)

Ferguson, James. 2006. *Global Shadows: Essays on Africa in a Neoliberal World Order.* Durham, NC: Duke University Press.

Foucault, Michel. 1978. *The History of Sexuality.* Trans. R. Hurley. New York: Pantheon Books.

Fukuyama, Francis. 1992. *The End of History and the Last Man.* New York: Free Press.

Gibson, James L. 2004. *Overcoming Apartheid: Can Truth Reconcile a Divided Nation?* New York: Russell Sage.

Gore, Charles, and Charles Pratten. 2003. "The Politics of Plunder: The Rhetorics of Order and Disorder in Southern Nigeria." *African Affairs* 102(407):211–40.

Gray, John. 1998. *False Dawn: The Delusions of Global Capitalism.* London: Granta.

Gupta, Akhil. 1995. "Blurred Boundaries: The Discourse of Corruption, the Culture of Politics, and the Imagined State." *American Ethnologist* 22(2):375–402.

Haggerty, Kevin D. 2001. *Making Crime Count.* Toronto: University of Toronto Press.

Hale, Charles R. 2005. "Neoliberal Multiculturalism: The Remaking of Cultural Rights and Racial Domination in Central America." *Political and Legal Anthropology Review* [*POLAR*] 28(1):10–28.

Hall, David. 1999. "Contracts, Concessions and Corruption in the Water Sector." United Nations Centre for Human Settlement (Habitat). http://www.unhabitat.org/HD/hdv6n3/contracts.htm (accessed 7 July 2005).

Hall, John A., and Frank Trentmann, eds. 2004. *Civil Society: A Reader in History, Theory and Global Politics.* Basingstoke: Palgrave Macmillan.

Hann, Chris, and Elizabeth Dunn, eds. 1996. *Civil Society: Challenging Western Models.* New York: Routledge.

Hansen, Thomas Blom, and Finn Stepputat. 2005. Introduction to *Sovereign Bodies: Citizens, Migrants, and States in the Postcolonial World,* ed. T. Blom Hansen and F. Stepputat. Princeton: Princeton University Press.

Harbeson, John W., Donald Rothchild, and Naomi Chazan, eds. 1994. *Civil Society and the State in Africa.* Boulder, CO: Lynne Rienner.

Harter, Pascale. 2005. "Egypt: Shouting for Democracy." *BBC Focus on Africa* 16(3):20–22.

Haynes, Jeff. 1997. *Democracy and Civil Society in the Third World: Politics and New Political Movements.* Cambridge: Polity Press.

Hibou, Béatrice. 1999. "The 'Social Capital' of the State as an Agent of Deception, or the Ruses of Economic Intelligence." In *The Criminalization of the State in Africa,* ed. Jean-François Bayart, Stephen Ellis, and Béatrice Hibou. Bloomington: Indiana University Press; Oxford: James Currey in association with the International African Institute.

Hobbes, Thomas. 1995. *Three Discourses: A Critical Modern Edition of Newly Identified Work of the Young Hobbes.* Ed. Noel B. Reynolds and Arlene W. Saxonhouse. Chicago: University of Chicago Press.

Joseph, Richard. 1987. *Democracy and Prebendal Politics in Nigeria: The Rise and Fall of the Second Republic.* Cambridge: Cambridge University Press.

Kaminski, Antoni Z. 1997. "Corruption under the Post-Communist Transformation: The Case of Poland." *Polish Sociological Review* 2(118):91–117.

Kaplan, Robert. 1994. "The Coming Anarchy." *Atlantic Monthly* 273(2):44–76.

Karlstrom, Mikael. 1996. "Imagining Democracy: Political Culture and Democratization in Buganda." *Africa* 66:485–505.

Karstedt, Susanne. Forthcoming. "Democracy and Violence." In "Violence," ed. Pieter Spierenburg. Special issue of *Theoretical Criminology.*

Kasfir, Nelson, ed. 1998. *Civil Society and Democracy in Africa: Critical Perspectives.* London: Frank Cass.

Klug, Heinz. 2000. *Constituting Democracy: Law, Globalism and South Africa's Political Reconstruction.* Cambridge: Cambridge University Press.

Levi, Michael. 1998. "Organizing Plastic Fraud: Enterprise Criminals and the Side-Stepping of Fraud Prevention." *Howard Journal* 37(4):423–38.

Lewis, Peter. 1996. "From Prebendalism to Predation: The Political Economy of Decline in Nigeria." *Journal of Modern African Studies* 34(1):79–103.

Makinda, Samuel. 1996. "Imagining Democracy: Political Culture and Democratisation in Buganda." *Africa* 66(4):485–505.

Mamdani, Mahmood. 1990. "State and Civil Society in Contemporary Africa." *Africa Development* 15(3–4):47–70.

———. 1992. "Africa: Democratic Theory and Democratic Struggles." *Dissent,* Summer, 312–18.

Marenin, Otwin. 1987. "The Anini Saga: Armed Robbery and the Reproduction of Ideology in Nigeria." *Journal of Modern African Studies* 25(2):259–81.

Marsh, James L. 2001. *Unjust Legality: A Critique of Habermas's Philosophy of Law.* Boulder and New York: Rowman and Littlefield.

Marx, Karl. 1936. *Capital: A Critique of Political Economy.* Vol. 1, *The Process of Capitalist Production.* Ed. Frederick Engels, revised and amplified according to the 4th German ed. by Ernest Untermann. Trans. from the 3d German ed. by Samuel Moore and Edward Aveling. New York: Modern Library.

Mbaku, John Mukum. 2000. "Minority Rights in Plural Societies." *Seminar,* 409, "African Transitions: A Symposium on the Continent's Engagement with Democracy." http://www.india-seminar.com/2000/490.htm (accessed 7 July 2005).

Mbembe, Achille. 2000. "At the Edge of the World: Boundaries, Territoriality, and Sovereignty in Africa." *Public Culture* 12(1):259–84.

———. 2001. *On the Postcolony.* Berkeley and Los Angeles: University of California Press.

———. 2002. "African Modes of Self-Writing." *Public Culture* 14(1):239–73.

Miliband, Ralph. 1969. *The State in Capitalist Society.* London: Weidenfeld and Nicholson.

Monga, Célestin. 1996. *The Anthropology of Anger: Civil Society and Democracy in Africa.* Trans. Linda L. Fleck and Célestin Monga. Boulder, CO: Lynne Rienner.

Navaro-Yashin, Yael. 2005. "Confinement and the Imagination: Sovereignty and Subjectivity in a Quasi-State." In *Sovereign Bodies: Citizens, Migrants, and States in the Postcolonial World,* ed. Thomas Blom Hansen and Finn Stepputat. Princeton, NJ: Princeton University Press.

Niger-Thomas, Margaret. 2001. "Women and the Arts of Smuggling." *African Studies Review* 44(2):43–70.

Olivier de Sardan, Jean-Pierre. 1999a. "African Corruption in the Context of Globalization." In *Modernity on a Shoestring: Dimensions of Globalization, Consumption and Development in Africa and Beyond,* ed. Richard Fardon, Wim van Binsbergen, and Rijk van Dijk. Leiden: European Inter-university Development Opportunities Study Group.

———. 1999b. "A Moral Economy of Corruption in Africa?" *Journal of Modern African Studies* 37(1):25–52.

Oloka-Onyango, Joe. 2001. *Constitutionalism in Africa: Creating Opportunities, Facing Challenges.* Uganda: Fountain Publishers.

Oomen, Barbara. 2004. "Vigilantism or Alternative Citizenship? The Rise of *Mapogo a Mathamaga.*" *African Studies* 63(2):153–71.

O'Toole, Sean. 2005. "Devaluing Mandela." *BBC Focus on Africa* 16(3):52–57.

Owusu, Maxwell. 1997. "Domesticating Democracy: Culture, Civil Society, and Constitutionalism in Africa." *Contemporary Studies in Society and History* 39(1):120–52.

Pinzón, Martha Lucia. 2003. "Latin America's Constitutions: Achievements and Perspectives." *Commentaries,* Summit of the Americas Center (Latin America and Caribbean Center), Florida International University. http://www.americasnet.net/Commentators/Martha_Pinzon/pinzon_94_eng.pdf (accessed 29 July 2005).

Przeworski, Adam, Michael E. Alvarez, Jose Antonio Cheibub, and Fernando Limongi, eds. 2000. *Democracy and Development: Political Institutions and Well-Being in the World, 1950–1990.* Cambridge: Cambridge University Press.

Rankin, Ian. 2004. *Fleshmarket Close.* London: Orion.

Rayner, Richard. 2002. *Drake's Fortune: The Fabulous True Story of the World's Greatest Confidence Artist.* New York: Doubleday.

Reno, William. 1995. *Corruption and State Politics in Sierra Leone.* Cambridge: Cambridge University Press.

———. 2000. "Clandestine Economies, Violence, and States in Africa." *Journal of International Affairs* 53(2):433–59.

Richburg, Keith B. 1997. *Out of America: A Black Man Confronts Africa.* New York: Basic Books.

Richter, Kelly. 2005. "From U.S. Funded Death Squads to L.A.-Bred *Maras:* The Rise of Transnational Salvadoran Youth Gangs." *Diskord* 1(3):8–11.

Robins, Steven. 2004. "'Long Live Zackie, Long Live': AIDS Activism, Science and Citizenship after Apartheid." *Journal of Southern African Studies* 30(3):651–72.

Roitman, Janet. 2005. *Fiscal Disobedience: An Anthropology of Economic Regulation in Central Africa.* Princeton, NJ: Princeton University Press.

Schneiderman, David. 2000. "Constitutional Approaches to Privatization: An Inquiry into the Magnitude of Neo-liberal Constitutionalism." *Law and Contemporary Problems* 63(4):83–109.

Siegel, James T. 1998. *A New Criminal Type in Jakarta.* Durham, NC: Duke University Press.

Sissener, Tone Kristin. 2001. *Anthropological Perspectives on Corruption.* Bergen: Chr. Michelson Institute.

Standing, André. 2003. "The Social Contradictions of Organised Crime on the Cape Flats." Institute for Security Studies, Pretoria, South Africa, Occasional Paper no. 74.

———. 2005. "The Threat of Gangs and Anti-gangs Policy." Policy discussion paper, Institute for Security Studies, Pretoria, South Africa, Paper no. 116.

Steinberg, Jonny. 2004. *The Number.* Cape Town: Jonathan Ball.

Stiglitz, Joseph E. 2002. *Globalization and Its Discontents.* New York: W. W. Norton.

Tilly, Charles. 1985. "War Making and State Making as Organized Crime." In *Bringing the State Back In,* ed. Peter B. Evans, Dietrich Rueschemeyer, and Theda Skocpol. Cambridge: Cambridge University Press.

Torre, Giuseppe Dalla. 1998. "A Strong Moral Conscience for a Culture of Legality." *Jubi-*

laeum, "Tertium Millennium," no. 1. http://www.vatican.va/jubilee_2000/magazine/documents/ju_mag_01021998_p-8_en.html (accessed 1 August 2005).

United Nations. 2005. *Report on the World Social Situation, 2005: The Inequality Predica-ment.* http://www.un.org/esa/socdev/rwss/media%2005/cd-docs/media.htm (accessed 29 August 2005).

Veloso, Leticia Medeiros. 2003. "Remaking the Future: Childhood and the Paradoxes of Citizenship in the Brazilian Democratic Imagination." PhD diss., University of Chicago.

Venkatesh, Sudhir. 2000. *American Project: The Rise and Fall of a Modern Ghetto.* Cambridge, MA: Harvard University Press.

Wacquant, Loïc. 2001. "The Penalisation of Poverty and the Rise of Neo-Liberalism." *European Journal of Criminal Policy and Research* 9(4):401–12.

Wedeen, Lisa. 2004. "Concepts and Commitments in the Study of Democracy." In *Problems and Methods in the Study of Politics,* ed. Ian Shapiro, Rogers M. Smith, and Tarek E. Masoud. Cambridge: Cambridge University Press.

———. Forthcoming. *Peripheral Visions: Political Identifications in Unified Yemen.*

Wedel, Janine R. 2003. "Mafia without Malfeasance, Clans without Crime: The Criminality Conundrum in Post-Communist Europe." In *Crime's Power: Anthropologists and the Ethnography of Crime,* ed. Philip C. Parnell and Stephanie C. Kane. New York: Palgrave Macmillan.

Woods, Dwayne. 1992. "Civil Society in Europe and Africa: Limiting State Power through a Public Sphere." *African Studies Review* 95(2):77–100.

Young, Tom. 1993. "Elections and Electoral Politics in Africa." *Africa* 63(3):299–312.

The Mute and the Unspeakable
Political Subjectivity, Violent Crime, and "the Sexual Thing" in a South African Mining Community

Rosalind C. Morris

Violence has been the single most determining factor in South African political history.

TRC REPORT

IN THE BEGINNING, as it were, all states are founded upon a primal confusion between law and lawlessness, for every state must institute the authority and produce the forms by which law can express itself. Before this moment, its power is not distinguished from its capacity to exercise force. Yet it is rare to recall the violent acts by which law is first asserted. The exception is provided by those instances in which a new state emerges from the wreckage of an old one or from an empire whose foreign rule has at last collapsed in the face of an emergent sovereignty. Nonetheless, few states have been confronted with a more acute problematization of the political and the criminal than has that of postapartheid South Africa. And few governments have staked their claims to relative political legitimacy so firmly on their capacity to control crime as has that of the African National Congress (ANC). Not surprisingly, the period of transition, as this awkward moment of still-youthful legitimacy in South Africa is termed, has been marked by a perceived efflorescence of criminality and by a sensation of political crisis.

Sexual violence is widely thought to lie at the heart of this crisis of crime and is often read as the symptom of a failure both in the formation of the public sphere and in the restoration of previously damaged institutions like the family.[1] Its elevation to the status of metonym for the history of criminality in South Africa has taken two somewhat antithetical forms. On the one hand, sexual violence has been recognized, retrospectively, as a possible mode of political violence (instrumentalized in the struggles between the apartheid state and its opponents). On the other, its recent proliferation is read as evidence of the failure of the new polity to extend the rule of law (even into the domestic sphere) in such a way as to prevent or contain sexual violence.

The fact that sexual violence can be read, simultaneously, as a possible

form of political activity and as the absolute limit of the political suggests
that the most fundamental institutions and principles of social order in
this newly liberalizing state are currently in question. The relationships between personal agency and political subjectivity, between the family and
the state, between the private and the public, are all being refigured. More
fundamentally, the relationships between desire and language, violence
and law, are being redrawn. This is why an understanding of the history of
crime in South Africa requires an account of the changing significations
that are attached to sexual violence. But the reverse is also true. To understand the changing significations of sexual violence requires an analysis of
the transformations in the relationships between language and law, the
family and the state. This essay is an attempt to trace these relationships
and their transformations in a particular place: a gold-mining community
at the heart of South Africa's economic history.

It should be said, at the outset, that an analysis of violence and its significations is not the same as an analysis of motives or intentions. Sexual
violence in particular appears to be an individual act, even an intimate act,
irreducibly connected to the desire of one or more agents—even when performed in the service of such tendentiously political ends as "racial separatism" or gang warfare. But the communicative force of an act is not determined by what motivates its perpetrator or by the effect that he or she
hopes to achieve. It is determined by the ways in which the act is interpreted, and this is itself contingent upon the context and the discourses
that mediate that act (for the perpetrator, for the victim, and also for the
communities that they inhabit). Moreover, the "same" act or form can
have radically different effects in different moments and milieus. In this essay, I am not concerned with what the perpetrators of violence think they
are doing or accomplishing, nor with the retrospective understanding that
they may have of their acts, now or in the past. In any case, statements
made by such individuals are as important for what they reveal about the
limits of self-knowledge as for what they reveal about the meaning of an
event that those subjects produced. Rather, I am seeking to comprehend
the historically specific structures that solicit or mediate, repress or fore-
close, certain kinds of violence, either extending the communicative force
of that violence or blunting it. Such structures may possess people, but
they are not necessarily operative in the form of individual intentionality
even when that possession produces desire. This does not mean that violence is not also, and always already, a question of agency. Indeed, violence
is the experience of an injury whose causality can be attributed to an agent.
But personal agency must be distinguished from intention, as well as from

political subjectivity. Indeed, as I hope to demonstrate in the pages that follow, it is precisely in the aporia between personal agency and political subjectivity that sexual violence tends to erupt.

This aporia has been opened wide in the period of South Africa's transition, as new rights and new forms of political representation are distributed, sought, or, as is sometimes the case, felt to be lacking or even being withdrawn. But if, under all circumstances, sexual violence wounds its victims, repudiating completely the sovereignty that would have been achieved in the act of negation, in the woman's or child's refusal to consent, its communicative force nonetheless changes from time to time and place to place. It may be contained in the family or staged in the public realm. It may demonstrate the presumptive immunity of the former to the state's interventions or call the attention of the state to its own inadequacy. It may express the solidity of patriarchal authority as the absolute right to exercise force, or it may be a means for asserting sovereignty in the face of competing and uncertain claims to power. And this is true of all violence. The very attribution of criminality to a particular act of violence constitutes the means by which the state gathers power to itself, thereby opening a gap between itself and its subjects. Similarly, the decision to withhold or repudiate such an attribution demarcates the state's limit, the point of its becoming impotent. It is therefore necessary to begin an analysis of the changing force of violence and especially sexual violence with a history of its shifting status in the discourse of criminality. From there, it will be possible to consider how and why the thwarted drive to achieve political subjectivity in language may be linked, for some, to the violent exercise of desire's force.

Histories of the State of Crime

For decades, the apartheid regime legitimated its violence against the majority black population and those aspiring to democratic rule with labyrinthine laws, which were enforced by police and military security forces. Their extrajudicial killings, torture, and preemptive detentions buttressed a draconian state apparatus and ensured a nearly exclusive monopoly on violence. Or rather, they sustained a monopoly on political violence. Intimate violence that occurred between familiars, whether these were understood to be members of a single household, a family, or, in the case of black communities, the township itself, constituted a kind of "visible invisibility," a public secret and an object of taboo. Known to exist, it was nonetheless rarely prosecuted or punished if it did not entail interracial violence involving white women. And except in the latter case, it was not construed as a threat to the state. As the authority of that regime began to wane, however, the nature of political violence changed, diffusing itself (with the encouragement of the state) throughout an ethnicized population, such that violence came to be perpetrated as much by nonstate actors—mainly in rural and township areas—as by state representatives.[2] After the Sharpeville massacre of 1960, and increasing after the Soweto uprising of 1976, the white government's failure to prosecute nonpolitical crime in the townships, and its cultivation of counterinsurgent forces in mining hostels and townships, converged with the ANC's and South African Communist Party's (SACP) policy of ungovernability.[3] The result was a gaping fissure into which both the aspiration to power and the passion for punishment rushed. In this context, sexual violence also acquired a political dimension. Its politicization may have ensured that, in the aftermath of apartheid, the depoliticization of all violence would leave an awful remainder, one whose eruption would be split between new and acute forms of incestuous violence (as the family comes to supplant race as the point of affiliation) and random acts carried out in a still-tenuous public sphere, one even more beholden to the logics of spectacle than was the apartheid world, which, after all, conducted its war against multiracialism partly as a war against mass-mediated collectivities.

Today, South Africa is an energetically mass-mediated space. Transmitted along a myriad vectors, in televisual serials, newspaper columns, radio broadcasts, and music lyrics, crime is the phantom that haunts the new nation's imaginary. Macabre tales of heavily armed robbers and single-minded carjackers, of remorseless murderers, and—most remarked of all—pedophilic rapists[4] feed a national press that is insatiable for news of personalized catastrophe with which to signify or prophesy political failure. More often than not, the face of crime is the face of youth, and in this respect, the discourse of crime bespeaks a sense of generational crisis. Or rather, it metaphorizes a perceived crisis of authority and political legitimacy as an unleashing of youthful and especially masculine ambition which has neither been socialized nor restrained by the weight of history.[5] Stories about random but deeply personalized crime committed by youths invert earlier narratives emphasizing the sociopolitical nature of conflict and even, during the eighties and nineties, the predicament of civil war. Nonetheless, another set of narratives bears the images of more socialized violence; gangsters and vigilantes with elaborate codes of honor are represented as inhabiting the chasm left by a financially crippled and deeply distrusted police force.[6] What these stories share in their myriad forms is a historical metanarrative organized by the perception that crime during the apartheid years was mainly political, while that which followed has been primarily extrapolitical and even antipolitical.[7] Sexual violence figures in both of these moments, as we shall see, but its nature and its relationship to both law and the category of the political have changed.

The causes of crime's transformation are nonetheless usually construed in political terms. Thus, contemporary crime is variously understood to be the legacy of apartheid, a function of the dismantling of the apartheid regime's nexus of security and policing institutions, or an expression of poverty or of in-migration from more impoverished regions of Africa. Encompassing all of these explanations is the idea of excess; whether it is conceived as the corruption of the political from within or as the repudiation of the political from without, crime marks the boundary of the polis as much as any other wilderness.[8] Looking to such a limit while in the grip of fear, many South Africans now yearn for immediate, expiatory types of retributive justice. Whether in restored forms of state-sanctioned corporeal and capital punishment, in "traditional" forms of community discipline meted out by elders, or in cruelly militaristic tribunals like those operated by the Self-Defense Units (SDU) during the apartheid years, punishment offers itself here as the instrument of social restoration.[9]

Such vindictive aspirations nonetheless sit in paradoxical proximity to a growing desire for more abstractly mediated forms of justice, administered by the state according to principles of universal human rights and due process.[10] Legal rhetoric suffuses everyday discourse in rural and urban areas, inflecting everyday idioms in many languages with the lexicons of legal procedure—and, not infrequently, the clichés of American television's courtroom melodramas. Such language often appears fetishistic, with legal terms acquiring a nearly magical aura. Perhaps ironically, it is the very material density of this language that reveals the generalizing value of law (even and despite the rise in crime). Even more ironically, the gathering authority of law may be associated with the exercise of force in those areas that lie on the periphery of the public domain. This is because the desire for universality that is cultivated by discourses of the rule of law can be satisfied only in a substitutional mode for those with limited access to the public sphere. And that substitutional mode is mass-mediated crime.

Like rumor, of which it is the technological supplement, the mass media give to crime a communicative force that permits it to traverse the social field—not as meaningful action encoded in messages of universal legibility but as pure effectivity. The more that the former (the value of law) is upheld, the more that the latter (the force of crime) aspires to mirror it.

Thus, a petty thief may refer to both his stolen goods and his own property as "alleged," revealing his slender grasp of the word's meaning, but in his insistence on representing himself before a magistrate's court, he also expresses a newfound faith in the rule of law.[11] Indeed, he both transgresses the law and summons it, exercises his will and submits himself to an abstract power. In short, he lives his life as an incarnation of liberalism's ambivalence: convinced of his own sovereignty while at the same time believing it to emanate from law and, despite his bravado, seeking recognition for it from the state. Nor is he alone in this ambivalence.

Ten years into its new history as a democratic polity, South Africa's citizens and subjects live suspended in thrall to the specter of crime, but equally to a rule of law which has itself been spectralized. This rule, it turns out, is doubled. Not only is it that of liberal political theory, according to which all persons function as equivalent bearers of rights and responsibilities. It is also a libertine rule, the phantasmatic image of universal power, exercised beyond or beneath the political—at the point where the will-to-power collapses into a will-to-violence without, at the same time, ceasing to be social. The proliferation of new forms and discourses of sexual violence emerges here as evidence of this other rule (the rule of desire's law) at points of blockage, where histories of political exclusion coupled with the expectation of political presence effect their most insidious conflations—for the sexual is the domain in which violence achieves, to the highest degree, its communicative and hence political dimension without having to become mimetic or representational. This is why, in the end, it is the image of rape as much as murder that constitutes the most remarked sign of an old but changing crisis of the political in South Africa. In what follows, I consider the space in which the crime discussed in this essay takes place.

Carletonville/Khutsong and the Place of Mining

Merafong City was created in 2000 as a new administrative area, gathering together the formerly white towns of Carletonville and Fochville and their historically black townships of Khutsong and Kokosi, as well as Gatsrant, Southern DC, and Wedela. The name means "place of mining." Today, Merafong is home to several of the world's deepest gold mines—some over two miles in depth—and has, for decades, been the fulcrum of gold production for South Africa. The AngloGold Ashanti, Harmony, and Goldfields mining companies dominate the local space, along with the Blyvooruitzicht Gold Mining Company (owned by Durban Roodeport Deep) and the Canadian firm Placer Dome. Until 1994, Carletonville was an almost exclusively white town, its "colored" population having been evicted and transported to the neighboring township of Lenasia under the Group Areas Act. Its black population comprises migrant laborers temporarily resident in hostels and longer-term residents who were previously confined to the area beyond the railroad, a sprawling but rationally planned township in which neighborhoods are divided by language and ethnicity. For the past decade or so, black residents with sufficient monetary resources have been leaving the township of Khutsong for the town of Carletonville, but the township itself has become a scene of additional informal in-migration. On its outskirts, a sprawling squatter settlement grows, and today, it dominates the formal settlement.[12]

The railway divides this world in two and marks the point of radical difference. Carletonville is a modernist dream town with broad boulevards and neatly planted trees, its handsome schools and regular bungalows interspersed with churches, shopping malls, and private medical clinics.[13] In Khutsong, by contrast, the orderliness of urban design cannot conceal the generally unpaved roads, the absence of medical facilities, and the open drainage ditches. The schools are woefully ill equipped, the libraries nearly empty, the police stations mere shells. Brick churches with tin roofs dot the neighborhoods, but their poor congregations do not have the means with which to repair the cracking walls. And such cracks are legion because Merafong is built on a bed of porous dolomite and is subject to constant subsidence, or sinkholes. These sinkholes have appeared regularly over the past decades, and into their gaping spaces houses, crushing plants, tennis courts, and roads have fallen—along with the people who happened to be there at the moment of disaster.

Sinkholes are not merely the evidence of geological events, however; they are also potent metaphors. They give concreteness to the ideology of accident, which is so central to life in the mines. Their very form seems to echo that of the mine shafts, although they have generally been represented (by the mines and their representative body, the Chamber of Mines) as meaningless facts: merely natural phenomena.[14] At best, corporate officialdom considers them, like other accidents in the mines—from methane gas explosions and fires to collapses and floods—to be an inevitable risk in an industry where the elimination of "accident" stands on the threshold of impossibility. The idea of accident is, of course, the mode in which the violence of an extractive industry assumes the form of second nature. Accident is the experience of violence when such violence cannot be named as crime. This is why, as Shula Marks and Neil Andersson can rightly say, that "it is the acceptance of accident as normal that marks the violent nature of the society" in South Africa.[15] In South Africa, then, crime must be understood in an oppositional relation not only to the political but to the accidental. Neither social exigency nor coincidence will explain it; which is to say, crime, or rather, criminality, is a discourse of agency and, as we shall see, of agency interrupted.

The "sinkhole" is a particularly acute form through which to naturalize violence, for it both represents and sublates the historical relationships between mining, the experience of violence, and something called crime. It is telling, in this context, to observe the recent metamorphosis in the colloquialisms of technocrats and urban developers, who now use the term "sinkhole" to refer to "properties that are slummed, abandoned, overcrowded, poorly maintained, used for illegal or unsuitable uses (shebeens, some clubs, sweatshops, panelbeaters in homes, etc.)."[16] Through a chain of metaphoric substitutions and metonymic associations, then, the place of mining in South Africa has become the iconic locus of both accident and crime—and thus the location of the new state's most demanding tests.

Crime and Crisis: The Language of Violence

Not coincidentally, Nelson Mandela chose Khutsong as the location from which to deliver the eighty-fourth-anniversary oration of the ANC. On 8 January 1996, not quite two years after South Africa's first democratic election and on the eve of the convening of the Truth and Reconciliation Commission (TRC), he addressed a crowd of more than ten thousand people and spoke of a "struggle which intensifies with each passing day, to define the agenda of the democratic order." He was speaking of the struggle to end violent crime, especially in KwaZulu-Natal and in the mining hostels, where tensions between Zulu and other ethnic groups had been mobilized and manipulated during election campaigns (as they had during apartheid). The division between political and nonpolitical crime was strained in Mandela's speech, as he called upon audience members to "ensure that the people themselves take up the struggle for an end to violence and the creation of a climate conducive to free political activity."[17] With the architects of the TRC, he was articulating the new state's claim to legitimacy as well as its right to a monopoly on violence. At the same time, he was eschewing any political claims that might be made on behalf of crime—not only by Buthelezi's Inkatha Freedom Party[18] but also by the victims of apartheid who might otherwise imagine vengeance as an adequate mode of justice, and by those individuals who, frustrated by the limited opportunities to assert their new but much-touted rights, might attempt to demonstrate their sovereignty and their will-to-power in and through violence.

To a certain extent, Mandela's call for an end to violence as the condition of possibility for political activity implied an absolute antithesis between violence (violent crime) and political processes, and it indexed a nearly Habermasian conception of the political as a space of transparent communicative relations between all people. With its capacious multilingualism and recognition of eleven official languages, South Africa's new constitution materialized that conception in an overt form. In order to make such a statement, however, Mandela also had to construe "political violence" as an exception, indeed as *the* exception on which the new social order would be based. Such exceptionalism also provided the axiomatic ground for the TRC, which indemnified the new state against civil liability for the violence committed by its precursor and offered amnesty to individuals if they could demonstrate that their offenses were committed "with political objectives and . . . in the course of the conflicts of the past."[19] While the TRC and its members recognized the effects of "structural violence" in the generally high rates of nonpolitical crime throughout South African society, it nonetheless offered amnesty only for those deeds intentionally and proportionately perpetrated in terms of the fight for and against apartheid.

Two extreme cases of "criminality" marked the limit on either end of what could be encompassed within the political, and tellingly, they occurred within the fold of legitimate policing and security operations. The first case comprised the "clearly criminal deeds" committed by "bad apples" in the security forces. Though recognizing their criminality, the TRC granted amnesty to such perpetrators if their acts had been condoned or had gone unpunished over a long period of time, and hence could be said to reflect the policy of the state's security apparatus. The second was represented by the case of *kitskonstabels* (instant constables), who were recruited into the police force as part of a "contra-mobilisation force" after minimal training. Typically black men, they were accused of using the power of their office and the force of their quickly acquired arms to harass and terrorize politically active community members. The TRC chose to "view these acts within their political context" and generally granted amnesty *"unless acts committed were clearly aberrations."* The examples of aberration cited by the TRC report are "shooting the owner of a shebeen, or *raping someone in circumstances which indicated that it was a random crime."*[20]

The first instance appears to be a straightforward crime of economic self-interest, and one that would have been useless to the counterinsurgency. It is, however, the second that draws our attention, suggesting as it does that rape might be enacted in a random manner but also that it might on occasion constitute a political act. We will return to this question of the possibly political nature of sexual violence below. Here, it is important only to note that, in its demand for full confessions, the TRC institutionalized (and theatricalized) a deeply ironic concept of individuated political accountability: those acts which expressed a will-to-political-subjectivity would be amnestied only if they could be explained as politically over-determined and hence as acts which actually reflected the limit of the personal as the basis for political agency. Meanwhile, those illicit acts which had been carried out in a context that was saturated with political violence but which lacked political purpose remained criminal and unavailable for amnesty. As such, these latter acts came to represent a doubled failure, particularly in masculine subjects: the failure to be political (or to channel disaffection into political struggles) and the failure of the previous regime to recognize all persons equally as full political subjects. Here, as admissions of accountability came to entail the surrender of any notion that individual acts could be a legitimate mode of achieving social justice, the political emerged as a category denoting the limit of the personal. Thus would permanent social confrontation and an explosion of general desires for retribution be avoided.

Yet, in a milieu increasingly saturated with legal discourse, where tele-visual dramas of law and order and promises of political enfranchisement reinforce but also distort each other, the distinction between political responsibility and individual indemnity, on the one hand, and personal culpability understood as guilt or innocence, on the other, was lost. Its effacement can be seen in the petitions for amnesty in which perpetrators believed they were being given an opportunity to proclaim their innocence, rather than to admit their guilt, as the means to freedom. It can, perhaps, also be seen in the forms of violence that seem to have proliferated in the very wake of the TRC: sexual and domestic violence, incestuous rape, assaults on elderly people, and the transformation of economic crime into personalized and often sexually violent crime. I want, therefore, to consider some examples of this confusion from the records of the TRC concerning cases in the Merafong area.

Hearings and Overhearings: The Trials of Khutsong Youth

> And at this stained place words
> are scraped from resinous tongues
> wrung like washing, hung on lines
> of courtroom and confessional,
> transposed into the dialect of record.
> INGRID DE KOK, "Parts of Speech"

In 1993 a number of individuals from Khutsong township were brought before the Potchefstrom Circuit Court and tried for murder and other crimes committed in conflicts between local gangs and the ANC Youth League in 1989, 1990, and 1991. Mpayipheli William Faltein, twenty-three, and Johnson Thembe Ncube, twenty-five, were charged with the 24 December 1990 murder of David Mayeko, as well as the attempted murders of Sgotlo (last name unknown) and David Maseko. Ncube was also charged with robbery and malicious damage to property.[21] Both men had been found guilty, and a judgment handed down on 10 September 1993 had sentenced them to concurrent terms of twelve, six, and six years for each of the respective offenses. Almost exactly three years later, on 3 September 1996, they filed for amnesty under section 18 of the Promotion of National Unity and Reconciliation Act, no. 34, of 1995.[22] On the same day, nine other men also made application for amnesty, six of them members of the ANC Youth League or the South African Youth Congress who had been found guilty of murder which they now claimed was political, and three of them members of the white nationalist Afrikaner Weerstandsbeweging (AWB) who had been convicted of both murder and robbery in May 1991.

The amnesty hearings of Faltein and Ncube attracted a great deal of attention, mainly because they revealed the possibility that the Khutsong ANC had actually armed youths to fight against the gangs, which were manipulated by both the police and the Carletonville business elite. Khutsong had become a tense scene of youth and other political conflict, as well as so-called vigilante justice following the uprising in Soweto, especially in the late 1980s and early 1990s. The tension reached its peak in the early 1990s, at which point the township was engulfed in a general state of conflict often referred to as the "Reef Township War." From January 1990 until December 1992, between 3,166 and 4,815 people died annually in South Africa in violence associated with antiapartheid protests, counterinsurgency, and related activities. Several more thousands were injured, though death rates were higher than injury rates. The West Rand was relatively quiet, when compared with the neighboring East Rand and more distant parts of KwaZulu-Natal. Nonetheless, more than seventy-seven violent incidents (including "massacres," in which more than four people were killed) occurred during protests each year on the West Rand, and by far the majority of those committed in 1990 occurred in Oberholzer, the district within the Pretoria-Witwatersrand-Vaal Triangle that included Carletonville, Khutsong, and Toekomsville (now included within Merafong).[23] Popular uprisings and violence associated with hostels were accompanied by retributive violence directed at black policemen, ostensibly for complicity with the apartheid system. In the brief period between 1 and 31 January 1990, three Khutsong policemen were burned to death in three separate incidents, a black councilor's home was petrol-bombed, and the homes and single quarters of black policemen were stoned and fire-bombed. These incidents accounted for 13 percent of police deaths in the entire country during that period.[24]

In the end, however, the TRC hearings left as many questions as answers for historians of the Struggle in the townships surrounding Johannesburg. They revealed a state of near-constant war, fought mainly by youths in their midteens. They also revealed a population of schoolchildren whose "education" had led them to fetishize forms of proceduralism and what they perceived to be juridical terminology, without giving them the means to appropriate any place in the language of the state. In several instances, the hearings broke down in confusion, as judges and lawyers, witnesses and confessors, spoke past each other in spasms of mutual untranslatability. Not incidentally, the blockages that are recorded in the transcripts coalesce around a particular set of questions about witnessing and the status of claims to "having been there." Often, the missed encounters, the events which the youths nonetheless claimed to have seen, concerned sexual violence.

In their decisions on Ncube, TRC members J. Mall, J. Wilson, J. Ngoepe, C. De Jager, and S. Khampele granted Ncube amnesty and stated:

> The applicant was a member of the Self Defense Unit (SDU) as well as a member of the African National Congress Youth League (ANCYL) in Khutsong. The victims were members of a vigilante group. According to the applicant, the vigilante group sowed terror in Khutsong, working in collaboration with the South African police. Political activists were harassed, for example, the applicant's house was burned down and the applicant had to flee Khutsong at some stage. The ANCYL members had to acquire firearms in a clandestine manner in order to repel the attacks.[25]

Accordingly, they granted Ncube amnesty. However, the same commissioners withheld amnesty from Faltein on the grounds that he refused to admit guilt or even participation in the offenses for which he sought amnesty. They continued, "the applicant was not prepared to, and in fact did not, make a 'full disclosure of all the relevant facts' to us as required by Section 20(1) of the Act."[26]

William Faltein, as he is identified in the transcripts, began by claiming membership in the ANC Youth League of Khutsong, but his testimony was quickly interrupted by a confusion regarding the names of victims in his narrative. The commission members had mistaken David Maseko, a state witness, for David Mayeko, who had been killed by Faltein and Ncube. According to Faltein, "David Mayeko that we killed was a member of the gangster group called vigilantes that was harassing the activities in the location and victimising all activities and killing people around the location and they burnt our house as well and they burnt all our property in the house."[27]

Faltein's speech was breathless and the simultaneous translators, who were charged with facilitating the smooth flow of discourse in the multilingual context of the TRC, had difficulty keeping up. He answered a question about why he "felt that [Mayeko] had to be killed" simply enough, with an accusation—that Mayeko was a vigilante—and a claim of self-defense. With regard to the latter, Faltein stated that he and Ncube had been told Mayeko was looking for them and that when they initially confronted him—he was armed and in the company of his gang—they had fled. Ncube, said Faltein, had shot back, not because he wanted to kill Mayeko but because he wanted to "scare him away."[28]

The TRC members were perplexed, to the point of asking him to "concentrate on the question." One of them wondered aloud whether poor translation or even the haste of Faltein's testimony was precipitating general confusion. Nonetheless, they continued with their questions. As they did so, Faltein vacillated between saying that the vigilantes were "a group that was killing and raping people without any reasons" and that "it was a political thing. They used to kill all activists in the location if you are affiliated to the ANC, they will kill you with the police."[29] The same acts appeared to be meaningless and political for him, by turns. And it was, perhaps, this seeming conflation of violence without reason and political violence that irked the TRC commissioners.

Faltein's testimony came under even greater scrutiny when he described the burning of his parents' home, for he had not seen the event himself. He was "away sleeping at [his] brother's place." He added, by way of explanation for his claim to knowledge about that event, that "they [the vigilantes] were seen by my sister who was at school."[30] The young man's claim to having witnessed an event at which he was not present, and from which even his sister, through whom he claimed proximity, was absent, stymied the TRC members. It solicited not only confusion but epistemological doubt, and the specter of rumor was palpable. A host of other confusions about the identity of the state's witness and the fact that he did not testify in a case that resulted in a guilty verdict made matters worse. Nor could Faltein describe the events leading to the shooting of Mayeko in any convincing manner: "When he went out of the yard [685, an address in Khut-song] he called us. We just ran away and then he was shooting in the air as we were running across the streets. And then when we thought that he had turned away, we thought he was away but the co-accused [Ncube] shot him."[31] Judge Ngoepe[32] was dismayed: "You are giving your evidence in a very telegraphic manner that I don't understand what you are saying. . . . Mr. Faltein, why do we struggle like this to get information out of you? Were you not told that when you make application for amnesty you must come and give all the details all the information to us?"[33] With a certain degree of pathos, Faltein said that he had "read the whole booklet" and that his victim had attempted to shoot at him and his colleague. He would later admit to hearing only a single shot, but Johnson Ncube would claim this as his own, denying that their victim had fired at the SDU members, and hence denying the self-defense claim. But although Faltein claimed to have picked up his weapon after it was abandoned by fleeing gangsters in a street war, he acknowledged the fact that Youth League members had received guns as donations from the "location community." Unlike Faltein, Ncube understood that it was guilt rather than innocence that the TRC sought as the grounds of freedom. Guilt could be forgiven, because its agency could be reassigned to political forces. But innocence could be claimed only in a court of law, where its acknowledgment would preserve a subject's claims to agency precisely as a force that had been kept in reserve.

When Faltein explained that he had known Mayeko for a long time, the latter's grandmother having lived in the same neighborhood, the Xhosa section of Khutsong, the TRC was so dumbfounded that they asked "which question are you answering?" while explaining to him that they were interested only in a narrative of events, not a history of the failed social relations from which they emerged.[34] Here, however, the rupture of the supposedly smooth space of the juridical domain revealed something else, namely the difficult passage between speech and violence, between relation and negation, as it occurred that fateful Christmas Eve, somewhere near number 685. Yet what ultimately threatened to interrupt the proceedings was not so much the intransigence of the witness or even his refusal to admit to the crime for which he had sought amnesty. It was not merely the impossibility of ascertaining whether mistranslation had undermined the hearings or whether the witness, as Judge Ngoepe worried, really understood the questions to which he offered his improbable responses.[35] The risk to the proceedings and the vision of the public sphere that the TRC sought to theatricalize lay in the confusion between talking and fighting at the heart of Faltein's testimony. The following exchange reveals, with particular clarity, the dilemmas that Faltein's testimony represented:

> JUDGE NGOEPE: How did you ensure that people were not being attacked by the vigilantes?
>
> MR. FALTEIN: We kept on guard all the time to make sure that everybody is safe, escorting people from the busstops to home.
>
> NGOEPE: If people were to be attacked what would you do?
>
> FALTEIN: We would help them by fighting against the people who are trying to attack them.
>
> NGOEPE: How would you fight those people?
>
> FALTEIN: We would try and find out from them as to why are they attacking these people and try and defuse the matter.
>
> NGOEPE: How would you fight those people?
>
> FALTEIN: We would try fighting them by trying to talk to them and we would fight with them after talking to them.
>
> NGOEPE: That is not fighting, talking to them. How would you fight those people?'
>
> FALTEIN: As I said, that we would fight but we try stopping this person, but if they don't listen we would try to stop the person doing from whatever they want to do [sic].
>
> NGOEPE: Do you lack the courage to say that as a member of the SDU, if necessary, in defending the community I would produce a gun and shoot people who were terrorizing the community? Do you lack that courage to say so, if that was the case?
>
> FALTEIN: I wouldn't just shoot people without a reason.[36]

In this extraordinary episode, a judge and TRC commissioner not only strains to decide the difference between talking and fighting, but he inserts himself into the domain of violence through an act of linguistically mediated, imagined reciprocity. Accusing the confessor of lacking the courage to speak and to own violence through the confessional speech act, he does what Faltein seems incapable of doing, namely appropriating the position of the speaking "subject" as the one who can admit to having knowingly transgressed language *and* the law. He substitutes himself for the youth in language, the only place in which such mutual substitution can be undertaken, becoming the one who would say "I"—precisely by addressing a comparably situated "you."[37] And though tentative—this appropriation is spoken and redacted in the conditional tense—it is nonetheless based in the fantasy of (retributive and preemptive) violence: "I would produce a gun and shoot people who were terrorizing the community." The entire exchange runs aground here, as the judge undertakes this act of reciprocity in order to think its failure in the moment that a gun is fired. For his part, Faltein continued to insist that he never intended to kill anyone and that his acts were always, and only, defensive, responsive, and reactive.

An entire theory of the political and its relationship to violence resides here. Judge Ngoepe states the matter bluntly in his effort to counterpose "saying" with "fighting," language with violence. Violence is what happens when language fails for him. And the termination of violence in and through negotiations, as happened in Khutsong following Mayeko's death, when representatives of both the ANC Youth League and the vigilantes agreed to a cessation in their hostilities, is peace. In this sense, violence is the limit, the outside, and the interruption of the political sphere. It is also the provocation of speech, the ground on which the virtue of political discourse becomes visible. Applicants are, after all, granted amnesty only insofar as they can claim that they acted violently because the political was at risk. As Dan Ndzeku, one-time ANC organizer in Carletonville and mayor at the time of his testimony, put the matter, "what was at stake was a free political activity"—this in a context that he described as one of "war," in which "pitched battles [were being] fought."[38] Strangely, the symptoms of that state of emergency were not to be found in a mass of corpses; Ndzeku could name only David Mayeko as a certain casualty of the fighting (although other hearings conducted by the TRC made clear that there had, in fact, been many other deaths, and national and regional statistics for the period corroborate this). Rather, the symptom of gang warfare was to be found in the rape of activist women by vigilantes.[39] Faltein had, in fact, begun his testimony by describing the vigilantes as "a group that was killing and raping people without any reasons,"[40] and Ndzeku reiterated this, although he framed his discussion of rape with suspicion. It is important to understand the place of rape in this economy in which language and violence are opposed, but to pursue that topic requires that we move away from the hauntingly vague invocations of a commonplace sexual violence to a more overt discussion.

Mimetic Justice, or The Specter of Law

At the same time as Faltein and Ncube brought their applications for amnesty to the Potchefstrom hearings of the TRC, Peter Lebona, Solomon Lekitlane, and Elias Bosakwe made application under the same act for the murder of Zenzile Joseph Dlamini (or Nglamini or Ndlameni—the spelling changes by document) in July 1991, in Orkney, a mining town not far from Carletonville/Khutsong. The context was comparable: conflict between the ANC Youth League and local gangs had erupted into armed combat. In this case, the murder victim had been a comrade who had changed his affiliation and attached himself to a local gang, called the Kofifi. Although Zenzile was murdered following a meeting of the ANC, both Peter Lebona and Solomon Lekitlane commenced their narratives by identifying Zenzile as the perpetrator of a particularly violent rape, in which a local ANC woman, Mrs. Maleto, was assaulted in her home by Zenzile and his companions. According to the men's TRC testimony, when she was commanded to pay the gangsters and indicated that she could not do so, Zenzile allegedly bound her husband before raping her in his presence and then crushed her skull with a stone. Other rapes were also invoked in Lebona's testimony, and in fact, it was in the aftermath of their dragging Zenzile to the police station in the hopes that charges would be brought against him for those earlier rapes that the ANC Youth League members determined that there was a conspiracy between the gangsters and the local police force. Nonetheless, after apprehending Zenzile and taking him to an ANC meeting, at which he ostensibly confessed to the "killing" and apologized on the grounds of drunkenness, the ANC marshals determined to hand him over to the law enforcement agents in the township. Lebona and Lekitlane were marshals for the organization, and it was while they were transporting their charge, they said, that he drew his gun (he had not been patted down). There, between the spectacle of collective but not legal adjudication and the institutions of state power, they shot him. Or rather, Lebona shot him, but not fatally. Lekitlane stabbed him to death as he lay bleeding and then poured petrol on his head in the anticipation of necklacing—an act that would have mimicked the method of terrorization for which Zenzile was himself famous. A third comrade, Elias Bosakwe, intervened, however, on the grounds that Zenzile was already dead and therefore not to be further brutalized (burning is here the mode of an execution, not that of disposing of the corpse).

The hearings of Peter Lebona, Solomon Lekitlane, and Elias Bosakwe like those of Faltein and Ncube, were troubled by the questionable status of witnessing on which the applicants rested their explanatory narrative. They were also troubled by what emerged as a failure of communication within the hearing and, ultimately, a certain excess of juridical form. In the first instance, they could not demonstrate that they had seen the rape, and although Lebona admitted to accompanying the deceased on many occasions, he could say only that he had seen Zenzile enter the house of the woman who was to be so cruelly attacked. Lebona also dismissed the origi-

nal testimony he gave in his own defense at the original trial as "lies."[41] The
TRC members were unconvinced, and their doubt about the petition was
intensified when they learned that in his written statement to the TRC
Lebona had omitted to mention a gun, Zenzile's use of which was adduced
as grounds for self-defense in the oral testimony. When Lebona explained
this omission by stating that he "forgot to include that in my statement but
he had a gun," the lead commissioner could only reply, "You forgot to
mention perhaps the most important element."[42] The commissioner and
his colleagues were even more confused when informed that the woman
whose murder had ostensibly precipitated the informal trial had not, in
fact, actually been killed after being raped.

Nonetheless, the commissioners' doubt about Lebona's testimony was
stimulated less by the information that differed from that provided in his
written application to the TRC than by the similarity of the applications
of the three men; for example, each of the written applications began with
the eloquent explanatory preamble, "Post February 1990-era marked a
significant hallmark in the history of our democratic revolution."[43] The
formality and literacy of these documents, which claimed a political origin for the crime of murder, were markedly at odds with the broken speech
and grammatically awkward enunciations of their oral testimony.

Lebona defended the mirroring between his application and that of his
coapplicants by saying, simply, that "what we said was prevailing then."
However, the presiding commissioner doubted that "three people relating
what had happened in the past would use identical wording for a four page
statement." At best, he would acknowledge that one statement was legitimate and that the others had been copied. Still frustrated at the end of the
hearing, he called upon Lebona's attorney to offer some "explanation as
to how it came about that all these statements are in the same language."
He added that "oral testimony would be far better" than any affidavit that
Lebona might produce to supplement his questionable application statement. In the end, Lebona's attorney revealed that initially Lebona and the
coapplicants had been in the same prison cell as a third-year law student,
who not only took the statements down but redacted them in a manner
that gave to them the respectability of law.[44]

Imagining themselves to bear the authority that would accrue to one
who spoke in the language of the courts, the three men seem to have imagined that legal truth is precisely the kind of truth that is iterable, and even
reiterable. In this sense, they expressed an understanding of law akin to
that propounded by pragmatist philosophers of language, who argue that
the performative force of law derives from its structure of iterability.
Lebona and his peers did not so much mistake the nature of law, then, as

they mistook their own relationship to it; for, if law is made operative in the moment that a primordial authority is invoked and reiterated, the subject of law acquires authenticity only to the extent that he or she can express the uniqueness (the noniterability) of his or her experience. The misrecognizing testimony of the youths is all the more poignant, then, for its errors. It demonstrates with uncommon clarity the virtue and the potency of legality in the minds of even murderous young men. For them, the repetition between statements was not an index of dubiousness but a sign of the truth-value of their statements, if not the authenticity of their voices. Unfortunately, they lacked any sense that such truth-value should be correlated with a unique voice. For their part, the TRC members embraced a nearly lyric theory of truth as that singularity which requires unique expression.[45] Ironically, of course, the TRC commissioners needed evidence of authentic subjectivity as the ground for confession, just as they needed confession as the ground for emancipation, but in this respect the written statements offered nothing but the specter of serial individuality. Perhaps this is why the chairman's recourse to the virtues of "oral testimony" came as a shock to the applicants. After the laborious processes by which written applications had been made—by men who, their attorneys admitted, may not have fully understood the questions put by the TRC—a call for straight talk seemed ignominiously inadequate to the grandeur of the occasion.

Lekitlane's testimony, which followed Lebona's, suffered even more from the disjuncture between the style of the written discourse and that of the oral testimony. As in the hearing of Faltein and Ncube, the language question arose most pointedly around the matter of witness. Lekitlane claimed to have seen the rape of Mrs. Maleto but admitted that he had not been present, that he had only seen Zenzile enter the woman's house. Moreover, the issue was complicated by a knot of kinship terms which eluded the TRC members and remained opaque even after the hearings.

> JUDGE NGOEPE: When you say that you saw the deceased committing all these crimes, did you mean that you saw that with your own eyes?
> LEKITLANE: What I have seen which he did with my own eyes is when he entered a certain house, I was with him on that day when he did that terrible action, that woman who came and make an allegation that her husband is giving her trouble then he said to the father of that house to say, he told that husband to say he must never come into that house again, if he come I'm going to kill you. When I came I found out that this is the house for the deceased, he is the father[46] of the house.
> CHAIRMAN: What do you understand by that? Maybe because of language

difficulties I didn't understand what the witness is trying to say. Is it possible for you to clear up what he is trying to say?

COUNSEL: Chairperson may we ask him to repeat it again, I didn't understand
actually what was said?

CHAIRMAN: Please I want you to give your answer in such a way that we can
understand what you are saying, step by step, understand?

MR. DE JAGER: What language is he speaking?

COUNSEL: Sotho.

MR. DE JAGER: Are you satisfied that it's being interpreted correctly?

CHAIRPERSON: Would you please just answer again because we had some difficulty understanding what was said?

LEKITLANE: I was together with the deceased to realize that he was doing evil
things, as we were walking a woman came to us and she said my husband
is giving me troubles in the house. Myself and the deceased we went into
this woman's house to try and bring solutions, but the next day when I
go back to the house the deceased was now the father in the house and
when I requested the answer, the next door neighbour told me that no,
the father has been chased away because now the brother that I see now
in this family is now the new father of this house.

Later, Lekitlane was asked what he saw with his own eyes. He responded as follows: "Many things which I've seen that he do, I was afraid
to walk with him because he was raping. What I've seen that he is doing he
has a bad heart, he hit a certain woman with a stone and then we thought
the woman has died." But Lekitlane was not present at the rape. He admitted, "I was not there." But if he could not claim the authenticity of the
witness, he could claim the moral authority of one for whom rape represents evil, even when not seen: "What I've seen the deceased do, I have
never seen him do something but I know that what he did I didn't like."[47]

In the light of the magisterial prose of the application, the blunt, confused, and nearly infantile words of the hearings could only consolidate
doubt about the applications being made. Precisely because of their raw-
ness, however, the words reveal something about the ways in which the
young men perceived events in the moment that gangsterism confronted
an organized political apparatus and the shadow forms of a state represented by the ANC. The youths were, it appears in retrospect, acting out
of horror and obedience. This doubled relation was fuelled in part by the
fact that the crimes being committed were being done under the false auspices of the organization to which they had pledged their allegiance. Zenzile was famed not only for the merciless violence of his acts but for the

degree to which he claimed to be acting as a representative of the ANC. Even more than his "crossing over," it was his continued masquerade that upset the youths, who believed they could avoid any potential perception of complicity with him (and they had often been in his company) only by destroying that with which they might have been associated. Precisely as members of the ANC, they had to eschew the criminality that had emerged within their cell. A sacrificial act of killing was the means by which they attempted to draw the line between legitimacy and illegitimacy, discipline and criminality. They conducted themselves with all the pomp and circumstance of judges and policemen in an order ruled by the law of efficiency. When blood lust and vengeance seduced them with an awful pleasure beyond utility's bounds, Elias Bosakwe called them back. The man was dead, he had reminded them; burning would have been excessive.

A nearly identical set of issues emerged in another case during the same TRC amnesty hearings, one from the town of Fochville (some fifteen miles from Carletonville on the other side of the mines, and now part of Merafong). In that case, a group of ANC youths who had fled the violence in Khutsong established a new branch in the Fochville township of Kokosi. One of the key organizers later became the subject of rumors that he had turned coat and joined a vigilante group. Tsietsi Gideon Thloloe and Andreis Johnny Mageti Motluong killed their former comrade for his putative betrayal and for undertaking criminal acts while continuing to claim allegiance to the party.[48] Robbing, killing, and raping in the name of the ANC was not only criminal but violently subversive because it blurred the distinction between gangsterism and the party. Because both were officially extralegal and hence criminal, the claim to legitimacy could be made only through mutual negation and was extremely fraught.

The Sexual Thing: Violence and/as Language

> *Rumor, than whom no evil thing is faster:*
> *speed is her life; each step augments her strength.*
> VIRGIL, *Aeneid* (trans. Frank Copley)

It is precisely in the context of rumor that the question of sexual violence became so important. In the labor to distinguish similitude from identity, public discourse from rumor, legitimate political violence from criminality, the "Sexual Thing" emerges as a peculiarly potent force. In his response to the judge's question as to why Zenzile Dlamini might have attacked the woman whose rape and possible murder he had been accused of, Peter Lebona revealingly remarked that the act had been the manifestation of a more general desire: "this woman was a member of the ANC Women's League . . . and Zenzile *was really intending to kill the activists* of the ANC that is why he chose to do that act."[49] Effectively, he attributed to the rape a metonymic status. The rape and murder (the latter now questionable) were not, precisely, representational or even representative acts. However, they were signifying acts, capable of forging connections between the wounded and the wounding parties, and especially the witnesses—including those distant auditors who would become "witnesses" through overhearing.

In addition to the awful injury to which the woman was subjected, the act was performed on the woman, before her husband, in a way that encouraged the circulation of stories and oral testimony (however mediated). It therefore both specularized the aspiration to power in the form of violence and threatened to foster further fraternal conflict.[50] One might even say that this sexualization of violence performed a specularization of the general condition of violence defining life in the townships after 1990 (at which time political organizations had been banned by the state). Moreover, it was in response to a rape undertaken in this communicating mode that Lebona and Lekitlane acted—as representatives of an alternative judicial process. Their effort to retrospectively clad their acts in the appearance of law dramatizes this yearning toward a legitimate violence.

It must be remarked that violence against women was not exclusively a symptom of the conflict between gangsterism and the ANC or a mark of the increased tensions that defined the last panicked years of the apartheid state. It had been an irreducible part of the economy of both white and black masculinity, and it had been especially central to the world of the gangs as these had emerged in the gold-mining towns around Johannesburg. Keith Breckenridge called "the capacity for violence" the "heart of masculinity for both groups of men [black and white]" working in the mines.[51] For most writers, this tendency toward sexualized violence against women and the aesthetics of violence that sustained it are linked to apartheid, if only to the extent that the system of racialized natural-resource-based capital is seen as a force that amplifies and reinforces indigenous forms of gendered hierarchy. Thus, for example, Clive Glaser suggests that the only domain in which otherwise-emasculated black male subjects could maintain a sense of the "ascendant" was in the hyperbolically masculine spaces of the gangs.[52] Without attributing a causal force to the apartheid system, Catherine Campbell links it to sexual violence when she asserts, "The ability of men to control women . . . and the use of violence to ensure this control, is one area where the power of working class men has not been threatened by a racial capitalist society."[53] Glaser's analysis, however, goes further in not only comprehending the prevalence of sexual violence in terms of apartheid but suggesting that sexual violence actually constituted one of the definitive practices of (urban) gangsterism: "Although many urban youth gangs mugged and robbed ordinary residents, probably the majority were not engaged consistently in serious property-related crime. Rather, the *most common manifestations of gang violence involved sexual coercion and inter-gang feuding.*"[54]

What does it mean to suggest that sexual "coercion" constituted a central activity of the gangs? Glaser and Kynoch, like most Marxist-influenced writers on the topic, read the centrality of such violence in economic and utilitarian terms. To quote Kynoch, "the control of women has been crucial to the economic survival of the gangs." Women, says Kynoch, were used as lures to seduce miners into spending their money in establishments run by the gangs, and were also deemed to enhance men's power through their praise singing. But they were also always eligible to become "spoils of war" or "trophies," and Kynoch quotes a gang member describing the ideals of masculinity as the capacity to "to kill, commit robberies, and kidnap women."[55]

Invariably, it seems, arguments about violence against women devolve into these economistic explanations. While it seems to me an unassailable claim that women in severely patriarchal contexts are the objects of a fierce extractive process, such explanations do not ultimately explain violence, and certainly not the forms of violence that are in evidence in the gang wars of Khutsong or the other towns and townships of the area. Those forms are differentiated in complex but also coherent ways, and this differentiation suggests that they partake of language, that they are communicative. Among other things, they communicate the nature of power.[56] Visibility is a primary vector of such power, and this is true in two senses. First, publicly performed acts of violence communicate a force, whose eruption they endlessly threaten to repeat. As an expression of power, this force is vulnerable, however, to its dependence on witnesses—even remote witnesses such as Lebona and Lekitlane, who must apprehend events through rumor and hearsay or mass-mediated instruments. Such violence, and the power of its perpetrators, are affirmed in being discussed. In contrast, acts of violence may express power precisely to the extent that they prohibit their own revelation. Such secret and invisible violence exercises its force through a threat of violence, but what is threatened in this case is the injury of the witness. Secret violence is perpetrated, in South Africa and perhaps elsewhere, by those who claim a monopoly over it, in circumstances that may be more or less limited. It includes both the state-organized disappearance and torture of dissidents and the incestuous violence performed in domestic households. Power that demands silence rather than discursive repetition—whether this silence is enforced through the logics of shame, the rhetoric of sexual prerogative, or the idea of sovereign right—will only be exercised when its perpetrator is injured rather than enhanced by visibility and/or mimicry. In the case of sexual violence, I would like to suggest, secrecy is sought and presumed mainly by those who can identify with the ideal forms of political subjectivity operative in the public domain. The revelation of this kind of violence would radically undermine the status of the perpetrator, and hence its enactment depends on the willingness of the state to cede the domestic sphere as the autonomous domain of patriarchal desire, no matter how violent its manifestations. When a state intrudes to secure victims against violence in their own homes, it repudiates this autonomy, declares such violence to be both abnormal and illegal, and asserts the universality of its law.

It is important to recognize that the criminalization of violence constitutes the moment of a perpetrator's utter debasement, but it is debasement in an individualizing form. It recognizes the agency of the perpetrator, even if only as a perverse one. If, however, the domestic sphere is either so weakly defined, so porous or broken, or so penetrated by the state that its inhabitants can presume no privacy (as has been the case in most townships throughout South Africa's history), matters tend to be rather different. The state may refrain from intervening, on cultural grounds, arguing that such violence is normal in particular contexts or sanctioned by tradition (contemporary debates about the nature and possible limits of African patriarchy hinge on precisely this issue). Or the state may explain it as a function of and effort to compensate for massive social dislocation, which is then read as either inevitable or historically irreversible. In either case, it is normalized. This normalization does little to buttress the claims to power that violence acts out. Indeed, such normalization actually functions to withhold recognition of perpetrators' individual agency. Accordingly, that recognition must come from elsewhere. This is the aporia of which I wrote earlier, when arguing that sexual violence often erupts in the abyssal space between personal agency and political subjectivity. One therefore understands that aspirations to power that take the form of violence (and certainly not all such aspirations take this form) will have to solicit the attentions of a phantom collective subject when they take place beyond, in opposition to, or in the spaces evacuated by the state. In the aspiration to such recognition, these acts forge a direct link between the desire of the one and the acquiescent-because-terrorized will of the many. And this is why episodes like those narrated in the amnesty hearings of the TRC in Potchefstrom seek not to be hidden in the dark and secret spaces of a criminal underground—or a domestic space—but demand to be looked upon as they are transmitted in and by others who are equally alienated from the languages of power.

Mimetic Violence, or The Specter of War

So, then, a question: How is sexual violence an act of communication? Is this not a preposterous mistaking of its nature, a confusion of the sort that inverts what Judge Ngoepe believed to be the fundamental enmity between violence and speech? Here, I want to consider for a moment what might be learned from structural-anthropological accounts of power and kinship, politics and familial relations. The lessons learned from ethnography and from structural-anthropological theory, it turns out, are mutually transformative—although this is as much because of the failure of the latter as because of the truth that needs to be confronted in the former.

It is Lévi-Strauss who tells us that war and matrimonial relations are bound by the shared objective of obtaining women. But it is Lévi-Strauss's student Pierre Clastres who demonstrates this in his melancholic account of the Guayaki Indians, wherein he describes an elaborate process by which this indigenous people of Paraguay conduct marriage so as to "bring the element of violence in the matrimonial exchange [defined as an act binding two potentially antagonistic social groups] into the open rather than hide it." In marriage among the Guayaki, he writes, people do "not . . . make war" but "mime it." Clastres goes on to argue that what is mimed is not marriage but the abduction of women, which would have defined relations between patriarchal communities in the case of warfare. Clastres describes the event as one that is "reduced to pure gesture" and that culminates in an act of vengeance. The father of the woman who will go to live with the man who has laid claim to both sexual and economic rights in her responds to his loss with an outburst directed not against the usurping young man but against (surprisingly enough) his own wife: "By punching his own wife" the marriage is consummated—or at least it will be after the son-in-law brings his new wife's parents game and grubs.[57]

For Clastres, an exchange of women by men takes place in the symbolic realm, and this means that it both reproduces and substitutes for a more primary kind of agony.[58] His emphasis on the gestural and the mimetic nature of the relation needs, however, to be counterposed to that form of discourse which constitutes the true essence of the political for Clastres, namely talk. In the Paraguayan instance, the chief's function is to speak, even if this means merely repeating what people know. And the community is generally infused, in Clastres's reading, with a desire "to dissolve in words whatever aggressiveness or bitterness inevitably arises within the group."[59] The symbolic, the realm of language, always differing from the world even as it seeks to replicate it, is identical with political life—even in those contexts where politics is not institutionally differentiated from other kinds of practice.

This would be a meaningless digression if Clastres's structuralism did not share something with the prevailing concepts about crime and violence and about the relationships between the public and the domestic sphere in South Africa. What, then, do we learn from this digression? The status of the injury to the woman, which Clastres renders as the mimesis of war, needs to be thought in terms of the more general order of power and violence within which it operates. This is one in which the society is sociologically structured by a prohibition against the identification of power with violence,[60] one not unlike that imagined in Judge Ngoepe's speech. Thus, Clastres writes, "A chief for them is not a man who dominates the others, a man who gives orders and is obeyed . . . he did not exercise his authority through coercion, but through what was most opposed to violence—the realm of discourse, the word." Dependent upon the recognition of the community, the chief constantly seeks to persuade and to demonstrate that "the law of the group is one with [his] desire."[61] His speech will retain its performative authority only insofar as the group accedes to this claim. Moreover, this latter identity is what prevents the leader from transgressing a law that has been made autonomous and rendered independent of any individual, including the chief. However, it does not save the people from violence per se. Warfare is still waged with other groups, and marriage, that mimesis of warfare on whose ground the community erects its homage to the identity of the chief's desire and the group's law, still culminates in an act of violence.

One could read this as a taxonomy in which a primal tendency toward violence is attenuated the more that it is mediated: in the gestural performance of the wedding, it is reduced to a mere punch; in political discourse, it is reduced to rhetorical flourish and exclamations. But in what sense is the punch a mimesis of violence? Does violence mime itself? Is the rape of the ANC woman the mere shadow image of a more real wounding that would occur in a war between the men of the gangs and the ANC youth group? Certainly this is implied when sexual violence is described, as it is in so much of the Merafong youths' testimony, as substitutional violence which occurs where a more political (fraternal) violence found itself blocked in its drive to expression. In the case of the Guayaki, the derivatively violent attack on women in marriage, which both commences and consummates marriage, begins to appear like a fold in social practice, a doubling which assumes the appearance of difference only by repressing the continuity between, in this case, war and the violence against women. How might we understand a comparable continuity between war and sexual violence in South Africa, where gangsterism and political conflict, as well as more random acts of aggression in abandoned social spaces, can all entail public rape?

Clearly, the world of South African gangs today is radically different from that of Paraguayan Indians—not only in its historical particularities but in the form of the political which governs it. It is also different, in different ways, from that of South Africa during the apartheid years. Gangsterism is also oriented by the claims of leaders that their desire and the law of the group are one, but it occurs against the backdrop and in a field wherein the hegemonic discourse of politics is one of representationalism, of the state. Such a field emphasizes the distinction between power and the persons who, as occupants of a particular bureaucratic position, can lay claim to it. And it rests on what Claude Lefort describes as "an irreducible gap between the idea of law and positive laws as well as between the idea of truth and the effective development of various forms of knowledge."[62]

Much can be learned if we consider the mode of politics that drives gangsterism as one that seeks to assert the identity of a leader's desire with the law of a group, within a context that has asserted (even if it has betrayed in a totalitarian and/or privatizing antisocial mode) the fundamental distinction between law and positive laws, between force and power. Indeed, I would like to suggest that the contradiction between these modes of thought and political being has not been attenuated but has, instead, radically intensified in the wake of the new constitution. Moreover, this intensifying contradiction is implicated in the transformation and possible intensification of rates of sexual violence, and especially specularized sexual violence that can be seen across South Africa but especially in townships and decayed inner-city communities where the privatization of the police function in security companies has been matched by the rise of incompletely commercialized vigilante forces and the evacuation of those powers that would otherwise authorize and oversee the deployment of "legitimate violence."

Activists, feminists, and political reformers agree that there is much to worry about in terms of sexual violence in South Africa. The most recent national report issued jointly by the Crime Prevention and Research Resources Center and the Medical Research Council estimated current rape rates in South Africa to be 244 incidents of rape and attempted rape per 100,000 women per annum (as of 1997).[63] This is the highest rate of reported rape in the world, and although there was a brief downturn in rates between 1996 and 1998, there was a resurgence immediately after the institution of the new constitution in 1998.[64] More than 40 percent of these incidents concerned the rape of children, defined legally as the rape of those under the age of eighteen. Such numbers are indeed awful, but they are not unique and it should be noted here that a US Justice Department report released in 2000 states that an astonishing 54 percent of rapes and attempted rape in the United States are experienced by individuals under the age of seventeen. Moreover, 21.6 percent of all such cases refer to violence directed at girls under the age of twelve.[65]

Child rape, including the exceptional and highly commented upon incidents of the rape of children under the age of three, is nonetheless metonymically inscribed in the narratives that circulate in the mass media about South Africa, as the sign of a unique failure and often as a sign of crisis whose narrative context is that of national decline. There is some reason for this insofar as some small studies have suggested that this category may account for nearly 20 percent of child rapes in South Africa.[66] At the same time, it has been observed by Latasha Treger, programme officer at the Women's Health Project in Galashewe township of Kimberley, where a major survey on child rape was conducted under the auspices of the Medical Research Council of South Africa, that a significant number of people (20 percent of those interviewed) do not consider intercourse with a child under ten to be eligible for the category of rape. It is unclear what, precisely, such acts are understood to be, other than "sex," but it is possible that, insofar as agency cannot be attributed to the child, who has no full command of language, and insofar as refusal is part of the negative (dialectical) condition for defining rape in legal terms (it is sexual intercourse to which one has not assented), such individuals are implicitly recognizing an aporia in the legal definition of child rape. It is an aporia that appears most visibly in those contexts where an absolute opposition between agency and enslavement, mastery and servitude, refusal and consent, is presumed.[67]

In addition to this instability in definition, however, the reports by the Medical Research Council testify to the fact that, beyond its status as event in the lives of victims and perpetrators, sexual violence is a discourse, and one that is increasingly central to the operations of the state. This official discourse is inextricably bound up with the popular discourse about such violence, with the rumors and phantasmatic images that circulate in gossip and televisual drama. Indeed, it rests on that which it would seek to contain. This containment is far from secure, which is demonstrated by the low rates of criminal prosecution and conviction. Less than 50 percent of all reported rape cases go to trial, and in 2000, less than 8 percent of these led to convictions.[68] Yet the increasing visibility of discourse about sexual violence and the public assertions that such rates must be improved, reveal the degree to which sexual violence has itself become a test for the new state. Let us then consider how this discourse operates.

In both its official and popular forms, contemporary discourse about sexual violence in South Africa is dominated by two specters. The first is that of random acts perpetrated in public spaces—usually in impoverished urban areas or in townships. The others is of the incestuous violence enacted upon either very young children or elderly women, the latter often associated with demands for payment in households where pension checks provide the only source of income. Between these "extremes," there is violence that appears to be common, normal, or at least legible within the collective understanding of what is likely to occur.

It is important to note, in this context, that while TRC policy focused on a single binary opposition, that between personalized or random violence and political violence, random sexual violence actually stands in opposition to two others forms: that which occurs in the household and that which occurs in the political field. Domestic sexual violence is the object of criminalizing discourse. Political sexual violence is the object of historicizing discourse, for as the new state consolidates its monopoly on violence, the category of political violence recedes. There is, from the perspective of the new state, no longer any legitimate political violence; there is only criminality and the state's response to it. Hence, sexual violence can no longer function in its service. Gangsterism, having been dissociated from the political struggle for which it was mobilized in the 1980s and 1990s, appears now only as the object of a fierce repression.

The constant remarking of random sexual violence[69] cannot help but render it as an excess, implicitly normalizing, though not normativizing or legitimating, that which occurs less randomly, and especially between familiars. This is the perhaps-unintended effect of the numerous statistical reports that describe sexual violence perpetrated by a known person, or by someone in the victim's household, as the most common form. Yet the understandable surfeit of rhetoric (compared to prevalence) about infant and elder rape also expresses a sense that the relative normalcy of incest and domestic violence has limits.[70] Beyond these limits, sexual violence is generally thought to be especially egregious. So, then, the household emerges as the imaginary space within which sexual violence occurs as both normalcy and criminality. Normalcy is spoken in countless interviews with victims who assert that, though they did not want or like the sexual advances to which they were forced to submit in their own households, they nonetheless came to expect them and knew that the same thing happened in other households just as often. But in those appalling instances in which sexual violence cannot be thus accommodated as unpleasant but unavoidable—that is, when infants or elderly women are its victims—it appears to call for the state's intervention into the household. Its eruption into public discourse through media coverage and criminal proceedings constitutes an acknowledgment that the family is actually incapable of fulfilling the role of containment.

These ambivalent discourses bespeak an extraordinary pressure that is currently being put on the family. Indirectly, then, they also reveal the emerging significance of the family for the state. From the perspective of the new millennium, when virtually all nations are beholden to one or another ideology of family values, family and state can appear to be virtually primordial forms of social organization. Yet this historical naturalization of "the family" needs to be examined. Other principles may also be crucially entailed in a given order of social reproduction, principles as diverse as chieftainship, clanship, race, class, and ethnicity. The particularly charged nexus of family and state is neither given nor inevitable, and its emergence demands some explanation. In postapartheid South Africa, the family as a concept acquires its particular value in opposition to race.

Crime, or The Discourse of an Impossible Relation

With the end of apartheid, the primary structuring principle of race has begun to give way to that of the opposition between family and state, and the multiplicity of putatively "separately developing peoples" has been supplanted by a new nationalism that aspires to generate a people. Meanwhile, the racialized class system has given way to a new system of class and national capital that seems to thwart the emergence of an organic collectivity called the people, even as it harbors the ghosts of racial inequality. The seeming displacement of what we can now call politically sexual crime and the apparent intensification of both domestic and random sexual violence need to be understood in terms of these other developments.

Sexual violence in its new form, in the form of both random crime and incestuous outrage, the form that terrorizes the remotely controlled readers of the mass media, is a discourse that mediates between the family and the state. It inserts itself in response to the appearance of an incapacity within families to maintain order, to control those forces (including the force of desire) that it cannot control. This, at least, was James Siegel's conclusion for the Indonesian case, where a discourse of *kriminalitas* operates through the narration of events of sexual abuse and especially incest, as well as the rescue of victims by the police. Siegel suggests that, in the aftermath of the Indonesian revolution, as the category of the "people" was thwarted by the emergence of class division, the discourse of *kriminalitas* provided the mechanism by which those "who, lacking a voice, burst onto the public scene nonetheless." This eruption into the public, and into visibility, was mediated in and by language, but it did not take the form of anyone "finding a voice." Rather, as Seigel says: "What is revealed in the reports of the crimes of incest and sexual abuse is the force that calls out for the law. There is not only the supposedly inherent disgust that incest stimulates in those who discover it. There is also the path of communication that the discovery engenders, leading as it does outside the family, to 'others.' It passes through these others to the police. The law and with it the state appears in response to desire."[71]

In this essay, I have not focused on incest; and the conditions in mining communities cannot properly be described in terms of the family's monopoly on legitimacy since the communities discussed here were, in their early days, defined by the segregation of the sexes and, in certain areas (especially hostels), by the exclusion of women. Nor did the apartheid state describe itself in the metaphorics of a single family. Nonetheless, the end of apartheid was widely anticipated, especially within the ANC, as the possibility for inaugurating a national formation grounded in a concept of a liberated multiplicity, a nonracial, non-ethnonational "people."[72] This people would materialize itself in the process of communicating across previously untraversable boundaries, and in that process, it was assumed, the state itself would be established as the bearer of both meaning and legitimacy, as these emerged in the representation of the will of a people. It was because this new state presumed the necessity for those communicative pathways by which others are brought into relation with each other that the new constitution enshrined the rights of all language speakers and elevated eleven different languages to the status of official national tongue. Thus, the "Founding Provisions" of the Constitution of the Republic of South Africa, state in chapter 1, section 6, "The official languages of the Republic are Sepedi, Sesotho, Setswana, siSwati, Tshivenda, Xitsonga, Afrikaans, English, isiNdebele, isiXhosa and isiZulu." They also state, "Recognising the historically diminished use and status of the indigenous languages of our people, the state must take practical and positive measures to elevate the status and advance the use of these languages."

A democratic state, the constitution's drafters clearly believed, is one in which everyone has language, and in which everyone can use that language to negotiate with the state. The difference between having a recognized language and having language might be understood as being akin to the difference between having speech and having a voice. And hence, reflecting upon the broken and sclerotic testimony of the TRC hearings cited above, we are forced to confront what is, at present, the problematic, if not altogether interrupted, relationship between those who long at last to have a voice—if only for the purposes of soliciting the state's recognition—and those who, still possessing the language of power, cannot hear what is being said in languages that the state's agents recognize but do not understand.

There are, moreover two additional issues to be considered here. The first is that the effort to recognize different languages can only work if it is presumed that speech is the disclosure of individual will and intention. The TRC attempted to both cultivate and promulgate this equation between speech and intentionality by granting amnesty only to those who disclosed all of the facts of their cases, who spoke the "whole truth." But the second, related, and more difficult issue concerns the degree to which the new state presumed that communicative transparency between all "people"—as the means of universalizing citizenship—could replace complicitous violence as a mechanism for linking some people in opposition to others. This could happen only if everyone had equal access to language, and if the lines of communication were both open and reversible.

What was perhaps not anticipated was the degree to which anticipation of a fuller capacity to appropriate language and therefore self-representational possibilities has been thwarted or retarded thus far by inadequate resources and the limited capacities for translation that reside within the political apparatus and, perhaps, within language itself. When such a promise is thwarted and when political subjectivity is contingent upon one's ability to speak and to be understood, agency may attempt to assert itself in the constricted light of the private domain, one of the few spheres in which one may attempt to identify one's own will with the rule of the group. It is here, I want to argue, that we understand both the continuities and the contemporary intensification of sexual violence, that awful violence which pretends to be the mere mimesis and hence displacement of that pure violence which is war, but which is, as much as anything else, the realization of a communicative power within violence. Here women and feminized men[73] become not only the ground of a signification as violent as any scarification rite but the very means by which a false division is made between violence and its mimesis.

A crucial development in the history of such violence within mining communities can be traced to the relatively recent accommodation of families in the spaces of black miners and the supplanting of migrant labor by more permanently settled workers. Indeed, it may be the case that mining communities have been especially subject to the changes described in this essay because they have seen such a compressed and material transformation of social organization, beginning with the massive dislocation of familial forms and then the dramatically rationalized reinstitution of familial residential structures over the past two decades. During earlier periods, hostels were the primary residential structure for black mine workers and were spaces inhabited only by men. Much has, in fact, been written on the forms of same-sex intimacy and rivalrous domestic relations of the factions that lived in the hostels, but such a state of affairs was largely displaced by changes in state legislation that permitted family residences on mining property after the 1980s, the time at which the Struggle began to accelerate and competition for political authority reached its apogee.[74] A fuller history of the transformations in the nature of violence in the mining communities would have to account for this change in policy and its eventual materialization in new living arrangements, but the question of sexual violence cannot be understood as a function of proximity to women, for it is not simply the objects of violence that have changed but, as has already been claimed, the forms and meanings attached to sexual violence. What we see is that sexual violence partakes of the transformations in the more general social sphere and is, in fact, a scene for their enactment.

Conclusions, or Future Histories

Sexual violence is not new. And yet, as an object of discourse, it can be experienced as the mark of the new. To the extent, then, that its significations are new, it must be thought in relation to the emerging power of both the family and the state, in opposition to both race and class—as these latter categories are disentangled from each other with the growth of a black bourgeoisie. And it must be thought in relation to the conflict generated at the point where the memory of patriarchal prerogative meets the still-unrealized aspiration for liberal democratic forms of political subjectivity. There are, in short, three histories of the future converging in the present, histories that are neither teleological nor uniformly liberating and that are contained within the broader history of patriarchy. One history entails efforts to displace racialism and to depoliticize violence, despite the fact that the legitimacy of the new state emanates in part from its representative status vis-à-vis a black majority population and despite the fact that the institutions through which the state would monopolize violence are in competition with a privatized security industry. Another charts the attempt to instill the desire for a rule of law in a context that has not (yet) seen the institution of a true multilingualism or the equitable distribution of political and economic rights, and that has, at the same time, rested on the dissociation of personal agency and political subjectivity such that longed-for sovereignty often seems to find its purest expression in acts of transgressive violence. Finally, there is the history by which the family is being revalorized in communities where it has been most viscerally undermined—by both the historical organization of mining capital and, now, the ravages of the AIDS epidemic. These are the histories that are revealed in the confused and confusing testimony of Merafong youths, whose sometimes successful, sometimes misrecognizing petitions demonstrate so acutely the nature of life lived at such a tumultuous crossroads.

Longing for postracialism and an end to war, seeking justice and full political representation for those who have lacked a voice, attempting to repair the wounded fabric of intimate social life, South Africans are nonetheless afflicted by the constant eruption of new violences—in this case, the unsignifying and seemingly random (because personalized) violence in the public domain, and extreme forms of incest—where old ones have already left their scars. In the discourse about such eruption we see not only the phantasmatic shape of fear's new object but also the unconscious drive to contain force in the family and to make that force the ground of a new state's power. Perhaps the most symptomatic tale of this painful effort to contain and transmute the effects of a painful history can be found in the course of the women's hearings of the TRC.

One recalls here the criticism that the amnesty hearings received precisely because they required women to narrate the losses of their sons, husbands, brothers, and lovers but provided little opportunity for them to narrate their own experiences of violation. An entirely distinct hearing was established for women, but this marginalization (and necessary protection) only bespoke the difficulty of addressing the sexual within the political. Moreover, it has been remarked, with particularly acute and poignant bitterness, that even in the hearings devoted to "women's issues," the possibility of describing incidents of sexual violence was deeply limited by the lack of vocabulary, the difficulty of translating deeply personal idioms of sexual experience, and the additional burden of shame that befell those who attempted, however, unsuccessfully, to claim rape as an experience of violence rather than as a sign in the rivalrous relations between groups. When such events were narrated, they tended to overwhelm everything else; sexual violence was circumscribed either by silence or a discursive excess, and women's political subjectivities were doubly disappeared.[75]

It is not incidental in this context to observe the different function that language performed in the hearings wherein simultaneous translation was undertaken. Pumla Gobodo-Madikizela describes the difficulty of translating women's testimony about their own violation as the risk of over-identification. In her recent book, *A Human Being Died That Night,* she describes a case in which an antiapartheid activist had been raped by soldiers. The woman testified to the shame occasioned by her realization that the men were the same age as her children. Translating the terse descriptions, Gobodo-Madikizela was overwhelmed by her own recollections of a comparable incident in her own life, and, possessed by her own trauma, she found herself identifying with the woman for whom she was merely supposed to be translating. In her account of the event, Gobodo-Madikizela pulled herself back into the enframing narrative of the TRC through a strange act of redoubled identification: "Forcing myself to return to the role of facilitator, I repeated something that Mrs. Khutwane had said earlier in her testimony, more like talking to myself in order to understand the full implication of the soldier's terribly wounding act than as a way to help Mrs. Khutwane tell her story: 'The soldier could have been my son.'"[76] Such an act of imagination would, in Gobodo-Madikizela's eyes, constitute the ground of forgiveness, and hence a basis for the establishment of a new society. In her eyes, the production of a new language, the act of forgiveness, and the institution of democracy are all linked: "An important condition for the possibility of democratization after totalitarian rule is the forging of a vocabulary of compromise and tolerance, especially in the aftermath of mass tragedy. For the exercise of forming that vocabulary is part of the project of creating the operating rules of the democratic game. . . . to make the transition into a properly functioning democracy is therefore to create conditions that encourage replacing enmity with, if not love or friendship, then at least regard for others as fellow humans." She concludes, "the absence of enmity . . . separates people."[77]

The production of empathy by the raped woman is an extraordinary act, not only for the enormous measure of generosity that it would entail but because it nullifies the political valence of the rape by imagining it as that which could have been contained in the family: incest as the alternative to gang rape. It thereby demonstrates, from the aching other side of this scarred national body, just how political rape could become in South Africa and just how central the division between the domestic and the public sphere is to the constitution of liberal democracy. But more can be said. To imagine the literalization of that nightmare to which Mrs. Khutwane was subjected and to which Mrs. Gobodo-Madikizela subjected her imagination is to imagine the predicament of the townships today, where sexual violence has become one of the increasingly restricted avenues for asserting a masculine agency that had to renounce itself in order to be recognized as political and that had to be political in order for violence to be legible.[78]

The contradictory status of this predicament, and the awful conclusions that it seems to beg, cannot be explained away with recourse to notions of drives, frustrated or not, nor to the fact of apartheid, nor even to the multiplicity of cultural traditions within which violence against women and coerced sexual relations were normalized. What demands attention now, what solicits the labor and fidelity of the analyst now, is the way in which these forms of sexual violence are being transformed by the mediating function that they are asked to perform vis-à-vis the familial and the political, the domestic and the public. There will never be a typology or a history of the traumatic experiences suffered by women who are raped in South Africa or anywhere else, but there can be a critical anthropology of their structuring into and their symbolic effacement in society.

Notes

This essay was initially presented at the Harvard workshop organized by Jean and John Comaroff and entitled "Law and Disorder in the Postcolony." The essay benefited from conversations with other participants, but especially with Jean and John, who first introduced me to the anthropology of South Africa. It also received useful criticism and input from other readers at various points in its history: Yvette Christiansë, Bruce Grant, Tony Morphet, Beth Povinelli, and Gayatri Spivak all have my gratitude. Thanks are also due to Reney Warrington for her research assistance and to Deborah Posel of the Wits Institute for Social and Economic Research for her support and conversation on related matters. Most profoundly, I am indebted to the many people of Merafong who shared their stories with me and who trusted me with the task of understanding the questions to which they themselves are concerned to respond. Partial funding for this research came from Columbia University.

1. In her account of women's testimony at the Truth and Reconciliation Commission (TRC), Fiona Ross argues that the privileging of the sexual in accounts of political violence against women is based on a double failure, the first emanating

from a presumption that sexual and/or corporeal injury constitutes the "primary event of harm," regardless of the context or the nature of other injuries suffered; the second based in a related refusal to recognize women's capacity to survive the effects of physical violence as political subjects. She rightly notes the excessive emphasis that the press gave to accounts of sexual violence during the TRC hearings, even though women tended to recount other kinds of loss much more frequently. See Fiona Ross, *Bearing Witness: Women and the Truth and Reconciliation Commission in South Africa* (London: Pluto, 2003), especially pp. 91–92. My point here is not to suggest that sexual violence occurs (or occurred) more frequently than other kinds of violence, or that it constitutes a violence of a more primary sort; rather, I am attempting to understand the discourse of sexual violence *and* the fact of frequent sexual violence in terms of the organization of the public sphere and the political economy of masculinity in a changing social formation. The very discursive excess of which Ross writes demands analysis, and not mere dismissal as "overstatement."

2. Brandon Hamber, "'Have no doubt it is fear in the land': An Exploration of the Continuing Cycles of Violence in South Africa," *South African Journal of Child and Adolescent Mental Health* 12, no. 1 (1999): 2–3. This is not to say, however, that "nonpolitical" crime was absent in South African life prior to the 1960s. To the contrary. There are many eloquent testimonies to the experience and social cost of crime and especially violent crime in the lives of black South Africans, who bore the main brunt of both state-sponsored and nonpolitical crime throughout the century. In a series of journalistic articles written for *Drum* and the *Rand Daily Mail,* for example, Nat Nakasa described the "Victims of the Knifemen" and quoted a Baragwanath Hospital physician, who said of the daily violence in Johannesburg, "You'd think there's a war raging just outside." Nakasa indicted the thugs whose "false idea of 'toughness'" he reviled as much as the dehumanizing conditions of apartheid in which it flourished. And, as early as the 1950s, he wrote of the terror afflicting taxi-drivers and their passengers. See *The World of Nat Nakasa,* ed. Essop Patel, introduced by Nadine Gordimer (Johannesburg: Ravan/Bateleur, 1975), especially pp. 14–16, 37–39. The relative failure to provide security for black South Africans is well documented. Nonetheless, it is the intentional mobilization of crime, either through encouragement or nonprosecution by the state, that constitutes crime's politicization.

3. There is perhaps no better statement of the principle of "ungovernability" than that uttered by Steve Biko in the Stubbs interview, posthumously published in the *New Republic,* 7 January 1978, p. 152: "I only understand one form of dealing with police, and that's to be as unhelpful as possible." Cited in *Steve Biko: No Fears Expressed,* ed. Millard W. Arnold (Johannesburg: Skotaville, 1987), p. 57.

4. For an account of the incidence and discourse surrounding child rape, and even "baby rape," see Sarah Nuttall, "Girl Bodies," *Social Text* 22, no. 1 (2004): 17–33. Nuttall cites reports in 2001 that indicated 21,000 cases of child rape per year in South Africa (p. 19). Her article nonetheless focuses on the deployment of these figures and actualities by technological industries that "capitalize" on the racialized fear of such events by proliferating discourses and selling instruments for preventing them.

5. Stephen Ellis, "The New Frontiers of Crime in South Africa," in *The Crimi-*

nalization of the State in Africa, ed. Jean-François Bayart, Stephen Ellis, and Béatrice Hibou (Oxford: James Currey; Bloomington: Indiana University Press and the International African Institute, 1999), pp. 52–55; Jeremy Seekings, "The 'Lost Generation': South Africa's 'Youth Problem' in the Early-1990s," *Transformations* 29 (1996): 103–25. Seekings argues that although the objective conditions for crime are generated by the conditions described above, "moral panic" about crime and especially about youth crime exceeds actuality. For him, this panic is essentially political and "corresponds to periods of crisis in the negotiations" between parties over constitutional change" (107).

6. It has been suggested (rightly, I believe) that so-called vigilante violence is the mirror, but down-class, image of the privatized policing services that operate in wealthy neighborhoods as armed security companies. This is perhaps the largest growth industry in the new South Africa. See Hamber, "'Have no doubt it is fear in the land,'" p. 6; also M. Schönteich, "Vigilantes: When the Judicial System Fails . . . ," *Frontiers of Freedom* 20 (1999): 18–23.

7. Deborah Posel and Graeme Simpson note that the TRC and the nation-building project that it facilitated rested on a "somewhat sanitised version of the past," which relied on the possibility that one could "cultivate . . . a clear distinction between political and criminal violence, with 27 April 1994 (the date of South Africa's first democratic election) standing like an unbreachable wall between the era of political violence and the era of antisocial, criminal violence." They conclude that "the TRC arguably did more to mask than to reveal some of the most deeply rooted and sustained patterns of social conflict under apartheid." See Deborah Posel and Graeme Simpson, "The Power of Truth: South Africa's Truth and Reconciliation Commission in Context," in *Commissioning the Past: Understanding South Africa's Truth and Reconciliation Commission,* edited by Deborah Posel and Graeme Simpson (Johannesburg: Witwatersrand University Press, 2002), p. 10.

8. For a range of competing but also often complementary explanations of the high rates of violent crime in South Africa, both before and during the transition, see Ellis, "The New Frontiers of Crime in South Africa," pp. 49–68; Hamber, "'Have no doubt it is fear in the land'"; Bronwyn Harris, "'As for violent crime that's our daily bread': Vigilante Violence during South Africa's Period of Transition," Violence and Transition Series, vol. 1, Centre for the Study of Violence and Reconciliation, Braamfontein, May 2001; Shula Marks and Neil Andersson, "The Epidemiology and Culture of Violence," in *Political Violence and the Struggle in South Africa,* ed. N. Chabani Manganyi and André du Toit (New York: St. Martin's, 1990), pp. 29–69; Mark Shaw, "Crime, Police and Public in Transitional Societies," *Transformations* 49 (2002): 1–24; G. Simpson, *Explaining Endemic Violence in South Africa* (Johannesburg: Centre for the Study of Violence and Reconciliation, 1993). In many cases, and especially those that rely on materialist theories of poverty to explain crime, the persistence and even escalation in crime following the end of apartheid is an anomaly to be explained. In other cases, the disjuncture between the expectation of poverty reduction and political enfranchisement and the actuality of high rates of unemployment, epidemic disease, and the slowness of political change is held accountable for this increase. There is evidence that some people hold the rule of law itself responsible for the rise in crime, insofar as it inserts time between crime and its retribution, despite evidence to the

contrary. This is perhaps especially true of sexual crime. Thus, a respondent to the survey on vigilante crime undertaken by the Centre for the Study of Violence and Reconciliation remarked that rape itself is a function of the attenuation of punishment: "During the time when people were hanged, there were no rape cases. . . . and we black people never used to discuss anything with a rapist, we used to pull him with a rope and beat him up or hang him straight away" (Harris, "Violent Crime," p. 29).

9. Durkheim, of course, saw punitive justice as the opposite of restorative justice (in a structural analogue of the opposition between penal and civil law), but he understood the latter category to be the form of a contractual relation by which individuals would be recompensed for losses caused by the violation of contracts. He did not foresee the kind of situation in which the return to punitive justice would itself be rendered as the restitution of order in a historical milieu where the state is precisely the organ thought to have violated the social contract. See Émile Durkheim, *The Division of Labor in Society,* trans. George Simpson (New York: Free Press, 1933).

10. Here I part somewhat from Posel and Simpson's otherwise-perspicacious analysis. They intimate naivety on the part of the TRC commissioners, noting their "assumption that restorative justice would contribute to the re-establishment of the rule of law in South Africa, as if the post-apartheid thief or carjacker would somehow come to respect the legitimacy of the law, despite the fact that the political assassin was literally getting away with murder" (Posel and Simpson, "The Power of Truth," p. 11). My own sense is that the fantasy of a rule of law and the actuality of criminal practice are not mutually exclusive, if law is understood in proceduralist terms. Hence, criminals are as likely to make use of, to desire, and to presume the rule of law as anyone else. It is the paradoxical coexistence of criminality, on the one hand, and a phantasmatic investment in law, on the other, that defines the current situation and that demands accounting.

11. This example is drawn from personal experience of a case brought before the Cape Town magistrate in 1996. The thief was arrested following a chase, in which one of his victims and several passersby apprehended him. Although a gathering crowd threatened to execute him on the spot (with a revolver, handily produced by a bystander), the police were called and charges laid. The thief declined legal representation, despite a magistrate's concerned admonitions that he risked self-incrimination; he was found guilty and sentenced to one year's imprisonment, which was, at the time, a rather severe sentence given the minor and nonviolent nature of the crime.

12. John W. Jenkins, "Urbanisation and Security in South Africa: The Continuation of History," *African Security Review* 6, no. 6 (1997), www.iss.co.za/ASR/6No6/Jenkins.html. Efforts by the national government to reassign Khutsong, moving it from wealthy Gauteng Province (which includes Johannesburg and Pretoria) to the relatively poor North West Province are currently being contested by local residents.

13. Private medical facilities are maintained by the mining companies for employees, but in addition, Carletonville has a large public hospital. In-patient treatment for illness associated with HIV is generally provided at the latter institution, and most black residents receive care there.

14. In the mid-1960s, the Chamber of Mines and the mining companies vehe-

mently denied that there was a relationship between the mines and the sinkholes, and they pointed to "naturally occurring" sinkholes that predated the mines. However, it is now widely recognized that the pumping out of water evacuates spaces in the dolomite, and that this induced vulnerability then makes the area susceptible to higher rates of sinkhole formation than would otherwise have been the case.

15. Marks and Andersson, "Epidemiology and Culture of Violence," p. 44. Marks and Andersson cite an AngloGold report stating that 90 percent of their workers experience a reportable accident some time in their careers.

16. JHI Real Estate Group, "Johannesburg Market Trends" (2003), p. 1.

17. Greg Rosenberg, "Battle Is On against Legacy of Apartheid," *Militant* 60, no. 8 (February 26, 1996).

18. From the Xhosa-dominated ANC perspective, of course, the Inkatha Freedom Party was merely a function of apartheid logics as these met, resonated with, and were embraced by a patriarchal Zulu monarchism. Buthelezi's ethnic politics ran contrary to both the multiethnic solidarity advocated by Biko and the Black Consciousness movement (which represented all nonwhites as black) and the non-racialism of the ANC and the SACP. On the history of the Black Consciousness movement, see Gail Gerhard, *Black Power in South Africa: The Evolution of an Ideology* (Berkeley and Los Angeles: University of California Press, 1978).

19. Truth and Reconciliation Commission, *Truth and Reconciliation Commission of South Africa Report,* vol. 1 (Johannesburg: Juta for the TRC, 1998), p. 117.

20. Ibid., p. 85, emphasis added.

21. TRC, Amnesty Committee, "Application in Terms of Section 18 of the Promotion of National Unity and Reconciliation Act, No. 34, of 1995," Johnson Thembe Ncube Applicant (AM 0121/96), AC/97/0004; TRC, Amnesty Committee, "Application in Terms of Section 18 of the Promotion of National Unity and Reconciliation Act, No. 34, of 1995," Mpayipheli William Faltein Applicant (AM 0120/96), AC/96/0001. In the application documents and the transcripts, the spellings "Thembe" and "Themba" are both used.

22. Faltein and Ncube both sought amnesty for the murder. Ncube also applied for amnesty in regard to the robbery and malicious-damage charges, though he later withdrew the applications for the latter.

23. A. de V. Minnaar, *An Analysis of the Scope and Extent of Conflict in South Africa with Specific Reference to the Identification of High Conflict Areas* (Pretoria: Centre for Socio-political Analysis, Human Sciences Research Council, 1994), pp. 11, 16, 18. These figures are confirmed by the Independent Board of Inquiry's report, *Fortress of Fear* (Braamfontein, 1993), which reported levels of violence associated with hostels on the West Rand to be substantially lower than levels on the East Rand but significantly higher than those in the Johannesburg area (p. 48).

24. Wayne Safro, *Special Report on Violence against Black Town Councillors and Policemen* (Johannesburg: South African Institute of Race Relations, 1990), pp. 5–6.

25. AC/97/0004, p. 2.

26. AC/97/0001, p. 4.

27. Faltein testimony, in *Amnesty Hearings 09–13 September, Potchefstrom,* Internet edition, http://www.doj.gov.za/trc/amntrans/potch1/potch.htm, p. 1.

28. Ibid., p. 2.

29. Ibid., p. 3.

30. Ibid., p. 4.

31. Ibid., pp. 8–9.

32. Note that although Ngoepe is a judge, and although De Jager and others bear the title of advocate, their role at the hearings was that of commissioner (not judge or advocate). The TRC had no capacity to determine innocence or guilt, only to assess the nature of the act and to determine whether it was fully disclosed. In this sense, it was a pseudolegal institution, operating by virtue of law but not as the instrument of law.

33. Ibid., p. 9.

34. Ibid., p. 26.

35. Ibid., p. 27.

36. Ibid., p. 32.

37. I am relying here upon Émile Benveniste's concept of language as the terrain of subjectivity. His argument is most neatly encapsulated in the following passage: "Language is . . . the possibility of subjectivity because it always contains the linguistic forms appropriate to the expression of subjectivity, and discourse provokes the emergence of subjectivity because it consists of discrete instances. In some way language puts forth 'empty' forms which each speaker, in the exercise of discourse, appropriates for himself and which he relates to his 'person,' at the same time defining himself as *I* and a partner as *you.*" See Émile Benveniste, *Problems in General Linguistics,* trans. Mary Elizabeth Meek (Coral Gables, FL: University of Miami Press, 1971), p. 227.

38. Ndzeku testimony, in *Amnesty Hearings 09–13 September, Potchefstrom,* Internet edition, http://www.doj.gov.za/trc/amntrans/potch1/potch.htm, p. 86. Dan Ndzeku was the first black mayor of Carltonville, a man who established improbable credibility with mine management, white businessmen, and the largely ANC-leaning population of the township. When I interviewed people in Carltonville in 1997 and 1998, I was impressed by his wide base of support and noted also that his popularity was the object of nostalgia via-à-vis the subsequent occupier of the office, a flamboyant member of the ANC Woman's League whose inaugural address advocated radical land reform and, if necessary, the expropriation of white farms.

39. Ibid., p. 93.

40. Faltein testimony, p. 3.

41. Lebona testimony, in *Amnesty Hearings 09–13 September, Potchefstrom,* Internet edition, http://www.doj.gov.za/trc/amntrans/potch1/potch.htm, p. 125.

42. Ibid., pp. 120, 122.

43. Ibid., p. 119.

44. Ibid., p. 129.

45. I mean to invoke the notion of "lyric" quite literally. Anglophone conceptions of the lyrical voice as the expression of a unique subjectivity are historically coemergent with the understanding of truth as both singular and relatively perceptible. To repudiate a statement's truth-value on the grounds that it could not appear in the same form twice is not merely to suggest that the testimony might have been produced artificially but to invoke an entire power/knowledge system. It is perhaps possible to see the struggle of the young men as having been conducted

within an epic framework and the commission as having operated within a lyrical one. In any case, the commission's confessionally based logic was one in which authenticity was identified with the expression of a unique subjectivity, a logic that could only have been felt as an obstacle by those whose acts originated in the blockage of access to both linguistic and political subjectivity.

46. "Father" here means only "head of household," identifying the man who bears the sexual prerogative within the household.

47. Lekitlane testimony, in *Amnesty Hearings 09–13 September, Potchefstrom,* Internet edition, http://www.doj.gov.za/trc/amntrans/potch1/potch.htm, pp. 125, 136.

48. TRC, Amnesty Committee, "Application in Terms of Section 18 of the Promotion of National Unity and Reconciliation Act, no. 34, of 1995," Tsietsi Gideon Thloloe First Applicant (AM1333/96) and Andreis Johnny Mageti Motluong Second Applicant (AM1325/96), AC/99/0321. Amnesty was granted to the applicants on 10 November 1999.

49. Lebona testimony, p. 103, emphasis added.

50. One cannot help but note here the similarity between this narrative and that which structures J. M. Coetzee's apocalyptic novel about the sexualized form of racial warfare and the fantasy of a postracial society in South Africa; see J. M. Coetzee, *Disgrace* (London: Secker and Warburg, 1999). However, in the case I am discussing, the act was not mediated by race nor directed toward a white patriarchal gaze. It may therefore suggest the need to separate out the logic of specular sexual violence from the paranoid fantasy of proxy warfare.

51. Keith Breckenridge, "The Allure of Violence: Men, Race and Masculinity on the South African Goldmines, 1900–1950," *Journal of Southern African Studies* 24, no. 4 (1998): 669.

52. Clive Glaser, "The Mark of Zorro: Sexuality and Gender Relations in the Tsotsi Subculture on the Witwatersrand," *African Studies* 51 (1992): 62.

53. Catherine Campbell, "Learning to Kill? Masculinity, the Family and Violence in Natal," *Journal of Southern African Studies* 18, no. 3 (1992): 625. Campbell's argument is more ambiguous than that of Belinda Bozzoli, who first took leave of materialist orthodoxy (and the presumption that indigenous cultural logics had been radically effaced by mining capital) when she described the condition of social life in South Africa as a "patchwork of patriarchies," in which competing forms of masculinist authority coexisted, overlapped, and reinforced each other. See Belinda Bozolli, "Marxism, Feminism, and South African Studies," *Journal of Southern African Studies* 9, no. 2 (1983): 149.

54. Clive Glaser, "Swines, Hazels and the Dirty Dozen: Masculinity, Territoriality and the Youth Gangs of Soweto, 1960–1976," *Journal of Southern African Studies* 24, no. 4 (1998): 719, emphasis added.

55. Gary Kynoch, "'A Man among Men': Gender, Identity, and Power in South Africa's Marashea Gangs," *Gender and History* 13, no. 2 (August 2001): 252, 252–53.

56. Language here is the system of differentiation, whether construed in a Saussurian sense, in which the system can be conceived as a relatively closed entity, or in a Derridean sense, in which the fact of temporality entails the endless deferral of that closure which would allow the meanings within language to be fixed.

57. Pierre Clastres, *Chronicle of the Guayaki Indians,* trans. Paul Auster (New York: Zone, 1998), pp. 226, 231.

58. It would be more precise to say that the symbolic is produced in and through this exchange, in Clastres's Lévi-Straussian reading. In this context, it is well to recall that such an exchange is, in Lévi-Strauss's analysis, driven by the incest taboo, which he describes as the archetypical form of the rule, indeed of all rules, being both social and presocial. This rule stands on the threshold of culture while also being the condition of its possibility. Although Lévi-Strauss imagines the rule to be one that bids men exchange women, there is no reason to presume that the rule must take this form; it can equally be construed as the limitation of both men's and women's sexual relations. Sexual violence, whether incestuous or not, can then be understood as the means by which some subjects, usually men, attempt to render themselves the unique and relative bearers of the symbolic function. See Claude Lévi-Strauss, *The Elementary Structures of Kinship,* trans. James Harle Bell, John Richard von Sturmer, and Rodney Needham (Boston: Beacon Press, 1969), especially pp. 12, 30, 43, 63–65.

59. Clastres, *Guayaki Indians,* p. 237.

60. There is a certain convergence here with Hannah Arendt's typological spectrum positing power and violence as antithetical poles, each negating the other. See Hannah Arendt, *On Violence* (New York: Harcourt Brace and Co., 1970).

61. Clastres, *Guayaki Indians,* pp. 106, 107.

62. Claude Lefort, "Reflections on the Present," in *Writing: The Political Test,* trans. and ed. David Ames Curtis (Durham, NC: Duke University Press, 2000), p. 268.

63. A national survey conducted in 1998–99 reports that 63 percent of all women covered in the survey ($N = 1,000$) believed themselves to have been the subject of sexual violence, and 76 percent described themselves as victims of physical abuse. See Shahana Rasool, Kerry Vermaak, Robyn Pharoah, Antoinette Louw, and Aki Stavrou, *Violence against Women: A National Survey* (Pretoria: Institute for Security Studies, 2002), p. 27. The survey authors note the difficulty of basing statistical analyses of sexual violence on police statistics given that, while 92 percent of the women believed that the most serious instance of abuse committed against them constituted a crime, only 46 percent had reported it to police authorities (p. 112).

64. There were 50,481 reported cases of rape in 1996 and 49,280 in 1998, but by 2000, the number of reported rapes was 52,975. See South Africa Police Service Crime Statistics, www.rapecrisis.org.za/statistics.htm.

65. Patricia Tjaden and Nancy Thoennes, "Full Report of the Prevalence, Incidence, and Consequences of Violence against Women: Findings from the National Violence against Women Survey," National Council of Justice, November 2000, p. iii.

66. The *Mail and Guardian* quotes a study of the Teddy Bear Clinic in Johannesburg, where 42 of 227 child rape cases involved children less than three years old. See "The Reality behind Child Rape," *Mail and Guardian,* 8 November 2002. These facts are, of course, also the ground for a discursive elaboration which translates them into the sign of a more general catastrophe. See Jean Comaroff, "Con-

suming Passions: Nightmares of the Global Village," in "Body and Self in a Post-colonial World," ed. E. Badone, special issue, *Culture* 17, nos. 1–2 (1997): 7–19.

67. On related and perhaps analogous grounds, Rachel Jewkes, director of the Health and Gender Unit at the Medical Research Council, calls for the jettisoning of the category "rape" and the use instead of the notion of "coerced sex." See "The Reality behind Child Rape."

68. "Most Rapists Go Unpunished, Says Report," *Mail and Guardian,* 15 November 2002.

69. To give some indication of how prevalent media coverage of the issue of rape is, the *Mail and Guardian,* one of South Africa's most restrained venues, published 165 stories on rape in South Africa during the one-year-period between 1 January and 31 December 2004.

70. Statistical significance must always be differentiated from symbolic significance, and there is no necessary correlation between them. The rarest phenomena may be those invested with value and significance; the most common may be the least capable of bearing meaning. Indeed, this is the logic that appears to operate in the discourse on sexual violence in South Africa.

71. James T. Siegel, *A New Criminal Type in Jakarta: Counter-revolution Today* (Durham, NC: Duke University Press, 1998), pp. 4, 87.

72. As stated above, this nonracial imagination won out over the alternative vision proposed by the Black Consciousness movement only gradually, and it is possible that emergent ethnic politics will compete with it in the future.

73. There is an emerging discourse and consciousness about the sexual violence directed toward men in South Africa, especially within prisons. But this discourse functions quite differently, insofar as it does not presume a normative sphere within which same-sex violence is relatively common. Instead, it relies upon a different set of oppositions that reinforce those operative within the discourse of sexual violence against women, namely that masculinity is equivalent to sexual sovereignty.

74. On the changing nature of accommodations in the mining sector, see Wilmot G. James, *Our Precious Metal: African Labour in South Africa's Gold Mining Industry, 1970–1990* (Cape Town: David Phillip, 1992), especially pp. 79–88. On male same-sex relations in the context of the segregated compounds, see Charles van Onselen, *Studies in the Social and Economic History of the Witwatersrand, 1886–1914,* 2 vols. (Johannesburg: Ravan, 1992), especially vol. 2, *New Nineveh;* Robert Morell, "Of Boys and Men: Masculinity and Gender in Southern African Studies," *Journal of Southern African Studies* 24, no. 4(1998): 605–30; T. D. Dunbar Moodie, "Migrancy and Male Sexuality on the South African Gold Mines," *Journal of Southern African Studies* 14, no. 1 (1988): 228–56.

75. Ross, *Bearing Witness.*

76. Pumla Gobodo-Madikizela, *A Human Being Died That Night: A South African Story of Forgiveness* (New York: Houghton Mifflin, 2003), p. 91. Fiona Ross suggests that it was Gobodo-Madikizela's interventions that prompted Yvonne Khutwane to even recount her tale of sexual violence in the first place, and remarks, as did Martha Minnow (*Between Vengeance and Forgiveness: Facing History after Genocide and Mass Murder* [Boston: Beacon, 1998], p. 84), that the

sexual violation was not mentioned in Khutwane's original written testimony. Ross quotes an e-mail (with permission) in which it is the identification (rather than the later consciousness of a risk of overidentification, which appears in Gobodo-Madikizela's book) that leads Gobodo-Madikizela to elicit this testimony from Khutwane (*Bearing Witness,* p. 88). For her part, Ross appears to believe that Khutwane would not have offered the testimony if not encouraged to do so and suggests that it may have distorted the proceedings, producing Khutwane as a "victim" while negating her political activity and the complex explanations that she herself offered for the acts of violence to which she was subjected (including jealousy, rivalry with other women in the community, etc.). See Ross, *Bearing Witness,* pp. 87–94.

77. Gobodo-Madizkela, *A Human Being Died That Night,* pp. 126–27.

78. The highly publicized trial of former ANC deputy president, Jacob Zuma, has crystallized discussion about masculinity, sexuality, and public politics in South Africa. It is interesting to note, in this context, the degree to which Zuma's own self-defense in the public arena entailed a demand that his political 'family' defend him. Njabulo Ndebele, Vice Chancellor of University of Cape Town, responded to Zuma's family rhetoric with an observation of the ironic expulsion of female rape victims from the inner sanctum of the ANC Family. In doing so, Ndebele observes not only the degree to which the state and the family have come to provide each other with metaphors, but also how precarious is the position of women within either domain. See Njabulo Ndebele, "Why Jacob Zuma's bravado is brutalizing the public," *Sunday Times,* March 5, 2006. Available at: http://www.adminnews.uct.ac.za/docs/5cb878a4b688f960dc7fc5fcd9f8bab1.pdf.

"I Came to Sabotage Your Reasoning!"
Violence and Resignifications of Justice in Brazil

Teresa P. R. Caldeira

INCREASING URBAN VIOLENCE is one of the most intractable problems of contemporary Brazil and one the most significant challenges to the effective democratization of Brazilian society. In the last two decades, both urban violence and democracy took root in Brazil, in a context in which neoliberalization was also transforming the institutions of the state and reshaping economic and social life.[1] Instead of serving to deter each other, violence and democracy expanded in interconnected, paradoxical, and sometimes simply surprising ways. Democratization unfolded in Brazil as the result of the inventive engagement of citizens, especially in social movements in the urban peripheries. After twenty years of democratic rule, procedures and imaginaries of democracy are deeply rooted among Brazilians, even if this democracy is disjunctive. Increasing urban violence is one of the processes that challenge democratization most directly and simultaneously ruin the conditions of life in cities.[2]

In the last twenty years, the most different social groups in Brazil— from politicians to prisoners, from members of social movements to policemen, from rich to poor, from white to black—have become acquainted with the language and procedures of democracy. They have learned to make use of notions of rights, justice, and citizenship to put forward their claims, indicating the extent to which democracy has become hegemonic politically. Yet, in spite of their legitimization, the meanings associated with notions such as rights and justice have remained unstable and contestable and are also associated with quite contradictory social practices.

In this essay, I analyze three ways in which notions of rights and justice have been articulated in democratic Brazil. The first example shows how urban social movements have engaged with notions of rights to force the recognition of the poor residents of the urban peripheries as citizens and to demand that the state transform urban policies and improve the places where they live. The movements for urban reform indicate one of the ways in which democratization has taken root in Brazilian society and how the grassroots experience of local administration, legal invention, and popular mobilization has made its space in federal law. The second example refers directly to the question of violence and crime. It is in relation to this universe that some of the most perverse articulations of notions of rights and justice occur. The cases I analyze include a campaign to contest the legitimacy of human rights claims, expressions of support for police violence, and some demands by organized-crime groups. In all instances, the references to rights and justice are associated with attempts to undermine democratic practices and institutions. The third example also refers to the question of violence. I focus on hip-hop movements and their attempts to control the proliferation of violence and death among young residents of the poor peripheries. They use music, dance, and graffiti to articulate what they call "attitude," a new code of behavior that might allow poor young men, especially black, to survive in the midst of widespread violence. For the hip-hop groups, democratic institutions are ineffective, unjust, and suspicious. Therefore, their discussions of justice are framed from a moral and sometimes religious perspective.

For the three analyses, data come mostly from the city of São Paulo, where I have been doing fieldwork since the late 1970s. This essay's juxtaposition of such different engagements with issues of rights, justice, and citizenship reveals the uncertainty and contestation that exists in relation to these notions in contemporary Brazil. Moreover, it suggests that the main challenge to the expansion of democracy and to the control of violence is to create public spaces where issues of inequality and racism can be addressed without cynicism and denial and simultaneously to create institutions capable of giving meaning to notions of justice and of protecting the lives and bodies of subaltern people.[3]

Rights to the City

There is no doubt that Brazil has democratized in the last two decades. There is also no doubt that democratization has not touched several dimensions of Brazilian society. As James Holston and I have argued elsewhere, it has been an uneven process, in which the political system represents its most successful aspect, and justice and civil rights its most unsuccessful.[4] In the last two decades, elections have been free and fair, political parties and civil associations organize freely, the media are uncensored, and political prisoners ceased to exist. Nevertheless, the institutions of order—the police and the justice system—have been systematically incapable of guaranteeing public security, justice, and respect for civil rights even at minimal levels. The urban spaces of Brazilian metropolitan regions, especially their poor peripheries, constitute a dimension of Brazilian society in which we can observe both an inventive engagement with democratization and some of its most dramatic limits.[5]

In São Paulo, as elsewhere in Brazil, poor workers have settled by building their own houses in the periphery. On the outskirts of the city, workers bought cheap lots of land sold either illegally by outright swindlers or with some kind of irregularity by developers who failed to follow city regulations regarding infrastructure and land registration. In São Paulo, as elsewhere in Brazil, workers have always understood that illegality is the condition under which they can become property owners and inhabit the modern city. And in São Paulo as elsewhere, metropolitan regions are marked by a dichotomy between the "legal city" (i.e., the center inhabited by the upper classes) and the illegal peripheries. In streets without pavement and infrastructure, workers build their own houses by themselves and without financing in a slow and long-term process of transformation known as autoconstruction. It is also a process that symbolizes perfectly progress, growth, and social mobility: step by step, day after day, the house is improved and people are reassured that sacrifice and hard work pay off. Thus, during the last half century and especially during the years of intense urbanization from the 1950s to the 1980s, workers in São Paulo have moved to the "bush" to build their houses and in this process were the agents of the peripheral urbanization of the city.

Starting in the mid-1970s, numerous neighborhood-based social movements appeared in the poor urban peripheries of Brazilian metropolitan regions, frequently with the help of the Catholic Church. Movement participants, a majority of them women, were new property owners who realized that political organization was the only way to force city authorities to extend urban infrastructure and services to their neighborhoods. They discovered that being taxpayers legitimated their "right to have rights" and their "rights to the city," that is, rights to the legal order and the urbanization (infrastructure, piped water, sewage collection, electricity, telephone service, etc.) available in the center. With the social movements, rights extrapolated the labor sphere, in which they have always been legitimated and enforced in regulated form. At the root of their political mobilization were the illegal/irregular status of their properties and the precarious situations of their neighborhoods, which the public authorities had failed to provide with services and infrastructure, alleging exactly their irregular status. Thus, a central inspiration for these movements was an urban and collective experience of marginalization and abandonment, in spite of individual efforts of integration through work and consumption.

The urban social movements were central actors in the political process that brought the military dictatorship to an end. Their influence was especially important during the Constitutional Assembly, which extended notions of rights and citizenship even further. The 1988 Constitution institutes a long list of rights as a consequence of the approval of a series of popular amendments that urban movements and organized minority groups presented after unprecedented political mobilization. The rights range from reproductive rights and paid paternity leave to the right of urban adverse possession (*usucapião urbano*).[6] The new conceptions were also expressed in new practices. Brazilians learned to invoke their rights standing in line at banks and public-service agencies as well as in the tribunals in which they demand their rights to urban property and in the services in which they affirm their consumption rights.

The works of the Constitutional Assembly and of the numerous state and municipal assemblies that followed it mark an important moment in the formation of a new conception of citizenship grounded in the popular construction of the law and the exercise of new kinds of rights through legislation. One of the most significant sources of this process of innovation is popular participation in urban reform and municipal administration. In many major cities, groups associated with the National Movement of Struggle for Urban Reform have succeeded in developing this conception of urban citizenship into innovative municipal codes, charters, and master plans.[7] One of the most important pieces of legislation is the remarkable Estatuto da Cidade (City Statute), a federal law of 2001 that institutes a new model for urban legislation.[8] Incorporating the language and concepts developed by the urban social movements and various local administrations since the 1970s, the Estatuto da Cidade establishes that the city and urban property must fulfill a "social function." It frames the directives for urban policy from the point of view of the poor, creates mechanisms to overhaul patterns of irregularity and inequality, and requires urban policy to "guarantee the right to sustainable cities, understood as the right to urban land, housing, sanitation, urban infrastructure, transportation and public services, work, and leisure for present and future generations" (art. 2, par. I). Moreover, it requires that local urban policies be conceived and implemented with popular participation. Thus, it takes into consideration the active collaboration and involvement of the private organizations and interests of civil society. Unmistakably, the Estatuto da Cidade is the result of the insurgent citizenship movements of the previous decades.[9]

The Estatuto da Cidade and the practices that have inspired it are important indications of one of the ways in which democratization and notions of rights and citizenship have taken root in Brazilian society. Other examples indicating important expansion of rights and citizenship could certainly be added. Nevertheless, there is one crucial aspect of Brazilian life in which the transformations either did not take root or produced little effect. As James Holston and I have argued elsewhere,[10] this is the universe of civil law, justice, and individual rights. It is in the sphere of violence, crime, justice, and civil rights that the process of democratization gets stuck and that some of the most perverse articulations of notions of rights and justice emerge.

Violent Democracy and the Perversion of Rights

Violent criminality has increased continuously in Brazil since the early 1980s, to the point that by the late 1990s the rates of homicides of several of the country's metropolitan regions ranked among the highest of the world (around 65 per 100,000 inhabitants in São Paulo, or more than 6,500 homicides per year).[11] In São Paulo, although these rates have decreased in the early 2000s, homicide has become the main cause of death of young men (the third for the total population) and has made life expectancy for men decrease four years in the last decade.[12] More dramatically, the police have been responsible for about 10 percent of the homicides in São Paulo's metropolitan region in the last twenty years. The police are therefore part of the problem of violence and co-responsible for its high level.[13] Finally, most cases of murder remain uninvestigated and therefore unpunished, and various types of racial and gender biases in criminal trials have been clearly documented.[14] Thus, the population's distrust of both the police and the justice system has a solid basis. This increase in violence and distrust of the police has not impeded democratic consolidation or the legitimization of the imaginary of citizenship and rights inherent to it. But it has certainly marked them in peculiar ways.

The question of human rights is emblematic of numerous paradoxes generated by the intertwining of crime and rights, violence and democracy. In the context of the democratic transition in the mid-1980s, the human rights movement that had originated in the demand for amnesty for all political prisoners expressed for the first time the defense of human rights of common prisoners and exhibited publicly the degrading conditions of Brazilian prisons. The reaction against this defense was immediate and strong and probably marks the first and most perverse resignification of rights made with the objective of undermining these same rights and their defenders. Here is a quotation from a manifesto of the Association of Police Chiefs of the state of São Paulo directed to the population on 4 October 1985 in the context of mayoral elections and while the state governor was trying to reform the police forces to restrain their use of lethal force:

> The situation today is one of total anxiety for you and total tranquillity for those who kill, rob, rape. Your family is destroyed and your patrimony, acquired with a lot of sacrifice, is calmly being reduced. Why does this happen? You know the answer. Believing in promises, we chose the wrong governor, the wrong political party, the PMDB [Partido do Movimento Democrático Brasileiro]. How many crimes have occurred in your neighborhood and how many criminals were found responsible for them? You also know this answer. They, the bandits, are protected by the so-called human rights, something that the government considers that you, an honest and hardworking citizen, do not deserve.

Human rights were resignified as "privileges for bandits."[15] This was a skillful articulation based on the popular notion that justice and rights in Brazil are enforced as privileges. The justice system is seen by the majority of the population as biased and inefficient, as something guaranteed only to a few—those who have access to its intricate mechanism, can pay good lawyers, and have enough power to manipulate the system. If justice is a privilege and if the majority of citizens have their rights disrespected systematically, why assure rights (privileges) to criminals?—asked those campaigning against the notion of human rights. Thus, a mark of inequity and social inequality was articulated to destabilize the expansion of democracy and to undermine an attempt to expand respect for citizens' rights.

The power of this articulation of rights and privilege was such that it took the movements defending human rights more than a decade to start to unmake some of the images consolidated in the attack on the "privileges of bandits." The new articulation became evident in the National Plan for Human Rights approved by the federal government in 1996 and then adopted by various states. This plan defines human rights as "rights of all citizens." Thus, it tries to remove human rights from an exclusive association with prisoners and criminals and tie them to the rights of all marginalized groups. This rearticulation was possible because a series of clear human rights violations (e.g., in Eldorado dos Carajás, Favela Naval, and Cidade de Deus), which the media intensively exposed, provoked a shift in public opinion. Among those episodes were several police strikes in which armed policemen from different police forces confronted each other on the streets and directly threatened the population in the streets.

Public security and the police forces certainly constitute one of the main fields in which the intersection of criminality and democracy continues to be fertile in the production of paradoxes and perversions. To frame the practices of the police forces according to the parameters of the rule of law is one of the biggest challenges of any democratic transition. In new democracies with a long history of authoritarianism and in which the police are accustomed to acting outside the boundaries of legality, the problems of controlling police violence and enforcing police accountability can be especially complicated. In Brazil, the limits to police and prison reform have been especially obvious, as indicated by constant accusations of police corruption and data on abuse of the use of lethal force and on disrespect of the rights of suspects and prisoners by policemen. The police forces have resisted the reforms strongly, as indicated by their various strikes. Nevertheless, not even the police forces have remained immune to the democratization process. The Military Police of the state of São Paulo, for example, felt compelled to change its public image. It adopted some new initiatives, such as community policing, and tried to ameliorate its image as an institution that abused the use of lethal force and disrespected people's rights on an everyday basis. One of its new Web sites presented citizenship and the opinion of citizens as parameters for the actions of the members of the institution. This is an indication of the legitimacy that notions of citizenship and rights have acquired in contemporary Brazil. Nevertheless, when one pays attention to the ways in which those notions are articulated, one notes their peculiarities. Here is a quotation from the site:

> The 1988 Constitution brought a new concept that became strong in our society: citizenship. People became more aware of their rights, more demanding in relation to the Institutions, and this was an invitation to those willing to serve well to revise their posture.
>
> The question was not only to expand services but also one of attitude. . . . With the new established order, something more was necessary than just placing ourselves in the clients' position and imagining new products. It was necessary to listen to them. . . . It was an invitation to a cultural change. . . . It was necessary to shift from a bureaucratic model . . . to a new model, the managerial, which was introduced at the Military Police of the state of São Paulo through a Program of Quality Improvement. Its goal is to get closer to the population via the improvement of the services rendered to the population.[16]

At the military police Web site, citizenship becomes an invention of the 1988 Constitution, citizens are clients, and public security is a product offered by the Military Police to demanding clients. The reference is, not the rule of law, but the market. This suggests that the Military Police is in fact tuned into the requirements of the neoliberal age more than into the liberal interpretation of citizenship and rights.

Moreover, although there has been a change in the discourse and even in the organization of the Military Police, the same cannot be said about its practice. In spite of the determination of Governors Mário Covas and Geraldo Alckmin to control police violence in São Paulo, to reform the police forces and unify some of their operations, to create community policing, and to institute an ombudsman for the police (Ouvidoria) and training in human rights, the Military Police of São Paulo have continued to kill civilians. The number of civilian deaths caused by policemen was higher than one thousand per year in 1991 and 1992, when a famous massacre of 111 prisoners at the Casa de Detenção occurred. Civilian deaths caused by police diminished in 1996–97 but started to go up again after 1997, exactly at the moment when the new managerial philosophy was implemented. In 1999, there were 664 deaths caused by the two police forces (the majority at the hands of the Military Police); in 2000, 807; and in 2001, 703. These figures correspond to approximately 10 percent of the total number of homicides in the metropolitan region. Between 1990 and 2001, there were at least 11,700 confirmed deaths of civilians by policemen. The majority of the people killed had no criminal history, as indicated by investigations done by the Ouvidoria da Polícia (the police ombudsman) in 1999 and 2000.

The fact that these violations continue to occur in spite of the best intentions and the political will to control them indicates some of the limits of the process of democratization. In the context of the naturalization of police violence, many people understand the abuse of police lethal force as their "right." Moreover, the difficulties in controlling police abuses indicate one of the most perverse ironies of this universe: the fact that the police who kill may, in fact, be acting according to the expectations of citizens who are frustrated with the inefficacy of the justice system and who cannot believe in the possibility of security in a system with immense social inequality. Thus, the violence of the São Paulo Military Police may perversely end up satisfying their "clients," the citizens who have learned to interpret their violence as efficiency. This happens even when the majority of those who articulate the defense of the tough police who kill come from the same social group as the victims of the police: the poor residents of the neighborhoods in the peripheries. In a total reversion of meaning, the police who kill are seen as fulfilling their duties and enforcing the "rights" of poor citizens for justice and security. Here is this perspective articulated by an eighteen-year-old resident of São Paulo's peripheries:

> I wish the Esquadrão da Morte [Death Squad] still existed. The Esquadrão da Morte is the police who only kill; the Esquadrão da Morte is justice done by one's own hands. I think this should still exist. It's necessary to take justice in one's own hands, but the people who should do this should be the police, the authorities themselves, not us. Why should we get a guy and kill him? What do we pay taxes for? For this, to be protected. . . . It is not worth it for us to lynch. They [the police] should have the right, they have the duty, because we pay taxes for this. . . . The law must be this: if you kill, you die.

But probably one of the most striking rearticulations of the language of rights and justice comes from organized-crime groups. Brazilian prisons have always been spaces of brutal and widespread violation of rights, a situation that was first exposed by the defenders of human rights. In the last years, prisons have become the domains of a series of organized groups that call themselves "commands" or "parties." These commands impose a violent order inside the prisons at the same time as they control crime on the outside with the providential help of cell phones, smuggled by the hundreds into the prisons. With the use of cell phones that the police fail to control and confiscate, the commanders of these groups organize prison revolts, kidnappings, assaults, and especially the extermination of people they consider dangerous or simply not loyal. Their actions are not only criminal and violent but usually cruel. The most experienced forensic doctors, policemen, and human rights activists have declared themselves shocked by the monstrous inventiveness of the violations. They evoke the notion of cruelty to express the frequent spectacle not only of dead bodies but also of corpses that are exaggeratedly mutilated, violated, and exhibited.

In spite of this, not even those commands do without the language of rights and justice. Their declarations therefore represent the most perverse form of the intertwining of the language of democracy and the practice of prisoner violence. They talk about justice and rights and they describe the abuses to which they have been subjected in terms similar to those used by human rights reports, but all of this to justify their own violence and abuses, their crimes, and their cruelty. The Statute of the PCC, the Primeiro Comando da Capital (First Command of the Capital), a command organized in São Paulo's prisons, exemplifies this trend:

> 11. Primeiro Comando da Capital—PCC, founded in the year 1993, in a gigantic and tireless struggle against the oppression and the injustices in the

concentration camp annex to the Casa de Custódia e Tratamento de Taubaté, has as absolute themes: liberty, justice, and peace.

13. We must remain united and organized to avoid another massacre similar to or even worse than that of the Casa de Detenção on 2 October 1992, when 111 prisoners were killed, a massacre that will never be forgotten in the consciousness of Brazilian people. Because we from the Command will shake the system and make the authorities change prison practice, which is inhuman, full of injustice, oppression, torture, and massacre in the prisons.

7. That one who is in liberty and well set up but forgets to cooperate with the brothers who are in jail will be condemned to death without pardon.

16. . . . In coalition with the Comando Vermelho—CV, we will revolutionize the country inside the prisons and our armed arm will be the terror of the powerful, oppressors, and tyrants who use the annex of Taubaté and Bangú I, in Rio de Janeiro, as instruments of society's vengeance and of fabricating monsters.[17]

Another example of the same trend comes from a letter that is attributed to the Comando Vermelho and that was distributed to the population of Rio de Janeiro on 24 February 2003. On that day, owners of shops in central neighborhoods in Rio kept the doors of their establishments closed and alleged that by doing so they were following the orders and threats of the Comando Vermelho. The letter confirms that those who disobey the order will be "radically punished." The reason for the closedown was to protest against police actions and decisions of the justice system.

Now is the time to react firmly and with determination and to show this repulsive and oppressive politics that we deserve to be treated with respect, dignity, and equality, because if this doesn't come to pass, we will no longer stop causing the chaos in this city, because it is absurd that all of this keeps happening and always remains unpunished. . . .

Also the judiciary continues doing whatever it wants with its power, especially the division of penal executions, because with a total abuse of power they are violating all of the established and legal laws and even the Lawyers are targets of hypocrisy and of abuse, and they can do nothing, so if someone has to put a stop to this violence, that someone will have to be us because the people don't have the means to fight for their rights, but clearly they know who is doing the robbing and massacring and this is what is important, because the time has passed when the bandit was from the *favelas* and behind prison bars; well, these days those one finds living in a *favela* or behind prison bars are nothing more, nothing less than humble and poor people, and our president Luiz Inácio Lula da Silva, the country only counts on you to get us out of this mud, because would there exist a violence greater than robbing the public treasuries and killing the people with poor diet, without decent minimum salary, without hospitals, without work, and without food? Will this violence succeed in ending this violence? Violence generates violence. Does there exist among those imprisoned in this country one who has committed a crime more heinous than killing a nation with hunger and misery?

So ENOUGH, we only want our rights and we are not going to give them up, so the businessmen have to keep the doors closed until midnight on Tuesday (02/25/2003), and he who dares to open the doors will be punished one way or another, we are not joking, those who are joking are those in politics, with this total abuse of power and with this widespread robbery; the judiciary must start to evacuate the prisons and act within the law before it is too late. If the laws were made to be followed, why this abuse?

Although this letter is supposedly defending the rights of prisoners and of poor people abused by the police forces, the logic of its arguments is quite similar to that used to attack the defense of human rights of prisoners since the mid-1980s. In both cases, the attack is built on a contrast between crime, police abuse, and the failure of the justice system, on the one hand, and poverty, absence of public services, and bad living conditions of the majority of the population, on the other. However, in the twenty years that separated one articulation from the other, a significant slippage occurred. In the 1980s, the campaign against human rights was articulated by self-proclaimed "good citizens" (including members of the police forces and the justice system) outraged at the fact that "criminals" might be entitled to rights. To oppose this idea, they argued that the government should not extend "privileges to bandits" and spend on their care the sparse resources badly needed to provide services such as hospitals and schools and better living conditions to the majority of the population. Consider, for example, the following quotation from the radio program of state deputy Afanasio Jazadji, one of the most popular radio stars in São Paulo in the 1980s and one of the main articulators of the campaign against the defense of human rights:

> Someone should take all those irredeemable prisoners, put them against the wall, and fry them with a blowtorch. Or instead throw a bomb in the middle of them: pum! End of the problem. They have no family, they don't have anything, they don't have anything to worry about, they only think about doing evil, and why should we worry about them? . . . Those bastards, they consume everything, millions and millions a month. Let us get this money and transform it into hospitals, nurseries, orphanages, asylums, and provide a respectable life for those who really deserve to have this dignity. Now, for

those types of people . . . people? To treat them as people! We're offending humankind! (Rádio Capital, 25 April 1984)[18]

Although this view continues to be popular, twenty years later it coexists with another one. The newer discourse is articulated by prisoners and their organizations, people who had no voice in the previous debate. Now they threaten the population, speak in the name of the poor—as do the so-called *justiceiros* (literally, "justice makers"), or vigilante groups—accuse the politicians of corruption and of denying the people the hospitals, salaries, and food they need, and demand to be treated with "respect, dignity, and equality" and to have their rights respected. Supposedly, their rights in this case are to be released from the prisons or maybe to have access to some of the "privileges" they have lost in the last months, such as the use of cell phones and the ability to communicate freely with their organizations outside the prisons.

From the point of view of the rule of law and of the principles that supposedly found a liberal-democratic polity, both articulations are perverse. But to say so is not enough either to elucidate the complex relationships among poverty, violence, crime, disrespect of rights, and injustice that sustain these articulations or to clarify the slippage between them. The association of these same elements will be encountered once again in the new forms of artistic movements proliferating in the peripheries of São Paulo in the last years. By looking at some of these movements, I hope to contribute to clarifying paradoxical articulations among poverty, the imaginary of rights, and violence in Brazil.

The Periphery

One of the main symbols that hip-hop and other recent artistic movements of São Paulo elaborate is that of the periphery. It is important, then, to add some information about it, especially considering that the periphery imagined in the raps and texts of the so-called marginal literature in São Paulo is quite different from the periphery that the social movements made popular.

In the last fifteen years, the peripheries of São Paulo have undergone contradictory processes of improvement and deterioration. The social movements, in addition to their crucial role in the democratization process and in the constitution of a new conception of citizenship, provoked a significant transformation in the urban environment of the peripheries. The state administrators in São Paulo who received the demands of social movements immediately responded to them. The city of São Paulo (and many others in Brazil) borrowed heavily to invest in urban infrastructure, especially in sanitation, to the point that Brazil became the World Bank's largest borrower in the area of urban development. As a result, the peripheries of São Paulo (and of other metropolitan regions) improved substantially in terms of urban infrastructure (asphalt, sewage, sanitation, electricity, etc.) and in terms of indicators such as infant mortality. City administrations also responded to the demands for legalization of urban land and offered various amnesties to illegal developments, enlarging substantially the amount of legal property on the peripheries. This combination of legalization and infrastructural improvement radically changed the status of the periphery in the cityscape, a transformation analogous to that of the political status of its residents obtained through the social movements.

Nevertheless, as the peripheries improved, and as democratization took root in Brazil, the conditions that sustained industrialization, developmentalism, and social mobility eroded. They started to collapse in the 1980s with what is called the "lost decade," the deep economic recession associated with changes that significantly transformed Brazilian society and many others in Latin America and all around the world. They continued to change as a result of the adoption of "structural-adjustment" policies. Although this is not the place to analyze these changes in more detail, it is important to mention the most important of them because they affected the metropolitan region of São Paulo in the 1980s and 1990s. They include a sharp decrease in population growth; a significant decline in immigration and increase in out-migration, especially of upper- and middle-class residents; a sharp drop in the gross national product (GNP) and rates of economic growth; a drop in per capita income; a deep reorganization of industrial production associated with large unemployment and instability of employment; a redefinition of the role of government in the production and management of urban space; and a significant increase in violent crime associated in part with the restructuring of urban segregation.[19] As a result of the economic crisis and related changes, the distribution of wealth—already bad—worsened, and perspectives of social mobility shrank considerably. In the peripheries, important aspects of the urban inclusion achieved by the social movements eroded. Many people could no longer afford a house of their own, and the reduced horizons of life-chances seemed to preclude even the dream of autoconstructing one. The number of people living in *favelas* in the city increased from 4.4 percent in 1980 to 9.2 percent in 1991 and 11.2 percent in 2000.[20]

Certainly, one factor that contributes in significant ways to the deterioration of everyday life in the peripheries is the sharp increase in violent crime. As I mentioned above, the annual murder rate of about 65 per 100,000 in the late 1990s made São Paulo one of the most violent cities in the world. Even with the decrease in the rate in the early 2000s, many of the neighborhoods on the periphery still have a homicide rate of more than 60 per 100,000, compared to fewer than 5 in the city's central districts.[21] Moreover, most of the cases of police abuse and killing by the police happen in the peripheries.

In sum, although the urban space of the peripheries has improved and political citizenship has been extended to their residents, their civil rights have shrunk and their everyday lives have deteriorated in certain respects. Peripheral neighborhoods are more legalized, have relatively better infrastructure, and in spite of impoverishment their poor residents have much more access to consumption, information, and communication (from cell phones and computers to radios and phonographic electronic technology) than the older among them had ever dreamed they might. Nevertheless, daily life in these areas is harsher and more uncertain than before because of the expansion of violent criminality, police abuses, unemployment, the increasing precariousness of conditions of employment, and the partial dismantling of an already-precarious welfare state. It is this periphery, where the marks of social inequality are quite obvious and the conditions of everyday life are especially difficult, that became a symbol for a series of cultural movements and artistic forms that proliferated with democratization and with the broader access to resources of information and communication.

Many things can be said about the crystallization of the periphery into a symbol of precariousness, deterioration, violence, and inequality, and several will be discussed below. However, it is important to preface them with two observations. First, although the symbol of the periphery tends to homogenize, the conditions of life in the peripheral areas of the city are far from homogeneous. For this reason I keep writing "peripheries." The processes that transformed the metropolitan region of São Paulo in the last years affected these areas differently. The areas that improved the most became middle-class neighborhoods; in some areas that continue to be poor one can encounter upper-class enclaves; *favelas* are everywhere; and many autoconstructed houses improved so much that several neighborhoods have lost the precarious appearance that they used to have. Even violence and crime are not distributed equally, and some regions are significantly more violent than others. But as the peripheries diversified in both urban and social terms, they were homogenized symbolically by movements such as hip-hop to express the worst types of inequalities and violence.

Second, not all residents of the peripheries, and not even the majority of them, share the interpretation of the periphery articulated in this recent symbol. For most of them, life in the peripheries is still interpreted in positive terms, regardless of the obvious setbacks of the last years and of the increase in violence. The people who share the views of rappers, marginal poets, and graffiti artists are probably only a minority of the residents of the peripheries. However, the rest of the population cannot ignore the view that represents them so powerfully and that places their areas once again at the center of political debate.

The diversity of views about the periphery also expresses, I suggest, a generational shift in the group that elaborates the dominant view from the outskirts of the city. The previous image of the hardworking and resourceful periphery was elaborated by the generation of migrants who first settled there and later organized the social movements to claim their "rights to the city." The members of these movements, although young, were mostly homeowners and parents. A significant proportion of them were women. They came to São Paulo to work and strongly believed in the possibilities of social mobility and incorporation into the modern society offered by hard work and education in the city. The members of the contemporary artistic movements may be described as their children. They are mostly young, the first generation of children of migrants born in the poor neighborhoods that their parents built while dreaming of becoming property owners and modern citizens. Although many of them have children, they usually do not have independent households and almost never are homeowners. The conditions they encounter in the peripheries are quite different from those of their parents. They are part of the first generation to come of age under both a democratic political system and the effects of neoliberal policies, such as high unemployment, less formal jobs, and a new "flexible" culture of labor. From many perspectives, their parents succeeded in their dreams of social mobility, and their own insertion into the city, into its modern consumption market, and into its public sphere of political debates and communication are signs of this success. However, while their parents believed in progress, they feel that they have few or even no possibilities for social mobility. They think of themselves as marginal and excluded, not as citizens, although they exercise daily their citizenship rights of participating in public debate and creating a public representation of themselves. They grew up at a moment in which possibilities of incorporation were matched by their immediate undermining, when the expansion of consumption came with unemployment, broad access to the media with the realization of their distance from the worlds the media represent, formal education with its disqualification in the job market, better urban conditions with more violent crime, democracy with injustice. From this location they create one of the most powerful critiques of social inequality, injustice, racism, and disrespect for human rights ever articulated in Brazil.

Hip-Hop: Speaking from the Neoliberal Periphery

> *I have an old bible, an automatic pistol, and a sentiment of revolt. I'm trying to survive in hell.*[22]
>
> MANO BROWN, Racionais MC's, "Genesis"

The artistic and cultural movements that appeared in the peripheries of São Paulo in the last decade are quite diverse. The most visible of them is hip-hop (which includes rap, break dance, and graffiti), but they also include the so-called marginal literature, prison literature, clandestine radio stations (labeled community radio), and sometimes other media, such as video clips. Many of these forms, especially hip-hop, are globalized forms of youth culture with numerous incarnations around the world.[23] They represent languages and styles appropriated by groups suffering from discrimination and prejudices worldwide to reelaborate their identities and expose the injustices to which they are subjected. Each of these appropriations simultaneously establishes a dialogue with people in similar situations everywhere and creates a particular local rendition of the style. In what follows, I will focus mostly on the local circulation of some of these forms in São Paulo. Although I leave the detailed analysis of their relationships with other global movements, especially North American hip-hop, for another occasion, it will become clear that São Paulo's rap replicates various of the themes and styles of American rap. Moreover, I will concentrate my analysis on one form, rap music.[24]

The São Paulo cultural movements proliferating in the peripheries in the last years are movements of protest and confrontation. Although they have various internal differences, they share some common references. By portraying the conditions of life of the poor in the peripheries and critically incorporating the prejudices usually voiced against them, the members of these movements articulate a powerful social critique. They position themselves in the periphery, identify themselves as poor and black, express an explicit class and racial antagonism, and create a style of confrontation that leaves very little space for tolerance and negotiation. Their raps and literature establish a nonbridgeable and nonnegotiable distance between rich and poor, white and black, center and periphery. Racism is one of their more important denunciations, and in this sense these movements represent a significant departure from the ways in which racial problems have traditionally been addressed in Brazil. The members of these movements not only are mostly black but also assume publicly and confrontationally their racial identity in a society that has preferred to evade black racial identification in the name of an illusory "racial democracy."[25] They are also mostly men, in a society in which women of their generation are more educated than men, more integrated into the job market, and substantially less involved with and victimized by violent crime and police abuse (women represent only around 7 percent of the victims of murder in São Paulo). In spite of their poverty and exclusion, members of these movements are plugged into globalized circuits of youth culture, whose styles they reinterpret and adopt, and into an equally globalized consumption market that includes not only clothes and cars but also pagers, cell phones, computers, and the equipment necessary to produce and circulate their music and literature.

One of the most famous groups of the hip-hop movement in São Paulo is the Racionais MC's (Rationals MC's), formed by Mano Brown, Ice Blue, Edy Rock, and KL Jay. Their last two CDs sold more than 500,000 copies, mainly in the alternative market, and are strong references not only for the youth living in the periphery but also for those of the middle classes. I will concentrate my analysis on their raps not only because they are well known and a constant reference in people's conversations, but also because they have supplied some of the main metaphors and symbols of the culture of these various movements. People know by heart some of the very long rap lyrics, sing them at balls and in shows, and cite them constantly. The Racionais MC's give the poor youth of the peripheries an interpretation and a language to speak of experiences that had been silenced before—or at least that have not had this kind of powerful and confrontational interpretation.

The Racionais MC's speak from the periphery about the periphery. They also talk to its residents, especially the young males, whom they want to make aware about the periphery's predicaments and whom they hope to convert to their particular view of the periphery. They use many terms to refer to these young men, whom they consider friends, people who share similar life experiences. One of the most common terms is *sangue bom,* "good blood."

> Wake up *sangue bom.*
> This is Capão Redondo, man,
> Not Pokemon.

> Zona Sul is inverse, stress concentrated,
> A broken heart by square meter.[26]

The elaboration of place and the constant reference to the local spaces where the rappers are from is one of the distinctive features of hip-hop. In São Paulo, as in Los Angeles or New York, raps are interpretations of the conditions of life in the deteriorated spaces of postindustrial cities offered by their young residents and constantly name these spaces.[27] *Periferia* is the referential space of the Racionais MC's. And "periphery is periphery (anywhere)," they proclaim, expanding the dimension of their brotherhood.[28] In rap after rap, the Racionais MC's describe the poverty and the precariousness of the periphery where they live and where they circulate, its everyday violence, and its lack of alternatives. Frequently, they name the diverse neighborhoods, such as Capão Redondo, one of the most famous of the southern periphery (Zona Sul), which has one of the highest murder rates of the city and where two members of the Racionais MC's live. Displaying a deep knowledge of the local geography, they evoke village after village of their area, taking them out of the usual anonymity experienced by the spaces of the poor. But all these individualized spaces share the same conditions: they are the periphery. Many times, the Racionais MC's contrast life in the peripheries with that in rich neighborhoods. "Fim de Semana no Parque" (Weekend in the Park; by Mano Brown, 1993), one of their earlier and most famous raps, is an example. Following a common pattern, it starts with a dedication that is spoken instead of sung:

> 1993, strongly coming back, Racionais!
> Using and abusing our freedom of speech,
> One of the few rights the black youth still has in this country.
> You are entering the world of information, self-knowledge,
>   denunciation, and entertainment.
> This is the x-ray of Brazil. Be welcome.
>
> To the entire poor community of the Zona Sul![29]

The reference to the right of free speech that starts this rap is one of the very few mentions of any type of rights by the Racionais MC's. It comes with one of their rare uses of the word *negro*, the politicized term for black people. Rights that can be exercised are not part of what they describe as the universe of the black people of the periphery. But it is exactly this rare right that sustains the project of the Racionais MC's—and, in fact, of a considerable part of the hip-hop movement, that known as "radical" or *consciente* in the São Paulo context.[30] Their project is to use words as weapons, to make people think, to be rational, to circulate information, to denunciate, to build an x-ray of Brazil. Their mission is to take the *mole-cada* (which refers to a group of *moleques*, "boys"; usually the connotation is of young and poor boys who spend time hanging out in the streets) out of the path of drugs, alcohol, and organized crime. For them, this is the only alternative in a universe basically without alternatives, the only chance of life.[31]

In what follows in "Fim de Semana no Parque," the Racionais MC's contrast the life style of the *playboyzada* in a rich neighborhood close to theirs, to that of the *molecada* of their area on a sunny Sunday afternoon. The term "playboy," always used in English, refers to middle- and upper-class white males and invariably carries very negative connotations. It is opposed to *sangue bom* and to *mano* (brother). In "Fim de Semana no Parque," they observe families going to the park, playboys wasting water to wash their cars, fathers jogging, motorcycles, bicycles, whores, upscale clubs.

> Look at that club, how cool!
> Look at that court, look at that field, look!
> Look how many people!
> It has an ice-cream parlor, movie theater, heated pool.
> Look at that boy, look at that girl!
> Drown that whore in the swimming pool.
> They go cart racing, one can see,
> It's exactly like the one I saw yesterday on TV.
> Look at that club, how cool!
> Look at the little black boy seeing everything from the outside.
> He doesn't even remember the money he has to take
> To his father, plastered, screaming inside the bar.
> He doesn't even remember yesterday, where, the future.
> He only dreams through the wall.[32]

The luxury world of the upper classes became especially visible to residents of the peripheries recently. On the one hand, television is almost universal in the poor neighborhoods, and the upper-class lifestyle is "exactly like the one I saw yesterday on TV." On the other hand, recent changes in the pattern of urban segregation have brought poor and rich closer spatially and made the rich areas quite visible to the residents of the peripheries. This is especially the case of the neighborhoods in the southern zone where the Racionais MC's live. A trip to this area involves crossing the richest neighborhoods in town. Although the middle- and upper-class residences, offices complexes, and malls are all fortified, poor youths look through the walls on their way home and simply observe the differences.

These observations make them "automatically imagine" the *molecada* of their neighborhood, running and playing ball barefoot on unpaved streets, screaming bad words, without videogames or even television, counting only on the protection of Saint Cosme and Saint Damião.[33] In their everyday life there is not much to play with: all is on the other side, that obscene side described with hatred and disdain and that is revealed to the *"pretinho vendo tudo do lado de fora"* (the little black boy seeing everything from the outside). Zona Sul, "the number number one of low income in the city," is an area of closely built houses that the Racionais MC's sometimes call *favelas*.[34] In the periphery, sometimes a kid finds a "silver toy shining in the middle of a bush" and may decide to use its bullets to improve Christmas. There you can find dead bodies on the street, no public investment, no spaces for kids to entertain themselves. However, in the periphery you also find dignity, human warmth, overall happiness, and loyalty. The Racionais MC's belong to the periphery. There are their brothers, there are their friends, and the majority of the people look like them—they are black.

As the Racionais MC's describe the opposed universes of poor and rich, they repeat a dichotomy that has traditionally structured the worldview of the São Paulo working classes: the rich have material goods but they lack moral qualities (especially women, repeatedly called whores).[35] Moral qualities are characteristic of the poor people (human warmth, dignity, and loyalty are their marks).[36] However, in the last years, this traditional opposition became more complicated. The periphery of the late 1970s and early 1980s, the periphery of the social movements, was described by its residents as a space of hope and opportunity where moral qualities abounded in spite of the overwhelming poverty. In the description of the Racionais MC's, however, although periphery still means "dignity," it is also a space of despair:

> Believe me, by the ranking,
> The number number one of low income in the city,
> Community Zona Sul is dignity.
> There is a body on the big stairs; the woman goes down the hill.
> Police, the death! Police, help!
> Here I don't see any multisports club
> For the *molecada* to go. No incentive.
> The investment in leisure is very scarce.

The community center is a failure.
But, then, if you want to destroy yourself,
You're in the right place.
Alcohol and cocaine are always around,
At every corner, 100, 200 meters.

.   .   .   .

I'm tired of this shit, all this nonsense.
Alcoholism, vengeance, *treta,*[37] *malandragem,*[38]
Anguished mother, problematic son,
Destroyed families, tragic weekends.
The system wants this, the *molecada* have to learn.
Weekend in Parque Ipê.
Believe me! Racionais MC's and Negritude Junior together
We're going to invest in ourselves,
Keeping a distance from drugs and alcohol.[39]

In rap after rap, the Racionais MC's reiterate the elements of this space
of despair: the constant violence, the naturalness and proximity of death,
drugs, alcohol, organized crime, and feuds among brothers. These are the
things one has to resist to be able to survive. Poverty is something people
can deal with. The trick is to avoid these things that lead to death. *"Malandragem de verdade é viver"* (the true trick is to live). This is their argument
in another famous rap, "Fórmula Mágica da Paz" (Magic Formula of
Peace; by Mano Brown), from 1997.

It took time, but today I can understand
That the true trick is to live.
I thank God and the *orixás;*
I stopped in the middle of the way and looked back.
My other *manos* have all gone too far:
São Luís Cemetery, "here he lies."[40]

"Fórmula Mágica da Paz" is one of their many poignant descriptions of
the presence of death and of their attempts to find the "magic formula
of peace" that would allow them to survive. Its first verse is "This shit is a
mined field."[41] Among the things that make it so dangerous are the lack of
money and opportunity, joblessness, the desires for consumption, "evil on
your head all day long," women ("you know very well what she wants . . .
find one with a character, if you can"), relatives in prison, and above all
"lots of funerals." "To die is a factor" (*morrer é um fator*). But although the
periphery is a mined field, they cannot or do not want to escape. "I won't

betray who I was, who I am," they continue, "I like where I am and where I came from. / . . . / teachings of the *favela* were very good for me."[42] This notion of loyalty to what they are is crucial—and also relates to their blackness, as we will see. Members of the Racionais MC's especially emphasize this, refusing to enter the logic of fame and social mobility that their success as artists could give them access to. They continue to live in their peripheries, where they form their posses (such as Negritude Junior) to try to deal with the situation of the young brothers. They refuse to appear in the mass media. Rooted in the periphery, they feel they have a legitimate right to appeal to the young men around them and to ask them to pay attention.

This appeal is careful: "as I was saying, good bloodies, this is not a sermon. Listen, I have the gift. I know how it is." Their appeal cannot sound like any well-known form of moralizing used in relation to the poor and the young. It is an appeal among equals: "nobody is more than anybody else, absolutely!" This is why they address each other as *manos*, "brothers." What qualifies them as speakers, though, is the fact that they have so far escaped the common destiny of many of their friends—the cemetery. "Here one who speaks is one more survivor." As survivors, they became rappers to enlist others to their *malandragem* and to their kind of war.[43]

The 1997 CD *Sobrevivendo no Inferno* (Surviving in Hell), which includes "Fórmula Mágica da Paz," crystallized the notions of the periphery as hell and of the survivor. The rappers are survivors because they escaped the lack of alternatives of the periphery, or rather, they escaped its destiny, the main alternative it presents to the young men: fratricide. There is always the violence of the police, but the main cause of death is the poor brothers killing each other. Their description of a process of widespread reciprocal violence reminds us of what René Girard calls a sacrificial crisis, a crisis of distinctions in which men are leveled by violence and in which there is an impossibility of maintaining the difference between good and evil.[44] The survivor in "Fórmula Mágica da Paz" is confused as he leaves the hospital where another brother is going to die. He does not know who is right, who is the biggest son-of-a-bitch: "black, white, police, robber, or me?" All he knows is that:

> Each place, a law, I know.
> In the extreme south of the southern zone all is wrong.
> Here your life is worth very little,
> Our law is faulty, violent, and suicidal.
> . . . .
> Scary it is when one realizes

That all turned into nothing and that only poor people die.
We keep killing each other, brother, why?
Don't look at me like this, I'm like you.
Put your gun to rest, put your gun to rest,
Enter the train of *malandragem,*
My rap is the rail.[45]

All he sees is brothers going to the cemetery. His mother could be one of those crying and laying down flowers by the gravestones: "to die is a factor." In the indistinction of the universe of violence and death, they try to trace a line. They discover that the real trick is to live. And they want, maybe romantically, to use rap to show to other young men (yes, only men, as they do not talk to women, do not see them as equal, and in fact only despise them—more on this later) what may separate life and death. *"Descanse o seu gatilho, entre no trem da malandragem, meu rap é o trilho!"* (Put your gun to rest, enter the train of *malandragem,* my rap is the rail!").

The presence of death and the hopes offered by rap are central themes in São Paulo's hip-hop. In fact, its main event, the month-long hip-hop festival Agosto Negro (Black August) in 2003, had as its slogan the phrase "Hip-Hop Saves."[46] The Racionais MC's elaborate the counterpoint between life and death, the hopes embedded in their raps and the "death factor" of the periphery, in many ways. Several of their raps are painful to listen to because of the powerful way in which they describe the proximity of death, refer to various dead friends, and express the vulnerability of life in the periphery. The theme of the naturalness of mimetic or reciprocal violence is described sometimes in terms that seem to come straight from Girard's analysis—if it were not for some distortions added by context. Another example is the disturbing rap "Rapaz Comum" (Common Guy; by Edy Rock, 1997). The narrator is a regular guy who is dying. He was shot to death while watching a soccer game on TV at home. He describes his feelings and thoughts as he is rushed to the hospital to die and then goes on to describe his own funeral. He wonders about the banality of death and the difficulty of remaining alive in terms that are recurrent in other raps:

To survive here, one has to be a magician.

. . . .

Death here is natural, it's common to see.
Shit! I don't want to have to find it normal
To see my *mano* covered with newspaper!
It's bad! Suicidal everyday life![47]

Describing himself as another common boy whose life was wasted, the narrator asks about the value of life, reflects about the series of people he has seen die since an early age, feels the tears of his mother praying by his side and holding his hand as he dies, feels afraid, and promises revenge to his killer: he will be an *encosto* in his killer's life, that is, a spirit that will be attached to him, weighing him down:

> One who enters only has a one-way ticket!
> Tell me! Tell me: what does this bring?
>
> . . . .
>
> The frontier between heaven and hell is on your hands.
> Nine millimeters of iron.
> Coward! Stupid! What shit are you?
> Look at the mirror and try to understand.
> The weapon is bait to lure.
> You are not police to kill!
> It is like a snowball.
> One dies, two, three, four.
> Shortly another one dies.
> I feel it on my skin; I see myself entering the scene.
> Taking shots like in motion picture films.
> "Clip, clap, bum!"
> Common guy.[48]

If the police had the monopoly of the use of force and used it according to the parameters of the rule of law and human rights, maybe it would be less bizarre to remind someone that he is not the police and should not kill. But "Zona Sul is inverse." There the police basically kill and so the monopoly of force is represented in this perverted way that only adds to a cycle of violence instead of stopping it. When the police's monopoly on the use of force is a masquerade, when there is no authority to stop feuds and protect life, and when death is natural, common to see, one leads to the next and happens just like in the movies; in this universe of widespread mimetic violence one has to be a magician to survive.

Moreover, the line separating life and death, right and wrong, heaven and hell, and violence and peace is thin indeed. Distinctions are unstable and, therefore, there is always ambiguity. The Racionais MC's live side by side with brothers (still brothers) who made other choices, who did not have the strength to resist the drugs, the money, the appeal to consume, or crime. And they understand what makes them make these choices. Members of the hip-hop movement carry guns, as do so many *manos* in the periphery, and they display them on the covers, inserts, and sleeves of their CDs. They sympathize with those inside prisons. On *Sobrevivendo no Inferno* there is a rap that was written by Jocenir, a prisoner in the Casa de Detenção, infamous for a massacre in 1992 in which the police killed 111 prisoners. The rap is called "Diário de um Detento" (Diary of a Prisoner) and describes the feelings of a prisoner on the day of the massacre. The culture of the prisons is elaborated using the language of hip-hop. Rap is an important genre among the prisoners, and almost every wall of the Casa de Detenção was covered by graffiti. These prisoners are always present in the raps, as they are also a central reference in the everyday life in the peripheries. Moreover, literature produced by prisoners and social-science literature about prisons have become important references in the peripheries and beyond. Books by prisoners have been edited by mainstream publishing houses and reviewed positively by the press.[49] Recent issues of literary magazines have published and discussed this new "marginal literature." And in the few libraries that exist in the peripheries, the most frequently borrowed book is *Estação Carandiru* by Drauzio Varella, an account of everyday life in the Casa de Detenção written by a doctor who worked there.

What does allow them to trace this narrow path that separates life and death? First of all, there is reason. They think, they are the Rationals, right? But they alone do not have so much power. Thus, they evoke God and the *orixás* (the gods and goddesses in Afro-Brazilian religions) to help them to "stop in the middle of the way." Gods and the old bible end up being the only guarantors of the distinctions between good and evil, right and wrong, life and death. Although they stand for justice, justice is conceived in moral terms more than in legal and institutional terms. Loyalty, a moral compass, and vigilantism are notions closer to their reality than the rule of law. Moreover, justice, citizenship, and rights are usually identified with "the other side," the side of the white and the upper classes, and are accordingly treated with disbelief and disdain. In the absence of a trustworthy justice system and given the impossibility of trusting the authorities, above all the police, who only kill, there is God. The CD *Sobrevivendo no Inferno* has the short track "Genesis," which I cited as the epigraph for this section ("I have an old bible, an automatic pistol, and a sentiment of revolt. I'm trying to survive in hell").[50] It also has a cross on the front cover, a gun on the back cover, and a picture of the group holding a bible in the insert. Both covers also include the inscription of parts of Psalm 23, "The Good Shepherd." Its verses 3 and 4 are the reference for the title of one of their most famous raps:

there he revives my soul.
He guides me by paths of virtue
   for the sake of his name.
Though I pass through a gloomy valley,
   I fear no harm;
beside me your rod and your staff
   are there to hearten me.[51]

Here are selections from the rap "Capítulo 4, Versículo 3," by Mano Brown:

60% of the young people in the periphery without criminal record have
   already suffered police violence;
out of every four people killed by the police, three are black;
in the Brazilian universities, only two percent of the students are black;
every four hours, a young black dies violently in São Paulo;
here is Black Cousin speaking, one more survivor.[52]

My intention is bad, empty the place!
I'm on top of it, I want it, one two shoot!
I'm quite worse than what you are seeing.
Black here has no pity, is 100% poison!
The first goes "bum!" the second goes "bam!"
I have a mission and I won't stop.
My style is heavy and makes the floor tremble!
My word is worth a shot, I have lots of ammunition!
In the fall or in the rise, my attitude goes further!
And it has a disposition for evil and good!

.   .   .   .

I came to sabotage your reasoning!
I came to shake your nervous system and your blood system!

.   .   .   .

Look, nobody is better than nobody else, look.
Look, they're our brothers too.
But from cocaine and crack, whisky and cognac,
The *manos* die quickly, without notice.
But who am I to talk about who sniffles and smokes, not possible
I've never given you anything!
You smoke what comes, clog your nose,
Drink whatever you see,
Make the devil happy!

You will end up like that other *mano* there, who was a "type A" black.
Nobody messed with him, big style:
Calvin Klein's pants, Puma sneakers,
Yes, . . . a humble way of being, working, going out.
Liked funk, played ball,
Picked up his black girl at the school door.
Example for us, high moral, high IBOPE![53]
But he started to hang out with the white guys at the mall,
That was it!
Ih! *Mano,* another life, another mood,
Only elite girls, parties, and various drinks
Whores from boutiques, all that shit.
Sex without limit, Sodom and Gomorra
Hah, it has been like nine years . . .
I saw the mano 15 days ago . . .
You'd have to see, asking for a cigarette at the bus stop,
Bad teeth, empty pocket.
The guy smells, you'd be scared!
High, I don't know of what, early in the morning!
No longer poses any danger:
Addicted, sick, fucked, inoffensive! . . .
Brother, the devil fucks everything around him!
Through radio, newspaper, magazine, and billboard,
He offers you money, speaks softly.
He contaminates your character, steals your soul,
Then throws you in the shit alone!
Ya! transforms a "type A" black into a wimpy black!
My word alleviates your pain, illuminates my soul,
Praised be my Lord!
Who doesn't let the *mano* here go astray.
Ah! and neither attack a stupid guy!
But no son-of-a-bitch ignores my law:
Racionais, chapter 4, verse 3!
Alleluia, Alleluia!
Racionais!

. . . .

For the *manos* from Baixada Fluminense to Ceilândia,[54]
I know, streets are not like in Disneyland!
From Guaianases to the extreme south of Santo Amaro,[55]
to be a "type A" black is hard!

It's fucked!
I had no father, I'm not an heir.
If I were that guy who humiliates himself at the traffic light
For less than a buck,
My chance would be little.
But if I were that punk
Who cocks the gun and puts it in your mouth
"For nothing." Without clothes, you and your girl,
One, two! Not even saw me! Already disappeared in the fog!
But not . . .
I remain alive, I follow the mystic!
27 years old, contradicting the statistics!
Your TV advertisement doesn't deceive me.
Hah! I don't need either status or fame.
Your car and your money no longer seduce me,
And neither does your blue-eyed whore!
I'm only a Latin American guy
Supported by more than 50 thousand *manos!*
Collateral effect made by your system,
Racionais, chapter 4, verse 3.[56]

To be a "type A" black who defies the statistics and remains alive is hard. He must escape violence, always, but also resist many other seductions and temptations that transform *"um preto tipo A num neguinho!"* (a "type A" black into a wimpy black): consumption, women, the white culture, the rich, what is said on TV, all the capitalist universe of evil. He must not humiliate himself by performing jobs that pay less than a dollar. He must not become a thief and a murderer. In addition, nobody is better than anybody else; drug addicts and criminals are still brothers—who are the Racionais MC's to say anything about them? The only source of protection is God, *"que não deixa o mano aqui desandar"* (who doesn't let the mano here go astray). But in this context, if a young black man survives, he is subversive. He sabotages your (our) reasoning.[57] And the sabotage seems to be multiple. He sabotages the system, the statistics, the reasoning of the elites, the racist status quo that destines him to death in the periphery. He sabotages the pattern of reciprocal violence and indistinction that makes the brothers kill one another. But he may also sabotage the usual ways of conceiving of democracy and a democratic public sphere by marking a nonnegotiable position of exclusion, drawing rigid boundaries to the brotherhood, and testing the values of tolerance and respect for

difference. He sabotages the assurance of a democratic project that ignores
the task of protecting the bodies of the subalterns.

For the Racionais MC's, what makes a "type A" black is attitude. This
expression, "attitude," which is also present in the lexicon of American
hip-hop, acquires a more prominent and central role in São Paulo's hip-
hop. *Ter atitude,* or "to have attitude," means to behave in the proper way,
which supposedly will help to keep one on the side of life. It means to avoid
drugs, alcohol, and crime; to be loyal to your *manos;* to be proud of the
black race; to be virile; to avoid ostentatious consumption and the values
of the middle and upper classes; to avoid the mass media; to be loyal to the
universe of the periphery; to be humble; to avoid women. In other words,
the brotherhood is kept together by this strict code of behavior that those
who consider themselves its spokesmen do not hesitate to enforce in quite
authoritarian terms. One example is the rap "Juri Racional" (Rational
Jury; by Mano Brown, 1993), in which they condemn in the strongest
terms a black man whom they consider to be a traitor to the race. In this
rap, they use mostly the politicized term *negro* instead of *preto.*

> You have no self-esteem man!
> You shame us, think you're the best,
> But are not more than a shameless guy.
> If you dare, dare to define your personality,
> But deep inside, what you feel is inferiority.
> You give the dirty racists
> Enough reasons to keep fucking us as before.
> White sheep of the race, betrayer!
> To sell the soul to the enemy: you abjured your color!
> But our jury is rational, doesn't fail.
> Why?
> We are not fans of bastards!
>
> . . . .
>
> It gives me hatred and indignation
> Your indifference to our destruction!
>
> . . . .
>
> This is Mano Brown, a contemporary black descendant.
> You're in the rational jury and will be tried, stupid!
> For having played on the adversary team.
>
> . . . .
>
> I like Nelson Mandela, admire Spike Lee.
> Zumbi, a great hero, the biggest here.

They are important to me, but you laugh and turn your back.
So, I know what is the shit you like:
To dress like a playboy, to go to dance clubs,
To please the whores, to watch soap opera every day,
What shit!
If this is your ideal, it's lamentable!
It's quite probable that you'll get fucked a lot.
You destroy yourself and want to include us.
But I don't want to, I won't go, I'm black, I can't,
I won't admit it!
What are clothes worth, if one doesn't have attitude?
And what is blackness worth, if you don't put it into practice?
The main tactic, inheritance of our mother Africa,
The only thing they couldn't steal!

. . . .

Many among us have advised your mind,
But you, unfortunately,
Don't even show an interest in freeing yourself.
This is the question: self-esteem.
This is the title of our revolution.
Chapter 1:
The real black has to be able
To row against the tide, against any sacrifice.
But with you it is difficult: you only mind your own interest.

. . . .

"Unanimously, the jury of this tribunal declares the legal action
    justified
And considers the defendant guilty
Of ignoring the struggle of the black ancestors,
Of despising the millenary black culture,
Of humiliating and ridiculing the other brothers,
Being a voluntary instrument of the racist enemy.
Case closed."[58]

From the brotherhood are excluded not only the usual suspects (rich, white, policemen, politicians) and those with the wrong attitude. Excluded also are their sisters—all women. The only women treated with respect in the raps are their mothers, who suffer, cry for them, raise them by themselves, and give them character. Verses despising women abound. The most concentrated expression of their prejudices is the rap "Mulheres Vulgares" (Vulgar Women; by Edy Rock and KL Jay) from the CD *Holo-causto Urbano* (Urban Holocaust), from 1990:

> Derived from a feminist society
> That considers that we are all *machistas,*
> She doesn't want to be considered a sex symbol,
> Struggles to reach power, to prove her morality
> In a relationship in which
> She doesn't admit to being submissive,
> But she walks backward.
> She demands equal rights
> But what is the other side of the coin?
> Believe me!
> For her, money is the most important.
> Vulgar being, her ideas are repulsive.
> She's an idiot who shows herself naked as an object.
> She's a worthless person who makes money from sex,
> In the bedroom, the motel, or movie screen.
> She's another live being, obscene.
> She struggles for a special place,
> Fame and money with a soccer king! (ah, ah)
> She wants to get together with a magnate
> Who commands her steps with a suit and a tie (stupid).
> She wants to be the center of attention anywhere.
> . . . .
> She wants to make headlines.
> We are Racionais, different if not the same.
> Vulgar women, one night and nothing more.
> She's beautiful, delicious, and sensual
> Her lipstick and makeup make her banal.
> To be the evil one, fatal, fine, bad . . . She doesn't care!
> She only wants money, finally.
> She gets anyone involved with her ingenuous look.
> In fact, behind rules the most pure mediocrity.
> She dominates you with her promiscuous way of being.
> As one changes clothes, she trades you for another one.
> Many want her forever,
> But I just want her for one night, do you get me?[59]

São Paulo hip-hop is almost exclusively a male universe. There are only a few women rappers in Brazil and there is only one that I know of with a

CD circulating broadly, Nega Gizza (from Rio de Janeiro). In spite of the fact that some women in the periphery identify with hip-hop, which they consider the only movement expressing their racial problems adequately, there is always a kind of discomfort with their presence. The reasons are obvious. The *manos*—at least as expressed in rap verse—do not trust them and do not respect them. And obviously no one likes to be treated in the terms described in the above rap or to be under constant suspicion of disloyalty and betrayal.[60] The list of faults attributed to women is more de-tailed than those attributed to rich whites, and sometimes the words used to refer to them are more offensive (as are those used to refer to the black "traitor"). There are several possible conjectures to be made in relation to such an anxiety in relation to women, a trait that also marks American hip-hop.[61] It could be remembered that women in the periphery seem to have another relationship with the position of marginality and exclusion, as they continue to be educated (both in the school system and in a series of informal courses in which they learn computer skills, for example), to enter the labor force and find jobs, to support and head households, to raise children by themselves. They have also been using a language of rights, and the critical reference to this use is one of the few ways in which "rights" figure in the raps of the Racionais MC's (the other being the right to free speech). I would argue that the denigration of women (even if black) and the harsh judgment of the black "traitor" are part of the same trend. This is the need to police the boundaries of a community that is kept to-gether on the basis of "attitudes" and that has little tolerance for differ-ence. This task of policing is easy in relation to the obvious "others" but becomes a cumbersome deed when it has to separate those who are "equal but not quite."

The constant fear of betrayal and the policing of behavior are pervasive in a universe held together on moral grounds and in which everyday life is highly unpredictable given both economic uncertainties and the fragility of life. The last CD of the Racionais MC's, the double album *Nada como um Dia depois do Outro Dia* (Nothing like a Day after Another Day; 2002), has various discussions about betrayal and envy. The raps repro-duce alleged accusations by people who doubt that the members of the group will remain loyal to the *manos* now that they are famous. There is also the repetition of the notion that it is very hard to trust people, for there are always bad people everywhere. Trust is badly needed to keep the brotherhood alive—but how to trust people if even Christ, "who died for millions," was betrayed by one of the twelve who walked with him and ended up crying? In the rap "Jesus Chorou" (Jesus Cried; 2002) they express their doubts, their fears, and their vulnerability as they ask for help and evoke "a lot of people I trust, like, and admire, struggled for justice and in peace got shot: Malcolm X, Gandhi, Lennon, Marvin Gaye, Che Guevara, Tupac, Bob Marley, and the evangelical Martin Luther King."

In this recent album, the Racionais MC's elaborate the concept of *vida loka* (crazy life), but the word *louca* is deliberately misspelled as *loka*. The letters *c* and *k* have the same sound in Portuguese, but *k* is in disuse and normally appears only in foreign words imported into Portuguese.[62] The cover shows a shiny, big, old stylish car, like a 1960s Cadillac, a fancily dressed man shown only from the waist down, and a bottle and a glass of champagne—quite a departure from previous covers, which featured weapons, prison bars, drugs, and crosses! *Vida loka* is certainly not a clearly stated notion. I read it as the affirmation of their positioning in that ambiguous space of the periphery in which it is hard to separate good and bad, violence and nonviolence, consumption and crime. The first person to live a *vida loka* in history was Dysmas, they argue, the "good thief" who was crucified beside Jesus. Unlike the other thief, Dysmas believed in Christ and was pardoned by him. Maybe in selecting Dysmas to symbolize the *vida loka* the Racionais MC's were aware of the fact that both thieves who were crucified beside Christ belonged to a special category: they were social bandits who robbed the rich to give to the poor. Regular thieves were not crucified.[63] So, by evoking Dysmas, the good thief, the social bandit, to begin the lineage of the type of life they lead, the Racionais MC's reaffirm their ambiguous positioning in the universe of the periphery and of violence, as they also reemphasize their reliance on the "old bible" to make sense of their predicament.

They start the rap "Vida Loka, Part 2" with the sound of a champagne toast for a new year and go on to describe their jewelry and clothes. Signs of consumption are added one after the other, as they introduce the issue of the envious gaze upon them:

> Take your eyes off me!
> Take your eyes off me, forget me!
> I sleep ready for the war.
> I wasn't like this, I have hatred,
> I know it's bad for me,
> But what can I do, if it's like this.
> *Vida loka,* unfortunate,
> The smell is of gunpowder,
> And I prefer roses.[64]

Vida loka seems to represent another kind of immersion in the sphere of ambiguity that marks the universe of the Racionais MC's. Consumption is not discarded totally but is accepted as a possibility or maybe as an inevitability. "The question is that abundance makes the sufferer happier," they affirm, adding a few verses later: "Money is a whore and opens the doors of the sand castles you want." It seems that they are willing to revise some of their rigid principles. Although religious references continue to be strong, Judas the traitor and Dysmas the thief come to the forefront, and the God that guarantees life is represented as Jesus, who was betrayed and cried. As the rap "Vida Loka" unfolds, they go back and forth between preferences and reality. They seem to be always saying: "I don't like to be like this, but what can I do?" "I prefer roses, but the smell is of gunpowder." "A black man would prefer a simple life, but in São Paulo God is money," and so on. Instead of struggling to keep distinctions in place, they seem to have chosen, at least temporarily, to become immersed in the space of ambiguity that is constitutive of the periphery and of their lives, a space of ambiguity that is constitutive of violence.

I have interpreted the anxieties expressed by rappers in relation to women, other black men, and the envious gaze in terms of the need to police the boundaries of a community that is kept together on the basis of "attitudes" and that has no tolerance for difference. I have also argued that this task of policing is especially complicated in relation to those who are "equal but not quite." It seems to me, however, that this interpretation is not yet sufficient and that other elements shaping everyday life in the periphery should be brought into consideration.

Rappers characterize the periphery as a space of despair. It is a space of blatant social inequality and lack of opportunities. It is a space in which the presence of death is overwhelming. In both senses, it is a space of huge uncertainties. The generation of youth to which rappers belong grew up within a scenario completely different from that of their parents. The strong belief in progress and social mobility that structured the lives and actions of the previous generation of residents of the periphery has vanished. Moreover, the culture of labor that anchored the working class and their sense of dignity, especially for men, has faded in the context of unemployment and flexible labor relationships. When these losses of certainty combine with the constant presence of police harassment and murdered friends, "daily life becomes a perpetual dress rehearsal for death. What is being rehearsed . . . is ephemerality and evanescence of things that humans may acquire and bonds that humans may weave."[65] No wonder, then, that anxieties about betrayal, loyalty, appearance, and envy should be high and that trust becomes something to be carefully constructed and difficult to obtain.

In analyzing similar anxieties in American gangsta rap, Paul Gilroy argues that they signal a transformation in the black public sphere in which "old patterns" are replaced by a new "bio-politics" in which "the person is identified only in terms of their body."[66] In the periphery of São Paulo, as in the American inner city, the black male body is at the center of struggles for life and death, power and powerlessness. In this context, it is possible to understand why sex comes to the forefront of politics and why misogyny and preoccupation with the boundaries of life and death pervade rap. "As old certainties about the fixed limits of racial identity have lost their power to convince, ontological security capable of answering a radically reduced sense of the value of life has been sought in the naturalizing power of gender difference and sex as well as in the ability to cheat death and take life."[67]

Democracy and Enclosed Spaces

In recent years, numerous movements in Brazil have exposed the inequalities and injustices that condition the lives of the working poor and their spaces. The social movements of the 1970s and 1980s are the most well known. But their perspective had two crucial differences in relation to that of hip-hop. First, the social movements countered the negative images of the periphery by presenting a positive image of a unified, "solidarity" community of hardworking families and property owners. In other words, these movements questioned the elite's images of the periphery and its residents but not the elite's values of property and progress. They learned the notion of the unified community from liberation theology. The ethics of hard work as a tool of betterment and guarantee of dignity has structured the worldview of the working poor during the whole period of industrialization and urbanization of São Paulo. Second, they articulated their demands from a position of inclusion. They placed themselves inside the political sphere and indeed forced the expansion of its parameters so that they could fit in. They articulated their inequality as the basis for their demand for equal rights. In this demand, they affirmed inclusion, belonging, and membership.

The law and the state that the residents of the periphery engaged with and that incorporated them during the democratization period have protected their political rights, improved at least partially their spaces, changed the way in which the management of urban space is conceived, and even protected their property rights. But law and the state were unable to protect their bodies and lives, especially if black and male. It is this vulnerability and some of the stark limits to the inclusion of the working classes in Brazilian democracy and social life that the Racionais MC's and the hip-hop movement dramatically express. As they do this, however, they articulate for themselves a position of enclosure.

Hip-hop members use the only right they think that poor blacks like them still have, the right of free speech assured by democratization, to try to bind their brothers' bodies and help to keep them alive. Under the rubric of "attitude," they articulate a rigid ethic (even if they doubt and contradict it at times):[68] no drugs, no alcohol, no conspicuous consumption, no contact with whites, no trusting women, and so on. The brotherhood produced by this ethic and good behavior is kept together by the invocation of God (and sometimes the *orixás*), by *manos* patrolling each other's behavior, and by the authoritarian "rational trials." There is no institution other than the dispersed hip-hop groups and posses to articulate the rules and functioning of the brotherhood. These groups avoid relationships with outside organizations. As Ferréz, a famous writer from Capão Redondo and one of the publishers of marginal literature repeats: *"é so eu e meu povo!"* (it is only me and my people!). With this gesture he dismisses the collaboration of any well-intentioned middle-class volunteers and even of the new type of institution trying to develop programs in the periphery, the nongovernmental organizations (NGOs). "NGOs exist to tame things. There is a problem in the periphery, well, send an NGO to tame it, to give a little course in the periphery," ironizes Ferréz. In this view, the NGOs are worthless because Ferréz and people in his posse do not think that they can be helped by outsiders. They feel that they are alone: *"É nós por nós!"* (It is us for us!).[69]

Undoubtedly, the young and black residents of the periphery have many reasons to be skeptical of assistance and of institutions. Undoubtedly, too, it is hard for them to find notions such as justice, rights, and belonging, as articulated by the institutions of the current democratic state, relevant to them. However, it is important to note that they evoke the same notions, rearticulated, as part of their ethics. Nevertheless, their self-enclosure and intolerance for difference (any difference, in fact; remember the sisters) set limits to the kind of community and politics they may create. They think of the periphery as a world apart, something similar to the American ghetto, an imaginary that has never been used before in Brazil to think of the peripheries. *"É nós por nós!"* Moreover, "democracy" is not a word in their lexicon. It is, in fact, a notion that belongs to the other side, the side of the white, rich society. Their evocations of justice are not necessarily those of citizenship and the rule of law—as were the ones of the social movements. (And in this sense their demands for justice sometimes have a troubling similarity with the way in which the commands of organized crime use the same notions.) Theirs is a moralistic order, and one in which difference has no place. It is also an order in which the notions of justice and rights are disconnected, as the former is articulated in religious terms and the latter refers to a notion of citizenship.[70] Thus, the Brazilian hip-hop movement gives another indication of how concepts that many theories of democracy assume co-occur are in fact articulated in unexpected ways in different social contexts.

The construction of a position of self-enclosure by the hip-hop movement is especially problematic when one considers that it is paralleled by other practices of enclosure, this time by the upper classes. For some time, groups from the upper classes have been creating spaces of isolation for their activities, from housing to work, from entertainment to consumption. These are secluded in fortified enclaves and kept under the surveillance of private guards. When both sides of the wall think of themselves as enclosed and self-sufficient, what are the chances of democratization? What are the chances for the construction of a less unequal and less segregated city and a democratic public space when intolerance is evoked to build the communities on both sides of the wall?

Notes

"I came to sabotage your reasoning" is a verse from the Racionais MC's rap "Capítulo 4, Versículo 3," *Sobrevivendo no Inferno.*

1. Brazil was ruled by a military dictatorship between 1964 and 1985.

2. Violence is certainly not the only process provoking transformations in Brazilian cities. The cities have also been affected by neoliberal policies, industrial restructuring, and, in São Paulo, the concentration of new forms of services, especially those associated with global finance and communications. As violence increased and political and economic conditions changed, a new pattern of spatial segregation also took shape in the city. Its main effect is to enforce boundaries and separations. Thus, new forms of violence, socioeconomic change, and spatial segregation have occurred along with democratization in interconnected and sometimes surprising ways. I analyze São Paulo's new pattern of spatial segregation in *City of Walls: Crime, Segregation, and Citizenship in São Paulo* (Berkeley and Los Angeles: University of California Press, 2000).

3. I would like to thank the participants of the Radcliffe Institute for Advanced Study conference for their comments on this essay. Especially, I would like to thank Jean Comaroff, John Comaroff, J. Lorand Matory, Ben Penglase, and Ajantha Subramanian.

4. For an analysis of this uneven process, which resulted in what we label "dis-

junctive democracy," see Teresa P. R. Caldeira and James Holston, "Democracy and Violence in Brazil," *Comparative Studies in Society and History* 41, no. 4 (1999): 691–729.

5. The urban social movements are not the only example of processes that contribute to expanding citizenship and consolidating democracy. I choose them here as examples because they share with the other cases I analyze the same references to the peripheries and their social conditions. Another successful case would be the feminist movements, the expansion of women's rights, and various changes in gender relations.

6. "Urban adverse possession" is the legal process through which people who have been in possession of urban land that they acquired in good faith but do not have title to can claim their ownership titles.

7. The National Movement of Struggle for Urban Reform was founded in 1986 and was later consolidated in the National Forum of Urban Reform, which congregates numerous nongovernmental organizations (NGOs), social movements, and trade union organizations interested in urban reform. The Forum is still quite active in promoting urban legislation at all levels of government.

8. For an analysis of the new urban legislation and the City Statute, see Teresa P. R. Caldeira and James Holston, "State and Urban Space in Brazil: From Modernist Planning to Democratic Interventions," in *Global Assemblages: Technology, Politics, and Ethics as Anthropological Problems,* ed. Aihwa Ong and Stephen J. Collier (London: Blackwell, 2005), pp. 393–416. In that essay, we argue that the City Statute and legislation that followed it in fact consolidate a new type of urban planning and engagement with city management that we term democratic. We contrast this model with the modernist-developmentalist type of urban planning that had prevailed in Brazil and elsewhere from the 1950s on and which was based on a notion of total plan, usually implemented in a very authoritarian fashion.

9. The concept of insurgent citizenship is developed by James Holston in his "Spaces of Insurgent Citizenship," *Planning Theory* 13 (1995): 35–52.

10. Caldeira and Holston, "Democracy and Violence in Brazil"; James Holston and Teresa P. R. Caldeira, "Democracy, Law, and Violence: Disjunctions of Brazilian Citizenship," in *Fault Lines of Democracy in Post-transition Latin America,* ed. Felipe Agüero and Jeffrey Stark (Coral Gables, FL: North-South Center Press/University of Miami, 1998), pp. 263–96.

11. James Holston and I developed the following discussion of violence and the perversion of democratic rights together. His interpretation of these issues appears in James Holston, *Insurgent Citizenship: Disjunctions of Democracy and Modernity in Brazil* (forthcoming).

12. Maria Helena Prado de Mello Jorge, "Violência como Problema de Saúde Pública," *Ciência e Cultura* 54, no. 1 (2002): 52–53. According to Seade (Fundação Sistema Estadual de Análise de Dados), homicide rates in the city of São Paulo decreased 36.8 percent between 2000 and 2004, when it was 37 per 100,000 (http://www.seade.gov.br/noticias.php?opt=107). However, the homicide rate for young people (fifteen to twenty-four years old) is more than double the city rate: 110 per 100,000 (*Veja SP,* 6 July 2005, p. 27). Although the reasons for the decrease are not well researched yet, it seems that they include an intensification of the work of NGOs in areas of high incidence of homicide, a campaign for disarm-

ing the population that has collected more than 110,000 weapons in the state of
São Paulo between January 2004 and July 2005, and improvements in police
equipment and training.

13. See Teresa P. R. Caldeira, "The Paradox of Police Violence in Democratic
Brazil," *Ethnography* 3, no. 3 (2002): 235–63, for a discussion of police violence,
popular support of it, and the failure of various governmental initiatives to control it.

14. Sérgio Adorno, "Discriminação Racial e Justiça Criminal em São Paulo,"
Estudos Cebrap 43 (1995): 45–63; Danielle Ardaillon and Guita Debert, *Quando
a Vitima é Mulher: Análise de Julgamentos de Crimes de Estupro, Espancamento
e Homicídio* (Brasília: Conselho Nacional dos Direitos da Mulher, 1988); Danielle
Ardaillon, "Cidadania de Corpo Inteiro—Discursos Sobre o Aborto em Número
e Gênero" (PhD diss., Department of Sociology, University of São Paulo, 1997);
Americas Watch Committee, *Criminal Injustice: Violence against Women in
Brazil* (New York: Americas Watch Committee, 1991).

15. For an analysis of how this resignification of human rights was articulated,
see Caldeira, *City of Walls,* chap. 9.

16. http://www.polmil.sp.gov.br/qtotal/evolucao.asp (accessed 7 December
2001).

17. The Statute of the PCC is available at the following Web site: http://www
.jt.estadao.com.br/editoriais/2001/02/21/ger040.html. The texts by prison organizations frequently contain grammar mistakes and inarticulate phrases. This is the
case with the two examples I cite here.

18. Jazadji was elected state deputy of São Paulo in 1986 on the basis of his attacks and has been reelected since then.

19. Rates of population growth that had been above 5 percent annually until
the 1960s dropped to 0.8 percent in the 1990s. Fertility rates decreased sharply
(from 5.8 children per woman in 1970 to 2.9 in 1990), and the rich residents abandoned the city and its central quarters by the hundreds of thousands. Brazil's GNP
dropped 5.5 percent and the real minimum wage decreased 46 percent during the
period 1980–90. Between 1940 and 1980, the GNP had grown 6.9 percent annually (4 percent in per capita terms). Between 1980 and 1992, it grew only 1.25 percent annually and per capita income dropped 7.6 percent. See PNUD (Programa
das Nações Unidas para o Desenvolvimento) and IPEA (Instituto de Pesquisa
Econômica Aplicada), *Relatório para o Desenvolvimento Humano no Brasil*
(Brasília: PNUD-IPEA, 1996), p. 73. Inflation rates soared during the 1980s and
1990s and reached 2,500 percent a year in 1993, before they were controlled by
the Plano Real of 1994. The GNP of the metropolitan region of São Paulo dropped
from US$92 billion in 1980 to US$85 billion in 1990. The GNP per capita dropped
27 percent during the same period (Eduardo Marques and Haroldo Torres, "São
Paulo no Contexto do Sistema Mundial de Cidades," *Novos Estudos Cebrap* 56
[2000]: 155). The industrial sector that gives the region its identity has been especially affected by the crisis. Since the 1980s, São Paulo's share in the value of industrial transformation has dropped. It was 58.2 percent in 1970 and 41 percent
in 1991. In 1990, São Paulo was still responsible for 26.3 percent of the industrial
production of the country, but this was a much lower percentage than the 55 percent it represented in 1960. Industrial employment in the metropolitan region de-

creased 32 percent between 1989 and 1999 while general employment dropped 10 percent. During this period, the service sector increased 38 percent (Marques and Torres, "São Paulo no Contexto do Sistema Mundial de Cidades," p. 157). Unemployment increased from 9 percent in 1989 to 15 percent in 1996 and 20 percent in 1999, affecting two million people. Formal employment has decreased significantly more than informal employment. The interpretations of changes in the industrial sector vary. Although some talk about deindustrialization, it seems that what has been happening is industrial restructuring. In the context of the ending of subsidies and protectionism and an opening to external markets that framed the abandonment of the interventionism-protectionism model of import substitution, most industries adopted new technologies and styles of management and reorganized production. The results were an increase both in productivity and in unemployment. Moreover, it seems that there was an intense displacement of occupations from the industrial sector to various segments of the service sector (Alvaro Comin and Claudio Amitrano, "Economia e Emprego: A Trajetória Recente da Região Metropolitana de São Paulo," *Novos Estudos Cebrap* 66 [2003]: 53–76).

20. *"Favela"* refers to a set of shacks built on seized land. Although people own their shacks and may transport them, they do not own the land, since it was occupied illegally. Autoconstructed houses may sometimes look as precarious as *favela* shacks, but typically they are built on land bought by the residents. There have been various controversies about the number of people living in *favelas* in São Paulo. The estimates that I give are from Camila Saraiva and Eduardo Marques; "A Dinâmica Social das Favelas da Região Metropolitana de São Paulo" (São Paulo: Centro de Estudos da Metópole, 2004), http://www.centrodametropole.org.br/textos.html, accessed 22 July 2004. They argue against a famous study by FIPE (Fundação Instituto de Pesquisas Econômicas) that estimated the number of *favela* residents in 1993 as representing 19 percent of the population of the city.

21. Data for 2004 from Seade, http://www.seade.gov.br/noticias.php?opt=107 (accessed 14 July 2005). For an analysis of crime trends during the 1980s and 1990s, see Caldeira, *City of Walls*.

22. "Eu tenho uma bíblia velha, uma pistola automática e um sentimento de revolta. / Eu tou tentando sobreviver no inferno" (*Sobrevivendo no Inferno*, 1997).

23. See Tony Mitchell, ed., *Global Noise: Rap and Hip-Hop outside the USA* (Middletown, CT: Wesleyan University Press, 2001).

24. My interest in the hip-hop movement stems from my ongoing research on gender and youth in São Paulo. As I started to investigate a growing gender gap among São Paulo's youth, it was impossible to ignore hip-hop. This research focuses on young men and women from all social classes living in São Paulo and investigates the paradoxical and unprecedented ways in which they are re-creating gender roles. This re-creation is paradoxical because it simultaneously breaks with past models and reproduces in almost caricature fashion some traditional attributes of those roles, especially male aggressiveness and female sensuality. The most emblematic expressions of these trends are, for males, involvement with guns, crime, and artistic-stylistic expressions valorizing risk and aggressiveness, such as hip-hop; and, for females, the rising rates of pregnancy among adolescents and a preference for styles and careers that valorize the exposure of a sexualized body.

The re-creation of gender roles is unprecedented because it articulates in explicit ways two issues that traditionally have been either silenced or disguised in Brazilian society: racism and class antagonism. I conducted the fieldwork for this project between July 2001 and December 2002 and in the summers of 2003 and 2004. I would like to thank the institutions that have generously supported this research: J. William Fulbright Foreign Scholarship, Fundação de Amparo à Pesquisa do Estado de São Paulo, Núcleo de Estudos da Violência from the University of São Paulo, Program in Latin American Studies of the University of California, Irvine, and the Academic Senate Council on Research, Computing, and Library Resources from the University of California, Irvine.

25. I cannot discuss here the complex Brazilian system of racial relations. One of its marks is a flexible system of racial classifications that allows people to shift positions depending on circumstances. Under this system, the question of who is black is always open-ended. In this essay, I use the expression "black" because this is the way in which rappers represent themselves. There are two main words for "black" in Brazil: *preto* and *negro*. Historically, *negro* is the word adopted by the organized black movements. In the last years, organized black people have also started to use the expression *afro-descendente* (afro-descendant) to identify themselves. It is significant to note that rappers usually use the term *preto* to refer to themselves, therefore simultaneously establishing a certain distance from the black movements and speaking from the perspective of those who are discriminated against. They also tend not to differentiate between *pretos* and mulattos or among different types of *pretos,* something Brazilians in general are very careful about doing. Although the term *preto* has been used as a term of derogation in Brazil, it does not carry the same strong derogatory/abusive meaning as the English "nigger."

26. "Acorda sangue bom. / Aqui é Capão Redondo, Tru / Não Pokemon / Zona Sul é invés, é stress concentrado, / Um coração ferido por metro quadrado." ("Vida Loka, Parte 2," 2002, *Nada como um Dia Depois do Outro Dia*). In this CD, they do not identify individual authors of the raps. Translating rap lyrics is an incredible challenge, as they are not only rhymed but also full of slang and local references. Although I hope that the translations I present here convey the content of the verses, they certainly do not do justice to the form, as rhymes were eliminated in the translation. For this reason, I supply the Portuguese lyrics in the notes. Brazilian rappers rap exclusively in Portuguese.

27. It is unavoidable to notice the parallel between the image of the periphery elaborated by São Paulo's rappers and that of the inner-city neighborhoods of postindustrial Los Angeles and New York put forward by American rappers. There are many common features in those different postindustrial cities, although their poverty levels and homicide rates are not comparable. On the relationship between rap and the postindustrial city in the United States, see Tricia Rose, *Black Noise: Rap Music and Black Culture in Contemporary America* (Middletown, CT: Wesleyan University Press, 1994); Robin D. G. Kelley, "Kickin' Reality, Kickin' Ballistics: Gangsta Rap and Postindustrial Los Angeles," in *Droppin' Science: Critical Essays on Rap Music and Hip Hop Culture,* ed. William Eric Perkins (Philadelphia: Temple University Press, 1996).

28. "Periferia é Periferia (em Qualquer Lugar)," 1997, *Sobrevivendo no Inferno*.

29. "1993, fudidamente voltando, Racionais! / Usando e abusando da nossa liberdade de expressão, / Um dos poucos direitos que o jovem negro ainda tem nesse país. / Você está entrando no mundo da informação, auto-conhecimento, denúncia e diversão. / Esse é o raio-x do Brasil. Seja bem vindo! / À toda comunidade pobre da zona sul!" ("Fim de Semana no Parque," 1993, *Raio X do Brasil*).

30. This branch of rap shows a certain relationship with American "message rap" or "political rap." Nevertheless, the way in which each of these types of raps is articulated is quite different. In Brazil, there is no equivalent either to the Nation of Islam or to what is called "black nationalism" in the United States. The Racionais MC's also maintain a tie with "gangsta rap." See Kelley, "Kickin' Reality, Kickin' Ballistics"; Paul Gilroy, "After the Love Has Gone: Bio-politics and Etho-poetics in the Black Public Sphere," *Public Culture* 7 (1994): 49–76. The Racionais MC's 2002 CD *Nada como um Dia depois do Outro Dia* is dedicated to a good assortment of American rappers and Brazilian singers, indicating the type of influence they want to acknowledge: "To James Brown, Jorge Ben, Marvin Gaye, Tim Maia, George Clinton, Tupac Shakur, Bob Marley, Too Short, Cassiano, Fat Back, Gap Band, Snoop Dog [*sic*], Dione Worrick [*sic*], Cameo, Barkays, War, One Way, Notorius [*sic*] B.I.G., Run DMC, Public Enemy, George Duke, King Tee, Ice T, Clara Nunes, Isaac Hayes, Quincy Jones, Curtis Mayfield, All [*sic*] Green, Bebeto, 105FM and all the community radios. Thanks for the inspiration. *É desse jeito vagabundo!*"

31. In one of the most provocative analyses of Brazilian rap, psychoanalyst Maria Rita Kehl characterizes this mission of the Racionais MC's as their "civilizing effort." Using Freudian references, she describes the Racionais MC's as part of an orphan brotherhood (*fratria orfã*) that comes to occupy a new role in Brazilian society. This role is that of a "strong *brotherhood,* which trusts itself and is capable of supplanting the power of the 'father of the horde' and of erecting a symbolic father under the form of a just law that contemplates the necessity of all and not the voracity of a few" (p. 217, her emphasis). See Maria Kita Kehl, "A Fratria Orfã: O Esforço Civilizatório do Rap na Periferia de São Paulo," in *Função Fraterna,* ed. Maria Rita Kehl (Rio de Janeiro: Relume Dumará, 2000), pp. 209–44.

32. "Olha só aquele clube, que da hora / Olha aquela quadra, olha aquele campo. Olha! / Olha quanta gente! / Tem sorveteria, cinema, piscina quente / Olha quanto boy, olha quanta mina / Afoga essa vaca dentro da piscine / Tem corrida de kart, dá pra ver / É igualzinho o que eu ví ontem na TV / Olha só aquele clube, que da hora, / Olha o pretinho vendo tudo do lado de fora / Nem se lembra do dinheiro que tem que levar / Pro seu pai bem louco gritando dentro do bar. / Nem se lembra de ontem, de onde, o futuro. / Ele apenas sonha através do muro" ("Fim de Semana no Parque").

33. In Umbanda, a syncretic Afro-Brazilian religion, these are the saints that protect children.

34. As stated earlier, there is an important difference between *favelas* and the peripheral neighborhoods originated in autoconstruction: while *favelas* are conglomerations of shacks built on invaded land, autoconstructed houses are typically built on lots purchased by the owners, who are therefore property owners, even if they have problems registering their deeds due to various sorts of irregularities. To disregard the differences between *favelas* and autoconstructed areas of the periph-

eries is part of the process of symbolic homogenization of the periphery in which the Racionais MC's participate. This homogenization is deeply resented by residents, who make constant efforts to elaborate those differences.

35. To refer to women as prostitutes is something that São Paulo rap shares with American gangsta rap.

36. See Teresa P. R. Caldeira, *A Política dos Outros (o Cotidiano dos Moradores da Periferia e o que Pensam do Poder e dos Poderosos)* (São Paulo: Brasiliense, 1984), chap. 4, for a discussion of how the residents of the periphery describe themselves in opposition to the rich and conceive of their moral qualities and health as characteristics that more than compensate for their lack of material goods, which the rich have but which do not quite compensate for their poor health and lack of moral qualities. This book is an ethnographic study of part of the periphery of São Paulo in the late 1970s and early 1980s, at the moment in which social movements were starting to become strong in São Paulo. Between 1978 and the present, I have conducted a series of research projects in various neighborhoods in the peripheries of São Paulo. My observations about the direction of transformations in the peripheries are based on these studies, especially the above-mentioned book and my more recent one (*City of Walls*).

37. *Treta* is slang for "fight," "confusion," "disorder."

38. *Malandragem* is a complex concept. It means "trick," "trickery," "roguery," a way of circumventing rules and regulations of the established order without overtly crossing the line into illegality.

39. "Pode crer, pela ordem / A número número um em baixa renda da cidade, / Comunidade Zona Sul é dignidade. / Tem um corpo no escadão, a tiazinha desce o morro; / Polícia! a morte, polícia! Socorro! / Aqui não vejo nenhum clube poliesportivo / Pra molecada frequentar. Nenhum incentivo. / O investimento no lazer é muito escasso. / O centro comunitário é um fracasso. / Mas aí se quiser se destruir, está no lugar certo. / Tem bebida e cocaína sempre por perto, / A cada esquina, 100, 200 metros. / . . . / Tô cansado dessa porra, de toda essa bobagem / Alcoolismo, vingança, treta, malandragem / Mãe angustiada, filho problemático / Famílias destruídas, fins de semana trágicos. / O sistema quer isso, a molecada tem que aprender. / Fim de semana no Parque Ipê. / Pode crer, Racionais MC's e Negritude Junior juntos / Vamos investir em nós mesmos, / mantendo distância das drogas e do álcool" ("Fim de Semana no Parque").

40. "Demorou, mais hoje eu posso compreender / Que malandragem de verdade é viver. / Agradeço a Deus e aos orixás, / Parei no meio do caminho e olhei pra trás. / Meus outros manos todos foram longe demais: / Cemitério São Luís 'aqui jaz'" ("Fórmula Mágica da Paz," 1997, *Sobrevivendo no Inferno*).

41. "Essa porra é um campo minado."

42. "Não vou trair quem eu fui, quem eu sou. / Gosto de onde estou e de onde eu vim, / Ensinamento da favela foi muito bom pra mim" ("Fórmula Mágica da Paz").

43. "Então como eu estava dizendo, sangue bom, / Isso não é sermão—ouve aí, tenho o dom. / . . . Ninguém é mais que ninguém, absolutamente. / Aqui quem fala é mais um sobrevivente" ("Fórmula Mágica da Paz").

44. René Girard, *Violence and the Sacred* (Baltimore: Johns Hopkins University Press, 1977).

45. "Cada lugar, uma lei, eu tô ligado. / No extremo sul da Zona Sul tá tudo errado. / Aqui vale muito pouco a sua vida, / Nossa lei é falha , violenta e suicida. / . . . / Legal, assustador é quando se descobre . . . / Que tudo deu em nada, e que só morre pobre. / A gente vive se matando, irmão, por que? / Não me olhe assim, eu sou igual a você. / Descanse o seu gatilho, descanse o seu gatilho, / Entre no trem da malandragem, / Meu rap é o trilho" ("Fórmula Mágica da Paz").

46. The city administration of the PT (Workers' Party, 2001–5) consistently supported hip-hop events. In 2002, 2003, and 2004 the Secretary for the Youth sponsored the festival Agosto Negro, which featured daily hip-hop events in all regions of the city, including the periphery. A large number of hip-hop artists have participated in the festival. In 2004, a show by the Racionais MC's attended by more than 30,000 people closed the festival.

47. "Pra sobreviver aqui tem que ser mágico. / . . . / Morte aqui é natural, é comum de se ver. / Caralho! Não quero ter que achar normal / Ver um mano meu coberto de jornal! / É mal! Cotidiano suicida!" ("Rapaz Comum," 1997, *Sobrevivendo no Inferno*).

48. "Quem entra tem passagem só pra ida! / Me diga. Me diga: que adianto isso faz? / . . . / A fronteira entre o céu e o inferno tá na sua mão. / Nove milímetros de ferro. / Cusão! otário! que pôrra é você / Olha no espelho e tenta entender / A arma é uma isca pra fisgar. / Você não é polícia pra matar! / É como uma bola de neve. / Morre um, dois, três, quatro. / Morre mais um em breve. / Sinto na pele, me vejo entrando em cena. / Tomando tiro igual filme de cinema. / 'Clip, clap, bum!'" ("Rapaz Comum").

49. Examples of prisoner literature include Luiz Alberto Mendes, *Memórias de um Sobrevivente* (São Paulo: Companhia das Letras, 2001); Jocenir, *Diário de um Detento: O Livro* (São Paulo: Labortexto Editorial, 2001); André du Rap and Bruno Zeni, *Sobrevivente André du Rap (do Massacre do Carandiru)* (São Paulo: Labortexto Editorial, 2002); Antonio Carlos Prado, *Cela Forte Mulher* (São Paulo: Labortexto Editorial, 2003); William da Silva Lima, *Quatrocentos contra Um: Uma História do Comando Vermelho* (São Paulo: Labortexto Editorial, 2001).

50. "Eu tenho uma bíblia velha, uma pistola automática e um sentimento de revolta. Eu tou tentando sobreviver no inferno" ("Genesis," 1997, *Sobrevivendo no Inferno*).

51. *The Jerusalem Bible*, Reader's Edition, p. 693 (vv. 3–4). The literal translation of "Capítulo 4, Versículo 3" is "Chapter 4, Versicle 3." This seems to be the peculiar way by which the Racionais MC's refer to the psalm's verses. On the cover of the CD, each verse is called "Chapter."

52. "60% dos jovens de periferia sem antecedentes criminais já sofreram violência policial; / a cada quatro pessoas mortas pela polícia, três são negras; / nas universidades brasileiras, apenas dois por cento dos alunos são negros; / a cada quatro horas um jovem negro morre violentamente em São Paulo; / aqui quem fala é Primo Preto, mais um sobrevivente" ("Capítulo 4, Versículo 3," 1997, *Sobrevivendo no Inferno*). In this rap, the Racionais MC's use both *negro* and *preto* to refer to black people, and it would be interesting to analyze the switches. In this introductory statement, which again is spoken instead of sung, they use the politicized term *negro* three times when giving the statistics but switch to *preto* (Primo Preto, "Black Cousin") to identify themselves.

53. IBOPE is a well-known public-opinion polling firm: Instituto Brasileiro de Opinião Pública e Estatística.

54. Baixada Fluminense is a poor area of Rio de Janeiro and Ceilândia is a poor satellite city of Brasília.

55. Guaianases and Santo Amaro are neighborhoods in the periphery of São Paulo. Guaianases is on the eastern border of the city and Santo Amaro on the southern border.

56. "Minha intenção é ruim, esvazia o lugar! / Eu tô em cima, eu tô a fim, um dois pra atirar! / Eu sou bem pior do que você tá vendo / Preto aqui não tem dó, é cem por cento veneno! / A primeira faz "bum!," a segunda faz "tá!" / Eu tenho uma missão e não vou parar! / Meu estilo é pesado e faz tremer o chão! / Minha palavra vale um tiro, eu tenho muita munição! / Na queda ou na ascenção, minha atitude vai além! / E tem disposição pro mal e pro bem! / . . . / Vim pra sabotar seu raciocínio! / Vim pra abalar o seu sistema nervoso e sanguíneo! / . . . / Veja bem, ninguém é mais que ninguém, veja bem, / Veja bem, eles são nossos irmão também. / Mas de cocaína e crack, whisky e conhaque, / Os manos morrem rapidinho sem lugar de destaque! / Mas quem sou eu pra falar de quem cheira ou quem fuma / Nem dá / Nunca te dei pôrra nenhuma! / Você fuma o que vem, entope o nariz! / Bebe tudo que vê! / Faça o diabo feliz! / Você vai terminar tipo o outro mano lá, que era preto tipo A / Ninguém entrava numa, mó estilo! / de calça "Calvin Klein," tênis "Puma" / É . . . o jeito humilde de ser, no trampo e no rollé. / Curtia um funk, jogava uma bola, / Buscava a preta dele no portão da escola! / Exemplo pra nós, maior moral, "mó" IBOPE! / Mas começou "colar" com os branquinhos no shopping, / "Ai já era" . . . / Ih! Mano, outra vida, outra pique! / E só mina de elite, balada e vários drinks! / Puta de Butique, toda aquela pôrra! / Sexo sem limite, Sodoma e Gomorra! / Hã . . . faz uns nove anos . . . / Tem uns 15 dias atrás eu vi o mano . . . / Cê tem que ver, pedindo cigarro pro "tiozinho" no ponto / Dente todo "zoado," bolso sem nem um conto! / O cara cheira mal, cê ia sentir medo! / Muito louco de sei lá o quê, logo cedo! / Agora não oferece mais perigo: / Viciado, doente e fudido, inofensivo! / . . . / Irmão, o demônio fode tudo ao seu redor! / Pelo rádio, jornal, revista e outdoor, / Te oferece dinheiro, conversa com calma. / Contamina seu caráter, rouba sua alma. / Depois te joga na merda sozinho! / É . . . transforma um "preto tipo A" num "neguinho"! / Minha palavra alivia sua dor, ilumina minha alma / Louvado seja o meu Senhor! / Que não deixe o mano aqui desandar, / Ah! e nem "sentar o dedo" em nenhum pilantra! / Mas que nenhum filho da puta ignore minha lei: / Racionais, Capítulo 4 Versículo 3 ! / Aleluia! Aleluia! Racionais! / . . . Para os manos da Baixada Fluminense à Ceilândia: / Eu sei. as ruas não são como a Disneilândia! / De Guaianases ao extremo sul de Santo Amaro, / ser um "preto tipo A" custa caro! / É foda! / Não tive pai, não sou herdeiro. / Se eu fosse aquele cara que se humilha no sinal, por menos de um real, / Minha chance era pouca, / Mas se eu fosse aquele moleque de touca, / Que engatilha e enfia o cano dentro da sua boca, / De quebrada, sem roupa, você e sua mina, / Um, dois! Nem me viu! Já sumi na neblina! / Mas não . . . / Permaneço vivo, eu sigo a mística! / 27 anos, contrariando a estatística! / O seu comercial de TV não me engana, / Hã! Eu não preciso de status nem fama. / Seu carro e sua grana já não me seduz, / E nem a sua puta de olhos azuis! / Eu sou apenas um rapaz latino-americano / Apoiado por mais de 50 mil manos! / Efeito colateral que seu sistema fez, / Racionais, capítulo 4 versículo 3!" ("Capítulo 4, Versículo 3").

57. "Sabotage" is an important word in the universe of São Paulo's rap. It was also the name adopted by a São Paulo rapper who became well known for appearing in two recent movies (*O Invasor* and *Estação Carandiru*) dealing with crime in the periphery and prison life. Sabotage was shot to death in January 2003 close to his home in the southern periphery after he had accompanied his wife to her job at 6:00 a.m.

58. "Você não tem amor próprio, fulano! / Nos envergonha, pensa que é o maior. / Não passa de um sem vergonha, / Se ousar, ouse só definir sua personalidade. / Mas é inferioridade o que você sente no fundo. / Dá aos racistas imundos / Razões o bastante pra prosseguirem nos fodendo como antes. / Ovelha branca da raça, traidor! / Vender a alma ao inimigo, renegou sua cor! / Mas nosso juri é racional, não falha! / Por que? / Não somos fãs de canalha! / . . . / Me causa raiva e indignação / A sua indiferença quanto à nossa destruição! / . . . / Aqui é o Mano Brown, descendente negro atual, / Você está no júri racional e será julgado, otário! / Por ter jogado no time contrário. / . . . / Gosto de Nelson Mandela, admiro Spike Lee. / Zumbi, um grande herói, o maior daqui. / São importantes pra mim, mas você ri e dá as costas. / Então acho que sei da porra que você gosta: / Se vestir como playboy, frequentar danceterias, / Agradar as vagabundas, ver novela todo dia, / Que merda! / Se esse é seu ideal, é lamentável! / É bem provável que você se foda muito, / Você se auto-destrói e também quer nos incluir. / Porém, não quero, não vou, sou negro, não posso, / não vou admitir! / De que valem roupas caras, se não tem atitude? / E o que vale a negritude, se não pô-la em prática? / A principal tática, herança de nossa mãe África! / A única coisa que não puderam roubar! / . . . / E se avisaram sua mente, muitos da nossa gente, / Mas você, infelizmente, / Sequer demonstra interesse em se libertar. / Essa é a questão: auto-valorização. / Esse é o título da nossa revolução. / Capítulo 1: / O verdadeiro negro tem que ser capaz / De remar contra a maré, contra qualquer sacrifício. / Mas com você é difícil: você só pensa no seu benefício. / . . . / "Por unanimidade, o júri deste tribunal declara a ação procedente. / E considera o réu culpado / Por ignorar a luta dos antepassados negros / Por menosprezar a cultura negra milenar. / Por humilhar e ridicularizar os demais irmãos. / Sendo instrumento voluntário do inimigo racista. / Caso encerrado" ("Juri Racional," 1993, *Raio X do Brasil*).

59. "Derivada de uma sociedade feminista / Que considera e dizem que somos todos machistas. / Não quer ser considerada símbolo sexual. / Luta pra chegar ao poder, provar a sua moral / Numa relação na qual / Não admite ser subjugada, passam a andar pra trás. / Exige direitos iguais / E o outro lado da moeda, como é que é? / Pode crê! / Pra ela, dinheiro é o mais importante. / Sujeito vulgar, suas idéias são repugnantes. / É uma cretina que se mostra nua como objeto, / É uma inútil que ganha dinheiro fazendo sexo. / No quarto, motel, ou tela de cinema / Ela é mais uma figura viva, obscena. / Luta por um lugar ao sol, / Fama e dinheiro com rei de futebol! (ah, ah!) / Ela quer se encostar em um magnata / Que comande seus passos de terno e gravata. (otário.) / Quer ser a peça central em qualquer local. / . . . / Quer ser manchete de jornal. / Somos Racionais, diferentes, se não iguais. / Mulheres Vulgares, uma noite e nada mais! / É bonita, gostosa e sensual. / Seu batom e a maquiagem a tornam banal. / Ser a mau, fatal, legal, ruim . . . Ela não se importa! / Só quer dinheiro, enfim. / Envolve qualquer um com seu ar de ingenuidade. / Na verdade, por trás vigora a mais pura mediocridade. / Te domina com seu jeito promíscuo de ser, / Como se troca de roupa, ela te troca por outro. / Muitos

a querem para sempre / Mas eu a quero só por uma noite, você me entende?" ("Mulheres Vulgares," 1990, *Holocausto Urbano*).

60. Many books of the so-called marginal literature share this negative version of women. A clear example is the novel *Capão Pecado* by Ferréz (São Paulo: Labor-texto Editorial, 2000). In this novel, the female characters are either suffering mothers or seductive women responsible for the destruction of the men who get involved with them.

61. In the case of American hip-hop, two of the most provocative analyses of this anxiety in relation to women are Rose, *Black Noise,* and Gilroy, "After the Love Has Gone."

62. They have used the idea of *vida louca* before, but without transforming it into the same kind of symbol.

63. I thank Ana Flora Anderson, a Bible scholar, for this information and for assisting me in interpreting the biblical metaphors used by the Racionais MC's.

64. "Tira o zóio, / Tira o zóio, vê se me erra, / Eu durmo pronto pra guerra, / E eu não era assim, eu tenho ódio, / E sei que é mau pra mim, / Fazer o que se é assim, / vida loka, cabulosa, / O cheiro é de Pólvora, / E eu prefiro rosas" ("Vida Loka, Parte 2").

65. Zygmunt Bauman, cited in Gilroy, "After the Love Has Gone," p. 69.

66. Ibid., p. 70.

67. Ibid.

68. A fascinating topic still to be addressed is the relationship between the hip-hop movement and the various Pentecostal groups that have a strong presence in the periphery. This topic would include a comparison between the influence of the Catholic Church and liberation theology on the social movements and the influence of evangelic Pentecostalism on hip-hop.

69. Ferréz's talk during the cycle of debates "Metropolis XXI" at Ágora, São Paulo, 18 November 2002. See also his book *Capão Pecado* (São Paulo: Labor-texto Editorial, 2000). A question that still needs more elaboration is the influence of American hip-hop in constructing the periphery as a ghetto. The Brazilian periphery has never constituted a ghetto in the sense of the American ghetto, and residents of São Paulo, rich and poor, have never before conceived the periphery as an enclosed and excluded space similar to an American ghetto. Among hip-hop members, however, the image of the (American) ghetto is common and may be shaping their perception and construction of isolation.

70. It would be very interesting to compare hip-hop's moralistic articulation of justice with that of the corporatist state of the 1940s to 1960s. With Getúlio Vargas, workers learned that they had rights. The corporatist order that he put forward was based on the creation of legal labor rights. However, the law was not universal. Rather, it created different categories of workers with differentiated access to rights. Basically, workers entitled to labor rights were those with a legal labor contract and a profession recognized by the state. For the workers, though, rights were seen as universal but distributed according to moral criteria: they were "given" by good employers to employees who deserved them. The popular notion was that to have rights a worker had to be (morally) right and have his/her qualities recognized by a good boss. This notion was prevalent in the peripheries until the 1980s and began to be transformed only by the labor movements associated

with the social movements in the 1970s and 1980s. I discuss this topic in Caldeira, *A Política dos Outros,* chap. 4.

Discography

Racionais MC's. *Holocausto Urbano,* 1990. Zimbabue.
Racionais MC's. *Escolha o Seu Caminho,* 1992. Zimbabue.
Racionais MC's. *Raio X do Brasil,* 1993. Zimbabue.
Racionais MC's. *Sobrevivendo no Inferno,* 1997. Cosa Nostra Fonográfica.
Racionais MC's. *Nada como um Dia depois do Outro Dia,* 2002. Cosa Nostra Fonográfica.

Death Squads and Democracy in Northeast Brazil

Nancy Scheper-Hughes

BETWEEN 1964 AND 1985 Brazil was a military police state run by senior army generals. The 1964 coup, initially euphemistically described as a "revolution," ushered into power (with support from the CIA) a repressive military dictatorship that justified itself by claiming that it would stabilize a volatile and inflationary economy and a politically volatile population of rural workers. These workers were organizing in the backlands of Northeast Brazil under the Ligas Camponese (Peasant Leagues) while rural migrants to Brazil's cities settled their land problems by "invading" hillsides and other underutilized public land to create new shantytowns.

Under the tightfisted hand of the Fifth Army, Brazil's industrial economy flourished, ushering in the so-called Economic Miracle that turned the country into an economic powerhouse, the world's eighth largest economy. Not all sectors of Brazilian society benefited from the military years, however. Millions of rural workers, urban migrants, factory workers, domestic workers, as well as artists, intellectuals, and political dissidents, suffered from economic exclusions and political oppression. As for sugar plantation workers and rural migrants from the impoverished Northeast, the only economic miracle for them was that some managed to stay alive during the penitential military years.

During the late 1970s, the harshest period of the dictatorship, those suspected of subversive activities such as participation in outlawed social movements were illegally detained, "disappeared," tortured, some to their death, which forced thousands of Brazilians into exile (Archdiocese of São Paulo 1985; Amnesty International 1990). Although never approaching the horrendous situation in Argentina during the so-called Dirty War (1976–82), when the army there turned its force against ordinary citizens (Suarez-Orozco 1987), the military years in Brazil were ruthless enough,[1] the aberrations of a large and "nervous" state gone haywire. The operations of paramilitary "death squads" and the mere *rumors* of these were sufficient to frighten political dissidents into exile and the undifferentiated poor into silence.

The complicity of more affluent Brazilians with the succession of military generals derived from a belief that their country could "develop" only under authoritarian rule (Alves 1985). It was only when the "Economic Miracle" began to falter in the early 1980s that a demand for a gradual return to democratic structures emerged. But even here the military dictatorship left its mark by overseeing and managing the democratic transition (the *abertura*), which began in 1982 and culminated in the 1989 presidential elections that brought into power a mass-media-created populist named Fernando Collor de Melo, a corrupt politician from the old latifundist class who was rather quickly impeached and removed from office.

Nonetheless, during the shaky transitional years Brazil produced a new constitution (1988) that is one of the most enlightened, progressive, and admired documents of its kind. The special attention given to the social rights of women, children, prisoners, peasants, urban workers, squatters, and shantytown dwellers and to cultural and sexual minorities was a source of inspiration to other transitional democracies, including the authors of South Africa's new constitution. The famous preamble to the chapter on children's rights in the Brazilian Constitution states: "It is the duty of the family, society, and the State to guarantee the child and the adolescent, with absolute priority, the rights to life, health, food, education, leisure, professional training, culture, dignity, respect, freedom, family, and social life, and to protect them from all forms of negligence, discrimination, exploitation, cruelty, and oppression." The newfound rights of children and youth included the right to use public spaces; free expression; freedom of religion; participation in sports and leisure activities; participation in family, community, and political life; access to refuge and assistance; and freedom from violence. These same principles were adopted one year later at the UN Convention on the Rights of the Child. Once again, Brazil served as a model of radical consciousness with respect to recognizing the special needs and rights of unprotected children.

New laws were a fine beginning, but in a struggling democracy in which structural inequalities remained fierce, where authority was centralized within a weak federal state, and where "childhood" was revered for one class and despised for another (see Calligaris 1991 on the "two childhoods" of Brazil), new social and political institutions were needed to see that these rights were implemented and protected. Social movements, such as the National Movement of Street Boys and Girls (MNMMR) founded by activists and street educators, fought to organize and empower Brazil's street youth.[2] Their achievements were impressive: exposing police brutality, establishing street schools and alternative employment, fostering HIV/AIDS education and prevention, and advancing model legislation. One result was the 1990 Child and Adolescent Statute, which created

Children's Rights Councils and Child Rights' Advocates in each of Brazil's five thousand municipalities. These councils, made up of representatives from grassroots organizations, churches, commercial institutions, and local government, were meant to prevent the more egregious abuses against Brazil's millions of semiautonomous "street children"[3] and minority (mostly Afro-Brazilian) youth, who, during the military years, were routinely rounded up and thrown into state reform schools that were worse than prisons.

The paradox: during this phase of active consciousness-raising (*conscientizacão*) and "democratization," death squad attacks on vulnerable populations did not cease. They resurfaced with even greater vigor (Almeida and Berno 1991; Alvim 1991; Amnesty International 1992). By the mid-1990s it was clear that the targets of the new death squads were not only politically engaged "troublemakers," radical environmentalists, and members of Sem Terra and other militant groups but also ordinary people, most of them young, poor, semi-illiterate, and "marginal" (a term that is synonymous in Brazil with deviant and criminal). These attacks occurred in the absence of national (or even significant international) public outrage. To the contrary, public-opinion polls in Brazil showed strong popular support for social cleansing (*limpeza*) campaigns. In short, the demilitarization of Brazil's government was not accompanied by a demilitarization of everyday life.

The Racialization of Criminal Discourse

> *These violent criminals have become animals. . . . They are animals. They can't be understood any other way. That's why encounters with them can't be civilized. These people don't have to be treated in a civilized way. They have to be treated like animals.*
>
> MARCELLO ALENCAR, governor of Rio de Janeiro State, 11 May 1995, three days after state civil police officers killed thirteen suspected drug traffickers in the Nova Brasília *favela.*

Why would ordinary people accept violent attacks on street children and marginal youth as the legitimate business of the police? How does one explain this extraordinary consensus? As described in *Death without Weeping* (Scheper-Hughes 1992), the everyday experience of violence leads poor people to accept their own deaths and those of their children as predictable, natural, *cruel but usual* events. The history of authoritarian rule—whether by local landowners, political bosses, or military police—extinguished any incipient culture of protest. A deep lack of trust in the legal and judicial systems, which were largely untouched by the democratic transition, contributes to a cynical attitude toward the possibilities of real political change, as the recent scandals within President Lula's Workers' Party have reinforced.

The entrenched racism of Brazilian society, a social fact that has been successfully deflected by the Brazilian national sociology of "racial democracy" (which is at best the fleeting "sexual democracy" of the hammock or canvas cot in the maid's bedroom; see Freyre 1986), is manifest in the color of death squad victims. The crimes of the poor—of the *favela,* the housing project, and the shantytown—are viewed as race crimes, as naturally produced. Poor black youth are freely referred to as "bandits" because crime is "in their blood," because they are *bichos da Africa,* "wild African beasts." Unacknowledged class and race hatreds feed the popular support of violent and illegal actions against the poor.[4] The subtext of references to "street kids" is color-coded in "race-blind" Brazil, where most street children are black.

Meanwhile, despite democratization, Brazil lacks a viable political culture of civil rights (Zaluar 1994). The language of human rights entered Brazil in the 1980s in part through radicalized Catholic clergy who had come into contact with Amnesty International, Americas Watch, and other international "rights" organizations. In Brazil, however, claims made in terms of human rights were easily subverted by manipulating people's fears of escalating violence blamed on human rights "protectionism" toward common criminals. The problem is that while it has many surreal qualities, violence talk is not just the product of social and moral panics. The democratic transition in Brazil (as elsewhere in the world) was, in fact, accompanied by violence, a real spike in crime due to the simultaneous entry of Colombian cartels, international crime networks, and cocaine trafficking into the country.[5] The drug trade brought modern, upscale firearms into the Brazilian "ghetto" and into the hands of *favela* youth, who were readily recruited as drug couriers (Zaluar 1995; Zaluar and Ribeiro 1995; Pinheiro 1996).

As Teresa Caldeira (2000) has argued, to a great many affluent Brazilians the mere proximity of rural migrants, unemployed black and brown men, and loose children is seen as an affront to "decent" people. In response to the threat of "engulfment" by the "masses" of undifferentiated poor, once public spaces—the *rua* and the *praça*—were redefined as the *private* domain of middle-class and propertied people. The segregatory impulse is expressed in modern urban planning. The "utopian" model city in Brazil today is not Brasília, the failed experiment that looked to the vast Brazilian interior, but the internationally celebrated city of Curitiba,[6] a minutely planned, ecologically correct, public-transportation-minded community, supported by a peripheral working-class community of artisans, shopkeepers, and mechanics. The only thing "wrong" with the picture is the absence within this utopian bubble of rural migrants and the urban poor.

Marginal people (the poor and propertyless classes) are seen by a great many Brazilians, not as rights-bearing individuals, but rather as *bandidos*, public enemies, and rubbish people (*lixo*), those who often are better off dead. Thus, the introduction of human and civil rights embodied in the 1988 Constitution, promising civil liberties to the homeless, street children, vagrants, the unemployed, and prisoners, was counterintuitive to a great many people in Brazil. Every gain in civil rights law and in innovative public policies and programs was fought tooth and nail by those seeking to restrict the extension of civil rights to populations thought of as having no right to rights at all. Empowering marginals (read "criminals") was perceived as an attack on the freedom of respectable people, who began to fortify themselves inside buildings and on gated streets protected by mechanical security devices and by gun-toting armed guards (Caldeira 2000). And a strong popular backlash against the dangerous classes of subcitizens fueled "street-cleaning" campaigns, the Brazilian version of ethnic cleansing (with the support of police, political leaders, commercial firms, and armed response groups), in the *favelas, morros* (hillside shantytowns), and public-housing projects of Brazil's own inner cities.

Throughout the 1990s police and vigilante attacks on street children and marginal youth in São Paulo, Rio de Janeiro, Salvador, and Recife (see Dimenstein 1991; Milto, Silva, and Soares 1994; Louzeiro 1990; MNMMR 1991, 1992; Penglase 1993; Piccolino 1992; Vermelho and Mello 1996) produced youth mortality statistics that rivaled South Africa's during the armed struggle against apartheid (Scheper-Hughes 1996). Democratic Brazil had the demographic profile of a nation at war, which in a sense it was.

The transformation in political culture is captured in the very different feel and content of two acclaimed Brazilian films, one produced in 1981 at the close of the military years and the other in 2003, both treating the lives of marginalized youth in Brazil. Hector Babenco's *Pixote: A lei do mais fraco* (Pixote: The Law of the Weakest) is a film of social critique and political protest, a devastating exposé of the detention of streets children in brutal reform schools run by the military police. At the time, *Pixote* struck the conscience of the nation and inspired social protest. By the late 1980s, however, and well into the democratic transition, some 700,000 youths were still being housed in state correctional institutions in Brazil (Swift 1991). And in 1990 Pixote himself, the street kid turned national symbol, was shot dead in the city streets that remained his only home.

In 2003, an equally gripping Brazilian film, Fernando Merirelles's *Cidade de Deus* (City of God), presented a very different view of dangerous and endangered street children growing up in the peripheral housing projects of Rio de Janeiro: a portrait of savage, fratricidal violence among competing gangs (never mind that a few of the children are lovable and righteous). Rather than focus on the structural violence of race and class and the institutionalized violence of Brazil's police and state prisons, this film focuses on the intergenerational cycles of violence and the anarchy of the *favela* itself. It is a portrait compatible with Oscar Lewis's (1961) "culture of poverty" thesis and with a neoliberal ethos that attributes "equal agency" to all, including those with their backs up against a wall of social and economic exclusion. The film glorifies the solitary heroes who manage to escape their homes.[7]

Social Cleansing in Timbaúba

A legion of criminal children, known as thieves and glue-sniffers, and protected by the mantle of legislation appropriate to the patterns of a civilized country in the first world and consequently excessively protectionist, are free to rob and attack citizens in frank daylight. Many of these so-called minors are bearing arms and do not hesitate to use them. They practice extortion of local businesses, demanding contributions to maintain their gangs. Of course, behind these miniature bandits are the real mafia "chief's," who use them, train them, and maintain them for their own ends.
Manifesto of the Masons and Shopkeepers of Timbaúba, Pernambuco, April 2004

I first became aware of the violence practiced with impunity against young residents of the Alto do Cruzeiro, Timbaúba, in the late 1980s. Timbaúba (the "Bom Jesus da Mata" of my 1992 ethnography, *Death without Weeping*)[8] is a sprawling market town on the border of Pernambuco and Paraíba, in Northeast Brazil, a persistent pocket of the third world in Brazil and the site of my long-term anthropological and political engagements, which now span four decades. At the end of 1987 a half dozen young black men, all in trouble for minor infractions, were seized from their homes by masked men "in uniform." Two showed up dead several days later, their mutilated bodies dumped unceremoniously between rows of sugarcane. Police arrived with graphic photos for family members. "How do you expect me to recognize my man in this picture?" Elena screamed hysterically. "Ah, but this is the fate of the poor," she said bitterly some days later: "They don't even own their own bodies" (*Nem donos do corpo deles, eles estão*). Finally, "they" came late one night for the nineteen-year-old son of "Black" Irene, the boy everyone in the *favela* knew affectionately as Black De (Nego De). A death squad with ties to local police was suspected, but on this topic my shantytown friends were silent, speaking, when they did at all, in a rapid and complicated form of sign language. No one else wanted to be marked.

Even more troubling, however, was the public silence that accompanied these disappearances and deaths. The extrajudicial killing of shantytown men and street children in Timbaúba was not thought worthy of a column in the progressive "opposition" newspaper of the community. "Why should we criticize the 'execution' of *malandros* [good-for-nothings] and scoundrels?" asked a frequent contributor to the newspaper. The "Children's Judge" responded to my first tentative inquiries about the fate of several disappeared street children as follows: "How can one verify a bona fide 'disappeared' street kid from the multitude of runaways, or those who were murdered by death squads from those who died in street fights?" As for the older young men of the shantytown, those like Nego De, "executed" through some form of rough or vigilante justice, they were written off by "decent" citizens as *malandros* looking for trouble. "The police have to be free to go about their business," said Mariazinha, the old woman who lives in a small room behind the church and who takes care of the altar flowers. "They know what they're doing. It's best to keep your mouth shut," she advised, zipping her lips shut to show me. And many in the shantytown sided with the actions of the police and the death squads, commenting when one or another young thief was disappeared or murdered: "Good, one less" (*Bom—menos um*). It often escaped the tacit supporters of the Brazilian version of social and ethnic cleansing that their own sons had suffered from police brutality in prison and that the democratic reforms were meant to protect *their* social and economic class in particular.

Meanwhile, rumors surfaced about the disappearance of some street children, several of whom lived in the open-air marketplace taking shelter at night in between the stalls and under canvas awnings, foraging bits of fruit and starch from the crates and baskets. It was rumored that their bodies were wanted for spare parts to feed a growing international market in transplant organs. Roaming vans driven by medical agents for Japanese and North American medical centers were cited. On the Alto do Cruzeiro, where so many people are illiterate and where rumor is often the main source of information, everyday life has an almost *literary* quality, so that fact and fiction, event and metaphor, are often merged. While the educated classes scoffed at the organ-stealing rumors, young people in the shanty-town continued to disappear and then, some time later, to reappear dead, their bodies stripped of vital organs. "What do they want with all those body parts?" my research assistant Irene asked, certain that the death squads were working hand-in-glove not only with drug traffickers but with an organs mafia.[9] "So many of the rich are having plastic surgery and transplants we hardly know to whose body we are speaking anymore," she insisted.

Given the undeclared war against the shantytown, and the terror that prevented poor people from acknowledging even to themselves what was going on, the insecurity, the terror of it all, was expressed in bizarre and surreal ways. When the life-sized body of the Christ disappeared from the huge cross that gives the shantytown of O Cruzeiro (Crucifix Hill) its name, the more devout and simple, like Dona Amor, wondered whether Jesus, too, had not been kidnapped. The old woman wiped a stray tear from her wrinkled cheek and confided in a hoarse whisper, "They've taken him, and we don't know where they have hid him." "But who would do such a thing?" I asked. "The Big Shots" (*Os grandes*). "But why?" "Politics/Power" (*política*). Amor was referring to the politics and pathologies of power, to all the inchoate forces that accounted for the misery of their lives. *Política*—power—explained everything, including the size of one's coffin and the depth of one's grave.

The sad collusion of poor people with the authors of their own extra-judicial executions is a common phenomenon in situations of political ter-ror and instability. Perhaps the phenomenon is similar to the Stockholm Syndrome, whereby victims identify with their kidnappers or prison guards in a desperate bid for security and survival. The reluctance to speak out was reinforced by invoking the *lei de silencio*—the law of silence—and *deixa pra la,* leaving bad enough alone, as it were.

The complicity of Timbaúba's middle classes with the death squads is more consistent and "logical," if none the less devastating. The campaign of social hygiene intended to sweep the streets of its social garbage was a residue of the military years and a result of the "shock" of democratiza-tion. For twenty years the military state had kept the social classes segre-gated and the "hordes" of "dangerous" street youths contained to the *favelas* or in detention. When the old military policing structures loosened following the new dispensation, the shantytowns ruptured and poor people, especially unemployed young men and street children, descended from the hillsides and climbed up from the riverbanks and seemed to be everywhere at once, flooding downtown streets and public *praças* once the normal preserve of *gente fina* (cultivated people). The presence of the poor and working classes flaunting their misery and their "criminalized" needs "in broad daylight" and "in public" was seen as a direct assault on the social order.

Unwanted and perceived as human waste, shantytown youths and street children evoked contradictory emotions of fear, aversion, pity, and anger. Their new visibility betrayed the illusion of Brazilian modernity and made life feel very insecure for those with "decent" homes, cars, and other enviable material possessions. Excluded and reviled, the loose and abandoned street children of Timbaúba were easily recruited to work for local small-time "mafia" (as they are locally called), especially as drug messengers (*avioes*).

To repeat: death squads and vigilante justice are nothing new in Northeast Brazil (Scheper-Hughes 1992: chap. 6; Huggins 1997). During the colonial period up through the postcolonial years of the Republic, hired guns worked for sugar plantation and sugar mill owners to keep first their slaves and after abolition their debt-slaves cutting and milling sugarcane at the same levels of human misery. Then, during the military years, death squads returned in the employ of the state to deal with political dissidents. In the democratic 1990s vigilantes and *justiceiros* arose within a policing vacuum, an excessively weak state, and in the wake of a new transnational, transregional traffic in arms, drugs, and children for commercialized international adoption.

Dangerous and Endangered Youth

During fieldwork in 1992, 2001, 2004, and 2005 I turned my gaze from infant mortality to youth mortality, first following the "disappearances" and unexplained deaths of street children and later following the summary executions of other young "marginals" in Timbaúba. In 1992 (accompanied by Dan Hoffman) I followed a large and loosely defined cohort of street children who identified twenty-two of their *companheiros* (peers and buddies) who had been killed by hired guns (*pisoleiros*), by police (and thus classified as "legitimate homicides"), or by other former street children. Some had simply vanished (see Scheper-Hughes and Hoffman 1998).

Meanwhile, despite new laws that prohibit the incarceration of children and older youths in jails, we found several minors detained in Timbaúba's local jail alongside adult offenders. A former judge explained that

Street children in jail in Timbaúba, 1993. (All photos are by Nancy Scheper-Hughes)

they were being held there "for their own safety" in the absence of alternative shelters or other forms of protective custody. The youths, he explained, had been rejected by their families and were despised by local merchants, who described the younger ones as pests and flies and the older ones as criminals and bandits, whether or not they had actually committed a crime. Some of the bright-eyed children we met in jail in 1992 were indeed already "marked for extermination."

In one cell were Caju and Junior, two fifteen-year-olds whom I remembered as cute *molekes* (street urchins) who attached themselves to my field household in the mid-1980s. Since then Caju had been elected by his peers to attend the first National Convention of Street Children, held in Brasília, and his photo had appeared in a national magazine story about that historic event when street children from all over Brazil converged on the capital city to voice their grievances and to demand their human rights. Now, a few years later, Caju was imprisoned for the usual behaviors born of street life. But the "final solution" that awaited Caju was, as the judge suggested, even worse. When I next returned, in 2001, Caju was dead, the victim of summary execution, after he himself had become the member of an incipient death squad, recruited while he was still in jail. Before his release and summary execution, Caju had sent an absurd death threat to one of Timbaúba's most dedicated youth and child rights advocates, Ruth de

Lima Borba, who had been monitoring Caju's treatment in jail. In thanks
she received a letter from Caju. In his barely legible chicken scrawl, but
with all the normal Nordestinho courtesies, Caju wrote: "Dona Ruth, I
know who you are, *senhora,* and what you are doing. I have already killed
three people and I can kill more. Be careful!" As the guard at the local jail
reflected: "The life of a young marginal here is short. It's like this: for a
street kid to reach thirty years of age, it's a miracle."

More than five thousand children were murdered in Brazil between
1988 and 1990.[10] During the same period the Legal Medical Institute (the
police mortuary and forensic lab) in Recife, the state capital of Pernambuco, received the bodies of approximately fifteen children a month. Black
and brown (mixed-race) bodies outnumbered white bodies 12 to 1, and
boys outnumbered girls 7 to 1. In 80 percent of the cases the bodies had
been damaged or mutilated (Filho, Azevedo, and Pinto 1991: 42). These
routine extrajudicial executions represent an unofficial death penalty, one
carried out with chilling cruelty and without any chance of self-defense.
Official statistics identified the state of Pernambuco as the "champion" of
violence in Brazil, and Timbaúba, with a population of 57,000, as the
crime capital of the state between 1995 and 2000, with an estimated homicide rate of more than 30 per 100,000.

The state of political anarchy peaked in 2000 when an unexpected turn
of events led to the aggressive pursuit and arrest of fourteen local men associated with a single death squad (*group de extermino*) that had been terrorizing the city and its surrounding rural areas. A small band of local activists, some of them constitutionally empowered as human rights and
child rights advocates, joined forces with a fearless and headstrong
woman judge, indifferent to death threats, and a brilliant, tough-minded,
and independent *promotor* (public prosecutor) in a battle to wrest the
municipio from its murderous vigilantes.

These activists were armed with little more than the new constitution
and their passion for "human rights," a term of very recent currency in this
community, where Marxist and neo-Marxist analysis, sometimes in the
language of progressive education (as in Freire's radical pedagogy), sometimes in the language of liberation theology, was for generations the only
idiom of resistance against class and race oppression. In the face of a complicit and brutal police force, and with a general populace that was either
actively supporting the activities of the death squad or terrorized into
silent complicity, the work of these activists was something quite new and
unprecedented in the interior of Northeast Brazil. The tale of the initial
success of their struggle is worth telling, although its aftermaths indicate
that happy endings are usually premature.

Face-to-Face with Abdoral and His Guardian Angels

In the spring of 2001 I received a startling fax from Dr. Marisa Borges, a newly appointed judge, and Dr. Humberto da Silva Graça, a newly appointed public prosecutor in Timbaúba. The fax included a twelve-page report of the investigations by the prosecutor and the legal case against a man named Abdoral Gonçalves Queiroz and his band of accomplices who had been—depending on one's class position and politics—"protecting" or "terrorizing" this economically strapped interior town for the latter half of the 1990s. Abdoral's "public-security" operation, the Guardian Angels,[11] was, in the words of the prosecutor's brief, "a hyperactive death squad of hired killers—a *groupo de extermino*" charged with the executions of more than one hundred people, most of them street children and young men, poor, uneducated, unemployed, and black[12] ("You know, getting rid of all these excess people without a future," one working-class resident, still sympathetic to the local system of "popular justice" later explained to me). Prominent figures in Timbaúba society—well-known businessmen and local politicians—applauded the work of the death squad, also known as Police 2, and were themselves active in the extrajudicial "courts" that were deciding who in Timbaúba should be the next to die. Not one of these prominent citizens was detained or brought to trial; their fingerprints were not found on the smoking guns even if they had paid for the deaths, which could be purchased for as little as R$500 (US$217.00).

When a "job" was decided upon, normally in the hillside slums of Timbaúba, the vigilantes, dressed in black and armed with guns and automatic weapons, walked together in formation to their appointed destination. Doors and windows were quickly shut, and soon thereafter shots were heard. Everyone knew the assigned script: "I didn't see! I didn't hear! I don't know anything!" Depending on the gravity of the accusation, the victim might receive a warning or might simply be "rubbed out" without knowing what he was accused of. Abdoral's gang was also involved in the traffic and distribution of drugs and arms (rifles, 12-caliber guns, and pistols) throughout Northeast Brazil. The public prosecutor spoke of a "peaceful coexistence" between the parallel traffic in murder, arms, and drugs. Minors who delivered the drugs (*avioes*) were protected by Abdoral as long as they obeyed orders.

Abdoral himself came from a line of notorious outlaws. His father, Antonio Gonçalves, known as Antonio de Redes (Antonio of Hammocks), was a notorious cattle rustler and a paid gun who would shoot animals or people on demand. Antonio was the "strong man" for the powerful Heraclito family from the interior town of Limoeiro, on whose estate Antonio hid whenever the police were looking for him, which was, by all accounts, very infrequently. When Antonio killed a well-liked cowboy in the small border town of Itabaiana, he was finally arrested, brought to trial, and convicted despite ample interference by and protection from the town's most powerful businessman. When her husband was incarcerated in the agricultural prison of Itamaracá, Abdoral's mother went to work selling clothing and other sundries in the outdoor market in Timbaúba while also trying to provide protection to her three sons and daughter, who was apprenticed to her aunt, the notorious local midwife and pharmacist, Primativa, around whom many rumors of questionable conduct swirled during her long lifetime. By adolescence Abdoral had already developed a reputation as a hooligan, a marijuana and alcohol abuser, a virgin spoiler, and a petty thief. He broke benches in public plazas, harassed young girls, and was a public nuisance despite the fact that, like his father before him, Abdoral was "claimed" by an influential politician who tried to keep him out of prison if not out of trouble.

During the 1970s Abdoral was arrested for the rape and murder of a domestic (known as Tonha) who worked for the Levino Bras de Macedo family in Timbaúba, the owners of a large bakery. Tonha's body was placed on the Timbaúba train track that cut across the city. Abdoral and his accomplice (Sofonias) were tried and briefly imprisoned, but there is no record of his case in the local justice department. In addition to his natal home in Timbaúba, Abdoral acquired an impressive three-story house in Sapucaia (a scrubby new settlement on the outskirts of town) and a country house near the sugar mill of Curanji. The top floor in Sapucaia served as a lookout, while his country home functioned as headquarters for meetings with his band of killers. He also owned a garage in the small town of Ferreiros, which was used to store illegal weapons. Abdoral's wife, Fatima, herself a fugitive from the state of Alagoas, was her husband's primary accomplice, filling the role of Maria Bonita to her Lampião.[13] And very much like the notorious outlaw of the backlands, Lampião, Abdoral collected a weekly tribute from the majority of businessmen in Timbaúba, a tax to terrorize and to eliminate "problematic" individuals.

The list of Abdoral's victims included dozens of former Timbaúba street children. The following names of victims appeared in the prosecutor's brief: Jose Roberto De Lima (Nau Jabau), aged eighteen; Leonardo (Nego Leo), twenty-one; Carlos Fernando Da Silva (Nando Malaquia), eighteen; Geraldo (Coxinha), seventeen, member of a rival death squad; Antônio Belarmino (Tonho da Irmã), eighteen; Antônio (Tonho Pampa), twenty; Raimundo (Mifiu), seventeen; Isaias (Cabeleireiro), twenty; Marconi Farias, nineteen (who was assassinated with his two older brothers);

Pinana, twenty; Edson José Da Silva (Fofão), thirteen; "Peu," twenty-two; Rui, sixteen, a notorious young drug dealer; Luciano (Matuto), seventeen, member of a rival death squad; Severino, fifteen; Cláudio Júnior, eighteen; Pedrinho, twenty-two; Gilvam, nineteen; Marcos Fernandes (Marcos Malaquia), sixteen; Severino Gomes Da Silva (Guru), seventeen; Edilson, seventeen, member of a rival death squad, murdered in front of his common-law wife and children.

Abdoral's gang used intimidation, kidnappings, beatings, torture, and public execution. They staged train and car accidents and drownings and they hid the cadavers in clandestine graves in sugar plantations and in forest undergrowth. Over the years, a few members of the band were arrested and tried, but acquittals were always easily arranged by intimidating or bribing the jury members.

During the 1990s Timbaúba, a place where more than 80 percent of the population lives in deep poverty, became a primary transit point for the new regional traffic in drugs (primarily marijuana cultivated in the backlands of the arid *sertão*[14] but also counterfeit prescription drugs), arms, and stolen merchandise (motorcycles, cars, and trucks). At the same time, local brokers involved in black markets in babies preyed on young, poor, and disabled shantytown mothers to supply international adoption networks (Scheper-Hughes 1990). "Timbaúba is becoming famous for tudo que naõ presta [everything worthless]," I was told. The town's outlaw status had become so legendary that young boys took to wearing baseball caps with "#1 Mafia" sewn across the front. "What does 'Mafia' mean?" I asked a cute little street urchin who could not have been more than five years old. "I don't know—beautiful, right?" he replied.

It was in the midst of this transition that Timbaúba fell, like a ripe avocado, into the hands of Abdoral, a man who promised to deliver what the police were seen as no longer capable of providing: security and protection. Abdoral and his twenty-two-year-old right-hand man, José Eron da Silva, were of modest, but not miserable, backgrounds. They had some schooling, were literate, had wives and children and they had developed connections with powerful citizens of Timbaúba—plantation and factory owners, businessmen, police and political leaders, judges and juries. Abdoral and his men gave protection to local businesses, settled bad debts, carried out vendettas, protected stolen cargo, and ran drug and arms trafficking markets throughout the region. They could be "gentlemanly," almost courtly, as when they provided around-the-clock surveillance of a small cornmeal factory owned by the neurotic aunt of a town council member. And they could be ruthless, as when they accepted commissions to kidnap, torture, and humiliate young women caught in extramarital re-lations, such as the hapless seventeen-year-old girlfriend of a local married pharmacist ("Dr. George") who was fingered by his aggrieved wife.

But most of Abdoral's death squad activities involved condoned-neighborhood surveillance, protection, and "street-cleaning" (*limpeza*), ridding the *municipio* of vagrants, drifters, chicken thieves, troublemak-ers, sexual deviants, and, eventually, just plain poor people. Only disobe-dient drug runners in the employ of the extermination group were killed. Otherwise, local drug traffickers were safe. The small-business community of Timbaúba was grateful for the activities of the "Guardian Angels," which they saw as a gift to their social class.

As the band grew stronger, other groups and institutions fell under its control, from the mayor's office to the town council to the police to some members of the Catholic clergy. Those citizens who refused to pay for Ab-doral's protection were added to the hit list. Between 1995 and 2000 the squad killed most of Timbaúba's older male street kids. Gildete, a street-smart activist and one of the original child advocates appointed under the Estatuto da Criança e do Adolescente (the youth and adolescent codes of 1989, a major reform under Brazil's new constitution), played a strong role in providing information on the death squad to the new judge and prosecutor. She explained Abdoral's reign of terror as follows:[15]

> This "street cleaning" was ordered by businessmen. The idea was to rub
> out, to remove, all those street urchins who spent their days sniffing glue
> [*cheirando cola*], stealing, getting into trouble. They wanted them gone
> because they thought they were hurting businesses, keeping people away from
> shopping in Timbaúba. They said that business was declining because there
> were just too many "dirty flies" [street kids] in the marketplace. So Abdoral's
> group took care of them, but only after they used them. They recruited the
> kids to steal for them and to run drugs, creating a pretext to justify their
> cleanup operation and to show the shopkeepers that they really needed the
> protection they were selling.

Not only street children but those who dared to defend or shelter them or to report their deaths were executed as a warning. Such was the case of a forty-eight-year-old woman, whose violent death I found buried in death records kept at the *cartorio civil*, the privately owned municipal civil reg-istry office. Gildete recalled this execution, which had escaped the atten-tion of the judge:

> This victim, Josefa Maria da Conceicao, was actually killed by her lover, a
> former street kid himself. They were beginning to put a life together, when

suddenly he arrived home and shot her point blank. You see, she came from a poor, disorganized family and each of her three younger sisters was the mother of street kids who were "cleaned up" by Abdoral's group. As the eldest, she had the courage to seek justice. She went to the former prosecutor to lodge a complaint about the executions of her nephews and she even named the assassins. The next day her *companheiro* [partner] came home and killed her. No doubt, he was sent by the death squad to kill her. Maybe they gave him no choice.

Gildete explained a financial scam that resulted in many deaths during the late 1990s.[16] Rural people from surrounding areas came to Timbaúba on market days to purchase motorcycles and used cars on time payments. Local shop owners would take their down payments and arrange monthly installments, promising to deliver the receipts and registration materials after the last payment. But when the buyers requested the documents, the shopkeepers would pay Abdoral to have them killed, and then they would repossess the cars and motorbikes, claiming that they had been stolen.

When there was no concerted effort to stop them, Abdoral and his men became bolder. They began to conduct their activities in public, flamboyantly and in the company of high-profile citizens, members of the commercial and landed classes. Eventually, the mayor and members of the town council capitulated to the death squad. No one dared to raise a voice in protest when Abdoral's gunmen showed up at the town hall (the *prefeitura*) to collect their tribute from the city council or when Abdoral was seen in bars and restaurants hobnobbing with the mayor. Indeed, by the late 1990s no one in Timbaúba knew exactly where the local government began and where the death squad ended. Inevitably, the band of outlaws wormed their way into all levels of local government and gained control over the local police station and the courthouse. They assumed the functions of public administration, policing, and the judiciary. As Dr. Humberto put it: "The extermination group had become Timbaúba itself."

Things veered so out of control that at the 7 September (Seite de Setembro) national-holiday parade in 2000, Abdoral and a dozen of his men wearing matching jackets decorated with the insignia "Security: Guardian Angels" led the marchers, with the mayor and town council members in tow. They usurped the role normally filled by civil police. Thus, they brazenly announced in public their semiofficial role as a paramilitary unit. In short, the death squad became an official organ of the city.

Before Abdoral's reign of terror was interrupted, somewhere between one hundred and two hundred people had been murdered, execution style.[17] In a small town like Timbaúba, the death toll was like an *intifada,* but the "state of emergency" that existed in this backwater place would never be covered by the national, let alone international, media. Similar events were occurring elsewhere in Brazil, especially in urban slums, where gangs and drug lords also ruled the roost and exacted tribute and decided who should die. But *favelas* are not administrative units or *municipios*, and the fall of an old plantation town, known regionally for its small plantations and sugar mills, its failing shoe factories, and its handwoven, workaday hammocks, under the sway and thrall of a sociopathological death squad is, I believe, a unique instance.

Toward the end, Abdoral's band became involved in providing protection to highway robbers. Guardian Angels, dressed in black with insignia armbands, were observed providing armed escorts to truckloads of stolen and contraband merchandise. The squad began to be perceived as dangerous robber barons rather than the folk heroes of small businessmen. It had begun to exceed the outer limits of acceptability and its "usefulness" to the landowning agricultural and commercial classes. Emboldened, the Guardian Angels began to demonstrate their fascist tendencies in their loathing of "deviant" white working-class and middle-class people in addition to the more socially acceptable targets of hatred: poor blacks, the illiterate, the vagrants, and poor sick people. Sexual transgressors and sexual outlaws (public homosexuals, *travesti* [cross-dressers], and cross-racial and cross-class lovers) fell under their purview, under an alien code of puritanical morality that was not embraced by most Brazilians, even in this corner of rural Northeast Brazil. Had Abdoral and his gang kept their activities contained to the *favelas,* shantytowns, and rural "villas of misery" around Timbaúba they might still be in control today.

Anthropology and Human Rights

The fax I spoke of earlier caused considerable consternation in the Scheper-Hughes household. It included a request for me to return to Timbaúba to put my anthropological skills to work in supporting the human rights vanguard in its efforts to recapture the *municipio* from vigilantes. As Judge Borges explained the mission: "We are trying to restore 'the rule of law' and to extend basic rights to all the people of Timbaúba, including the shantytowns and peripheral rural districts." The choice of words—rule of law, basic rights, etc.—was jarring. It sounded odd, almost like promotional materials from Amnesty International or the Open Society Institute. Then came the question: "Will you join us in the struggle?"

Specifically, Judge Borges and Dr. Graça wanted my help in identifying the many still-unknown and unidentified victims and survivors of the death squad. The relatives of victims and survivors were afraid to come forward and testify. They did not trust the police or the courts. Thus, only a fraction of the executions had come to the attention of the public prosecutor and the judge. Some of the victims' bodies were buried in unmarked graves owned by small, Protestant churches. Some of the deaths were registered at the privately owned municipal registry office. I was asked to identify the hidden victims of the death squads by using the same skills I had employed in uncovering infant and child mortalities.

I hesitated. Was this an appropriate role? At what point does one leave anthropology behind and join a frankly political struggle?[18] Or was this a false dichotomy, as Pierre Bourdieu argued when he called for scholarship *with* (rather than opposed to) commitment.[19] In the end I really did not have a choice. I was already implicated in the arrests. Dr. Humberto Graça, the prosecutor, explained that my writings on "everyday violence" and on violence against young black men and street children of the Alto do Cruzeiro were noted in the proceedings against Abdoral and his band. Although I was unable to interest a Brazilian publisher in a Portuguese edition of my book, a Spanish translation of *Death without Weeping* (1997) had reached members of the local intelligentsia and emerging human rights communities in rural Pernambuco. Meanwhile, local activists in Timbaúba had a high school teacher produce a rough translation of chapter 6, "Bodies, Death, and Silence," which was copied and distributed to the judge, prosecutor, and local police force of Timbaúba.[20]

Thus, nearly a decade after its publication in English, some members of the local community had access to my then still rudimentary analysis of what was, at the time of my writing, a small and incipient death squad, restricted largely to poor and shantytown neighborhoods where the executions were protected by a culture of terror and a political culture of impunity. Brazil's democratic transition was incomplete, I argued, and the failure of the Economic Miracle to "trickle down" to the vast majority left the community vulnerable to urban violence, drugs, and crime. It was little wonder that social banditry and vigilante justice (see Hobsbawm 2000; Scheper-Hughes 1995) gave people a false sense of security, of "order and progress," the elusive promise of Brazilian modernity. At the time I could see no way out of the vicious cycle of poverty, hunger, crime, and vigilante violence. Brazil's new democracy seemed illusory, a cruel ruse played on the excluded and "deviant" majority.

I had not anticipated the opportunities afforded by the new constitution and its "bourgeois" vision of "human rights" and the institutions it allowed to flourish, including the watchdog positions created to protect the rights of children and other vulnerable people. In Timbaúba, those elected or appointed to fill the roles of child rights counselors and human rights advocates were largely working-class or "popular" intellectuals lacking professional credentials, material resources, or symbolic capital. Nonetheless, these rights workers mobilized around the Constitution to begin to rescue the endangered population of street children and unemployed young men of the shantytowns, the main targets of Abdoral's "hygienic exterminations."

The work of these organic intellectuals was slow and anything but steady, interrupted by police and government crackdowns during the military and even the postmilitary years. Nonetheless, rights workers gained force and courage, although they had to operate through networks of trust that were often betrayed by pernicious class interests. Those involved included radical lawyers, Catholic nuns, Marxist intellectuals, ordinary working-class and middle-class individuals who could no longer tolerate

Marcos (a child rights
activist) and a street child,
Timbaúba, 2005.

the egregious violations of justice and human rights. One is a local pharmacist in her early seventies. Another was a *farinha* (manioc flour) salesman in the market of Timbaúba before he became a poor people's lawyer. Another was the son of a failed shoe factory owner. One is a woman who grew up with local street kids and who talks rough and wears low-cut dresses. She, too, is planning a late-life career in civil rights law. Another is a German nun who works closely with a local black educator and rights activist. The activists are black, white, and in-between. It is politics, not race, that runs in their veins. They are married, single, celibate . . . and in-between. They are devout Catholics, skeptical agnostics, and quiet atheists. They have met over the years in small rooms to share dog-eared paperbacks and pamphlets. They read and passionately debate Marx, Gramsci, Leonardo Boff, the Scriptures, Paulo Freyre, Celso Furtdao, and Cristovan Buarque. They are critical thinkers and astute strategists who use the techniques of the *bricoleur,* taking advantage of every possibility, every theoretical or practical opening at hand. They make political alliances and just as quickly break them. They do not have reliable access to e-mail or the Internet. They campaigned and voted for Lula and had their hopes dashed when Lula cut deals and made coalitions with the forces of the old regime. While not cynical, they never expect to succeed, and when they do, they are quick to disparage their victories, mindful that optimism must be tempered by the expectancy of reversals and betrayals.

Among their initial successes was a program that took them to the streets to identify and gather up Timbaúba's most threatened street children into a safe house run in large part by the older children themselves and following the philosophy of empowerment espoused by the MNMMR and the new child and adolescent statutes. They worked diligently to expose a corrupt judge and prosecutor who were linked to commercial international child-trafficking adoption networks that preyed upon the poorest and weakest women of the community.

On my return to Timbaúba in the summer of 2001, accompanied by my husband, Michael, who is a clinical social worker with many years experience working in the field of violence against children, we took up residence in the community center run by Irma Sofia and her circle of local human rights and children's activists. As usual, the residents of Timbaúba had very mixed views about the activists' efforts. Many in the larger community had grown accustomed to the protection that the Guardian Angels seemed to provide in the absence of a "strong" or "efficient" police force, and they referred to the death squad terrorists as *justiceiros,* representatives of popular justice. A taxicab driver said, "Look, these people are like us, they came

Biu, whose son, Gilvam, was
murdered by Abdoral and
his death squad in 2000.

from the base [the grass roots]. The police should not have arrested them.
If there was no peace under the *justiceiros,* today there is even more street
violence. Now the police have their hands tied by the new woman judge
and the little bandits [street kids] are again free to roam the street."

For those residing on the two hillside slums of Alto do Cruzeiro and Independencia, the hardest hit by Abdoral and his men, the near nightly executions had turned them into shut-ins, living under self-imposed curfews.
Many recalled with horror a night in 1999 when six people were murdered
on the Rua do Cruzeiro, the principal street of the Alto. "During the revolution," Black Irene said, using the local idiom to describe the terror as a
war or revolution against the poor, "we all went underground. The streets
were deserted; we kept our doors locked and our wooden shutters closed
tight. We would slide in and out our back doors to go to work or to the
fields or to the market. You never knew when the exterminators might appear or why someone had been fingered." Irene knew well enough, having
lost two sons and her husband during the earlier phase of death squad activities in Timbaúba.

Biu, my fifty-six-year-old friend and key informant of many years, was among the last in Timbaúba to lose a family member to Abdoral's extermination group. Emaciated from cancer, her face drawn and her skin stretched tight as a drum over her high cheek bones, Biu explained how her twenty-four-year-old son had met his untimely end walking home along the main road leading up to the top of Alto do Cruzeiro. It was just after Christmas in 2000 and Gilvam was returning from a party. Neighbors heard the shots and screams, but they were too frightened to leave their homes. The next morning it was left to Gilvam's older sister, Pelzinha, to discover what was left of his body, sprawled over a mound of uncollected garbage. A crowd of greasy winged vultures had discovered Gilvam first, and Pelzinha could barely recognize her brother.

Well seasoned by a lifetime of traumatic events, including the suicide of a first husband, physical abuse, desertion by a second husband, and the deaths of several of her infants and toddlers, Biu was stoic, elliptical, and ambivalent about the murder of her son. She began with a disclaimer: "Gilvam was no angel. My family had turned against him, saying he was no good, a brawler, a drinker, and a thief who was always getting into trouble. In one fight he even lost an eye. But when they say to me that

Gilvam as a child working in the cane fields with his mother (back to the camera) in 1987.

Gilvam really had to be killed, I feel dead inside. He was still my son! But I can't tell anyone, except you, how much I miss that boy. My own niece said, 'Be grateful, *tia,* for the little bit of tranquillity that Gilvam's death has brought into your life.' What does she understand?"

The Banalization of Violent Death

In addition to collecting testimonies from old shantytown friends who had resisted going to the police or the court with their stories, I returned to my old stomping ground, the civil registry office, located in the municipal courthouse of Timbaúba. There, Michael and I reviewed all the dully and officially registered deaths from 1995 to 2000, the height of Abdoral's reign of terror. Officially recorded homicides represented, of course, only the tip of the iceberg, as most extrajudicial killings were disguised as accidents, suicides, and train- and car-related deaths. Many homicides were not registered at all and the bodies hidden in small, clandestine graves in the rural surrounds. The public prosecutor, Dr. Graça, explained: "One method used by Abdoral and his gang was called the Dragnet. He or his agents would beat up or shoot the targeted minor and then drag him into a car and take him to what would become his grave in a secret locale, often on the border of Paraíba, especially near Itabaiana and Itambé [small towns near Timbaúba], but unmarked graves were also found in Condado, Aliança, and Macaparana."

Gildete reviewed the data we gleaned from the death registry books, adding her own interpretations and recollections:

> Yes, this man you have down here, Sergio Pedro da Silva, he sure was a crazy kid, suffering from mental problems. He lived in the streets of Timbaúba since he was a child. Then suddenly he showed up dead. The people who saw what happened said that a sugarcane truck came rumbling down the street and just then there was a lot of commotion and traffic. It looked like Sergio just threw himself underneath the truck loaded with its cargo of sugarcane. We knew that the people were afraid to say that he was thrown under that truck. One of the main techniques of the death squads was to conceal the execution because if they just shot them there would be too many witnesses. So, instead, they invented accidents. Sometimes they pushed them into traffic and sometimes they shot them and then threw them under train cars or cars passing on the highway. That way they always had an alibi so that the police who really knew what was going on could say that the person died in an accident. With your list, we can go back to the police and reopen these cases.

In all, our search through death records at the registry office led to the identification of an additional thirty-one homicides that appeared to be linked specifically to Abdoral's "exterminations." In most cases, the police had not even been alerted. The relative of the deceased would arrive at the registry office and report the name, age, and cause of death—firearms, knife, beaten unconscious, concussion, whatever the case might be—to Amintina, the discreet record keeper. No questions asked, the death certificates would be signed and stamped with the municipal seal and the information was shelved. The only reason for reporting the deaths was so that the deceased could be buried in a free plot at the municipal graveyard. No one wanted any trouble with the law—which at that time happened to be the death squad itself.

Initially, I pretended to be looking for infant and child mortalities, reprising my familiar role in the civil registry office. After a few weeks however, I had to explain to the proprietor of the records what we were looking for, and although she expressed no emotion, she began to facilitate my search in subtle ways. "Here, look at this," she would say, shoving a book toward me with a particular page open.[21] A total of ninety-three homicides were recorded via handwritten entries in the monthly ledgers of the Timbaúba civil registry office between 1995 and 2000, roughly nineteen per year. Few of these murders were investigated, which is hardly surprisingly considering both the social invisibility of the victim population, on the one hand, and the likely involvement of civil and military police linked to Abdoral's death squad, on the other. The majority of recorded homicides were of young men between the ages of fifteen and thirty. The youngest homicide victim was a boy of twelve, and the oldest a man of forty-one. The average death squad victim, a subset of all homicides in Timbaúba, was a twenty-six-year-old black (*negro*) or mulatto (*moreno*) male, unemployed or casually employed and residing in one of the "informal" settlements on the hillsides and peripheries of Timbaúba. In the early 1990s most homicides were of street kids and vagrants; toward the end of the decade the homicides included those who had gotten tangled up in petty crimes, sexual and/or personal vendettas, and drug deals.[22] We presented our report on "likely" death squad victims to Dr. Graça, the public prosecutor, and to the Ministry of the Public in Timbaúba to be used in continuing investigations and arrests. But our work was not finished.

Camanhada contra Morte—The March against Death Squads

Our status as outsiders and our highly visible and matter-of-fact involvement in the ongoing criminal investigations was seized upon by the human rights vanguard of Timbaúba as a useful tool toward building a broader-based anti–death squad coalition. Our conspicuous note-taking on violent deaths, our open conversations in public spaces, and our visits to the homes of death squad victims and survivors flew in the face of the normal regime, which Dr. Graça described as "the law of silence, the law of 'let it be,' and the law of forgetting" (*a lei do silencio, a lei do deixa pra la, e a lei do esquecimento*) adhered to by most members of the community. The time seemed ripe, the activists felt, for a public denunciation of the death squad. A meeting called by the rights activists brought together a larger group of political leaders, teachers, and officials from the local Ministries of Education, Justice, and the Public, who planned a public demonstration, a *camanhada*, or march, against death squad violence and to declare a truce and a time of peace.

The unique event was held on 19 July 2001, marking one year following the arrest of Abdoral and several of his accomplices. While most residents were still too fearful of, or complicit with, the death squads (some members of which were still at large) to join the march, the municipal secretary of education declared the day a public-school holiday, and she herself fearlessly led the town's grade school children and adult school youths in the march down the main streets of Timbaúba. She was joined by a few brave citizens, including José Carlos Araújo, a bold radio journalist well known in the region for his popular freewheeling daily talk show on "community radio" (poor people's public radio), and his wife, Maria do Carmel. Although the day was miserably "cold" and rainy, hundreds of residents came out of their homes to watch the unheard-of event from the sidewalk, registering their amazement and their excitement that it could be happening in Timbaúba. A small rented sound truck accompanied the procession, with Marcelo, the poor people's lawyer, doing his best to animate the event and to call others from the sidelines to join the march against death. His broadly accented Nordestinho voice, announcing an "end to the reign of terror" and declaring a "cease-fire in the war against the poor" in Timbaúba, made him particularly vulnerable. But none were more vulnerable than the front lines of the demonstration, which were reserved for the surviving cadre of local street children, who were dressed in white, each carrying a wooden cross bearing the name of a sibling or a friend who had been executed by Abdoral's gang. Following immediately behind them were about two dozen women, the mothers, older sisters, aunts, and wives of the men and boys who had been murdered, making public for the first time what had happened to them. My closest friends on the Alto do Cruzeiro—Biu, Black Irene, Marlene, Tereza, and Severina— were among them, Irene laughing and shaking her head in disbelief that she could be so brave as to protest "in front of the world" the execution-

The march against death squads, led by street children, Timbaúba, July 2001.

murders of her husband and two young-adult sons. Biu was a more reluctant protester and she shyly hid herself in the midst of the others, refusing at first to carry the cross with the name of her murdered son, Gilvam. Thus, we took turns carrying the sign for her and to honor her executed son.

Suddenly, two heavily armed police jeeps appeared at the front of the march as though intending to interrupt it. Stifled cries of warning split the protestors in half, with the front lines of street children and human rights workers taking one street and the teachers and public-school children taking another. There was a moment of panic. Would the newly installed and human rights–trained police force show their true colors and turn on the demonstrators and open fire? But instead and to our relief, amazement, and delight, the police were going to accompany and protect the marchers. Moreover, inside one of the jeeps was the shackled figure of Abdoral Gonçalves Queiroz himself, who the police put on view before the marchers, forcing the leader of the death squad, his head initially bowed, to snap to attention and witness the spectacle of raised crosses bearing the names of the victims that he and his gang had brutally and wantonly murdered. Later, we learned that Judge Borges had arranged this dramatic "confrontation" as a display of the power of the law and a visible sign that the new police force would represent all the people of Timbaúba, even street kids and "marginals" from the *favelas* and peripheral, informal settlement of Timbaúba.

The march terminated in front of the town hall (*prefeitura*), and spontaneous, if somewhat nervous, speeches were made by the new mayor, who had replaced the corrupt former mayor and his henchmen, who had been allies of Abdoral and his gang. The current mayor and his staff were presented with a large brass plaque memorializing the end of the most recent reign of terror in Timbaúba. The organizers of the march requested that the plaque be placed on the wall of a small public square that faced the town hall and that they hoped could be renamed the Praça de Paz. The plaque read: "With the Gratitude of the People of Timbaúba for All Those Who Fought against Violence and for Human Rights. Commemorating One Year of Peace, July 19, 2001."

What made this march a politically significant event? It was unique enough that Brazilian national radio and television (Rede Globo) sent reporters to film the demonstration and to interview some of the participants and spectators. That evening people gathered on the Alto do Cruzeiro in groups at the few homes with operable television sets to observe the interviews with local residents, including residents of the Alto do Cruzeiro, along with the wrenching profile of an emotionally overwrought middle-class woman, the adoptive mother of a teenage girl who had been kidnapped and tortured by Abdoral's gang. As Holston (2001) has noted, citizenship includes the right to be visible and to be heard, the freedom to participate openly in politics and social movements in the public sphere. The claiming of these rights by "disgraced" and stigmatized populations residing in peripheral neighborhoods is new, and Holston's term "insurgent" citizenship captures the "revolutionary" feeling of those participating for the first time in public protest. Among other things, citizenship is about the right of *public* self-representation, self-expression, the right to be seen, and the acknowledgment of being seen. The television coverage represented a "coming out" (to the public) and "the public eye," underscoring the importance of seeing and being seen in the affirmation of the citizen-subject. For the mothers and wives of the death squad victims, the *camanhada* was their coming-out party. It made them feel strong and courageous, which of course they were.

Epilogue: A Death Foretold
And so, for the first time, I returned from the field with a relatively happy ending to a sad saga. I knew, of course, that violent deaths would not cease in Timbaúba, but at least for a time they would not be organized

by roving bands of professional paramilitary death squads. Although I checked in with my friends from time to time, my subsequent field trips to Brazil took me elsewhere and were concerned with human trafficking for organs.

While in Recife in February 2004 giving testimony at a parliamentary investigation of a gang of human traffickers who had infiltrated the slums and recruited desperately poor men to serve as paid kidney donors in Durban, South Africa (see Scheper-Hughes 2006), a contingent of human rights workers from Timbaúba arrived at the open session to relay discouraging stories of Abdoral and his henchmen, who were rearming themselves in jail and communicating with local bandits via cell phones, which are sometimes allowed to prisoners as a constitutional right. They also intimated that new death squads were forming, that Dr. Humberto Graça had been reassigned and Judge Marisa Borges, without Graça's moderating presence, was becoming something of a liability, a "cowgirl judge," brave but belligerent and less than a well-informed and dependable resource for the community. Some in the loosely formed group of human rights activists were receiving anonymous death threats, and they were feeling betrayed, subject to local "double agents," powerful citizens (especially in the local business community, the "commercial class," as they put it) who were playing dirty, appearing to support the rule of law and the rights of the poor but who actively supporting hired guns and arms traffickers from behind the scenes. A huge cache of arms, including illegal and restricted automatic weapons, had been discovered in the warehouse of a local shopkeeper, an affable fellow who sold children's toys, party favors, and cheap sports equipment. Additional stockpiles of illegal weapons and bullets were found in the garages of his friends and neighbors. The ringleader was arrested, tried, and convicted, but would his conviction and his prison sentence "stick"? My friends doubted it. "He has friends all the way up," said Marcelo. Even more personally tragic was their report of the death of my age-mate and friend, Biu, mother of fifteen children, only six of whom survived, hunger and diarrhea taking some of the little ones and bullets taking a few of the older ones, including her "baby," Gilvam. Is there a term for poetic injustice? If so, it applies to Biu's death from uterine cancer and multiple-drug-resistant tuberculosis.

Meanwhile, Edilson, the twenty-one-year-old son of Tereza and Manoel, whose mournful photo as a small wasted child in *Death without Weeping* predicting his own early death, was (I learned) apprehended by police for an aggravated assault with a deadly weapon on a young woman, a neighbor known to him and with whom he had no enmity. Edilson bran-

dished the gun in her face and made off with her plastic string bag containing nothing of material value unless one counted (as the criminal case
against him did) a personal diary, a note pad, two audio cassettes, two
bottles of common medicine, one religious medal, a book of raffle tickets,
a hair barrette, two strings of rosary beads, a prayer book, and three small
booklets of *cordel* folk poetry.[23] Edilson was caught red-handed, interrogated, and confessed his crime. He said he had found the revolver, broken
and nonfunctional, in a pile of street garbage. He patched it together with
masking tape. He had no ammunition. He is serving a three-year prison
sentence in a distant interior city. Edilson represents everything the local
death squads were determined to eliminate: he is sickly, underweight, uneducated, unemployed, and (the unfairness of the Fates) ugly (hence his
nickname "Becudo," a reference to his pinched-in, beaklike face).

Despite these discouraging reports, I still wanted to sing the praises of
this small band of rugged, ragtag "rights workers" who demonstrated
that, despite well-reasoned anthropological critiques of the limits and
deficiencies of constitutional and/or universal declarations of civil and
human rights (such as the UN Proclamation on the Rights of the Child),
these discourses can empower and enable (as Margaret Mead famously
put it) thoughtful and committed citizens trying to transform the world in
which they live.

Then, a few months after my meeting with the Timbaúba contingent in
Recife, word reached me of a death that could have been foretold. Timbaúba's loose cannon, the popular (indeed populist) working-class hero
and community radio talk show host José Carlos Araújo, was shot in the
chest, belly, and mouth by two young gunmen on motorbikes who am-
bushed Araújo at 7:30 p.m. on 24 April 2004 (during Holy Week) outside
his home in Timbaúba and in view of his wife, Maria do Carmel, and his
three children. The thirty-seven-year-old folk musician (he and his wife
and children performed *forro* music for dance parties throughout the
region) turned truth teller and "voice of the poor" had made enemies in
Timbaúba after denouncing the continued existence of death squads run
by criminal gangs and, even worse, revealing the involvement of well-
known local figures and businessmen in wanton murders in the region.
The local police later captured one of the suspected assassins, nineteen-
year-old Elton Jonas Gonçalves, who confessed to killing Araújo because
the journalist had accused him on the air of being a bandit. Gonçalves told
the local police chief that he did not commit *all* the crimes Araújo accused
him of and he resented the journalist for giving him a bad reputation on
the Alto de Independence, where he lived.

On my return in July 2005 I resumed my meetings with the dispirited activists of Timbaúba. Marcelo brought me to the home of Maria do Carmel and her grieving family. There, I had to confront the role of the rights activists—and our march against silence—in further inciting Maria's husband to name and disclaim Timbaúba's deadly killers. She gave me copies of his taped radio programs leading up to his death. In one of these José Carlos, in a fit of fury, screamed:

> People from Alto do Cruzeiro are calling us and giving us details about the murder of a young man from the Alto. I'll pass this information along to the police, to the sheriff, and his team. People are outraged! The boy was shot and killed last Saturday, about 7:30 a.m. in public in the open market! No kidding! . . . [the informants] are not yet ready to reveal the name of the assassin, but this guy knew what he was doing. The police patrol begins at 8 a.m., and he did his business at 7:30 a.m.! In other words, he is very smart. He uses his intelligence to do evil, to commit crimes. He could use his same skills for good deeds . . . but evil begets evil, and the police won't be demoralized forever. The [common] people will put pressure on the police, and they won't eat dust forever. They will eventually blow up, they will lose their patience and use the

Poster of José Carlos Araújo, thirty-seven, a grassroots journalist for Radio Timbaúba FM (community radio), who was killed by hired gunmen on 24 April 2004 outside his home and in the presence of his wife and children. Araújo hosted a popular talk show, *José Carlos Entrevista*, on which he had often denounced the involvement of well-known local figures in death squad murders in the region. July 2005.

power they have, within the law, to catch him. . . . I don't give a damn about
bandits or bums. They should all go to hell to smoke Satan's pipe. If the police
don't arrest him, even better. I hope they send him off [kill him]! If he had
respected fathers and good citizens, I would shut up. But this guy does evil in
his own community; he kills a father from his own neighborhood. To reign
in a community of poor people is not bravery, it's cowardly!

Some days later in a conversation with Timbaúba's chief of police the following dangerous exchange took place on the air:

CHIEF OF POLICE: I want to give a personal message to Antonio de Joana,
from the Alto do Independencia. Dr. Guilherme [a local businessman] and
I were up there on the Alto after a meeting last Friday looking for him
until 3:45 a.m. Then we spent all of Saturday looking for him. If it weren't
for the 'warning' sounded by a friend, we would have arrested him. But
don't worry, we'll catch you next time.

JOSÉ CARLOS: So, now he's the one, the latest cause of all evil, is that it?

POLICE CHIEF: Yes, he's been trying to get everyone from Alto de Independencia in trouble, but he should know that [we] are on his tracks and will
find him sooner or later. That's also true for Pio and Jonas. We know that
Jonas is bringing in people [reinforcements] from Recife, but it doesn't
matter: Antonio de Joana, Pio, and Jonas will fall any day now.

JOSÉ CARLOS: . . . So beware Pio, Jonas, and Antonio de Joana, you are all
in trouble. I always say that bandits and outlaws don't have much time
to live; you either end up in jail or in hell! Any day now! Today's show is
over. I'll be back tomorrow to talk more about violence.

In one of his final programs before the voice of the people was silenced for-
ever, José Carlos seems to be prepared for his end and bids farewell to the
people of Timbaúba and the surrounding areas:

My friends, I do my duty with a clear conscience. . . . But now it's time to
return to reality, to the world of God, a world where I will never be betrayed.
. . . At the end of my program I always say that life is very good, but it also
has difficult times. The way out of hard times is never to bow your head—
quite the opposite—it is time to rise up and keep going. Victory cannot be
bought or stolen. The sorrow and tears of being vanquished are more valuable than the shame of not participating in this journey and this struggle. And
it is constantly fighting for victory where you will find me later, anywhere,
anytime, at any corner, and you will say, "José Carlos, you were right." . . .
From the bottom of my heart I wish that God will be your main guide and
give you reason to live through difficult times.

As the ballad of "Frankie and Jonnie" ends, so does this tale about banditry and death squads in democratic Brazil, a story that has no (certain or stable) moral, and a story that has no end—at least not in the sight of this chastened anthropologist-*companheira*.

Notes

This essay was made possible through collaborative work with the human rights activists of Timbaúba, Brazil: Irma Sofia Christa Maria Salanga, Tânia, Rute Borba, Joao Marcelo Gomes Ferreira, Gildete, Celma Vasconcelos, and all the members of the Conselho de Direitos Humanos. Dr. Marisa Borges and Dr. Humberto da Silva Graça were inspirational in their moral courage and deep integrity. The members of the Union of the People of Alto do Cruzeiro and the Clube das Maes (Mothers Club) of Alto do Cruzeiro continue to struggle and to affirm their right to live while choking on their swallowed grief following the hundreds of "small wars and invisible genocides" that have turned their infants into angel babies and their sons into the living targets of race and class hatred in democratic Brazil. An earlier, brief, and more optimistic version of this essay, "Death Squads and Democracy in Northeast Brazil—Mobilizing Human Rights Discourses in the Defense of Children," was published in the 2004 annual report of the Harry Frank Guggenheim Foundation. Funding for the field research was provided by the Center for Latin American Studies of the University of California, Berkeley.

1. In 1985 an unofficial Truth Commission sponsored by Cardinal Arns, archbishop of São Paulo, with the support of the World Council of Churches, concluded that 125 people disappeared for political reasons between 1964 and 1979, an absurd underestimate of the violence suffered by Brazilian citizens under the military regime. Later estimates conducted by human rights organizations put the number of political deaths linked directly to the military dictators at 480. But these numbers do not include paramilitary death squad murders of "no account" people in rural areas who were seen as "enemies of the state" by virtue of their very existence. In 2003, the federal government reinstated the Commission on Dead and Missing Political Activists, which is linked to the Special Secretariat for Human Rights, for the purpose of indemnifying the relatives of victims of the military regime.

2. MNMMR 1991 and Alvim 1991 provide a rich chronology on the major events, including the work of human rights–oriented street educators and activists—denouncements, demonstrations, studies—that influenced the government to define measures to combat the violence against children. (Thanks to Benedito dos Santos for alerting me to these references.)

3. "Street children" is a global nongovernmental organization folk classification. Brazilian human rights activists include under the designation both children who live on the streets (*meninos da rua*) and children who may have a home but spend most of their day on the streets (*meninos na rua*).

4. As in the United States, the ugly and persistent legacies of colonial plantation slavery in Brazil have never been reckoned with, and those scholars who dare to link contemporary social problems in either country to that "long ago" historical period are accused of sociological naivety and/or anthropological nostalgia,

while political leaders in Brazil or the United States who call for national reparations are summarily dismissed on the grounds of the biological and racial diversity in their countries. Would social whites with black ancestry qualify for reparations?

5. Edmundo Campos Coelho (1988) argues that, until the 1960s, bank assaults were virtually unknown in urban Brazil, as were kidnappings for ransom. Drug dealings existed but lacked the well-structured network and entrepreneurial organization that emerged later, in the 1990s. In Rio de Janeiro and São Paulo, crime was basically an individual activity. While a few decades ago homicides were predominantly "crimes of passion," today homicides are an organized activity occurring within the conflict between drug-dealing gangs, clandestine death squads, and police (1988: 145). "Extermination squads," which had first targeted adults accused of being local criminals, later pointed their revolvers at the heads of children and adolescents. (Thanks to Benedito dos Santos for alerting me to this reference.)

6. See "Curitiba, Brazil: Three Decades of Thoughtful City Planning," www .dismantle.org/curitiba.htm.

7. In the 1960s Oscar Lewis developed the "culture of poverty" concept to describe the self-perpetuating aspects of entrenched poverty, its intergenerational and gestational aspects. His beautifully rendered but disturbing life histories of urban poor families in Mexico, Puerto Rico, and prerevolutionary Cuba analyzed the proximate and devastating consequences of poverty rather than the structural and political causes of the social disintegration described. Lewis failed to show the relations between structure and human action, although he clearly recognized that cycles of poverty could be broken by infusions of revolutionary optimism and revolutionary action. Lewis, in my view, was unfairly and selectively misread by both the political Left and Right in the United States.

8. I no longer believe that "protecting" the communities in which we work via pseudonyms is a defensible or ethical practice. Most pseudonyms are transparent in any case and only trivialize the people and communities studied. At best they offer a cover to the anthropologist/ethnographer. Those who are the targets of death squads and other forms of violence are hardly put at risk by traditional academic writings that are hardly read in English by academics let alone in Portuguese by the organizers of extermination groups.

9. When the organ traffickers did come to the slums of Recife in 2003, the men who were lured into traveling abroad to sell a kidney in Durban, South Africa, to Israeli transplant patients flown in by Israeli-based traffickers told me that, having grown up with organ-stealing stories, they were not so shocked by meeting the organ brokers in the flesh. See Nancy Scheper-Hughes 2006.

10. Federal police report cited in the *Journal de Comercio*, 19 June 1991.

11. The origin of the local term "guardian angels" was unknown to informants. Most were not aware of the similarly named Guardian Angels who arose in the South Bronx during a particularly dark period in that city's history (the late 1970s and 1980s) when massive budget deficits, law enforcement layoffs, and increasing crime "hollowed out" whole neighborhoods and left them in ruins. Planting and cleaning up vacant lots and boarding up bombed-out buildings, local youths with red head scarves managed to make this notorious inner-city neighborhood more livable. The movement spread to other neighborhoods, and the Guardian Angels involved themselves in everything from street education to neighborhood watch groups to riding the subways to protect the elderly from muggings. My

elderly mother, who traveled the subways on a daily basis, was very fond of the Guardian Angels, but there were accompanying critiques by many political leaders of their unacceptable use of "rough" vigilante justice.

12. Humberto da Silva Graça, Ministerio Publico do Estado de Pernambuco, Procurador Geral de Justica, Segunda Promotoria de Justica de Timbaúba, "(In)Sueguranca Publica em Timbaúba," Timbaúba, 30 March 2000.

13. Lampião and his sidekick, Maria Bonita, are perhaps the most famous outlaw-bandits of Northeast Brazil. During the 1920s and 1930s Lampião was the scourge of the backlands and a killer of police and soldiers, whom he always called *macacos* (monkeys). Lampião, the Robin Hood of Brazil, was a complex man, both religious and brutal. He was also extremely vain. His band rarely totaled more than forty men, but he fought many battles against militia and special police. Lampião wiped out entire households of enemies; he would assault small towns, killing police, asking local merchants for "contributions," and seizing anything he could carry off and distributing what he could not carry to the local population. Often women were raped. Early in his career, Lampião and about twenty of his band gang-raped the young wife of a soldier while the man was forced to watch. To this day, the exploits of Lampião are sung and recited in interior towns like Timbaúba.

14. The sertão is the drought-plagued interior of Pernambuco State.

15. The Brazilian Constitution of 1988 institutionalized the role of public child advocates (*conselhos tutulares*) in each of Brazil's *municipios*. These advocates, schooled in the new bill of rights, monitor the rights of all children to food, shelter, education, and protection from abuse by parents, teachers, and police. Brazilian street children have organized around another, more difficult and provocative right—the right to live in the street free of police harassment.

16. Gildete's data are based on records kept at the new office of public security in Timbaúba, where she is employed.

17. The numbers vary in different (civil versus police) reports. It may never be known exactly how many were killed by Abdoral's death squad because the families of the victims (see Biu's hesitant and hedged comments about the death squad slaying of her son) are still too terrorized or too ashamed to speak. And when questioned directly they will often deny that association for fear of those members of the gang who are still at large.

18. During 1964–66 I lived and worked as a neighborhood *visitadora*—a health "promoter"—in the largest hillside shantytown, Alto do Cruzeiro, of Timbaúba. After a fruitless year of immunizing children who died of hunger, I joined forces with a local peasant union and cofounded a shantytown association, the Union of the People of Alto do Cruzeiro (UPAC), and worked with them in the long struggle for clean water, a living wage, and the right to occupy the land on which they squatted. When I returned to Timbaúba as an anthropologist in 1982, for the first of many field trips there, the people of the Alto refused to cooperate with me unless I continued to be part of *a luta*, the political struggle. I tell part of this story in Scheper-Hughes 1993.

19. "To do so, writers, artists and especially researchers (who, by trade, are already more inclined and more able than any other occupation to overcome national borders) must breach the *sacred boundary*, inscribed in their minds, more or less deeply depending on their national tradition, between *scholarship* and *commitment*, in order to break out of the academic microcosm and to enter resolutely

into sustained exchange with the outside world (that is, especially with unions, grass-root organizations and issue-oriented activist groups) instead of being content with waging the 'political' battles at once intimate and ultimate, and always a bit unreal, of the scholastic universe. Today's researchers must innovate an improbable but indispensable combination: *scholarship with commitment,* that is, a collective politics of intervention in the political field that follows, as much as possible, the rules that govern the scientific field" (Bourdieu 1999).

20. The police, both civil and military, had frequently been involved in earlier death squad activities, and the mere idea of the local police in Timbaúba, reformed or not, knowing and reading what I had to say about their predecessors filled me with foreboding.

21. On my last trip, in the summer of 2005, that subtle help was not forthcoming, and I noted with alarm that the old ledger books I had so long and lovingly poured over on many field trips since the early 1980s would never again be so available. Amintina had wrapped stacks of the old books in what looked to me like blue laundry paper, sealed and tied. Instead of handing me the books, she offered to read the specific data I needed from across the long counter that separated us, an impossible offer and she knew it.

22. That is, drug deals that were not part of the death squads' own circuit of drug trafficking.

23. *Literatura de cordel* (string literature) consists of pamphlets or booklets that hang on a piece of string and are sold at peasant markets throughout Northeast Brazil.

References

Adorno, Sergio. 1995. "A violencia na sociedade brasileira: Um panel inconcluso em uma democracia nao consolidada." *Revista Sociedade e Estado* 10(2):299–342.

Almeida, Alfredo and Wagner Berno. 1991. *Violência contra crianças e adolescentes em conflitos de terra do Brasil (1980–1991).* Vols. 1 and 2. Brasília: Ministério da Ação Social/ CBIA.

Altoé, Sônia. 1991. "Jovens depois do internato." *Tempo e Presença* 258 (July– August): 26–28.

Alves, Maria Helena Moreira. 1985. *State and Oppression in Military Brazil.* Austin: University of Texas Press.

Alvim, R., coordinator. 1991. *Da violência contra o "menor" ao extermínio de crianças e adolescentes.* Rio de Janeiro: NEPI-CBIA.

Amaral e Silva, A. F. 1991. *O Estatuto da Criança e do Adolescente e a justiça infância e da juventude.* Vol. 6 of *Cadernos populares.* São Paulo: Sindicato dos Trabalhadores em Entidades de Assistência ao Menor e à Familia (SITRAEMFA); Centro Brasileiro para a Infância e Adolesência (CBIA).

Amnesty International. 1990a. *Brazil: Torture and Extrajudicial Execution in Urban Brazil.* Briefing (June). New York: Amnesty International USA.

———. 1990b. *FOCUS: Child Victims of Killing and Cruelty.* (September.) London: Amnesty International.

———. 1992. *Brazil, Impunity and the Law: The Killing of Street Children in Rio de Janeiro State.* London: Amnesty International.

Bezerra, Jaerson Lucas. 1992. "Assistencialismo e política." In *Os impasses da cidadania:*

Infância e adolescência no Brasil, ed. Almir Pereira Júnior, Jaerson Lucas Bezerra, and Rosana Heringer, pp. 36–49. Rio de Janeiro: IBASE.

Bourdieu, Pierre. 1999. Keynote address presented at the Modern Language Association meetings, Chicago, December.

Brooke, James. 1992. "Brazil's Police Enforce Popular Punishment: Death." *New York Times,* 4 November, p. A6.

Caldeira, Teresa Pires do Rio. 2000. *City of Walls: Crime, Segregation, and Citizenship in São Paulo.* Berkeley and Los Angeles: University of California Press.

Calligaris, Contardo. 1991. *Hello Brasil! Notas de um psicanalista europeu viajando ao Brasil.* São Paulo: Escuta.

Chauí, Marilena. 1990. "Criança ou menor?" In *A criança e o adolescente de baixa renda nas metrópoles.* São Paulo: Secretaria Municipal do Bem-Estar Social da Prefeitura de São Paulo.

Coelho, Edmundo Campos. 1988. "A criminalidade urbana violenta." *Dados* 31(2):145–83.

da Costa, Antônio Carlos Gomes. 1993. "O novo direito da criança e do adolescente no Brasil: O conteúdo e o processo das mudanças no panorama legal." In *A criança, o adolescente, o município: Entendendo e implementando a Lei No. 8069/90,* ed. Antônio Carlos Gomes da Costa, Edson de Moraes Seda, and João Gilberto Lucas Coelho, pp. 7–17. Brasília: Fórum Nacional Permenente de Entidades Não-Governmentais de Defesa da Criança e do Adolescente (Fórum-DCA).

DaMatta, Roberto. 1987. *A Casa & a Rua.* Rio de Janeiro: Guanabara.

de Carvalho, Maria do Carmo Brant. 1991. *O Estatuto da Criança e do Adolescente e a política de assistência social.* Vol. 9 of *Cadernos populares.* São Paulo: Sindicato dos Trabalhadores em Entidades de Assistência ao Menor e à Familia (SITRAEMFA); Centro Brasileiro para a Infância e Adolesência (CBIA).

de Oliveira Santos, Helio. 1995. *Criancas esquecidas.* Campinas, SP: Pontes Editores.

de Souza, Herbert. 1992. "As crianças de rua." *Carta Semanal do IBASE* (Instituto Brasileiro de Analises Sociais e Económicas), no. 89 (23 May).

Dimenstein, Gilberto. 1991. *Brazil: War on Children.* Trans. Chris Whitehouse. London: Latin America Bureau.

———. 1992. *Meninas da noite.* São Paulo: Editora Atica.

dos Santos, Benedito Rodrigues. 1992. "A implantação do Estatuto da Criança e do Adolescente." In *Os impasses da cidadania: Infância e adolescência no Brasil,* ed. Almir Pereira Júnior, Jaerson Lucas Bezerra, and Rosana Heringer, pp. 66–79. Rio de Janeiro: IBASE.

dos Santos, Ivanir. 1991. "Romper o silêncio e quebrar o mito." *Criança e adolescente trabalho e sindicalismo,* vol. 2, pp. 11–13.

Filho, Mario Simas, Eliane Azevedo, and Lula Costa Pinto. 1991. "Infância de raiva, dor e sangue." *Veja,* 29 May, pp. 34–45.

Freyre, Gilberto. 1986. *The Masters and the Slaves.* Berkeley and Los Angeles: University of California Press.

GAJOP (Gabinete de Assessoria Jurídica às Organizações Populares/Centro Luiz Freire). 1990. "Minors and the Death Squad in Pernambuco." Trans. Vera Mello Joscelyne. In *The Killing of Children and Adolescents in Brazil,* ed. André Papi, Marisa Brandão, and Jorge L. C. Jardineiro, pp. 20–21. Rio de Janeiro: Center for the Mobilization of Marginalized Populations (CEAP).

———. 1991. *Grupos de extermínio: A banalização da vida e da morte em Pernambuco.* Olinda: GAJOP.

———. 1992. *Estatuto da Criança e do Adolescente: Um ano construindo o novo.* Olinda: GAJOP.

Graça, Humberto da Silva. 2000. "(In)Sueguranca publica em Timbaúba." Timbaúba, 30 March. Unpublished public document.

Heringer, Rosana. 1991. "Movimentos de defesa da criança e do adolescente no Brasil." In *Os impasses da cidadania: Infância e adolescência no Brasil,* ed. Almir Pereira Júnior, Jaerson Lucas Bezerra, and Rosana Heringer, pp. 50–65. Rio de Janeiro: IBASE.

Hobsbawm, E. 2000. *Bandits.* Rev. ed. New York: New Press. (Originally published 1969.)

Holston, James. 1999. "Spaces of Insurgent Citizenship." In *Cities and Citizenship,* ed. James Holston, pp. 187–204. Durham, NC: Duke University Press, 1999.

———. 2001. "Urban Citizenship and Globalization." In *Global City Regions,* ed. Allen J. Scott, pp. 325–48. New York: Oxford University Press.

Holston, James, and Teresa P. R. Caldeira. 1998. "Democracy, Law, and Violence: Disjunctions of Brazilian Citizenship." In *Fault Lines of Democratic Governance in the Americas,* ed. Felipe Agüero and Jeffrey Stark, pp. 263–96. Miami: North-South Center and Lynne Rienner.

Huggins, Martha. 1997. "From Bureaucratic Consolidation to Structural Devolution: Police Death Squads in Brazil." *Policing and Society* 7:207–34.

Jornal do Commércio (Recife). 1991. "Quase 5 mil menores foram assassinados nos últimos 3 anos." 19 June, p. 11.

Júnior, Almir Pereira, and Angélica Drska. 1993. "O significado dos números." In *Os impasses da cidadania: Infância e adolescência no Brasil,* ed. Almir Pereira Júnior, Jaerson Lucas Bezerra, and Rosana Heringer, pp. 80–105. Rio de Janeiro: IBASE.

Louzeiro, José. 1990. "Genocide in the Baixada: Children Are Being Murdered." In *The Killing of Children and Adolescents in Brazil,* ed. André Papi, Marisa Brandão, and Jorge L. C. Jardineiro, pp. 18–19. Rio de Janeiro: Center for the Mobilization of Marginalized Populations (CEAP).

Milto, Claudia, Helio R. S. Silva, and Luiz Eduardo Soares. 1994. *Homicidios: Dolorosos practicados contra menores, no estado de Rio de Janeiro (1991 a Julho de 1993).* Brasilia: Ministry of the Public.

MNMMR (Movimento Nacional de Meninos e Meninas de Rua). 1991. "Guerra no centro da cidade." *O grito dos meninos e meninas de rua* 5(20) (June): 4. (Newsletter of the MNMMR, Pernambuco.)

———. 1992. *Vidas em risco: Assassinatos de crianças e adolescentes no Brasil.* Rio de Janeiro: IBASE.

Nascimento, Maria das Graças. 1990. "Street Children, the Right to Become a Citizen." In *The Killing of Children and Adolescents in Brazil,* ed. André Papi, Marisa Brandão, and Jorge L. C. Jardineiro, pp. 106–19. Rio de Janeiro: Center for the Mobilization of Marginalized Populations (CEAP).

Oliveira, Luis Claudio. 1991. "Crianças e adolescentes: Um desafio à cidadania." *Tempo e Presença* 258 (July–August): 5–9.

Penglase, Ben. 1993. *Final Justice: Police and Death Squad Homicides of Adolescents in Brazil.* New York: Human Rights Watch/Americas.

Piccolino, Alberta. 1992. "Killing the Innocents: The War on Brazil's Street Children." *Sojourners,* February–March, pp. 28–29.

Pinheiro, Paulo Sergio. 1996. "Democracies without Citizenship: Report on Crime." In "Injustice for All: Crime and Impunity in Latin America." Special issue, *NACLA: Report on the Americas* 30(2) (September/October): 17–23.

Prado, Antonio Carlos. 1991. "Documento da ESG sobre menino de rua causa polêmica." *Jornal do Brasil,* 19 June, p. 5.

Rizzini, Irene, Irma Rizzini, Monica Munhoz, and Lidia Galeano. 1992. *Childhood and Urban Poverty in Brazil: Street and Working Children and Their Families.* Innocenti Occasional Papers, The Urban Child Series, no. 3. Florence, Italy: UNICEF.

Rocha, Jan. 1991. Introduction to *Brazil: War on children,* pp. 1–15. Trans. Chris Whitehouse. London: Latin America Bureau.

Scheper-Hughes, Nancy. 1990. "Theft of Life: Illegal Markets in Children." *Society* 27(6):57–62.

———. 1992. *Death without Weeping: The Violence of Everyday Life in Brazil.* Berkeley and Los Angeles: University of California Press.

——— 1993. "The Way of an Anthropologist-*Companheira.*" In *Anthropology and the Peace Corps,* ed. Brian E. Schwimmer and D. Michael Warren. Ames: Iowa State University Press.

———. 1995. "Who's the Killer? Popular Justice and Human Rights in a South African Squatter Camp." *Social Justice* 22(3):143–64.

———. 1996. "Small Wars and Invisible Genocides." *Social Science and Medicine* 43(5):889–900.

———. 1997. *La muerte sin llanto: Violencia y vida cotidiana en Brasil.* Barcelona: Editorial Ariel.

———. 2002. "Min(d)ing the Body: On the Trail of Organ Stealing Rumors." In *Exotic No More: Anthropology on the Front Lines,* ed. Jeremy MacClancy, pp. 33–63. Chicago: University of Chicago Press.

———. 2006. "Kidney Kin: Inside the New Trans-Atlantic Slave Trade." *Harvard International Review* 27 (winter): 62–66.

Scheper-Hughes, Nancy, and Daniel Hoffman. 1998. "Brazilian Apartheid: Street Kids and the Search for Citizenship in Brazil." In *Small Wars: The Cultural Politics of Childhood,* ed. Nancy Scheper-Hughes and Caroline Sargent, 352–88. Berkeley and Los Angeles: University of California Press.

Soares, Leontina Célia. 1990. "Homicide: Author Unknown." In *The Killing of Children and Adolescents in Brazil,* ed. André Papi, Marisa Brandão, and Jorge L. C. Jardineiro, pp. 22–23. Rio de Janeiro: Center for the Mobilization of Marginalized Populations (CEAP).

Suarez-Orozco, Marcelo. 1987. "The Treatment of Children in the Dirty War: Ideology, State Terrorism, and the Abuse of Children in Argentina." In *Child Survival,* ed. N. Scheper-Hughes, pp. 227–43. Dordrecht, Holland: Kluwer.

Swift, Anthony. 1991. *Brazil: The Fight for Childhood in the City.* Florence: UNICEF.

Teixeira, Maria de Lourdes Trassi. 1992. *O Estatuto da Criança e do Adolescente e a questão do delito.* Vol. 3 of *Cadernos populares.* São Paulo: Sindicato dos Trabalhadores em Entidades de Assistência ao Menor e à Familia (SITRAEMFA); Centro Brasileiro para a Infância e Adolesência (CBIA).

Vermelho, L. and J. Mello. 1996. "Youth Mortality: Analysis Comprising the Period from 1930 to 1991." Paper presented at the International Meetings of *Social Science and Medicine,* Peebles, Scotland, September 1996.

Zaluar, Alba. 1994. *Condominio do diablo.* Rio de Janeiro: Editora Reven UFRJ

———. 1995. "Crime, medo e politica." *Sociedade e Estado* 10:391–416.

Zaluar, Alba, and Alexandre Isidoro Ribeiro. 1995. "Drug Trade, Crime, and Policies of Repression in Brazil." *Dialectical Anthropology* 20:95–108.

5 Some Notes on Disorder in the Indonesian Postcolony

Patricia Spyer

ALL TOO RARELY, it would seem, is violence addressed head on, in its own terms. This is perhaps even more the case in discussions of what is commonly called "communal violence." There, ready-made rubrics describing sociological processes and forms are reassuring because distancing designations of primordialism, tribalism, religious fanaticism, or other versions of the antimodern are invoked by social scientists, political analysts, policy makers, and mass-media representatives to cast violence within narratives that underscore the moral and cultural superiority of Euromodernity. This essay navigates between the pitfalls of the alleged certainties of social science and the models of political analysts, on the one hand, and, on the other, the more apocalyptic visions propagated by the mass media, which seize on the extremes of what is seen as radical otherness and societal disintegration (Allen and Seaton 1999). Intimately related, these are two sides of the same coin—the one invoking chaos and anticivilizational impulses; the other proposing the means and modes of government to cure it.

Taken-for-granted, hackneyed notions like transition to democracy, civil society, and crisis are more than the analytical stock and trade of neoliberal think tanks and organizations insofar as they simultaneously identify things to be fostered, abetted, and, especially, managed in countries of the South. At the very least, certain epistemological risks are involved when the very same terms used to describe the aims of government serve also as the analytical apparatus deployed by sociologists, political scientists, anthropologists, and the like. What is more, such concepts tend to mask and cover over highly subtle, complex processes and regimes of change—of which the outbreak and proliferation of violence, communal or otherwise, are deplorably an often telling dimension. Those who use such concepts impose temporal and logical directionality and linearity; they assume familiar outcomes and implicitly claim for themselves impressive powers of prediction. According to Achille Mbembe, such processes involve different temporalities and displacements; they take the form of fluctuations and destabilizations that can be quite dramatic, are often contradictory, and combine several regimes of change—from the more stationary and inert to the dynamic, chaotic, even catastrophic (Mbembe 2001: 66).

To be sure, the metatheoretical concepts of the social sciences invoked here, like others before them of an ordering kind, can also be quite useful and, at any rate, not done without. My aim here is simply one of interrogation: to pursue as closely as possible in the minutiae and momentum of a conflict that played itself out in the Moluccas (Maluku), at the far eastern end of Indonesia, between 1999 and 2002 the dynamics, modalities, and material technologies through which violence is produced, proliferates, and, crucially, becomes sedimented. The radical refiguration over time of what was previously considered possible, expected, or so taken for granted as to go unremarked and the concomitant breakdown of trust in what the everyday has to offer describe the particular kind of violence at issue here. Communal violence like that occurring on Ambon, for instance, is more dramatically totalizing in its effects than the state violence that insinuated itself into social life in multiple, varying ways under Indonesia's former president Suharto. When the familiar, habitual practices of everyday existence are rent by novel apprehensions and dangers that, in turn, abet the production of violence—forming a highly complex context in which violence becomes increasingly possible—then, I argue, is it possible to speak of the sedimentation of violence or the production of a context that is itself congenial to additional violence.

As I hope to show, the logic of such sedimentations of violence is one of movement, uncertainty, unpredictability. In radically transforming the banal conditions of quotidian life-worlds and exposing the limits of the possible, such sedimentations of violence necessarily go hand in hand with transformations in the construction of subjectivities. Thus, one salient characteristic of the communal violence outlined here is the deployment of a range of what I call anticipatory practices on the part of the actors most intimately involved. Such practices are aimed precisely at undermining and short-circuiting the unpredictability that becomes increasingly definitive of everyday existence. Operating in tandem, the mutually constitutive sedimentation of violence and production of anticipatory practices by social actors spawn supplementary effects that form the conditions of an inherently "violent situation."

Here, a "violent situation" is simply one that in the first place can be defined by the ongoing production of violence in the same way that, for instance, a colonial situation is characterized first and foremost by the relations of colonizer and colonized, metropole and colony. A violent situation is therefore more than the sum of any parts and cannot be under-

stood in terms of discrete individual or collective acts of violence and
atrocity. It is, once again, dramatically totalizing in its effects. I argue
against the atomization of violence, its culturalization or exoticization
with respect to the supposed inclinations of specific groups, and its reduction to "background" factors held to foster or enable its occurrence, and
I explore the dynamics of violence as it engenders the conditions of its own
ongoing and renewed possibilities. Elusive as this may sound, terms like
"climate," "ambiance," "atmospherics," and "milieu," often invoked in
descriptions of social and political violence, most closely approximate
what I am getting at. If tangential, these terms still conjure and gloss the
influence and effects of a certain presence that, while lacking any real precision, is understood, nonetheless, to have definitive power in the shaping
of events, human agency and identity, and the production of meaning.

Several telling dimensions of the problems addressed here can be as-
cribed to what scholars of the current world-historical moment often call
the postcolonial predicament. For Indonesia this "predicament" was cast
in especially high relief with the step-down of the country's longtime president Suharto in May 1998 in the face of far-reaching economic deterioration, mass popular protests and social turmoil, and a series of structural-
adjustment programs imposed by the International Monetary Fund. As
elsewhere, the ad hoc, provisional character of the hyphen conjoining
"nation" and "state" seems to be increasingly supplanted by a question
mark (J. L. Comaroff and J. Comaroff 2004).[1] Thus, while Indonesians
conventionally speak of the reach of their republic as extending between
the two symbolic pillars of Sabang in Aceh at the northwestern tip of
Sumatra to Merauke in southeastern Papua, hundreds of miles away, these
provinces currently figure as contested sites where struggles for independence or some degree of autonomy from the Indonesian state are both
most persistently waged and violently suppressed. More than any immanent threat of Indonesia's disintegration the refiguring of the relations
between nation and state in the era of Reformasi is rather the issue—one
that, moreover, was officially recognized in January 2000 with the imple-
mentation across the archipelago of the national program of regional autonomy (*otonomi daerah*).[2] Aimed at redressing the extreme imbalances
that characterized relations between the capital Jakarta and the country's
culturally and linguistically diverse regions under Suharto, regional autonomy assigns greater governmental responsibility and financial means
to the regency (*kabupaten*) level. Since its inception, regional autonomy
has also, in different places, provided the legal and imaginative framework
for the revival of custom (*adat*) and vernacular traditions of governance

(Avonius 2004; Sakai 2002), the resurgence of both a new and an older elite, the latter with restored titles and ambitions (van Klinken 2004), the foundation of a national alliance of indigenous peoples (Aliansi Masyarakat Adat Nusantara, or AMAN) (Acciaioli 2002), the institution of *shari'a* law in places like Aceh (Sumatra), Tasikmalaya, Garut (Java), and South Sulawesi, and the outbreak of conflicts waged on the basis of highly self-conscious ethnicized or religicized identities (Aragon 2001; Davidson and Kammen 2002; Peluso and Harwell 2001).

Following KRISMON (Krisis Moneter, or Monetary Crisis) and even KRISTAL (Krisis Total, or Total Crisis), Reformasi, the battle cry of protesting students in the heady spring of 1998, arrived with a slew of terms that were drawn equally from the language of democracy, good governance, and human rights—*demokrasi, transparan* (transparency), *masyarakat sipil* (civil society)—along with their alleged opposites, *korupsi, kolusi* (collusion), *nepotisme* (KKN). Political liberalization and media deregulation, the concomitant explosion of new media forms and venues (Sen and Hill 2000; Spyer 2002a), the mushrooming of international and national nongovernmental organizations (NGOs) across the country, and increasing numbers of young Indonesian activists engaged in the initiatives and struggles of Reformasi helped to spread and popularize this language and the aspirations for which it stands across the country. The already-excessive, spectacular character of violence in the postcolony has assumed new, if equally dramatic, forms, a situation that has only been enhanced by the mounting awareness on the part of social actors of the increasingly multiple, varied, and dispersed audiences to which they are attuned or aim to engage in their actions. Crucial, in other words, to the argument developed here is its attention to the agencies and the work of imagination on the part of those most immediately involved.

In what follows I focus on the role of the anticipated, the barely sensed, the possible, and the conditional in the structuring of ordinary people's perceptions and actions in extraordinary times of acute duress and chronic violence. I aim to trace in the workings of the conflict in the Moluccan provincial capital of Ambon, with occasional forays into neighboring Moluccan Islands, the sedimentations of a situation of violence and therein the coproduction of an enabling presence which could be glossed as "climate," "ambiance," "atmospherics," or "milieu." At the end of this essay I take up the problem of the law in relation to the postconflict situation and consider briefly the possible grounds for peace or, more accurately, postviolence in Ambon.

The town of Ambon, on the island of the same name (strictly speaking not reckoned among the original Moluccan spice islands),[3] developed around a Portuguese fort that was taken over by the Dutch East India Company (Vereenigde Oost-Indische Compagnie, or VOC) in the early seventeenth century. Rapidly the town became the epicenter of the highly lucrative spice trade (especially cloves but also nutmeg and mace), a site of aggressive competition between different European and Asian traders, and, by the end of the seventeenth century, a cosmopolitan colonial city populated largely by migrants (Knaap 1991). Already early on, the establishment of the draconically enforced VOC monopoly in clove cultivation on Ambon and the surrounding islands, the imposition of corvée labor to support the company's political and military infrastructure, the destruction of the Ambonese Muslim polities and traditional federations together with the continuation of the Christianization begun under the Portuguese, and the establishment of the VOC seat of power on the Christian Leitimor peninsula of Ambon Island set the general pattern of community relations that was to characterize Ambonese colonial society until the late nineteenth century (Chauvel 1990). With the demise of the VOC at the very end of the eighteenth century and the declining world market in cloves, Ambon went into a period of marked economic decline. Against this background but especially in light of augmented Dutch imperial ambitions across the archipelago, education in Christian communities was reformed and extended and the mass recruitment of Christian youth for the colonial army (Koninklijk Nederlands Indische Leger, or KNIL) and bureaucracy began. Considered loyal, these "Black Dutchmen"[4] enjoyed special privileges over other inlanders (indigenous peoples of the Netherlands East Indies), predominated in the KNIL and the lower ranks of civil administration, often worked and lived far from Ambon in military barracks and émigré communities on Java and elsewhere, and are highly visible in Dutch archives and photographs from the mid–nineteenth century until the Japanese occupation in 1942. Conversely, Ambon's Muslim population, much less an object of direct colonial intervention, maintained customary forms and practices and local language use to a much greater extent than is the case for the Christian communities and to a degree that remains noticeable today.[5]

The marked privileging of Ambonese Christians changed under Japanese occupation, which favored the Muslims, and then with the suppression by the young Indonesian Republic of the attempt at secession by the predominantly Christian Republic of the South Moluccas (Republik Maluku Selatan, or RMS) movement in the 1950s and 1960s, and, most explicitly, in the 1990s during the last decade of Suharto rule under the government's policy of "greening," or Islamicization.[6] While, to some extent, it is possible to speak, following van Klinken, of "long-term 'primordialist' social patterns" (2001: 3), the difference between Muslims and Christians was not necessarily or always defined in terms that were markedly religious. Generally in Indonesia, until quite recently, violence between majority Muslims (officially about 89 percent today) and minority Christians has been rare. In Ambon City especially, Christians and Muslims lived in proximate, familiar, and, occasionally, familial relations with each other in relative peace in the composite provincial capital—notwithstanding the inevitable resentments, tensions, and small-scale skirmishes that also marked intercommunity relations.

Since the outbreak of communal violence in Ambon City in mid-January 1999 up through the Malino II Peace Agreement of February 2002, much has been written about this conflict, which over time consolidated two polarized religiosities—one Christian and one Muslim—as the war's main obvious opponents. These writers include anthropologists and other social scientists, both within and outside Indonesia, activists and representatives of a range of local, national, and international NGOs, a number of protagonists within the conflict, as well as media practitioners based in Ambon and the surrounding islands, the capital Jakarta, or beyond the country's borders, especially in Australia, the Netherlands, and the United States.[7]

Ranging from highly engaged and informed analyses to the more codified versions of NGO-speak and the "contaminated" slanted stories that bolster the truth claims of one or another side, the origins, complicating factors and backgrounds, major events, and relevant national and international developments have been scrutinized and amply discussed in terms of their respective contributions to Ambon's violence. As so many theatrical backdrops against which the main action unfolds, important externalities and internal factors named as enabling and providing fertile ground for the outbreak of violence include such macropolitical and macroeconomic structures as the Southeast Asian financial crisis of 1997 and its aftermath, the step-down of Suharto and the transitions of Reformasi, and the behind-the-scene connivings of Jakarta's political elite and the military. Tensions among Ambonese Christians and Muslims, more specifically, are seen as having been aggravated over the long term as well as more recently by the religious division of labor established under Dutch colonial rule, which privileged Christians and marginalized Muslims socially, economically, and educationally; by the parallel processes of Islamicization and Christianization in the wake of World War II and the related erosion of the common ground of "custom" (*adat*) shared by Ambonese;[8] and by the "greening," or Islamicization, of Indonesia generally under the late Suharto regime, as evidenced in Ambon by the appointment of two Ambonese Muslims as provincial governors, leaving the Christians now the ones feeling that they were left behind. Add to this the increasing shortage of land, population pressure, and the in-migration of Muslims from South Sulawesi,[9] skewing the once more or less equal numerical balance on the island between Christians and Muslims, and the involvement of some, especially urban, Ambonese youth in gangs and criminality,[10] and one has a situation waiting to happen—waiting to happen perhaps, but still not yet, not quite, happening.

While many of the arguments and analyses that I have mentioned here have contributed to my understanding of the conflict in Ambon, I have also been troubled by the sense that something is missing. Some of this writing is just too grand, too abstract, and too removed from the volatile, fractured field where, throughout the violence, Ambonese men, women, and children pieced together their everyday lives out of the fears, contingencies, insecurities, and apprehensions that then weighed upon them. What tends to be passed over in foregrounding the influence of Indonesia's major political players, the networks of militant Muslims, the nefarious wheelings and dealings of thugs, the inbred violence, corruption, and partisan affections of the police and the military is, I argue, the character of the very space in which all of these figures, for better or for worse, deploy their schemes and make their dubious marks.

Too little heed is given to the work of the imagination and the construction of knowledge in violence's production and sedimentation and, specifically, how these compel and propel particular actions and shape those who carry them out. The mobile, dense, and murky terrain in which something that is waiting to happen does in fact happen is built on spirals of information, misinformation, and disinformation, on the revamping of criteria of credibility, customs of trust, and accountability, and on knowledge forms that blur the boundaries between what is seen and what is heard, what is known and what is suspected, what is feared and what is fantasized, what is fact and what is fiction.[11] This is what I understand by "climate." No mere backdrop, in Ambon, climate's infrastructure comprised the overt and covert representations and mobilizations of both mass and more small-scale, politically driven "tactical" media, the circulation and sedimentation of ideologically potent images and hard-edged reified positions, as well as rumors, graffiti, unknowables, and even unnameables. These haunted the terrain in which big men, regular folk, and shadowy characters moved, and these structured—equally but differently—their varied perceptions and actions. More blatantly than in other settings, agency in such circumstances also meant being acted upon—suffering bodily exposure, terror, and enforced passivity. Before I turn to some examples, an outline of the conflict will be helpful.

On 19 January 1999 a run-of-the-mill fight between a Christian bus driver and a Muslim passenger escalated into a full-scale battle between Christian red forces and Muslim white forces that was fought in the streets of Ambon with traditional or homemade weapons—knives, spears, machetes, arrows shot from slingshots, fishing bombs, and Molotov cocktails. By the end of the day, numerous houses, stores, offices, churches, and mosques had been destroyed or burned, scores of people had been displaced, and others wounded or killed. On the eve of the Malino II Peace Agreement, three years later, the International Crisis Group estimated that at least 5,000 and possibly as many as 10,000 people had been killed and close to 700,000 had become refugees—or one-third of a total Moluccan population of 2.1 million comprising also those fleeing violence on neighboring islands (see International Crisis Group 2002). In the largely residentially segregated city of Ambon, the kind of sectarian border skirmish that set all this off was common. Under normal circumstances it would also have remained a non-event—except, of course, for those immediately involved.

In what scholars have identified as the first phase of the war, lasting from mid-January 1999 until May 2000, periods of violent confrontation between native Ambonese Christian and Muslim mobs and mass destruction alternated with lulls in which attempts at reconciliation involving elite Ambonese from both sides were occasionally made (see Bartels 2003; Aditjondro 2001). Jakarta's blunders also began early on, with the dispatch of the first troops to quell the violence from South Sulawesi—that part of Indonesia from which the Muslim migrants driven out of Ambon during the conflict's first weeks also hailed—with shoot-on-sight orders and with a general lack of initiative and direction. This first phase was also marked by the outbreak of violence in the Kei Islands in southeastern Maluku in April 1999 and in the soon-to-be declared new province of North Maluku in August of the same year.

The second phase marked a qualitative change in the civil war with the arrival in Ambon in May 2000 of the so-called Laskar Jihad.[12] Called into existence out of a rising concern among Muslims that the Christians had the upper hand in the conflict, this militant Muslim organization with recruits from Java, Sumatra, and South Sulawesi provided both partisan humanitarian assistance and armed support. The Laskar Jihad emerged in the wake of a massacre of four hundred Muslims in a mosque in North Maluku in late December 1999 and was further authorized by a more general call for jihad during a mass rally in Jakarta held in early January 2000 under the auspices of such major Indonesian political figures as the country's former vice president, Hamzah Haz, and the People's Consultative Assembly Speaker, Amien Rais.

The number and sophistication of the weapons used in the war had grown over time, but the Laskar Jihad brought a surplus of professional arms to Ambon. It also introduced some order into the local Muslim militias, who initially at least welcomed these supporters, and it enjoyed the clear backing of segments of the armed forces. The Christians found themselves significantly outnumbered and outgunned, and casualties and devastation increased proportionally. By late June 2000 a state of civil emergency was declared in both Maluku and North Maluku Provinces, and a special conjoined force of elite troops was dispatched to Ambon. If the declaration of the state of emergency (*darurat sipil*, or DARSI) greatly curtailed civil liberties—not least of the press—and further enhanced the militarization of everyday life, it also gradually limited the number of large-scale confrontations.

This second phase of the conflict was further characterized by a deepening of the religious definition of the opposing parties and the crystallization of relevant extremist discourses—on the one hand, that of militant Islam and jihad, represented by the Laskar Jihad and the smaller, more covert Laskar Mujaheddin, and, on the other, that of nostalgic sovereignty and separatism, embodied by the Christian Front for Moluccan Sovereignty (Front Kedaulatan Maluku, or FKM). Posing as the successor to the former RMS movement (which in actuality exists only as a shadow of its former self among segments of the Moluccan population in the Netherlands), the FKM envisions its future as the nostalgic resurrection of an indigenous, "Alifuru" Moluccan identity and boasts a leader who models himself after Xanana Gusmao, current charismatic leader of former East Timor, which was, at the time, a very recent success story of national sovereignty.

With the decrease by 2001 of large-scale confrontations and their replacement by sporadic bombings and sniper attacks, the partial restraint of the Laskar Jihad under civil emergency conditions, and the signing of the Malino II Peace Agreement in early 2002, the period of postviolence may said to have begun. Civil emergency remained in effect, however, until mid-September 2003, along with the concomitant militarization of daily life and the restriction on foreign visitors to Maluku. The initial sense of euphoria in Ambon's streets following the 2002 Malino agreement was marred in the following months by intermittent explosions and attacks that many suspect were orchestrated by those who profit from the perpetuation of chronic, low-level violence—segments of the military and police, individual deserters from the same, local gangsters, militant groups, and possibly more shadowy protagonists.[13] For quite some time, the city remained divided into rigorously defended, religiously marked territories, or, as one source acutely observed, "concentrated pools of resentment and bitterness" (in other words, potential breeding grounds for more violence) alongside emerging neutral zones and places of resistance and peace (International Crisis Group 2002: 17). This, in broad strokes, is the war. Much has obviously been left out—not the least the kinds of atmospherics to which I alluded earlier.

Let me begin at the beginning—itself a point of bitter contention between Christians and Muslims since each side accuses the other of largely preparing and masterminding the onset of violence. As others have also pointed out, Ambon is not an island unto itself, which means that Christians and Muslims there are cognizant of violence elsewhere, especially when it is religiously inflected. As on Lombok, an island about one thousand miles west of Ambon, where following an outbreak of anti-Christian riots in early 2000, graffiti on a house read "this is in response to what was done to Muslims in Ambon" (Avonius 2004), so, too, may events in other places seize hold of the imaginations of Ambonese. Most accounts of the war name a fight between Ambonese gangsters at a gambling den in Ketapang, Jakarta, in November 1998, the ensuing anti-Christian violence and church burnings following the deaths of four Muslims, and the arrival of more than one hundred uprooted underworld *preman*[14] to Ambon as the prelude to trouble in January 1999.

What is usually not mentioned is a meeting convened by the governor in December 1998.[15] The governor impressed upon Ambon's Muslim and Christian communities the need to be prepared for violence, to be on the alert, and to guard against rumors. Meant as precautionary, the meeting instilled a sense of the possible in an already-nervous city, working as an augury of what might happen before it actually occurred. Both sides went home and set up *posko,* which are either communication or command posts (a slippage that suggests how easily the one slides into the other), with networks of mosques and churches connected by both cellular and regular phones.

In this case being prepared for the worst can in crucial respects be said to have produced the worst. When the fight broke out in the marketplace on 19 January, each side quickly mobilized its members—staging in no time at all a battle between reds and whites. Ironically, it is precisely this preparedness and visible organization that each side has repeatedly held out to the other as proof of their opponent's preconceived plan to mount an attack. It is also what many scholars have seized upon as evidence of large-scale, coordinated, behind-the-scene machinations.

My second example of how anticipation augurs what actually comes to pass also derives from that same first, fateful day—one that happened to coincide with Idul Fitri, the festive close of the Muslim fasting month Ramadan. In retrospect some may see 19 January 1999 as falling into the category of "likely violence days," a formulation coined by a US Embassy security officer in Israel in recognition of the patterned repetition of violent outbreaks on Palestinian commemorative occasions (Blumenfeld 2002: 54).[16] Whether conjoining identity and trauma or, as with Idul Fitri, religious celebration and community, such days are charged with a practiced, ritualized sense of collectivity. Yet in many parts of Indonesia and in Ambon, until the war, the celebration of Idul Fitri was also cross-cut, its alleged communalist potentiality complicated by interreligious conviviality, hospitality, and sharing.

In this way, a journalist acquaintance of mine found himself on that first day at the office of Ambon's *Suara Maluku* newspaper, alternately taking calls from a Muslim friend at home in the neighborhood where the battle subsequently broke out, making plans for the party that evening, and from a Christian friend with whom he was coordinating their joint attendance at the feast. On call from different ends of the city, his ongoing double conversation with his two friends and colleagues is itself an instance of the first stirrings of the conflict. After finalizing their plans, the Muslim friend immediately called back, telling my friend to bring his camera since a fight had broken out—a regular fight, he said, the kind of thing we have seen before. Then the other friend called again, too, saying he would not come because people were in the streets with machetes, up in arms because of a burned-down church. Caught in between, my friend heard of both mosques and churches being burned before any smoke was seen in the city. As he himself put it, the rumor preceded the event and, contrary to the laws of nature, where there was fire, no smoke had been seen. Indeed, the only fire around was a wildfire of misinformation and suspicion sweeping with incredible speed across Ambon.[17]

A strictly chronological account would fail to do justice to the erratic rhythms and unfoldings of the war, which depended as much on fantasy and desire as on apprehension and fear. Rather than try to extricate a causal chain, I argue that confounding any clear trajectory from which one might plot the actions of the various parties involved is a swirl of images, vocabularies, sound bites, slogans, and vectors introducing a host of mediatized and mediated elsewheres into the picture—or, inversely, projecting Ambon, with all its troubles and sufferings, onto a larger-than-local scale. It is in the thick of such things and their powerful effects that one may begin to address Ambon's violence.[18] And it is here, too, where violence can be addressed, as it were, on its own terms, that we may discern the operations of a process—mobile and without any clear direction—that spawns its own supplementary effects, which, in turn, are evidenced in new outbreaks of violence in other parts of the city, across Ambon Island, or even elsewhere in Maluku.

Take the difference between the Christian reds and the Muslim whites. Despite the common perception that these groups stood opposed from that first day as ready-made enemies, this is hardly the case. Contrary to easy discussions of "dehumanization" (as if it involves something that people wake up to one day and decide to do), the distancing that dehumanization presumes must actually be produced, with an enemy made and identities re-cognized and reforged in the heat of impending and ongoing confrontation. Once enmity is sealed in bloodshed and memory and codified through collective talk and imagery, dehumanization can apparently—horrifically and amazingly—become second nature for just about anyone, over time. Violence in Ambon, in this general sense, has a clear affinity to violence in places like Bosnia and Rwanda, an affinity that is regularly picked up on by journalists, who often all too eagerly gloss over equally important historical and political differences when they mainstream specificities within familiar stories about entrenched primordialisms (Allen and Seaton 1999).

The precise makeup of the distancing that forms a prerequisite of dehumanization has, in any given location, its own particular twists and turns. What it means to be "human" and, therefore also, "nonhuman" will, necessarily, be inflected by attitudes toward killing, suffering, and the body as well as by notions of vengeance, retribution, and reconciliation, among many other things.[19] To be sure, the cruel work of severing what was once the community of Ambon City and the congealing of difference into hardened binary identities resonate with other recent instances of communal forms of conflict elsewhere, where—much as in Ambon—ordinary people had for long tacitly agreed to live together with all their differences and therefore also, crucially, with greater or lesser degrees of communal tension. Yet within Indonesia itself, Ambon counts as just one more instance of the marked propensity throughout the Republic's history to "kill those in one's own image" or those not deemed "other" than oneself, in short, other Indonesians (Siegel 1998: 1–9).[20] In this respect, Siegel sees a difference between the various large-scale Indonesian killings and those of other peoples such as Hutus and Tutsis or Serbs and Croats, who murdered persons whom they considered constitutionally other than themselves or some version of the "nonhuman." Although I cannot pursue this argument here, I do believe that the extreme violence in the Ambon case is, at least in part, attributable to the need to turn "those in one's own image" into something else, with the violence figuring as part of the "work" involved in bringing about a radical difference. For all the underlying tensions, interreligious rivalry, dark legacies of the Suharto era, and even turf wars between the military and police, the civil war in Ambon was just that: largely fought out among Ambonese—that is, among former colleagues, friends, and neighbors. A refugee from the area even suggested that the differently colored headties worn from the beginning on both sides were imperative for telling each other apart—given, he said, that we are all Ambonese.

Perhaps such colors could not sufficiently conjure difference out of taken-for-granted sameness or bear the weight of growing fear and hatred as the experience of war with its trail of anger, loss, and grief increasingly shaped the terms of perception and action on either side. Perhaps hatred is precisely such a restless search for new names and new labels in which to provisionally shelter an emotion that inevitably exceeds them, or perhaps such search is simply part of the "work" that goes into the consolidation of a radical, hard-edged rift between those who previously—notwithstanding all their differences—lived as a community. Whatever the case, additional names and images of the enemy Other accreted along the way, further deepening the divide between Muslims and Christians and making it more difficult to imagine its undoing. A by-now-infamous public service announcement broadcast on national television and on several commercial channels some months after the violence began seems to have been compelling enough to emerge as an emblem of mutual enmity. Shortly after its airing the spot took on a life of its own—one quite different from that intended by its producer, who, as a result, claims to have suffered "trauma."

A sweet, sentimentalized vignette of only several minutes, "Voice of the Heart—Acang and Obet" features two young Ambonese boys, the Muslim "Acang," short for Hassan, and his bosom friend, the Christian

Robert, or "Obet."²¹ The scene is an abandoned, gutted-out basement of a large concrete building evoking the ravages and dislocations of war. The spot opens with Acang awaiting his friend, anticipation on his face, and the smiles and joy on both sides when Obet arrives. The two share a quick stolen conversation in which the more obvious problems afflicting Ambon's children somewhat stiffly parade by: Obet complains we can't go to school, see our friends, study at home, or sleep; Acang, that he misses school since moving to a refugee camp, where life is difficult. To Acang's question "Why did Ambon fall apart like this?" Obet responds, "I don't know, it's a problem of adults." Acang is left with the punch line: "It's an adult problem and we kids are the victims." The camera zooms in on the two friends, their arms around each other, speaking jointly from the heart, the one echoing the other, voicing the hope and mutual promise that "even if Ambon is destroyed like this, our bond of brotherhood should not be broken."

The spot has all the trappings of the documentary—sophisticated objectivist aesthetics and a credible backdrop bolstering cinema's illusory realism,²² authentic Ambonese dialect, Indonesian subtitles, and two emblematic Ambonese young boys. The drama resurrects the trope of friends torn apart by uncontrollable circumstances—seen on screen as early as D. W. Griffith's 1915 classic *Birth of a Nation,* set during America's Civil War, but also more recently with the Indonesian Revolution as setting in the film version of Hella Haasse's book *Oeroeg.* Strikingly though, unlike their predecessors—whether standing in for America's North and South or for the Netherlands and the birth of Indonesia—the Ambonese heroes of "Voice of the Heart" do not grow up.

To be sure, children are the future of any nation and emphatically so in Indonesia, where a large proportion of the population is under the age of twenty-five.²³ The war in Ambon has had terrible effects on everyone—not the least children, many of whom have been left fatherless, orphaned, homeless, in refugee camps, and out of school (Aditjondro 2001: 101). Many have seen and experienced horrific things and many, too, have participated in their making, serving as militia messengers on both sides, becoming skilled producers of crude, deadly weapons, torching houses and vandalizing neighborhoods after an attack. One source claims that between two thousand and four thousand children, aged seven to twelve (the same as Acang and Obet), took part in raids on "enemy" villages or assisted in defending their own. On the Christian side they were known as *pasukan agas,* "sandfly troops"; among the Muslims, *pasukan linggis.*²⁴

What fantasy, in brief, structures "Acang and Obet"? Letters and poems of refugee children testify indeed to their longings for former play-mates.²⁵ In contrast to these other children, Acang and Obet's cavelike shelter is a microcosm where, speaking from children's hearts, the pair evoke the *pela* blood brotherhood mythologized in Maluku and frequently invoked in peace and reconciliation dialogue. Their space is also a haven of apolitical innocence—located less beyond the upheavals of dislocation, refugee status, interrupted schooling, and everyday trouble, which the spot clearly names, than beyond the politics, power structures, and political-economy permeating and informing all of these. The diminutive child's world also serves to diminish the conflict—bringing it down to size, to that of spoken-from-the-heart childhood honesty and clairvoyance—and thereby trivializes its real impact on Ambonese children. In further blam-ing adults for Ambon's violence, the spot induces a double delegitimiza-tion: of the parents of all Obets and all Acangs, of *pemuda,* or "youth," a morally charged category on the crest of all fundamental change in In-donesia thus far, of students, and of all others excluded from the sheltered world of "Voice of the Heart." What remains after this pernicious erasure is an abstract, easily appropriable clarity—a schema amenable to all kinds of ends, including violence.²⁶

A name and face for the enemy is all that Ambonese took from the spot meant to foster peace among them. Refugee talk on my tapes from 2000 and 2001 is replete with phrases like "Acang attacked," "Obet's territory," and so on, testifying to the currency of the public service announcement's unforeseen afterlife, as well as to the irrepressible promiscuity of media and the unpredictability of "audience" reaction. As late as September 2003, the names hijacked from the public service announcement still cir-culated—cautiously if talking about the recent opponent but also exuber-antly in peace songs and propaganda. If, arriving unwittingly from else-where, Acang and Obet's message went awry in its adjustment to Ambon's conditions, so, inversely, did Ambonese actively borrow examples from other places held to approximate their own fraught world. Well before September 11, although I cannot date its emergence, the city's main divid-ing line between its Muslim and Christian parts was known colloquially as the "Gaza Strip," Jalur Gaza. This name was already prepared in the first days of the conflict when graffiti desecrating walls and buildings included insults of Jesus and the Prophet Muhammad, references to Jews, Israel, Muslim Power and Muslim Pigs, stars of David, and *allahu akbar* in Arabic writing.²⁷ Such fragmentary, free-floating bits of discourse work best in display mode—on T-shirts, banners, posters, headties, as visual and verbal slogans. Taken out of context they also transcend it, becoming both monumental and indexing a universe—one of closed ideological systems and stand-off positions.[28] Over time, the mirrored vocabularies and practices of Ambon's two intimate enemies, emergent out of their ongoing negative exchange, further sedimented the city's own Gaza Strip.

I am interested in this usurpation of a powerful name from elsewhere both because of its effects within the dynamics of the conflict—both more than local and less than global though feeding off of and beholden to much larger than national designs—and because of the mediatized, mediated realities of Ambon, as virtualized as almost anywhere these days, especially since the war. Akin to the "synchronic novelties" identified by Benedict Anderson with the beginnings of the imagination of community as nation—like New York, New London, Nueva Leon, Nieuw Amsterdam—Ambon's Gaza Strip could "arise historically only when substantial groups of people were in a position to think of themselves as living lives parallel to those of other substantial groups of people—if never meeting yet certainly proceeding along the same trajectory" (1991: 187–88). In our own globalized times, however, such neat parallelisms between metropole and colony have increasingly opened out, giving way to multifaceted and more rhizomatic forms of imagining.[29] Thus, the potent trope "Gaza Strip" not only assumed definitive power in Ambon but has also insistently cropped up elsewhere—even in what seems such unlikely a place as Venezuela—to characterize what appear to be the most hardened and intractable of violent situations. Twinning Ambon with this other, more famous, intensely mediatized war-torn place may have been one way of making the violence in Maluku—hardly a priority in Jakarta—matter, a way of lending local suffering and loss larger-than-local meaning.[30] It also demonstrates the theatricality and dramatic imagining of social actors in a world dominated by NGOs, international peacekeeping initiatives, Human Rights Watchers, and other important audiences.[31] One wonders, however, if the import of the conflict, once amplified, can thereafter so easily be scaled down[32]— adding an ironic twist to Marx's famous insight that men make their own history though not in conditions of their own making.

Such neat schema and ideologically compelling images, like those taken from "Voice of the Heart" and Gaza Strip, were part of a much larger arena of conflicting messages, fragmentary information, representational immediacy, and stark, clear-cut abstraction. They shared the same space with phantom letters that proved incendiary enough to trigger large-scale violence. One especially infamous incident involved a letter allegedly issued by Ambon's Protestant Church and calling for Maluku's Christianization. Once multiplied, read aloud over megaphones, and spread about, this letter led directly to the dislocation and deaths of numerous North Moluccans.[33] Such "dark" circuits underlaid, crossed, and competed for attention with partisan descriptions by the local press (the aforementioned *Suara Maluku* newspaper, for instance, having spawned a Muslim and a Christian part), village gossip presented as truth on Christian and Muslim Web sites,[34] Christian-inclined state radio vying with illegal Muslim stations, the latter dominating at one point all the airwaves in Ambon, crowding out other channels, and even infiltrating the handy-talkies of priests. These divergent and convergent voices and views drowned out, echoed, interrupted, and jostled each other in the cramped, ideologized, divided space of Ambon with all its mediated elsewheres, amplified, narrow-cast, obscure, and confusing realities.

Even the supposedly, on the face of it, simple problem of actors—the "who dun it" of the violence—could be hard to pin down. Take the abstract lexicon produced by some nonpartisan, pro-peace press journalists—people with the very best of intentions. In the aim of diminishing the conflict they often deliberately obfuscated the information about a violent exchange. Reading their accounts, one is left none the wiser—houses of worship are stripped of denomination, and only elusive actors are named: "certain parties," unidentified "political elite," "puppeteers," and the ever-popular "provocateur."[35] Only the numbers of casualties and ruined properties masquerade as precision. Whatever its aim, I have argued elsewhere that this lack of specificity with regard to agency may in fact produce a sense of phantom danger, lurking both nowhere in particular and therefore potentially everywhere in general, provoking fear and, perhaps even, new violence (Spyer 2006). Moreover, with the use of phrases like "Muslim cleansing," imported early on from Jakarta, and other vivid, slanted versions of war, a more neutral source is quickly marginalized since—as one Ambonese journalist put it—it appears ludicrous by contrast.

At first glance, the video CDs (VCDs) made by both Christian and Muslim sides but circulated only by the latter (and which I therefore highlight) fly in the face of these other, stark, stripped-down media reports. The VCDs' emotional appeal depends upon their sympathetic, almost tactile engagement with, especially, victims and their bodies—on close-ups of oozing wounds, bullets protruding from body parts, maimed and charred corpses, and the bodily contortions, moans, and screams of people's suffering too painful to watch. But they were watched—over and over again. Besides the victims, the occasional imam or Muslim NGO spokesperson, and the hands of surgical intervention (doctors themselves are rarely shown), the main action is that of mass scenes of attack and violence drawn from the war's earlier phases.[36] Very much in "the thick of things," these VCDs provide little perspective on events and often make no pre-tension to having a narrative—besides, that is, the insistent, repetitive one of victimization resurrected on and out of body parts (Spyer 2002b).

These VCDs are composite works; they range from the more profes-sional to the homemade though both often contain the very same clips, which were clearly shared and copied profusely. In Ambon I was told that, during the war, just as throughout Indonesia one could compile a CD of favorite songs, so, too, in some of the city's shops, could a compilation of select scenes of violence be put together on a personal VCD. Some of the clips were produced, or at least endorsed, by the military and feature sol-diers casually standing around or doing their thing, neither shying away from nor interrupting the camera. Others are said to have been filmed by doctor-volunteers who not only stitched wounds but lent their steady hands and surgical gazes to the close-up cinematic engagement of broken bodies. Many VCDs, at any rate, are pieced together, and many evidence the presence of different hands—some steady, others shaky, and some ap-parently entranced by the zoom function.

How did the mass appeal of the VCD genre translate into the actual creation of community and the shaping of perception and action in the conflict? This is a question with presumably somewhat different answers for Ambon's Muslim and Christian peoples and one that I cannot pretend to address here. If, however, community has anything to do with the cir-culation and consolidation of shared symbols, memories, and sentiments, then the nature of their mode of transfer and sedimentation is clearly im-portant. Among Christians in Ambon, VCD traffic was relatively small scale, difficult to break into, and closely controlled, with VCDs bearing advisory labels like "intended for our own group" (*untuk kalangan sen-diri*). The Muslim VCDs, by contrast, were not only mass-produced, sold during the war in the markets and streets of much of Indonesia, but are transnationally popular and quite homogeneous: Ambon's VCDs look much like Kashmir's, Bosnia's, and those of Palestine shown in Malaysia and elsewhere.[37]

For any of these VCDs to have had any effect—whether in the claus-trophobic enclave of Ambon's Christians or in the transnational Muslim space stretched thinly perhaps across the geopolitical mosaic of different Islams—at least two things were needed, which I can only name here. The first are codified discourses like those of the Laskar Jihad or Christian FKM, mentioned earlier, which serve as rallying cries or even captions that orient and provide a framework for perception and action. The second are, as Appadurai and Poole have suggested for other settings, what Raymond Williams called "social expressions in solution, as distinct from other semantic formations that have been precipitated and are evidently and more immediately available."[38] Neither institutionalized nor reflexively present, such social expressions in solution—or "modes of affect and feeling attendant on emergent social processes"—inhabit a patchy, dispersed terrain, constituting community only as a potential (Williams 1977: 132–34). Along with other factors and media, the highly mobile VCDs were themselves, of course, part and parcel of the making of this terrain.

One of the most professional VCDs in my possession is called *Maluku Utara berduka* (North Maluku's Suffering); it graphically intimates the kind of fluid, contingent expressions in solution that must have prefigured the Muslim community congealed on-screen.[39] There, the gathering, including several women and children, is bent to the common task of jihad in North Maluku but, I believe, in another situation, just as easily dispersed. Visibly at least, the community is an ad hoc collection of eclectic affinities: everyone more or less in white but some orthodox and sober, others inscribed from head to waist with *azimat* (magical charms dating to the Crusades), some in Saudi-style dress, others wrapped in Palestinian headscarves, and still others in Jihad-Central Javanese Yogyakartan style. Several carry southern Philippine Moro-type machetes, others have bows and arrows or spears, some have AK-47s, and a few even wield plastic guns, perhaps for their effect on unsuspecting audiences.

Throughout this essay I have stressed the role of the possible and the conditional—of which social expressions in solution form a part—or what I call anticipatory practice in the context of extraordinary, violent circumstances. It remains to give briefly some indication of what people caught in the midst do—with multiple influences and images impinging upon them. Once again, the general climate of fear, insecurity, and mental and physical exhaustion which Ambonese until recently inhabited every day is important to bear in mind. These are the conditions for what I call a hyperhermeneutic[40]—or a compulsive need to interpret and mine just about everything for hidden meaning, to see any trivial occurrence as a sign or omen of what might come. There is, relatedly, the drive to produce signs (headties, graffiti, and the like) for one's own community, for other social actors, for larger relevant audiences, and, not the least, for the enemy Other. Lest this seem too cerebral, the crucial dimension filling out this constellation of anticipatory practice is extreme, pervasive distrust: things are so thoroughly scrutinized because their nature and appearance are suspected of concealing something else.[41]

The prevalent assumption that things are other than they seem is nowhere more evident than in the discourse of disguise and revelation that followed an attack and ran through the more general talk about the conflict. A discourse of hidden depth, such talk revolved around the discoveries made when corpses were undressed, when the folds and pockets of garments were explored and turned inside out, disclosing a truer identity underneath—a jihad fighter with an army uniform under his robe, dates in a pocket indexing a devious connection to the Middle East, folded papers with talismans, and so on.[42] Crucially, this attempt to see through everything can emerge only in a situation where people in fact see nothing at all. This predicament—of being trapped in events beyond one's grasp and comprehension, of seeing no way out, of immersion in the thick context of terrible things—comes through poignantly in my taped conversations with Moluccan refugees from 2000 and 2001, in the voices and demeanor of Ambonese speaking on news reports before the 2002 Malino II Peace Agreement, and even in the recollections of men and women with whom I spoke in Ambon in September 2003.

More disturbingly even, as the war went on, more and more people claimed to discern just under the surface of your regular Ambonese face its "Christian" or "Muslim" contours. A striking indication of the sedimentation of violence, this claim stands in sharp contrast to the assertion of an Ambonese, cited earlier in this essay, who at the onset of war explained the Christian and Muslim practice of wearing differently colored headties as due to their mutual inability to tell each other apart—because, he explained, we are all Ambonese. While prepared in multiple ways and waiting, as it were, to happen, the hardening and primordializing of communal identities must be understood as an outcome and not the origin of Ambon's conflict—as one sign, among many, of violence's sedimentation. Although I cannot explore the implications of this outcome here, what the foregoing suggests is that, over time and to a much greater extent than previously was the case, the difference between Ambonese Muslims and Christians came to be something to be seen and, what is more important, something allegedly apparent beyond mere superficial distinctions of dress and manner. In short, during the war, religion acquired a highly elaborated, publicly visible dimension.

On 12 February 2002, the Malino II Peace Agreement was signed after over three years of intermittent and devastating warfare. Of the Malino agreement's eleven points no fewer than six invoke the rule of law, law enforcement, law and order, and human rights, while others refer to principles of transparency and fairness. The largely elite parties who took part in the two-day meeting convened by Indonesia's then Coordinating Minister of People's Welfare, Jusuf Kalla, were familiar with the new laws brought into being under Reformasi and, along with most Indonesians, undoubtedly regarded the law—however flawed and limited its application in practice—as somehow inherently just. The weight and value accorded to the law in Indonesia (which, following Dutch colonial tradition, is a *negara hukum* or, in Dutch, a *rechtstaat*—literally, a state of law or a constitutional state) have only increased as Indonesia's own dramatic changes have been inflected by the prevailing global discourse on democracy, transparency, rights, and human rights in the current Age of the International Community (Feher 2000). Since Suharto's fall a great deal of attention has been paid to legal reform, much of it focused on the courts, the police, and prosecution, in that order, and there have been some successes. As elsewhere, there is also a multitude of legally oriented NGOs focused on legal reform, corruption, rights, environmental issues, and so on at work in Indonesia and a new energetic and promising generation of young legal reformers and activists.

During the Ambon conflict, even after the imposition of civil emergency in June 2000, the security forces and police were, for a variety of reasons, virtually powerless when it came to taking legal action against those responsible for disorder. In a section on "the failure to uphold the law," an International Crisis Group report states that no fewer than 490 criminal cases were investigated and 855 suspects arrested as of July 2000, while a month later there was talk of holding trials on naval ships (International Crisis Group 2002). More than a year thereafter, however, in November 2001, the governor described the courts as still "paralyzed" and admitted that under the circumstances the law could not be upheld. In April and May 2001, some "symbolic" legal steps were taken against the extremist leaders on both the Muslim and Christian sides—the Laskar Jihad commander Ja'far Umar Thalib and the FKM leader Alex Manuputty—but, for different reasons in each case, prosecution has not been successful. What we have, in other words, is, on the one hand, a genuine regard for the law and repeated appeal to the judiciary as a privileged instrument deemed capable of restoring order and, on the other, a legal vacuum in terms of the means to enforce the law, considerable resistance to change by those schooled in the older system, and, in Ambon, the ongoing presence of the armed forces, which are generally known for lending their support to local clients.

Throughout the conflict, multiple attempts were made to reconcile the warring parties, many of which appealed to grounds other than the law but seen as possibly offering a solution or alternative to the war. These include *adat,* or customary law, most notably through the invocation of so-called *pela* (blood brother) ties linking some Muslim and Christian communities on Ambon,[43] and the mass media through the broadcasting of pro-peace public service announcements on radio and television and projects advocating peace journalism and more neutral forms of reporting, and on both sides the interventions of various charismatic leaders who at different times and through a variety of means tried to stop the fighting.[44]

It is hard to evaluate how much significance should, in the end, be attributed to the relative success of the Malino agreement and its appeal to the law given that this agreement benefited from the relative calm imposed over time by the declaration of civil emergency and given that it was met with skepticism by many ordinary Ambonese, who saw it as yet another elite move that touched minimally on their own immediate problems. Notably, many Ambonese I met in September 2003 spoke of four and not three years of war and insisted that whatever calm they then enjoyed was more than anything else a result of the extreme fatigue among the city's population and the feeling that they had suffered enough (and, though this was not stated, without any clear advantage won on either side). Others, as is common in Indonesia, attributed all the city's troubles to meddling by "outsiders," and especially to the operation of otherwise-unspecified politics in Jakarta.

Yet I do believe it significant that the relative détente that currently exists in Ambon has unfolded in what might be called "the shadow of the law" and, more broadly, within a wider global setting where the language of law, democracy, and rights is given increasing credence. Thus, if in this essay I have avoided, indeed rejected, any appeal to explanatory "backdrops" in tracking the sedimentations of violence within "the thick of things," with regard to peace I suggest, in fact, the opposite: namely, that the still-delicate peace that now prevails in Ambon was necessarily brokered against the backdrop of the law, something that may, indeed, be unavoidable under current globalized conditions. Against this backdrop other projects need to be staged in this radically changed city, projects that are more rooted in the life-worlds of ordinary Ambonese and in the ongoingness of the everyday, including that everyday shaped, importantly, by the recent violence.

Notes

The research on which this essay is based was conducted within the context of the "Indonesia in Transition" program funded by the Royal Netherlands Academy of Sciences. I would like to thank this institution for its support of this four-year research program (2001–4) and the members of the "Indonesian Mediations" subproject for their continual stimulation. Fieldwork has been carried out among predominantly Christian Moluccan refugees and among media practitioners in Manado and Bitung, North Sulawesi (May 2000, June–August 2001), among NGO activists and members of religious and humanitarian organizations in Jakarta and Yogyakarta (August 2001), and in Ambon City (September 2003, June–August 2005). I would like to thank John and Jean Comaroff for their incisive editorial suggestions, and Adrian Bedner, Daniel Lev, and Jan Michiel Otto for their valuable input on the law and judiciary post-Suharto. I am especially grateful to the media practitioners, NGO activists, and members of religious and humanitarian organizations for their time and contributions and to the many Moluccan refugees and ordinary Ambonese and Indonesians on whose stories, comments, and insights this essay draws.

   1. For another, earlier reflection on the "tiny hyphen" linking the "very different entities" of nation and state, see Anderson 1990.

   2. For an acute assessment of Indonesia's decentralization and its by-product *pemekaran,* or administrative fragmentation, see Jones 2004.

   3. The original clove-producing areas are the tiny north Moluccan islands of Ternate, Tidore, Moti, Makian, and Bacan. Nutmeg and mace, products of the same nutmeg fruit, come originally from the Banda Islands, southeast of Ambon.

   4. While this is the way many Christian Ambonese liked to refer to themselves, others in Indies society sometimes called them *anjing NICA,* or "dogs of the Netherlands-Indies civil administration" (de Graaf 1977: 279).

   5. In her fascinating discussion of the intricacies of sartorial practice in colonial Ambon, Marianne Hulsbosch (2004) emphasizes how her study was largely limited to Christian Ambonese due to the virtual absence of visual and written records on the Ambonese Muslim population.

   6. On the Islamicization of Indonesia under Suharto's late "New Order" government, see Hefner 2000, 1997.

   7. A selection of the many publications include, among the more academic, Aditjondro 2001; Bartels 2003; Bubandt 2001; Greiner 2000; van Klinken 2001; Manuhutu et al. 2000; Steijlen 2001; Tim Pengkajian Universitas Pattimura 1999. NGO and activist works include International Crisis Group 2000, 2002; Human Rights Watch 1999; Salempessy and Husain 2001; Sinansari ecip 1999; Institut Studi Arus Informasi 2000; Tim Penyusum al-Mukmin 1999. Other sources (including some by protagonists in the conflict) are Al-Jakartaty 2000; Husni Puruhena 1999; Kastor 2000a, 2000b; Kotan 2000; Front Kedaulatan Maluku 2000; Nanere 2000.

   8. For a good history of Ambonese society from the Dutch colonial rule of the late nineteenth century through the nationalist movement, independence, and the RMS movement of the 1950s, see Chauvel 1990. In her doctoral dissertation (1999) Juliet Patricia Lee provides a more recent assessment of Ambonese society, its transformations under the Suharto regime, and Muslim-Christian relations. On the widely publicized *pela,* or blood-brother, relations that conjoin some Muslim and Christian villages and kin groups, see Bartels 1977, 2003. For an excellent critical evaluation of the deployment of *pela* for political purposes as well as information on Ambon's Muslims, see Chauvel 1980.

   9. At issue here is recent migration dating from the 1970s. More generally,

Ambon has attracted migrants for several centuries—including peoples from South Sulawesi. See Knaap 1991.

10. For an insightful discussion and history of the category of "youth," see J. Comaroff and J. L. Comaroff 2005.

11. See Ann Laura Stoler's excellent article (1992). Her reading of the colonial sources within "the gossamered climates of violence" within which stories of a planter's murder were told was useful in thinking about Ambon's violence. Some of the differences between evaluating such murky events through written, archival documentation and my own more phenomenological approach based, among other things, on conversations and interviews with refugees and media practitioners are instructive. Some of the issues discussed here are also addressed in Appadurai 1996.

12. For one of the most informative discussions of the Laskar Jihad's background and activities, see Schulze 2002. See also Hasan 2002; Baker 2002. For a more general discussion, see International Crisis Group 2001.

13. On the problem of Ambon's "rebel soldiers" (deserters), see "Perang Tentara Pembangkang di Ambon," *Tempo* 10 (16 June 2002): 24–37.

14. *Preman* are thugs who tend to operate in gangs. Henk Schulte Nordholt calls them "traffickers in political violence" since they are often used as the henchmen of political parties and groups. See Schulte Nordholt 2001: 25 for a genealogy of the *preman* figure in Indonesia.

15. See, however, Human Rights Watch 2000: 6 and "Island of Ambon Is Worst Trouble Spot in Indonesia," *Radio Australia Indonesia Service,* interview with Moluccas specialist Richard Chauvel, Ambonese journalist Rudi Fofid, and Sidney Jones, Asian director of Human Rights Watch at the time, broadcast on 5 March 1999. My thanks to Rudi Fofid for a transcript of this broadcast.

16. I would like to thank Michael Fischer for bringing this book to my attention.

17. Any kind of balanced information was, not surprisingly, one of the first victims of the violence. Soon after the conflict broke out, the friends and *Suara Maluku* colleagues mentioned here could no longer come together, their office now located in the Christian part of the city and their printing press across the border in Muslim territory. Seizing a good business opportunity when it emerged, the *Jawa Pos* (the Surabaya-based owner of *Suara Maluku*) created a Muslim spin-off, *Ambon Expres,* of what, under the circumstances, increasingly defined itself as a Christian mouthpiece and community paper. For a general discussion of the press in Indonesia, including the business strategy of the *Jawa Pos,* see Sen and Hill 2000. See Allen and Seaton 1999 on the role of (especially) the mass media in situations of war. See also Philip Kitley's astute comments on media practice in conflicted situations (2002: especially 212–14).

18. With warm thanks to Philip Kitley (2002) for suggesting vectors as one way of tracking media effects in a confusing and changeable terrain and for advocating immersion in "the thick of things."

19. Writing of narratives of Partition violence from the Indian subcontinent, Chakrabarty speaks of the trope of "thingification" but also notes, crucially, that "for all the rendering of the human into a mere thing that collective violence may appear to perform, the recognition by one human of another as human is its fun-

damental precondition. . . . That is why it must be said that, even in denying the
humanity of the victim of violence, the perpetrator of violence and torture does,
to begin with, recognize the victim as human. In this unintentional practice of mutual human recognition lies the ground for the conception of proximity. The denial
of the victim's humanity, thus, proceeds necessarily from this initial recognition of
it" (2002: 142).

20. The violence on Ambon Island would be among the recent additions to
a series beginning with the fighting between nationalists and Communist-
nationalists in 1948 (in which killing was extensive), the massacre of Indonesian
Communists and those accused of being Communists in 1965, and the killing of
thousands of "criminals" by the Suharto government in 1983 and 1984 (Siegel
1998).

21. I would like to thank Victor Joseph and Wim Manuhutu for helping me
procure a copy of the public service announcement. The announcement was produced by Franky Sahilatua.

22. On the workings of backdrops, see Appadurai 1997; Gordon 1998.

23. For Maluku Province the proportion of people under twenty-five years of
age is 58.1 percent and more or less the same in rural and urban areas. In East Java
Province the corresponding percentage is 48.8 percent; Bali, 47.7 percent; Jakarta,
51.9 percent; while in the United States it is 35.7 percent and in Germany just 27.9
percent. See van Klinken 2001: 11, N11.

24. From the refugees I interviewed in Manado I heard only the term *pasukan
agas*. Other scholars of Maluku whom I questioned about the meaning of *pasukan
linggis* offered different explanations of the word *linggis*. Wim Manuhutu claims
linggis is a kind of fruit. James T. Collins offered a more historical interpretation.
In Indonesian *linggis* means "crowbar." During the Japanese era there was a song
(said, incidentally, to have been written by an Ambonese) the chorus of which was
as follows: *"Itu Inggris, kita linggis / Amerika kita seterika"* (The English we'll just
crowbar [prise] out / the Americans we'll iron flat). The Indonesian Communist
Party used the same melody and kept the chorus. The song, in other words, still
circulates, though I doubt most Muslim Moluccans would be aware of this genealogy. Collins further pointed out that both "team names"—*pasukan agas* and
pasukan linggis—are entirely Indonesian rather than Ambonese Malay. He also
suggested how the different names index the different self-images of the opponents
(and thus also, I would add, their intended or imagined effect on the enemy Other).
Agas simply cause trouble and misery but do not totally displace their victims.
Linggis, on the other hand, implies the entire removal and dislocation of the opponent. I thank both Wim Manuhutu and especially Jim Collins for their help in
unpacking these terms.

25. Many such poems and letters, as well as drawings, have been collected in
publications put out by NGOs or other humanitarian-oriented groups. At least
some of the children's work is produced in the context of postviolence trauma therapy and rehabilitation programs carried out by some of these organizations. See,
for instance, *Kisah di balik Kehidupan: Anak pengungsi Maluku Utara di Manado
dalam Gambar dan Puisi* (Manado: Yayasan Pelita Kasih Abadi/Catholic Relief
Services Indonesia, 2001); "Program Therapi Emosional Pengungsi Anak di Manado (Jan.–Maret 2001): Hasil Puisi," Yayasan Pelita Kasih Abadi/Catholic Relief

Services Jakarta, Manado, unpublished manuscript; "Kumpulan Puisi Sanggar Kreatif Anak Bitung (Sept.–Des. 2000)," Rakit Communication, 2005; *Rumah seng ada Pintu: Anak-anak Maluku "Korban Kerusuhan"/Een Huis zonder Deur: Molukse Kinderen: "Slachtoffers van Geweld"* (Utrecht: Stichting TitanE, 2001). On such projects, see "Ambon Children Express Trauma through Art," *Jakarta Post,* 20 May 2002, which begins with a letter from "Sukardi," a refugee in Makassar, to his friend "Tammi Aimi" in Ternate, North Maluku Province, in which he expresses longing for his friend but adds, "I'm scared, wondering if you, my friend Tammi, are willing to welcome me back, as we saw our family among those who attacked yours." These trauma and postviolence programs are highly complicated projects resting on specific conceptions of childhood, memory, violence, and the future and deserve further, in-depth study. My thanks to Katinka van Heeren for bringing the *Jakarta Post* article to my attention.

26. This privileging of children echoes other recent productions where children's faces and voices speak out against or serve as a sentimental antidote or contrast to violence, often defined as an adult problem and the result of their agency. These other recent productions also name or depict the abandonment by Indonesians of their duties as parent-citizens, the violent disruption of the father-child bond, or, more abstractly, children who appear alone in various renditions of "orphaned" landscapes. For a discussion of these issues, see, for instance, Spyer 2004a, 2004b, n.d.

27. Rudi Fofid and Zairin Salempessy, letter to the head office of *Aliansi Jurnalis Independen,* "Journalists in the Disturbances of Ambon" (Wartawan dalam Huru-hara Ambon), 10 February 1999 (jurnalis@idola.net.id). My thanks to Rudi Fofid for bringing this letter to my attention.

28. My discussion here is indebted to Susan Stewart's account of *multum in parvo,* or "miniaturized language" (1984: especially 52–53).

29. I am grateful to Christopher Pinney for alerting me to the rhizomatic character of this form of imagining. The use of the rhizome as a figure comes from Deleuze and Guattari 1987.

30. See James T. Siegel's excellent discussion (2000: 347–48) of how "Indonesian violence often stimulates a recourse to recognition outside the framework of the initial conflict," which he links to the more general lack of sedimented identities or their formulation in a narrow, dialectical sense.

31. More generally, the sense of audience is crucial to the production of political violence, as Ariel Heryanto, writing of the rapes of Chinese Indonesian women in May 1998, observes: "political rape, like all political violence, [is] statement making. [It] involve[s] some sort of authorship, medium, message, genre, style, and intended audience. The raped bodies are a sort of medium—comparable to walls vandalised with graffiti—on which the perpetrators inscribe messages directed towards an audience larger than those females directly assaulted" (1999: 299–334).

32. Such amplification can, incidentally, be quite literal, as on a mural featured in *Konflik berdarah Maluku,* one of the many Muslim-produced VCDs (video CDs). This VCD shows a mural of Jesus holding a globe and the camera zooming in on Israel, which is blown up to continental size. The term "amplification" comes from Sahlins 2005.

33. For a facsimile and discussion of the letter, see Nanere 2000: 63–80.

34. For a consideration of Ambon's war as fought out on the Internet, see Sen and Hill 2002; Bräuchler 2003.

35. Similarly, by informal agreement between the local government and journalists, the term *suku* (tribe) was omitted from newspaper articles and other journalistic reports in the wake of the violence between Dayak and Madurese in West Kalimantan. See Nooteboom 2004. Perhaps the most pernicious and explicit of these censoring omissions is the common practice of replacing the names of female rape victims with flower names like Mawar (Rose) or Melati (Jasmine) or even descriptives such as *gelas pecah* (broken glass). See Sushartami 2004.

36. If, as Henk Schulte Nordholt argues, violence has a history in Indonesia, so do, as elsewhere, representations of violence. One can speculate, for instance, that the cinematic preservation of mass, as opposed to small-scale, scenes of violence may lend credence to a communalist reading of the conflict. See Schulte Nordholt's nuanced discussion (2001).

37. My thanks to Farish Noor for this information.

38. See Appadurai 1996: 8–9, 153, on "communities of sentiment," mass-mediated sodalities of worship and charisma, and "structures of feeling" in ethnic violence. See also Deborah Poole's excellent discussion (1997: 107–41, especially 112–13) of the formation of transnational bourgeois sensibilities through the circulation of late-nineteenth-century *cartes de visite*.

39. The VCD is produced by the Dompet Sosial Ummul Quro, based in Bandung, Java. The organization's address, phone and fax numbers, and bank account information are all listed on the VCD jacket. It has a copyright from 2000.

40. I would like to thank Webb Keane for providing me with this term.

41. This kind of suspicion is common among intimate enemies such as those of Ambon's civil war. Appadurai links the extreme violence often characteristic of such conflict to the sense of betrayal between appearance and reality as "a perceived violation of the sense of knowing who the Other was and of rage about who they really turn out to be" (1996: 154–55).

42. For another example of the intimate coupling of pockets and identity, see Spyer 1999; also Spyer 2000: 92–100.

43. In contrast to Ambon, the appeal to *adat* in the context of the conflict in the Kei Islands, southeastern Maluku, was largely successful in bringing about reconciliation, something that most observers have attributed to the ongoing prominent position of custom and customary law in the lives of many Keiese. Regarding Ambon's *adat,* many would agree that its significance has been hollowed out and largely reduced to the performance of colorful dances on national television or at official state-endorsed ceremonies. At the same time, under the current national program of decentralization and the impetus it gives to regional identity, *adat* on Ambon seems in certain respects to be undergoing a revival. It remains to be seen, however, whether this revival amounts simply to more songs and dances or to the carving out of a more significant role for custom and by extension, perhaps, customary law. For a detailed assessment of the reconciliation process in Kei, see Laksono and Topatimasang 2003.

44. See, for instance, the somewhat congratulatory book that focuses on the bishop of Amboina, Monseigneur P. C. Mandagi MSC, as peacemaker in the conflict: Kotan 2000.

References

Acciaioli, Greg. 2002. "Re-empowering the 'Art of the Elders': The Revitalisation of Adat among the To Lindu of Central Sulawesi and throughout Contemporary Indonesia." In *Beyond Jakarta: Regional Autonomy and Local Societies in Indonesia,* ed. Minako Sakai, pp. 217–44. Adelaide, Australia: Crawford House Publishing.

Aditjondro, George Junus. 2001. "Guns, Pamphlets and Handie-Talkies: How the Military Exploited Local Ethno-religious Tensions in Maluku to Preserve Their Political and Economic Privileges." In *Violence in Indonesia,* ed. Ingrid Wessel and Georgia Wimhofer, 100–128. Hamburg: Abera Verlag.

Al-Jakartaty, Erwin H. 2000. *Tragedi bumi seribu pulau: Mengkritisi kebijakan pemerintah dan solusi penyelesaian konflik.* Jakarta: BukKMaNs.

Allen, Tim, and Jean Seaton, eds. 1999. *The Media of Conflict: War Reporting and Representations of Ethnic Violence.* London and New York: Zed Books.

Anderson, Benedict R. O. 1990. "Old State, New Society: Indonesia's New Order in Comparative Historical Perspective." In *Language and Power: Exploring Political Cultures in Indonesia,* ed. Benedict R. O. Anderson, 94–120. Ithaca, NY: Cornell University Press.

———. 1991. *Imagined Communities: Reflections on the Origin and Spread of Nationalism.* 2d ed. London: Verso. (1st ed., 1983.)

Appadurai, Arjun. 1996. *Modernity at Large: Cultural Dimensions of Globalization.* Minneapolis: University of Minnesota Press.

———. 1997. "The Colonial Backdrop." *Afterimage* 24(5):4–7.

Aragon, Lorraine V. 2001. "Communal Violence in Poso, Central Sulawesi: Where People Eat Fish and Fish Eat People." *Indonesia* 72:45–79.

Avonius, Leena. 2004. "Reforming Wetu Telu: Islam, Adat, and the Promises of Regionalism in Post–New Order Lombok." PhD diss., Leiden University.

Baker, Jacqui. 2002. "Laskar Jihad's Mimetic Stutter: State Power, Spectacular Violence and the Fetish in the Indonesian Postcolony." Bachelor of Asian Studies thesis (Honours), Australian National University.

Bartels, Dieter. 1977. "Guarding the Sacred Mountain: Intervillage Alliances, Religious Syncretism and Ethnic Identity among Ambonese Christians and Moslems in the Moluccas." PhD diss., Department of Anthropology, Cornell University.

———. 2003. "Your God Is No Longer Mine: Moslem-Christian Fratricide in the Central Moluccas (Indonesia) after a Half-Millennium of Peaceful Co-existence and Ethnic Unity." In *A State of Emergency: Violence, Society and the State in Eastern Indonesia,* ed. Sandra Pannell, pp. 128–53. Darwin: Northern Territory University Press.

Blumenfeld, Lori. 2002. *Revenge: A Story of Hope.* New York: Simon and Schuster.

Bräuchler, Birgit. 2003. "Cyberidentities at War: Religion, Identity, and the Internet in the Moluccan Conflict." *Indonesia* 75:123–31.

Bubandt, Nils. 2001. "Malukan Apocalypse: Themes in the Dynamics of Violence in Eastern Indonesia." In *Violence in Indonesia,* ed. Ingrid Wessel and Georgia Wimhofer, pp. 228–53. Hamburg: Abera Verlag.

Chakrabarty, Dipesh. 2002. *Habitations of Modernity: Essays in the Wake of Subaltern Studies.* Chicago: University of Chicago Press.

Chauvel, Richard. 1980. "Ambon's Other Half: Some Preliminary Observations on Ambonese Moslem Society and History." *Review of Indonesian and Malaysian Affairs* 14(1):40–80.

———. 1990. *Nationalists, Soldiers and Separatists.* Leiden: KITLV Press.

Comaroff, Jean, and John L. Comaroff. 2005. "Reflections on Youth, from the Past to the Postcolony." In *Makers and Breakers: Children and Youth in Postcolonial Africa,* ed. Alcinda Honnana and Filip De Boeck. Oxford: James Currey.

Comaroff, John L., and Jean Comaroff. 2004. "Criminal Justice, Cultural Justice: The Limits of Liberalism and the Pragmatics of Difference in the New South Africa." *American Ethnologist* 31(2):188–204.

Davidson, Jamie S., and Douglas Kammen. 2002. "Indonesia's Unknown War and the Lineages of Violence in West Kalimantan." *Indonesia* 73:53–87.

de Graaf, H. J. 1977. *De geschiedenis van Ambon en de Zuid-Molukken.* Franeken: Uitgeverij T. Wever B.V.

Deleuze, Gilles, and Felix Guattari. 1987. *A Thousand Plateaus: Capitalism and Schizophrenia.* Trans. Brian Massumi. Minneapolis: University of Minnesota Press.

Feher, Michel. 2000. *Powerless by Design: The Age of the International Community.* Durham, NC: Duke University Press.

Front Kedaulatan Maluku. 2000. "Tragedi Kemanusiaan Maluku dipersembahkan kepada dunia internasional atas nama rakyat Maluku yang menderita oleh Front Kedaulatan Maluku." Unpublished manuscript, Ambon, 24 August.

Gordon, Robert J. 1998. "Backdrops and Bushmen: An Expeditious Comment." In *The Colonising Camera: Photographs in the Making of Namibian History,* ed. Wolfram Hartmann, Jeremy Silvester, and Patricia Hayes, pp. 111–17. Cape Town, RSA: University of Cape Town Press.

Greiner, Andries, ed. 2000. *De Molukken in Crisis: Machteloos, ver weg, maar niet wanhopig.* No. 2691, 18 February. Lelystad: Actuele Onderwerpen.

Hasan, Noorhaidi. 2002. "Faith and Politics: The Rise of the Laskar Jihad in the Era of Transition in Indonesia." *Indonesia* 37:145–69.

Hefner, Robert W. 1997. "Islamization and Democratization in Indonesia." In *Islam in an Era of Nation-States: Politics and Religious Renewal in Muslim Southeast Asia,* ed. Robert W. Hefner and Patricia Horvawitch, pp. 75–127. Honolulu: University of Hawai'i Press.

———. 2000. *Civil Islam: Muslims and Democratization in Indonesia.* Princeton, NJ: Princeton University Press.

Heryanto, Ariel. 1999. "Race, Rape, and Reporting." In *Reformasi: Crisis and Change in Indonesia,* ed. Arief Budiman, Barbara Hatley, and Damien Kingsbury, pp. 299–334. Clayton, Australia: Monash Asia Institute.

Hulsbosch, Marianne. 2004. "Pointy Shoes and Pith Helmets: Dress and Identity Construction in Ambon from 1850 to 1942." PhD diss., Faculty of Creative Arts, University of Wollongong.

Human Rights Watch. 1999. "Indonesia: The Violence in Ambon." Human Rights Watch Report. March.

———. 2000. "Indonesia: The Violence in Ambon." Human Rights Watch Report, no. 6. March.

Husni Puruhena, M. 1999. *Buku putih-tragedi kemanusiaan dalam kerusuhan di Maluku: Sebuah prosesi ulang sejarah masa lalu.* Ambon: Lembaga Eksistensi Muslim Maluku (LEMM).

Institut Studi Arus Informasi (ISAI). 2000. *Luka Maluku: Militer terlibat.* Jakarta.

International Crisis Group. 2000. "Indonesia: Overcoming Murder and Chaos in Maluku." Report no. 10. Jakarta and Brussels. 19 December.

————. 2001. "Indonesia: Violence and Radical Muslims." *Indonesia Briefing.* Jakarta and Brussels. 10 October.

————. 2002. "Indonesia: The Search for Peace in Maluku." Asia Report no. 31. Jakarta and Brussels. 8 February.

Jones, Sidney. 2004. "What's Indonesia Going to Look Like in Five Years?" Keynote address at the Royal Netherlands Academy of Sciences conference "Indonesia in Transition: Reform, Crises, Conflicts, Continuities." Amsterdam, August.

Kastor, Rustam. 2000a. *Konspirasi politik RMS dan kristen menghancurkan ummat Islam di Ambon-Maluku.* Yogyakarta: Wihdah Press.

————. 2000b. *Suara Maluku Menbantah/Rustam Kastor Menjawab.* Yogyakarta: Wihdah Press.

Kitley, Philip. 2002. "Into the Thick of Things: Tracking the Vectors of 'Indonesian Mediations,' a Comment." In *Indonesia in Search of Transition,* ed. Henk Schulte Nordholt and Irwan Abdullah, pp. 207–17. Yogyakarta: Pustaka Pelajar.

Knaap, Gerrit J. 1991. "A City of Migrants." *Indonesia* 51:105–32.

Kotan, Daniel B., ed. 2000. *Mediator dalam Kerusuhan Maluku.* Jakarta: Sekretariat Komisi Katenetik Kwi.

Laksono, P. M., and Topatimasang, Roem, eds. 2003. *Ken Sa Faak: Benih-benih perdamaian dari Kepulauan Kei.* Yogyakarta: INSIST Press.

Lee, Juliet Patricia. 1999. "Out of Order: The Politics of Modernity in Indonesia." PhD diss., University of Virginia.

Manuhutu, Wim, et al. 2000. *Maluku manis, Maluku menangis: De Molukken in crisis.* Een poging tot verklaring van de geweldsexplosie op de Molukken. Utrecht: Moluks Historisch Museum/Moluccan Information and Documentation Center.

Mbembe, Achille. 2001. *On the Postcolony.* Berkeley and Los Angeles: University of California Press.

Nanere, Jan, ed. 2000. *Halmahera berdarah.* Ambon: Bimspela.

Nooteboom, Gerben. 2004. "A Madurese Family Network in East Kalimantan." Paper presented at the Royal Netherlands Academy of Sciences conference "Indonesia in Transition: Reform, Crises, Conflicts, Continuities." Amsterdam, August.

Peluso, Nancy Lee, and Emily Harwell. 2001. "Territory, Custom, and the Cultural Politics of Ethnic War in West Kalimantan, Indonesia." In *Violent Environments,* ed. Michael Watts and Nancy Peluso, pp. 83–116. Ithaca, NY: Cornell University Press.

Poole, Deborah. 1997. *Vision, Race, and Modernity: A Visual Economy of the Andean Image World.* Princeton, NJ: Princeton University Press.

Sahlins, Marshall. 2005. "Structural Work: How Microhistories Become Macrohistories and Vice Versa." *Anthropological Theory* 5(1):5–30.

Sakai, Minako, ed. 2002. *Beyond Jakarta: Regional Autonomy and Local Society in Indonesia.* Adelaide, Australia: Crawford House Publishing.

Salempessy, Zairin, and Thamrin Husain, eds. 2001. *Ketika semerbak cengkih tergusur asap mesiu: Tragedi kemanusiaan Maluku di balik konspirasi militer, kapitalis birokrat, dan kepentingan elit politik.* Jakarta: Sekretariat Tapak Ambon.

Schulte Nordholt, Henk. 2001. "A Genealogy of Violence in Indonesia." Lisbon: Centro Portugues de Estudos do Sudeste Asiatico (CEPESA).

Schulze, Kirsten E. 2002. "Laskar Jihad and the Conflict in Ambon." *Brown Journal of World Affairs* 9(1):57–69.

Sekretariat Komisi Kateketik KWI. 2001. *Mediator dalam kerusuhan Maluku.* Jakarta.

Sen, Krishna, and David T. Hill. 2000. *Media, Culture and Politics in Indonesia.* Oxford: Oxford University Press.

———. 2002. "Netizens in Combat: Conflict on the Internet in Indonesia." *Asian Studies Association of Australia* 26(2):165–88.

Siegel, James T. 1998. *A New Criminal Type in Jakarta Counter-revolution Today.* Durham, NC: Duke University Press.

———. 2000. *The Rope of God.* 2d ed., with two additional chapters. Ann Arbor: University of Michigan Press. (1st ed., 1969.)

Sinansari ecip, S. 1999. *Menyulut Ambon: Kronologi merambatnya berbagai kerusuhan lintas wilayah di Indonesia.* Bandung: Mizan.

Spyer, Patricia. 1999. "What's in a Pocket? Religion and the Formation of a Pagan Elsewhere in Aru, Eastern Indonesia." In "De bindkracht der dingen," ed. Hans Harbers and Sjaak Koenis. *Tijdschrift voor Empirische Filosofie* 1(23):37–49.

———. 2000. *The Memory of Trade: Modernity's Entanglements on an Eastern Indonesian Island.* Durham, NC: Duke University Press.

———. 2002a. "Indonesian Mediations: A Position Paper." With Ben Arps, Katinka van Heeren, Edwin Jurriens, and Wiwik Sushartami. In *Indonesia in Search of Transition,* ed. Henk Schulte Nordholt and Irwan Abdullah, pp. 177–217. Yogyakarta: Pustaka Pelajar.

———. 2002b. "Shadow Media and Moluccan Muslim VCDs." In *9/11: A Virtual Case Book,* ed. Barbara Abrash and Faye Ginsburg. New York: Center for Media, Culture, and History Virtual Case Book (VCB). http://www.nyu.edu/fas/projects/vcb/.

———. 2004a. "*Belum Stabil* and Other Signs of the Times in Post-Suharto Indonesia." In *Indonesia in Transition: Rethinking "Civil Society," "Region," and "Crisis,"* ed. Samuel Hanneman and Henk Schulte Nordholt, pp. 235–52. Yogyakarta: Pustaka Pelajar.

———. 2004b. *Why Can't We Be Like Storybook Children? Media of Violence and Peace in Maluku, Indonesia.* Jakarta: KITLV Press.

———. 2006. "Media and Violence in an Age of Transparency: Journalistic Writing on War-Torn Maluku." In *Media, Religion, and the Public Sphere,* ed. Birgit Meyer and Annelies Moors. Bloomington: Indiana University Press.

———. n.d. "Orphaning the Nation: Violence, Sentimentality, and Media in the Wake of Ambon's War." Unpublished manuscript.

Steijlen, Fridus. 2001. *Kerusuhan: Het misverstand over de Molukse onrust.* Utrecht: Forum.

Stewart, Susan. 1984. *On Longing: Narratives of the Miniature, the Gigantic, the Souvenir, the Collection.* Baltimore, MD: Johns Hopkins University Press.

Stoler, Ann Laura. 1992. "In Cold Blood: Hierarchies of Credibility and the Politics of Colonial Narratives." In "Imperial Fantasies and Postcolonial Histories." Special issue, *Representations* 37:151–89.

Sushartami, Wiwik. 2004. "Beauty Parade: Visual Representations of Women in Post-Suharto Media." Paper presented at the Royal Netherlands Academy of Sciences conference "Indonesia in Transition: Reform, Crises, Conflicts, Continuities." Amsterdam, August.

Tim Pengkajian Universitas Pattimura. 1999. "Analisis sosial tentang peristiwa kerusuhan berdarah di kotamadya Ambon dan sekitarnya januari–februari 1999." Ambon.

Tim Penysum al-Mukmin. 1999. *Tragedi Ambon.* Jakarta: Yayasan Al-Mukmin.

van Klinken, Gerry. 2001. "The Maluku Wars: Bringing Society Back In." *Indonesia* 71:1–26.

———. 2004. "Dayak Ethnogenesis and Conservative Politics in Indonesia's Outer Islands." In *Indonesia in Transition: Rethinking "Civil Society," "Region," and "Crisis,"* ed. Samuel Hanneman and Henk Schulte Nordholt, pp. 107–28. Yogyakarta: Pustaka Pelajar.

Williams, Raymond. 1977. *Marxism and Literature.* Oxford: Oxford University Press.

Witchcraft and the Limits of the Law
Cameroon and South Africa

Peter Geschiere

IN THE 1980s, state courts in Cameroon—notably in the East Province, generally considered as backward and infested with witchcraft—began to condemn "witches" to heavy sentences (up to ten years in jail and heavy fines). This was a striking reversal of previous jurisprudence, especially since the judges were now ready to accept the testimony of *nganga* (traditional healers) as conclusive proof. Until then it was the *nganga* who risked persecution (for defamation and disturbance). In the 1980s they became, on the contrary, crucial witnesses for the prosecution (see Fisiy and Geschiere 1990; Geschiere 1997: chap. 6).

In the 1990s, the new African National Congress (ANC) regime in South Africa came under heavy pressure to intervene against "witchcraft." Toward the end of apartheid, especially the northern parts of the country became the scene of violent witch-hunts, in which gangs of young people—often associated with the ANC[1]—played a leading role, supported by *inyanga* (experts in magic who are similar in many ways to the Cameroonian *nganga*). In 1995 the ANC government of the Northern Province (later rebaptized Limpopo Province) instituted the Commission of Inquiry into Witchcraft Violence and Ritual Murders in the Northern Province of the Republic of South Africa—commonly called the Ralushai Commission after its chairman—to look into the causes of these disturbances. In 1996 the report of this commission advised a change in the law so that not only *inyanga* and other specialists could be prosecuted but also any person "who does any act which creates a reasonable suspicion that he is engaged in the practice of witchcraft" (1996: 55).[2] One can wonder how the latter recommendation—which can be read as confirming the reality of witchcraft as a crime—is to be reconciled with the general trend of legislation under the postapartheid regime, notably with the modernist tenor of the new Constitution. In subsequent years the witch-hunts in Limpopo and in neighboring Mpumalanga seem to have abated somewhat. According to Isak Niehaus (2001) this is mainly due to the restoration of the authority of "traditional" chiefs in these areas.[3]

However, it is clear as well that the ANC government—like the Cameroonian regime—continues to be under heavy popular pressure to deal one way or another with witchcraft. The general panic about a supposed proliferation of witchcraft is certainly not limited to the rural regions. In several publications Adam Ashforth (1998b, 2000, 2005) has showed, for instance, that witchcraft panics became ever stronger in Soweto, the largest township in the country. He concludes that witches have replaced the former apartheid regime as an explanation for people's sufferings; and he adds that it might seriously affect the ANC regime's credibility if it does not show itself capable of dealing with this threat in one way or another. Indeed, in December 2004, the South African Parliament voted with great enthusiasm (clearly inspired by President Thabo Mbeki's call for an "African Renaissance," which implies proper respect for "African knowledge") for a new law that formalizes ways in which state officials can work together with *inyanga*. It is not yet clear what the practical implications of this law will be.

The aim of this essay is to compare these two efforts—prosecution and collaboration—to combat the rising fear of witchcraft. My question is whether one can expect the law—and I mean here state law—to contain this fear, which so many now see as a form of disorder that urgently needs to be addressed. In many parts of the African continent this is, unfortunately, a pressing question. At the same time it will be clear that this is also a very tricky topic: writing about it clearly entails the dangers of exoticizing—or even primitivizing—Africa as still beset by "traditional" forms of superstition. Especially in the United States, many African Americans (and also African colleagues working in the United States) tend to complain that discussing "witchcraft" implies "putting Africa back in the 19th century," as a colleague once remarked. It is certainly true that the term itself is a most unfortunate translation of African notions with much broader meanings. However, on the African continent itself, people—academics included—stress that the popular obsession with a supposed proliferation of "witchcraft" is an ever more urgent problem.[4] Clearly, it will not do to address such fears as stemming from the resilience of some sort of "traditional" relict that is seen as the very opposite of everything that is "modern." As Jean Comaroff and John Comaroff showed already more than ten years ago, in their seminal introduction to *Modernity and Its Malcontents* (1993), "witchcraft" has become, on the contrary, an integral part of people's vision of modernity. The often-disconcerting dynamics of these representations precisely in the more modern sectors of life—new forms of entrepreneurship, health services, sports, politics—show that they express not so much resistance to modernity but rather an effort to interpret modern changes and gain access to them.[5]

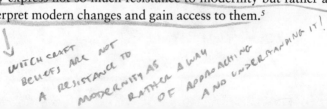

WITCHCRAFT BELIEFS ARE NOT A RESISTANCE TO MODERNITY AS RATHER A WAY OF APPROACHING AND UNDERSTANDING IT!

The consequence is that in many parts of present-day Africa—certainly not only in Cameroon or South Africa—there is increasing pressure on the government to intervene. It would be highly regrettable if political correctness made academics avoid such an urgent topic. Throughout the continent people complain that colonial governments (including the apartheid one) tended to protect the witches: they intervened against the "witch doctors," convicting them for defamation and disturbance of the peace. Many feel that, thus, the state allowed witchcraft to proliferate.[6] However, people expect the situation to be different in the postcolony: the new government should know what to do about witchcraft.

In this shadowy field, there is therefore certainly the tendency, signaled in the introduction to this collection, toward a "legalization" of everyday life. This tendency seems to be directly related to a widespread fear of looming and encompassing disorder. It is this fear—taking on, indeed, "metaphysical" dimensions—that directly reinforces the trend toward legalization. Yet there may be a paradox here, in the sense that this very appeal to the law to set things right, instead of appeasing popular fears of disorder, dramatically reinforces them. After all, it is a moot question whether the state, with its juridical sanctions, is at all capable of dealing with this explosive issue, and this can radically heighten people's feelings of intense insecurity.[7] There seems to be a worrying but almost inevitable logic involved in this: the modernist state with its claims to general control tends to spread its interventions ever more broadly; thus, it risks becoming bogged down in domains that are clearly at the margins of its scope. And it is precisely the failures of the supposedly all-powerful state that can make the fear of disorder attain metaphysical dimensions.

On this point, the question raised in the call for papers for our conference as to whether the "postcolony" is exceptional (or not) is highly relevant. At first sight the whole conundrum of witchcraft and the law may seem to highlight the exceptionality of the postcolony. It is true that the glaring contrast between the kind of rationality on which the modern state is built (at least formally) and the logics involved in witchcraft thinking can expose the limits to state interventions in this treacherous field all the more blatantly. However, in a broader perspective, similar tendencies seem to emerge, ever more strongly, in the supposedly modern countries of the West. There also a strong trend toward legalization—people invoking the law to tackle an increasingly broad spectrum of issues and problems—leads to unexpected dilemmas. To Jean Comaroff and John Comaroff (1999, 2000), the distinguishing mark of "millennial capitalism" is the proliferation of "occult economies": pyramid schemes, transnational financial speculations, smuggling on a global scale, Satanist networks on the

Internet, and so on—all pretty difficult challenges for the state, which is nonetheless expected to somehow remain in control. The predicament of the state sketched above is therefore not special to the African state (or even to the postcolonial one; see also Mbembe 2002). In the West as well the state seems to be drawn increasingly into fields that will inevitably highlight the limits to its power: think of the struggle over control of the Internet or the clumsy incursions into the family domain with its hidden currents of aggression.[8] Moreover, there is an intriguing paradox here. How does this trend toward legalization and state intervention relate to the now omnipresent belief in "the" market as the solution to all problems and the concomitant conviction that the state should restrain itself as much as possible in order to give free rein to "the" economy? Can the law in such a context indeed be expected to contain popular feelings of disorder?

However, the aim of this contribution is more modest. The central question concerns the ability of the Cameroonian and South African governments to deal with the tricky issue of witchcraft. There seem, indeed, to be good reasons to focus on the *limits of the law* in this context.[9] The Cameroonian example shows that a state offensive against witchcraft can be quite counterproductive. In practice it seems to have reaffirmed the popular obsession with witchcraft as an omnipresent danger. Moreover, the sanctions imposed proved to have completely opposite effects: what is the use of jailing supposed witches for several years when everybody is convinced that, by the time they are released, they will have become even more dangerous? However, such criticisms may seem to be quite gratuitous in view of the very real pressure on the government to do something. The question is, can South Africa do better?

Several factors make any attempt to control witchcraft difficult. The first is the circular and subversive character of witchcraft discourse. A precondition for any form of legislation—just as for our claims as academics—seems to be the creation of clarity and unequivocal distinctions. However, as soon as legislators have to deal with witchcraft, they—again just like academics—become entangled in a minefield of ambiguities and shifting meanings that seem to block any effort toward control.

A second factor, directly related to the first, is the problematic but crucial role of the local expert (*nganga, inyanga, sangoma,* healer, diviner, witch doctor—whatever term one prefers) as a key witness. Can judges ever establish proof in this occult domain without using their expertise? But how does one prevent this from being seen by the people as legitimating forces similar to those attributed to the witches? A related concern is the limited effectivity that the state's sanctions seem to have against witches, certainly in comparison to these local experts' forms of healing. In practice, it is precisely these indispensable intermediaries who entangle judges and legislators in all the ambiguities of witchcraft discourse.

However, first, a brief excursion into witchcraft as "disorder" might be helpful—all the more so in view of anthropology's persistent heritage of seeing these representations and practices as a very effective form of "social control." The rest of the essay will then focus on witchcraft as exposing the limits of the law.

[handwritten annotation: ↳ theme of my essay]

Witchcraft as Disorder?

In general, interventions by the law into the field of witchcraft—be it in present-day Africa or, for instance, in early-modern Europe—are based on the assumption that witchcraft constitutes a direct attack on the social order. During the heyday of anthropological witchcraft studies in the 1940s and 1950s, anthropologists certainly agreed with this view, but they gave it a special twist by also insisting on the role of these beliefs as very effective elements of social control. Max Gluckman, the guru of the so-called Manchester school, which produced a series of monographs on British "Central Africa" that deeply influenced anthropological views on witchcraft,[10] typically saw witchcraft as essential for the maintenance of the social order. He compared the morality ingrained in witchcraft beliefs to that expressed in an Anglican anthem and deemed it even more effective: "beliefs in the malice of witchcraft . . . do more than ask [you to love your neighbour] as an act of grace; they affirm that if you do not love one another fervently, misfortune will come" (Gluckman 1955: 94).

It was this threat that, in his view, made witchcraft so effective in obliging "men and women . . . to observe the social virtues" (Gluckman 1955: 94).[11] This peaceful view is, indeed, far away from the horrors depicted (both in writing and in photographs) in the Ralushai Commission report and from Peter Delius's shocking descriptions of how, in 1986, the "comrades" in two villages in Sekhukhuneland (present-day Limpopo Province) called in help from a local diviner, a certain Ramaredi Shaba, who no longer threw bones but instead had developed a more modern divining technique, called "African television." On her oversized screen the figures of the "witches" would appear who were then to be "necklaced" by the comrades (Delius 1996: 195). No doubt, Gluckman would have characterized such horrors as symptomatic of a period of transition. But then we may have to see the entire postcolonial period as one great transition. Indeed, since people increasingly feel that the whole world is in constant transition, the term seems to lose its meaning.

It might be more relevant to question Gluckman's (and many other an-thropologists') view of witchcraft as the opposite of the social order, serv-ing to keep this order in shape. My informants in East Cameroon, just like several people quoted in the Ralushai Commission report seem, rather, to see it as an integral part of the social order: it may be an extremely evil force, yet if channeled correctly it can also bring riches, luck, and power. Philippe Laburthe-Tolra (1977) concluded that among the Beti of Central Cameroon, *evu* (now always translated as *sorcellerie*) is seen as the dark side of power, extremely dangerous but yet at the same time necessary for making society tick. In these societies, the link between witchcraft and power seems to express the deep conviction that any form of power, even if it is necessary, is highly dangerous. And, again, it is striking that in the Ralushai report so many comments from informants, especially concern-ing the position of Venda chiefs, seem to echo this view.

This view, relativizing the distinction between good and evil in witch-craft discourse, that was so strongly conveyed to me by my informants from the Cameroonian forest area, has been strongly criticized by several colleagues. The French Togolese political scientist Comi Toulabor re-proaches me in his eloquent way for not making a clear distinction be-tween the "witch" and the "magician" (the first unequivocally evil, the second able to use his or her special powers only in a more positive way; Toulabor 1999). John Hund (now at the University of the North, South Africa) attacks me even more forcefully by naming me as an outstanding example of the academic writers who are "unfortunately some of the worst perpetrators of confusion." He is clearly shocked that I repeat my informants' view of the *nganga* (traditional healer) as being a kind of "superwitch" since she or he can heal only by using the same powers as witches tend to use. For Hund this is an "overwhelming misunderstand-ing" (Hund 2000: 369–70). He insists instead that healers (for him, espe-cially the *sangoma* of South Africa) should be radically distinguished from witches.

Of course, the whole witchcraft conundrum would be a lot easier to solve if such a separation could be applied so easily. The problem is, again, the subversive character of witchcraft discourse, which so easily erodes all such comfortable conceptual distinctions (in Africa, just as elsewhere in the world; see Favret-Saada 1977 on Europe and Taussig 1987 on Colom-bia). It is clear that there are wide differences in how African societies view central figures like chiefs and healers and in how they relate them to occult powers (or try to separate them from these powers).[12] It is true also that in the forest societies in Cameroon where I did my main fieldwork, the central notions (*djambe* among the Maka and *evu* among the Beti) are extremely broad and fluid, covering a wide array of different expressions of the occult, from highly negative to fairly positive—*djambe/evu* being potentially lethal but also essential for healing, exercising authority, or accumulating wealth. Elsewhere I tried to show (Geschiere 1997) that, for instance, in the more hierarchical societies of Cameroon's western highlands, there is a determined effort to "compartmentalize" the sphere of the occult through clear terminological distinctions between more negative and more positive forms. In these societies, the chief, though certainly associated with occult powers, is normally rigidly separated from the darker manifestations of these powers. However, it might be important to emphasize that such distinctions are always precarious and never self-evident. It seems to require a constant struggle to maintain them against the inherent fluidity of any discourse on the occult. For instance, recently, when many chiefs from the Cameroonian highlands got into trouble with their subjects for their continued support of the hated regime of President Biya, people were quick to accuse them of being real witches.

There may be good reasons therefore not to take the distinctions that are often emphasized in the literature on South Africa between "witch" and *sangoma*—or between the *sangoma* as a "priest-diviner" and the *inyanga* as his disreputable colleague— too much for granted. Even Hund (2000: 373) emphasizes that they all use "the same occult forces," but he insists that there is an "ontological" difference. Again, one can sympathize with his effort to differentiate the *sangoma* as a reliable ally in these dark struggles. But who makes this ontological difference between actors who are so closely involved with the same forces? And how can such a distinction be maintained in practice? It is clear that widely different views of the *sangoma* pertain in daily life. Several people quoted in the Ralushai Commission report (especially from Vendaland) say quite nasty things about *sangoma* ("with a lust for blood and easy money"; 1996: 268). Adam Ashforth (2000) quotes a *sangoma* (for whom Ashforth clearly had great respect) who told him that someone asked him to use his powers to kill another man, which the healer "of course," refused to do—yet the prospective client clearly had another idea of what *sangoma* do and do not do.

Rather than taking such terminological distinctions as givens, it might be more urgent to study exactly how—through what struggles and by what means—such compartmentalization is maintained. Apparently this will always entail a highly precarious struggle against the tendency of discourses on the occult to blur categories. It might be this subversive charge, undermining any clear-cut distinction between good and evil (or any attempt at a clear definition, whether by academics or by lawyers), that can help us to understand the impressive resilience of these discourses in the face of modern changes. It is also this blurring—think of the Comaroffs' characterization as "unroutinizable powers" (J. Comaroff and J. L. Comaroff 2004)—that makes it so difficult for the state to find reliable allies in its witchcraft struggle.

Subverting the Law: The Circularity of Witchcraft Discourse

A basic problem for any legislative intervention in the field of witchcraft is what might be called the latter's "circular" character. As mentioned, unequivocal terminology and clear-cut definitions are supposed to be crucial for any lawmaking (as they are for respectable academic research). It might be all the more important to emphasize that the very ambiguity and the fluidity of its core notions are at the heart of the resilience of witchcraft discourse. This seems to be an important reason why changes can be integrated so easily into this discourse and why it is able to explain whatever outcome an event has, making it impervious to any Popperian attempt to try and falsify it. It might also be an important reason why both lawyers and academics have such difficulty in making sense of this tricky field.

My first confrontation with the quite-alarming circularity of witchcraft talk was when my neighbors in the village in southern Cameroon where I had just settled started to gossip about my new friend Mendouga. The latter was a dignified lady of a certain age and with a somewhat enigmatic air who had already honored me twice with a visit. This was quite an honor since, at the time, she was generally seen as the greatest *nganga* (healer) of the area. But after her second visit, my assistant and his friends pointed out to me that "of course" this meant that she was a great *djindjamb* (literally, someone who has a *djambe*, "witchcraft"). Indeed, for them it was only because she had developed her *djambe* in an extraordinary way— thanks to the help of her "professor"—that she could "see" what the witches were doing (meaning that she had "the second pair of eyes"), fall upon them, and force them to lift their spell so that their victim (Mendouga's client) could be healed. Mendouga herself later on assured me, as all *nganga* will do, that her *djambe* was "different": her professor had bound her with heavy "interdictions" to use her powers only to heal and never to kill.[13] However, it was clear that my fellow villagers were not so sure of this: a *djambe* is a *djambe,* and there is always the risk that the basic instinct of the *djindjamb*—that is, to deliver one's own kin to be devoured by one's fellow witches—will break through. Indeed, *nganga* are always seen as highly ambiguous figures: they are the obvious persons to turn to when one feels attacked; yet they are also terribly dangerous. And, indeed, about all *nganga* there was constant gossip that they had betrayed their own clients, that they worked in league with the witches, and so on. Throughout the forest area of Cameroon, as in other parts of the continent, there is even a basic belief that, in order to become initiated, an aspiring *nganga* has to offer one of his or her own relatives to his or her professor.[14]

There is a basic circularity here: the *nganga* can heal only because (s)he has killed before. Moreover, the main protection against a *djambe* attack is to be found within the realm of the very same *djambe*. But by invoking the help and protection of a *nganga* one allows oneself to be drawn into *djambe*'s vicious circles. No wonder it is so difficult to escape.[15]

Again, it might be good to emphasize that this example has aspects that may be particular to certain parts of Cameroon (or maybe of the equatorial forest area). Yet the practical difficulties in keeping witch and healer apart—and the circularity this entails—seem to be much more general.[16] The question is what happens when the state with its judicial apparatus intervenes in such a tricky field?

The research by Cyprian Fisiy and myself on the witchcraft trials in the East Province of Cameroon began with a set of files from the Court of Appeal of Bertoua (the capital of the East Province) to which Fisiy succeeded in gaining access. The very language of these files shows what kind of confusion occurs when a witchcraft affair has to be dealt with in legal writing. The files are full of long vituperations by the judges against witchcraft as a basic evil: they expose it as the villagers' main form of subversion of government initiatives and as *the* explanation of why this province remains so backward. Like other civil servants, the judges clearly feel—at least in their official role—that witchcraft has to be exterminated at all costs. Any suspect who confesses to being a *sorcier* (witch) is, therefore, certain to be condemned to a heavy sentence (a longer term in jail, a heavy fine). The main witnesses against these witches are a small number of *nganga* whose expertise is clearly accepted by the court (in fact, their declarations that they have "seen" that the accused "went out"—that is, left his body at night to fly off to a meeting with his fellow witches—are in most cases the only form of "proof"). But when these *nganga* have to introduce themselves before the court in French, they announce themselves as Mr. So-and-So, *sorcier*.[17] Although this is completely in line with the local way of speaking (after all, the *nganga* are *mindjindjamb*), it goes directly against the unequivocal condemnation of *la sorcellerie* as such by the judges. But, of course, they will never take the *nganga*'s introduction of himself as a *sorcier* as proof of his guilt. Such terminological inconsistencies highlight the basic ambiguity of the judges' offensive against *la sorcellerie*: the very fact that the legal offensive hinges on the help of a *sorcier* (who, moreover, is seen by the locals as the main representative of the world of the *djambe*) makes it inconsistent in a very practical sense.

This inconsistency in the language of the files points to another ambiguity in the judges' position: like other civil servants, the judges may be quite insistent in their official condemnation of *la sorcellerie* when they perform their public duties, but in their private lives nearly all of them are deeply implicated in the *nganga* world. We often saw a big black Mercedes parked in front of the relatively modest house of our *nganga* friend Mendouga. This was a sure sign that one of her elite clients—Mendouga often boasted that elites from all over the region came to her to ask for help—had a consult with her, either to have themselves *blindés* (*bouima*, "armored") against treacherous attacks of their political rivals or possibly to ask her to attack these opponents. No wonder the judges did not see any inconsistency in accepting the help of these *sorciers* in their struggle against *la sorcellerie*.

The Ralushai Commission report is plagued by similar terminological slippages. In their effort to create clarity, Professor Nkhumeleni Ralushai and his coauthors point out an interesting inconsistency in the prevailing South African Witchcraft Suppression Amendment Act of 1957/1970. They point out that, although "the legislature's approach [in this act] is that witchcraft does not exist," the act nonetheless forbids people "from practicing witchcraft, when it is said that it does not exist" (1996: 57). However, the report itself hardly succeeds in avoiding similar ambiguities. For instance, a central term in the report is, as can be expected, "witchcraft killings." Yet, especially in the first chapters it is not clear whether this refers to the killing *of* witches or to supposed killings *by* witches. The case material that is so diligently accumulated in the report from various judicial archives in the Northern Province offers striking examples of both possibilities. In later chapters the authors seem to be conscious of possible confusion on this point, so they introduce alternative terms, like "witchcraft related killings," "witch killings," and "witchcraft violence." But, again, the terms are not clearly distinguished. Instead, the report introduces "ritual murders" as a separate category, referring to the so-called *muti* murders (the killing of innocent victims, mostly children, in order to use their body parts to produce "medicine" that will fortify the client).

The report convincingly shows that it was especially the increasing rumors about such *muti* murders that pushed the young "comrades" into a frenzy of witch-hunts. However, one can wonder whether these "ritual murders" can be so clearly separated from "witchcraft killings"—here also there seems to be a subversive circularity, if only because the same *inyanga* who were used as "witch finders" could also be easily accused of being involved in *muti* murders. The report is no doubt right in starting from local categories; yet some closer analysis of the ambiguities implied by these notions might help us to avoid being caught in the slippages of these very categories.

As is only to be expected, things become even more complicated when the report addresses the role of the local "experts," the *inyanga*.[18] In some passages the report seems to distinguish between "diviners" and "healers" (a distinction that is seen as basic to the representations of the occult in many Bantu societies). But in subsequent formulations this distinction is again neglected. And, indeed, the commission's case material shows how precarious such a distinction is becoming in present-day circumstances. In its recommendations the committee instead proposes another distinction: it severely criticizes the failure of "most of the legislation to draw a clear line between the so-called witch, the sorcerer, and the witchfinder" (1996: 61). The distinction between witch and sorcerer is not further elaborated in the report. But the aim of setting apart the witch finder is clear. To Ralushai and his fellow commission members the witch finder (in other passages the term *inyanga* is used) performed a key role in triggering the popular frenzy about a proliferation of witchcraft. And, no doubt with good reason, many of the report's recommendations aim to make it possible to undertake legal action against these witch finders.

Here again, the report seems to get entangled in the fluidity and circularity of these local notions. Its own case material shows in great detail how difficult it is to distinguish witch and witch finder. In many cases, an *inyanga* is accused of being a witch and even physically attacked. And, as said, many of the witches who were killed in the large-scale hunts around 1990 were apparently *inyanga*. The report's appendices spell out in detail how the "comrades" forced the accused to display all his or her herbs and pots in front of the house and explain their use. Only after this was the accused lynched. Often, the victim was explicitly accused of being involved in *muti* murders. Indeed, the *inyanga* figure as some sort of archetype of the witch; yet, as said, they also worked closely with the comrades as witch finders. Ramaredi Shaba with her "African television" screen in Sekhukhuneland (Delius 1996) may have been a particularly frightening example of what an *inyanga* could do, but she was certainly not exceptional. In nearly all documented cases of witch-hunts by the comrades, the latter explicitly sought the help of one or several *inyanga* to help them to expose the witches. Indeed, it is quite clear that the *inyanga* were often in some sort of catch-22 situation: if they refused to collaborate with the comrades they were in grave danger of being exposed themselves as witches to be lynched. After all, any *inyanga* is a self-evident suspect. There seems to be the same circularity here as in the Cameroonian examples above: apparently the very capacity of the *inyanga* to "see" witches indicates that they are involved with the same occult powers.

Ralushai's simple recommendation to "draw a clear line" between witch and witch finder might, therefore, be quite naive. Yet, at the same time, it touches upon a central issue in the whole conundrum: how are judicial interventions in the field of witchcraft to deal with the *nganga* and *inyanga?*

Cameroon: The *Nganga* as a Trojan Horse?

In earlier publications on the witch trials in eastern Cameroon, Fisiy and I compared the central role of the *nganga* in the judiciary offensive against witches to that of the Trojan horse that helped the Greeks to finally break the resistance of the proud city of Troy (Fisiy and Geschiere 1990; Geschiere 1997). As mentioned, the Cameroonian judges feel that the "expertise" of the *nganga* is crucial for establishing "proof." How else can they prove "beyond reasonable doubt" that the accused did leave their bodies at night to attack other people? However, as I said, to the Maka and other groups in the forest, the *nganga* is the most conspicuous representative of the world of *djambe* (or *evu* or *sorcellerie* or whatever term people use). The newly enhanced prestige of these local experts—who, instead of being persecuted by the courts, now play a central role during its sessions—seems therefore to confirm the popular belief in these powers.

This official recognition of their expertise seems to coincide with new aspects in the performance of these *nganga*. Especially after 1980, a novel, more modern type of *nganga* emerged. The *nganga* I knew in the Maka region during the 1970s (e.g., our friend Mendouga) were true villagers. They hardly spoke French and their knowledge of the exterior world was limited. Some were considered rich, but people would always comment that the wealth of witches, the *nganga* included, is based upon "delight without sweat," which seems to mean that it is easily acquired but does not last long. Most of the *nganga* lived in simple *poto-poto* houses (mud walls on a frame of poles), often situated slightly outside the village, not far from the bush. In everyday life they remained in the background: they were thought to operate in secret.

However, the *nganga* who figure in the court files as expert witnesses against the "witches" exhibit a very different profile. They present themselves emphatically as modern figures, also in everyday life. Often, they have worked for some time elsewhere, sometimes in public service. They speak French fluently and use, with certain ostentation, French (or even English) books on occultism, "Eastern magic," and other forms of secret knowledge. They brag about their modern education. One *nganga* (thirty-five years old) told me, for instance, that he had been admitted to a Swiss medical school when his ancestor "took" him. He remained paralyzed for six months. Then he started as a "traditional healer." But he still called himself "doctor." These modern *nganga* often emphasize that they work with the government as members of the new association of traditional healers. Their membership card is used as a sort of license and, more generally, as a symbol of their modern prestige.[19]

Baba Denis, a *nganga* who played a central role in several of the court cases we could follow, can serve as an example here. Baba established himself as a "traditional healer" in a village, close to the one where I lived, in the early 1980s. But his compound was very different from that of, for instance, our former friend Mendouga (who had died in the meantime; people said she had "lost her power" several years earlier). When I visited Baba in 1988, he lived in the middle of the village on the main crossroads. His house was adorned with several large signboards: not only "traditional Healer" but also "Astrologue" and "Rose-Croix" (Rosicrucian). Especially the last sign underscored the modernity of this healer: the Rosicrucians are supposed to be highly present among the new state elite (President Paul Biya himself is an acolyte). Indeed, Baba often spoke of his brother who was expecting to receive an important position in the president's office in the capital. He himself had the authoritarian air of a *fonctionnaire*, which was hardly surprising since he had served in the army for a long period. According to the villagers, he was sent home because of "problems." It was said that he even spent some time in prison. But this rumor only served to enhance his renown as a specialist, since—as said—people generally believe that in prison one meets the really dangerous sorcerers and learns their secrets. Baba himself, however, emphasized the scientific nature of his expertise: before the tribunal, he often explained how he applied "his science." Like his colleague referred to above, he called himself a doctor and talked about his compound as his "hospital."[20]

The high profile of such *nganga*, reinforced by the official recognition of their expertise, automatically enhances the popular idea that the *djambe* is everywhere. Of special importance in this context, moreover, is that these modern *nganga* are much more aggressive in recruiting clients and in unmasking suspects. In the 1970s, most *nganga* were still fairly discreet. They appeared in public only on special occasions, such as when the village notables invited them to perform a purifying ritual or an oracle. They were often hesitant to advance specific accusations, no doubt for fear of difficulties with the authorities but also because vague allusions seemed more useful to their forms of therapy. The treatments of a "healer" such as, for instance, Mendouga, were in fact mostly aimed at repairing family relations.

A "modern" *nganga* like Baba intervenes in a very different manner. In several of the court cases whose files we could read, it was he who took the initiative to "purify" a village, since he had "seen" that it was invaded by the witches (in one of these villages he even claimed to have destroyed a "nocturnal airstrip" where the witches "landed their planes"). During such purification actions, it was he who pointed out the witches and had them arrested by the villagers. Moreover, it was Baba who insisted that they should be handed over to the gendarmes. Other modern *nganga* as well have few scruples in hurling direct accusations against persons they often do not know. And they are constantly trying to attract new clients by warning them that they are the victims of occult attacks and that they urgently need protection against evildoers from within their close surroundings.

One reason for such aggressive behavior is clearly that these *nganga* hope to make quick money: the world of the *nganga* is becoming ever more based on money, and people often pay large sums for protection or purification. But *nganga* are also inspired by the new possibility of gaining some sort of official recognition as witch finders. It is, in fact, quite clear that the high profile of these new *nganga,* as expert witnesses before the tribunals and allies of the government, hardly contributes to putting an end to *la sorcellerie.*[21] On the contrary, it strengthens a general sense of "metaphysical disorder" among the people, since the omnipresence of these *nganga* seems to confirm that witchcraft is, indeed, proliferating.

The Ralushai Commission Report:
"Drawing a Clear Line . . ."

The patterns that emerge from the ways in which the South African courts try to deal with witchcraft and from the Ralushai Commission report differ from those in Cameroon. Yet there are also many similarities as far as the daily context is concerned. For instance, in everyday life in South Africa, *inyanga* are certainly as present as the *nganga* in the Cameroonian context. The Ralushai report quotes an article by Mihalik and Cassim (1992: 138): "By 1985 there were some 10,000 sangomas and inyangas practising in greater Johannesburg. These traditional healers were consulted at least occasionally by 85 per cent of all black households and were supported by a national network of approximately 40,000 traders in healing and magical herbs. The African Traditional Healers Association claimed a membership of 179,000 outnumbering western doctors by 8 to 1" (1996: 48).[22] These figures are quite convincing for anyone who has visited the Durban *muti* market, which serves as a magical hub for the whole of South Africa (and beyond). Moreover, it is also clear that these specialists played a key role in the outbreak of the shocking witch-hunts of the "comrades" in the Northern Province toward the end of apartheid. Delius's stories about Ramaredi Shaba and her fearsome African television screen are paralleled by many similar reports in the rich case material collected in the Ralushai report (see also Niehaus 2001). As in the judicial offensive against witchcraft in Cameroon, these local specialists were indispensable to the comrades' action against similar dangers: who else could "sniff out" the witches?

However, the eagerness with which the comrades—apparently encouraged by the changing political context—took matters into their own hands, and the violent consequences of this, gave the whole issue of witchcraft a somewhat different twist than in Cameroon (and many other sub-Saharan countries). In Cameroon, witchcraft as such became increasingly defined by politicians as the ultimate form of subversion of the state, sabotaging *le développement* and undermining the position of the state elite. Indeed, while I was living in the village in eastern Cameroon, I regularly witnessed officials haranguing the villagers and telling them that they should stop sabotaging the government's development projects with their eternal witchcraft, or else . . . The judicial offensive against witchcraft after 1980 seemed to be as much inspired by such worries among the Cameroonian authorities as by pressure "from below" (from the people) on the state to do something about the proliferation of occult attacks. In South Africa, at least in the former Northern Province, it was the proliferation of violent witch-hunts—the summary executions of witches by the comrades—rather than supposed conspiracies by the witches that posed an urgent threat to the state. As several observers noted, the witch-hunts seemed to indicate that the state was no longer in control in the area, which was highly problematic both for the apartheid regime and for the subsequent ANC government (see also Ralushai Commission 1996: 231). The vital question became, therefore, what the state courts had done—and could do—to contain these hunts. It is notably on this point that Ralushai and his coauthors evaluate the rich array of cases in the appendices of their report.

The authors note with clear dismay that in several cases the courts did not intervene at all. This seems to have occurred especially in those cases where chiefs were actively involved in the witch-hunts. The report sees this refusal of at least some courts to act as a crucial failure since it must have encouraged further witch-hunts (Ralushai Commission 1996: 236, 270). It notes also that in several cases where the courts did condemn the perpetrators of witch killings, they imposed punishments that were purely nominal, which again could only encourage the further spread of the hunts (240, 245). Only in a few cases were proper punishments imposed on the main culprits of the lynchings (247).[23] Moreover, the report notes that in none of these cases was judicial action undertaken against the *inyanga* who had been involved in "sniffing out" the witches; it clearly sees this as another failure of the judiciary apparatus (187, 269).

Indeed, Ralushai and his coauthors seem to recognize—and rightly so—that the *inyanga* were at the heart of the whole problem. Several of their most stringent recommendations are directed against the *inyanga* and the problematic implications of their role as witch finders. For instance, the new Witchcraft Control Act (which the commission proposed as a replacement for the Witchcraft Suppression Act of 1957 with its amendment of 1970) retains the article from the older law that declares guilty and "liable on conviction" anybody who "employs or solicits any witch-doctor, witch-finder or any other person to name or indicate any person as a wizard or a witch" (art. 1c, Ralushai Commission 1996: 55). Since it is central to the expertise of any *inyanga* (or any healer in general) that she be able to "see" the source of the occult aggression undermining the client's well-being, this article would mean that anybody who consults a local healer would risk prosecution. How is a client to stop the healer from exercising the gift that is supposed to be the secret to her powers? Not only the impressive figures quoted above but also the rich case material in the report's appendices vividly illustrates the omnipresence of the *inyanga* in everyday life. So how is this article ever to be applied with any degree of success?

The report's draconic recommendations against *inyanga*—understandable as they may be—are also difficult to reconcile with the emphasis in its opening pages on the need to take the popular concern about witchcraft seriously. For instance, after a few preliminary pages about the composition and the procedures of the commission, with eloquent simplicity the report raises right away what might be considered the crucial issue: "The question may be asked whether a community that still strongly believes in witchcraft can be blamed for insisting that the old man, who had made the threat [of witchcraft], should not be removed from the area" (1996: 13).[24] The question that automatically seems to follow from this is whether it is possible to take such concerns seriously without involving in one way or another a local expert? Indeed, in other passages as well the commission seems to highlight both how indispensable the *inyanga* are for reassuring the population and, at the same time, what dangerous and unreliable partners they are for any attempt by the government to intervene.

The report seems to look for a way out of this dilemma in the institution of a National Traditional Healers Association. No fewer than twenty-three pages of the report (1996: 64–87) concern a "Proposed Draft Legislation to Control the Practice of Traditional Healers." This draft is strongly influenced by the Zimbabwe example, where such an association has been functioning since the 1980s. Professor Ralushai himself and Mr. Ndou, another commission member, visited Harare and had a long interview with Professor Chavunduka, vice-chancellor of the University of Zimbabwe and president of the Zimbabwe National Traditional Healers Association. They also talked with other members of the executive committee of this association. The legal text they proposed on the basis of these interviews has a strikingly disciplinary character. It mainly consists of a long enumeration of all sorts of control boards and possible disciplinary measures against "improper or disgraceful conduct" by members. The text does not spell out what such conduct might be, but the rest of the report (notably the proposed text for the Witchcraft Control Act) makes it quite clear that this would especially be "to name or indicate any person as wizard or witch." As a consequence, the heavily disciplinary tenor of the proposed Traditional Medical Practitioners Act seems to have a very circumscribed view of what "traditional healing" is: if the whole aspect of "seeing" is cut out, what is left of this "healing"?

The basic problem is, again, the highly fluid character of notions of healing and healing power. The proposed act on traditional healers reminded me strongly of long debates in Cameroon on how to distinguish *"bonafide"* and *"malafide" nganga*. In Cameroon as well, some people advocate official recognition of a national association of traditional healers (which, as mentioned, has existed for some time but without clear official approval). The idea is here as well that it would help to separate charlatans—and in this context people often mention Nigerian "specialists"—from real *nganga*. Some insist that the line should be drawn between healers working with herbal medicine and other forms of "local knowledge," on the one hand, and those dabbling in "witchcraft," on the other. However, to the people in general such distinctions are never convincing: at least the capacity to "see"—to have "the second pair of eyes"—is believed to be crucial to any form of local knowledge. In this respect again, any distinction in the field of occult knowledge seems to be precarious and constantly shifting. There may be good reasons to doubt whether Ralushai's disciplinary Traditional Medical Practitioners Act could ever resolve the ambivalences of popular perceptions of healing and protection against occult aggression.

Conclusion

As mentioned, very different patterns emerge from the ways in which the state, or the law, get entangled with witchcraft in Cameroon and in South Africa. Yet somewhat similar vicious circles seem to stand out. In Cameroon, the results of the judicial offensive against *la sorcellerie* since the 1980s have been far from conclusive. On the contrary, it seems to have aggravated the popular obsession with the proliferation of witchcraft as an omnipresent form of disorder. A practical reason for this is the blatant inefficiency of the judicial apparatus. Court cases drag on for years. When people are finally summoned and come to the tribunal—often after a burdensome journey—they are told that one of the magistrates had urgent things to do elsewhere and that the *affaire* has once more been postponed, and so on. Witchcraft cases that are taken to court often attract a lot of attention, certainly in the village(s) concerned. And precisely the fact that such cases drag on and on reinforces the feeling of disorder. No wonder that lately people seem to look elsewhere for solutions, notably in the rapidly growing Pentecostal churches. Indeed, the Pentecostals seem to be much more efficient than the state in dealing with witchcraft dangers.[25]

At a more general level, this judicial offensive seems to be counterproductive because of its inherent inconsistencies. In their efforts to suppress witchcraft as a dangerous form of subversion, undermining even the state itself, the judges have to enlist the help of the *nganga*. How else can they ever hope to establish proof that the accused have, indeed, practiced witchcraft?[26] However, their alliance with the *nganga* as expert witnesses proved to have the opposite effect: it bestowed some sort of official recognition on these local specialists. And since for the population the *nganga* are the outstanding representatives of the world of the *djambe/sorcellerie*, this reaffirmed people's preoccupation with occult threats. Moreover, it promoted the emergence of a more modern type of *nganga* with a much more aggressive approach—both to potential clients and to people they accuse—who play a key role in the general excitement about the proliferation of witchcraft as a metaphysical form of disorder.

The dealings of the law with witchcraft in South Africa, though quite different, seem to be haunted by similar circularity and ambiguity. The members of the Ralushai Commission, like several other observers, identified the *inyanga* as having played a crucial role in the fierce witch-hunts in the former Northern Province, which threatened to destabilize this part of the country during the transition from apartheid to ANC rule. The commission's report severely criticized the courts for their leniency toward the perpetrators of these lynchings and especially toward the *inyanga* whose role as witch finders had been indispensable in starting the hunts. Moreover, it insisted (1996: 61) that the *inyanga* should remain apolitical— meaning that they should stay out of party politics. The commission clearly realized how dangerous it is to mix the world of occult healing with the politics of the state. However, the commission emphasized also that the legislator should take the popular fear of witchcraft more seriously. Therefore, it could hardly propose banning the *inyanga* altogether. As a consequence, without taking into consideration the fluidity and secrecy that is crucial to any form of occult healing, it launched a quixotic project to create an official association that would discipline the healers and select the "legitimate" ones.

Apparently any form of state intervention in this tricky domain runs up against the basic ambiguities of witchcraft thinking as personified by the *nganga/inyanga*.[27] Is there a solution to this stalemate? To an outsider (like me), it might be tempting to conclude from all these ambiguities and circularity that the state should stay out of this treacherous field as much as possible, and that adventurous interventions like those of the Cameroonian judges with their efforts to subdue *la sorcellerie* are highly inadvisable. Indeed, witchcraft and the minefield it offers to any judicial intervention seem to be a good example of the paradox highlighted above (and in chapter 1 of this volume) that the very trend toward ever further "legalization" reinforces the sense of disorder: the modern state is drawn into a terrain where it is not equipped to exercise control. How are judges to establish proof amid so much secrecy? What can the state do if its sanctions do not apply? The consequent failure inevitably creates an acute feeling of disorder, since even the state with all its pretence of control seems to be powerless.

However, from close range such a conclusion might be all too facile. Popular unrest is very real and hardly possible for the state to ignore.[28] There are, of course, alternatives. One of the reasons for the decrease in witch-hunts—at least the more open ones— in South Africa seems to be the reaffirmation of the chiefs' traditional prerogatives.[29] Indeed, the chiefs still have their own ways of dealing with the occult. However, it is clear that such dependency on "traditional" chieftaincy has its costs for a government intent on bringing development and progress.[30] In Cameroon, the rapid rise of Pentecostalism with its own forms of combating witchcraft (as the work of Satan) seems to have taken away some of the pressure on the state to do something about these occults threats. Yet the example of Ghana, where Pentecostalism appears to be intent on developing a political project that may take over the state, shows that this alternative also has its costs.

Is the best alternative then a drastic paradigm change of the law that allows the state courts to take witchcraft seriously? This is what both the Ralushai Commission and the national Commission on Gender Equality suggest; and authors like Hund (2000), Pelgrim (2003), and Ludsin (2003) seem to share this view. New legislation should allow the state courts, with the help of "legitimate" *sangoma,* to distinguish between false accusations and well-founded suspicions of witchcraft and, thus, to intervene against both false accusers and those ("the" witches?) who are, indeed, "engaged in harmful practices." The above might suggest that this approach has its dangers. If state politicians deem it necessary to link up, in one way or another, with the *nganga/inyanga* who dominate this field, they should at least take into account that these local experts are inherently ambivalent and that any effort to separate good from evil—construction from destruction, healing from killing—will always remain highly precarious in this field, just like any attempt to discipline these trickster figures. Moreover, the costs of the state's involvement in this minefield of ambiguity may be clear: if state officials pretend that they can play a role in the witchcraft struggle but find themselves mired in its ambivalences, the prestige of the state might be even more damaged than if the state had abstained from involvement in the first place. This seems at least to be the lesson of the Cameroonian example.

In my view, there is good reason to doubt whether the solution can be found at an "ontological level" (Hund 2000) or by launching a "paradigm change" (Commission on Gender Equality 1998) that tries to formally reconcile the bureaucratic logic of the modern state with witchcraft thinking. This might only reinforce the idea of a principled incompatibility of the two. However, this does not exclude more practical combinations. Jean Comaroff and John Comaroff (2004) suggest a very promising alternative. They discuss a case in which a local magistrate (at Lehurutse Magistrate's Court in South Africa's remote North West Province) succeeds in handling, within the limits of the law, a very "dangerous" affair with clear witchcraft implications. Witchcraft is discussed here not as an exotic belief—to be accepted or not—but as part and parcel of daily life. The whole affair is treated as a breach of contract—should the applicant still pay a certain sum of money to a healer?—rather than in terms of occult aggression (real or not). Thus, the magistrate succeeds in addressing "contemporary African concerns . . . without offending Euro-modern legal reason." His approach is in terms of practical social contextualization rather than ostentatious moral relativism. One can wonder whether such a pragmatic approach is possible when the issue is a supposed killing and not just payments of money—whether in such a more serious case it is possible to contain people's anger without either accepting or refusing the "reality" of such accusations. Nevertheless, it is clear that "legal code and local custom can act upon each other in supple, surprising ways" (J. Comaroff and J. L. Comaroff 2004: 199). Such a practical approach might fit better with all the ambiguities of the witchcraft conundrum than trying to find a once-and-for-all solution on an ontological level.[31]

Notes

Many thanks to Jean-François Bayart, Tlou Makhura, Achille Mbembe, Isak Niehaus, Barbara Oomen, Eric de Rosny, and the participants of the Radcliffe/Harvard conference—notably Arjun Appadurai, Adam Ashforth, Rosalind Morris, Janet Roitman, and Nancy Scheper-Hughes—and, of course, to the editors of the present volume for their valuable criticisms and suggestions.

1. The Ralushai Commission report (1996: 270, 273) refers to "revolutionary forces" which—toward the end of the 1980s—sought to "politicise the rural communities" and therefore "chose witchcraft and ritual killing to destabilize these communities."

2. Moreover, for this offense the Ralushai Commission report proposes the heaviest punishment of the three categories it distinguishes. Also characteristic seems the name of the new law proposed by the Ralushai Commission: Witchcraft *Control* Act, which was supposed to replace the old *Suppression* of Witchcraft Act of 1957 (my italics).

3. This is striking since the Ralushai Commission report (1996), in contrast, tends to emphasize the involvement of chiefs with witch-hunts. Regional differences might be involved here (Niehaus writes especially about the Lowveld/Mpumalanga while the commission's report is mainly based on findings from Limpopo (notably Vendaland). It is to be noted, moreover, that even though full-

scale witch-hunts became much less frequent, general panics about zombie practices, murders caused by *muti* (substances used by healers and sorcerers), and such hardly abated.

4. In many parts of the continent, public debates on this issue are waged using terms like "witchcraft," *sorcellerie,* etc. Therefore, it seems futile to try and avoid them in our analysis. It is true that these are Western notions but they have been appropriated on such a scale in public debates in Africa that academics would close themselves off from what is going on in society if they refused to use these notions.

5. However, as several authors have emphasized recently, Africa is certainly not exceptional in this. See, for instance, Jean Comaroff's seminal comparison (1997) of witchcraft fears in postcolonial Africa with the popular obsession with child abuse and Satanism in the West. See also Joan S. LaFontaine 1998 and my effort (1999) to highlight intriguing parallels with the upsurge of spirit cults in Taiwan during its economic boom and my comparison (2003) between "witch doctors" and "spin doctors" in, respectively, African and American politics.

6. Yet, there seem to be good reasons to nuance this contrast between the colonial state (as acting against witch doctors) and the postcolonial state (as more inclined to intervene against witches). Many colonial civil servants realized that, by convicting *nganga* (who had attacked or even executed witches), the government gave people the impression that they were protecting the witches. Therefore, officials often hesitated to take a clear stance. See Fields 1982 and also the very interesting research by Tlou Makhura (2002) on state interventions in the Lowveld (South Africa) in the early twentieth century. For parallels in West Africa see the drawn-out debate on this issue between British civil servants in Nigeria and Southern Cameroons in the 1930s (National Archives of Cameroon, Buea, Aa 1934, 16).

7. See Ashforth 1998a and 2005 on "spiritual insecurity" in Soweto. Jean and John L. Comaroff emphasize that, indeed, witchcraft marks the limits of the law—its "unroutinizable powers" making it a basic challenge, not only to (post-)colonial officials, but even to local rulers of earlier times (2004: 189).

8. Indeed, in the West as well, the family proves to be *un noeud de vipères* (*à la* Mauriac) not only for its own members but also for outsiders such as therapists, social workers, officials from child protection agencies, and many other government services. In this respect as well, the differences from witchcraft discourse, which, at least in many parts of Africa, invariably looks for the origin of occult aggression within the family, are not that great.

9. My title is a form of academic piracy from the title of one of the main research programs of WISER (Witwatersrand Institute for Social and Economic Research): The Limits of the State. Clearly, the latter title relates very well to present-day predicaments in South Africa (and elsewhere).

10. See, among others, Marwick 1965 and Turner 1954. Mary Douglas (1970) is probably right in emphasizing that these monographs might have been more influential than Evans-Pritchard's much quoted, but less followed, book on the Zande.

11. See also Douglas 1970, where she makes the ironical comment that for some time anthropologists managed to depict witchcraft as "domesticated" and "not running amuck"—in stark contrast to historians.

12. Such variations make it a bit disconcerting that Hund still speaks so easily of "African culture."

13. Thus, the *nganga* is the best example that witchcraft's evil forces can also be regulated and used in a highly constructive way: it is only because the *nganga* has learned to control his or her dangerous powers that he or she can heal. However, this control is always seen as precarious and so is, therefore, any distinction between more constructive and more destructive uses of the *djambe*.

14. Eric de Rosny (1981, 1992) describes this as a crucial moment in his own initiation as a *nganga* in Douala. De Rosny is a French Jesuit who has worked in Douala for more than forty years now. After his initiation as a *nganga,* he combined local forms of healing with Christian notions and practices in a very sophisticated and at the same time honest way. Luckily, in his case, the demand of his "professor" for *une bête sans poil* (an animal without body hair—i.e., a human being) could be met by offering a goat as a substitute.

15. See Geschiere 1997 for a more detailed analysis of Mendouga's vicissitudes (and those of other *nganga* in eastern Cameroon). See Ashforth 2000 for a very vivid (and therefore all the more disconcerting) description of how his friend from Soweto was sucked ever deeper into witchcraft's circular reasoning on his long quest among all sorts of healers. The overview of court cases in the Ralushai Commission report (1996) indicates also that a considerable number of "witches" killed by the youth gangs around 1990 were *inyanga*. Apparently, to the people *"inyanga"* and "witch" were more or less equivalent (which did not stop them from asking the help of other *inyanga* in "sniffing" out the witches within the community).

16. Such practical difficulties are certainly not special to Africa; for similar "confusions," see Favret-Saada 1977, on the Bocage in France in the 1970s.

17. The *nganga* who play a role in such court cases are mostly men. This is quite striking since locally *nganga* are at least as often women. But with the "modernization" of the profession (which occurred especially in the 1980s), men seemed to take over, especially when *nganga* performed in more modern contexts (as in the court room; see below and Geschiere 1997). Possibly this is only a temporary phenomenon, since there are signs that in the forest area of Cameroon female *nganga* are catching up with their modern male colleagues.

18. It is also striking that the report does not try to set up a clear distinction between *inyanga* and *sangoma* (the latter term is used only occasionally).

19. In Cameroon, this organization of traditional healers is still not officially recognized, in contrast to other countries (Ghana, Zimbabwe; see below), but it has some sort of semiofficial status.

20. Characteristic also is that he referred to his clients not only as his "patients" but also as *les coupables* (the guilty).

21. At stake here is not only the impact of the *nganga* on the courts but also, conversely, the effect of their performance before the courts on their role as healers. In earlier publications (Fisiy and Geschiere 1990; Geschiere 1997) Fisiy and I emphasized that the association of the *nganga* with the courts and the gendarmes in their offensive against *la sorcellerie* seems to turn them into disciplinary figures (auxiliaries of the authoritarian state). It remains to be seen how this will affect their performance as healers.

22. It is striking of course that these authors seem to take for granted that only black households make use of the services of *inyanga*.

23. "The harsh sentences imposed by the courts in the Venda Supreme Court

have also played a significant role in curbing these killings. Venda is quiet now except for the case at Mutale" (Ralushai Commission 1996: 270).

24. The quotation sums up, with admirable briefness, the basic dilemma of any official who has to deal with a witchcraft case. Fisiy and I came upon exactly the same problem in various parts of Cameroon. For instance, during an interview we had in 1992 with the new prosecutor at Kribi (in the Province of the South), he complained to us that right after his installation he had been caught in the same dilemma. Just before his arrival in Kribi, his predecessor had been confronted with a gang of young men from the village of Ntdoua who dragged an old man to his office and demanded that the man be locked up since he was a witch. His predecessor refused to do so. A few months later the young men set fire to the old man's house, who perished in the flames. Now the new prosecutor was stuck with the young men in his jail. "What can I do? If I have them accused of murder, the people will say the state is protecting witches. If I let them go, people might start murdering witches throughout the region." The prosecutor, therefore, tended to accept (clearly with some hesitation) the proposition that if a community wanted to expel a "witch," the state had to accept this decision (if only for the protection of the accused; see further Geschiere 1997: 185). The catch here is of course the notion of "community." Only in very exceptional cases will a whole community agree about a witchcraft accusation—rather, it seems to be in the nature of witchcraft that there is always disagreement over it. These quotations from the Ralushai report and from the Kribi prosecutor may show, therefore, that there is some urgency for anthropologists in debunking the notion of "community"—yet another of those notions that our forebears launched with so much success, also outside the discipline, but now come back to us with a vengeance.

25. See Meyer 1999. One may wonder to what extent the Pentecostals will be able to stay out of the vicious circles of witchcraft discourse. For instance, in Nigeria there seems to be a rapid increase in rumors about the involvement of the more successful preachers in pacts with the witches or Satan to get rich, etc.

26. In Fisiy and Geschiere 1990 and Geschiere 1997 we discussed two opposing explanations of the sudden reversal in the Cameroonian jurisprudence on witchcraft. Did the initiative for the judicial offensive against the witches come from above, from the government that was increasingly worried about witchcraft as a supreme form of subversion? Or was it rather pressure from below, from a population that was becoming ever more obsessed with the supposed proliferation of witchcraft, that made the judges intervene in this tricky terrain? Interestingly, there is a similar debate among historians of the great witch-hunts in early-modern Europe. Some (e.g., Muchembled 1978, 1981) see the witch trials as the logical outcome of an *offensive civilisatrice* by the absolutist state, supported by the church, in order to subdue popular culture. Others (e.g., Briggs 1996; see also Levack 1995; Marneff 1997) emphasize, in contrast, that the main epidemics of witch-hunting in early-modern Europe occurred in areas where the state was relatively weak; they try to show that the courts were often reluctant to give in to popular pressure to intervene against the witches. In the Cameroonian case there are signs that the government—with its hegemonic project of "nation building" and its constant appeals to *vigilance* against all the forms of *subversion* that seemed to threaten national unity (Bayart 1979)—became increasingly worried about witchcraft as a form of subversion that was especially hard to control. Yet it is clear as

well that there was heavy pressure on the courts "from below" to do something about occult threats.

27. It is striking that one of the few, more-or-less formal follow-ups to the work of the Ralushai Commission seems to be haunted by the same challenge of creating clarity in a by-definition highly ambiguous field. In September 1998, the participants in the National Conference on Witchcraft Violence convened by the Commission on Gender Equality in Thohoyandou (the capital of Vendaland, Limpopo Province) composed a highly committed declaration to put the issue on the national agenda. Like the Ralushai Commission report, they asked for new legislation to replace the 1957 Witchcraft Suppression Act, which was seen as "fuelling witchcraft." The new legislation would allow the separation of "those who are engaged in harmful practices . . . from those who are falsely accused." Apparently the implication is that not only the false accusers but also those engaged in harmful practices (the "witches"?—thus, implicitly, accepted as real?) should be "brought to book." To this aim the declaration requests "clear definitions for words and concepts such as 'witch,' 'wizard' and 'witchcraft'" and a "Code of Conduct" to control the practice of "traditional medicine" (Commission on Gender Equality 1998; see also Ashforth 2005: 256); Mavhungu n.d.). Again, this courageous declaration risks remaining an empty wish if the ambiguity of all positions and concepts in this field is not taken into account.

28. Eric de Rosny, the French Jesuit who had himself initiated as a *nganga* in Douala and has worked with issues of witchcraft and healing for more than forty years (see de Rosny 1981, 1992), insists that the state *has* to play a role in assuaging popular fears of witchcraft. For him the state, church leaders, and psychotherapists should form a common front to deal with these issues. In March 2005 he organized a conference on justice and sorcery at the Université Catholique de l'Afrique Centrale in Yaounde, which became a major event due to the presence of a huge audience and the participation of several judges and officials of the Ministry of Justice (the papers of this conference were published in de Rosny 2005). Riekje Pelgrim (2003) concludes, on the basis of a series of interviews with members of the police in Limpopo Province, that it is hardly possible for a state official to function if the state does not propose some sort of solution to the witchcraft conundrum. Adam Ashforth (2000, 2005) and Hallie Ludsin (2003) seem to share this view.

29. See Niehaus 2001. See also Oomen 2005 for a very rich analysis of how "traditional chiefs" (in earlier years often seen as stooges of apartheid) succeeded in reinstating themselves as indispensable spokesmen for and partners with the ANC regime, and possibly also in witchcraft affairs. However, the capacities of the chiefs and their customary courts in this field must not be overrated. The renaissance of chieftaincy certainly did not lead to a decrease in the popular anxiety about witchcraft (as evidenced by the continuing stream of rumors and cases of violence in relation to zombie practices, *muti* murders, and such). Moreover, if the chiefs increasingly become associated with the modern state, witchcraft as an "unroutinizable form of power" (J. Comaroff and J. L. Comaroff 2004) may become a hard-to-handle challenge for them as well (cf. similar trends in Cameroon; see Fisiy and Geschiere 1991; Geschiere and Ndjio 2003).

30. This is one of the less controversial theses of Mahmoud Mamdani's much-discussed book (1996).

31. Maybe such a more pragmatic approach could be undertaken by having the law give healers some leeway to try and reconcile cases—without formally collaborating with them but clearly setting limits to their actions. After all, any witchcraft discourse always contains its own procedures for attempts at reconciliation (or protection). Summary executions, as in the case of the comrades' witch-hunts, are not in accordance with "local custom"—certainly not if one has not first tried out the other solutions available (attempts to neutralize dangerous witchcraft, etc.); so it is certainly not clear why state courts should be especially lenient in these cases. Leaving some scope for alternative local arrangements for resolution—without making them part and parcel of the state's judiciary apparatus—might ease the pressure on the state to intervene. A hopeful sign is also the quite-surprising outcome of Riekje Pelgrim's recent research in parts of Limpopo Province. She notes a continuous increase of witchcraft affairs brought before the state courts in the 1990s. However, since around 1995—and in contrast to earlier periods—these concern mostly complaints about defamation (people starting a lawsuit against fellow villagers who openly accused them of witchcraft; Pelgrim 2003: 109–12). Apparently this change was promoted by Seth Ntaai, minister of safety and security for the Northern Province (he was also one of the main initiators of the Ralushai Commission). He made several tours through the area during which he strongly emphasized the possibility of bringing such accusations before the courts. This might be an example of a limited state intervention that did have certain effects. Again, a more piecemeal and varied approach seems to have more of a chance to diffuse people's anxieties about witchcraft and to relativize the representations involved than efforts to bridge the chasm between law and witchcraft discourse in ontological terms.

References

Ashforth, Adam. 1998a. "Reflections on Spiritual Insecurity in a Modern African City (Soweto)." In "Containing Witchcraft," ed. Diane Ciekawy and Peter Geschiere. Special issue, *African Studies Review* 41(3):39–69.

———. 1998b. "Witchcraft, Violence, and Democracy in the New South Africa." In "Disciplines et déchirures: Les formes de la violence," ed. Bogumil Jewsiewicki. Special issue, *Cahiers d'Études Africaines* 38(2–4):505–33.

———. 2000. *Madumo, a Man Bewitched.* Chicago: University of Chicago Press.

———. 2005. *Witchcraft, Violence, and Democracy in Post-apartheid South Africa.* Chicago: University of Chicago Press.

Bayart, Jean-Francois. 1979. *L'état au Cameroun.* Paris: Presses Fondation Nationales Sciences Po.

Briggs, Robin. 1996. *Witches and Neighbours: The Social and Cultural Context of European Witchcraft.* London: Fontana.

Comaroff, Jean. 1997. "Consuming Passions: Nightmares of the Global Village." In "Body and Self in a Post-colonial World," ed. Ellen Badone. Special issue, *Culture* 17(1–2):7–19.

Comaroff, Jean, and John L. Comaroff. 1993. Introduction to *Modernity and Its Malcontents: Ritual and Power in Postcolonial Africa,* ed. Jean Comaroff and John L. Comaroff. Chicago: University of Chicago Press.

———. 1999. "Occult Economies and the Violence of Abstraction: Notes from the South African Postcolony." *American Ethnologist* 26:279–301.

———. 2000. "Millennial Capitalism: First Thoughts on a Second Coming." In "Millennial Capitalism and the Culture of Neoliberalism," ed. Jean Comaroff and John L. Comaroff. Special issue, *Public Culture* 12(2):291–344.

———. 2004 "Criminal Justice, Cultural Justice: The Limits of Liberalism and the Pragmatics of Difference in the New South Africa." *American Ethnologist* 31(2):188–204.

Commission on Gender Equality. 1998. *The Thohoyandou Declaration on Ending Witchcraft Violence.* Johannesburg: Raven Press.

Delius, Peter. 1996. *A Lion amongst the Cattle: Reconstruction and Resistance in the Northern Transvaal.* Johannesburg: Raven Press.

de Rosny, Eric. 1981. *Les yeux de ma chèvre: Sur les pas des maîtres de la nuit en pays douala.* Paris: Plon.

———. 1992. *L'Afrique des guérisons.* Paris: Karthala.

———, ed. 2005. *Justice et sorcellerie: Colloque international de Yaounde (mars 2005).* Yaounde: Presses de l'Université catholique d'Afrique centrale.

Douglas, Mary. 1970. "Introduction: Thirty Years after 'Witchcraft, Oracles and Magic.'" In *Witchcraft Confessions and Accusations,* ed. Mary Douglas, pp. xiii–xxxviii. London: Tavistock.

Favret-Saada, Jeanne. 1977. *Les mots, la mort, les sorts.* Paris: Gallimard. Translated by Catherine Cullen as *Deadly Words: Witchcraft in the Bocage* (Cambridge: Cambridge University Press, 1980).

Fields, Karen. 1982. "Political Contingencies of Witchcraft in Colonial Central Africa: Culture and State in Marxist Theory." *Canadian Journal of African Studies* 16(3):567–93.

Fisiy, Cyprian, and Peter Geschiere. 1990. "Judges and Witches, or How Is the State to Deal with Witchcraft? Examples from Southeastern Cameroon." *Cahiers d'Études Africaines* 118:135–56.

———. 1991. "Sorcery, Witchcraft and Accumulation: Regional Variations in South and West Cameroon." *Critique of Anthropology* 11(3):251–78.

Geschiere, Peter. 1997. *The Modernity of Witchcraft: Politics and the Occult in Postcolonial Africa.* Charlottesville and London: University Press of Virginia.

———. 1999. "Globalization and the Power of Indeterminate Meaning: Witchcraft and Spirit Cults in Africa and East Asia." In *Globalization and Identity: Dialectics of Flow and Closure,* ed. Birgit Meyer and Peter Geschiere, pp. 211–39. Oxford: Blackwell.

———. 2003. "On Witch Doctors and Spin Doctors: The Role of 'Experts' in African and American Politics." In *Magic and Modernity: Interfaces of Revelation and Concealment,* ed. Birgit Meyer and Peter Pels, pp. 159–83. Stanford: Stanford University Press.

Geschiere, Peter, and Basile Ndjio. 2003. "Democratization and the Uncertain Renaissance of Chieftaincy: Varying Trajectories in Cameroon." Paper presented at the conference "Chieftaincy, Governance, and Development Projects," Accra, January 2003.

Gluckman, Max. 1955. *Custom and Conflict in Africa.* Oxford: Blackwell.

Hund, John. 2000. "Witchcraft and Accusations of Witchcraft in South Africa: Ontological Denial and the Suppression of African Justice." *Comparative and International Law Journal of Southern Africa* 33:366–89.

Laburthe-Tolra, Philippe. 1977. *Minlaaba: Histoire et société traditionnelle chez les Bëti du Sud Cameroun.* Paris: Champion.

LaFontaine, Joan S. 1998. *Speak of the Devil: Tales of Satanic Abuse in Contemporary England.* Cambridge: Cambridge University Press.

Levack, Brian. 1995. *The Witch-Hunt in Early Modern Europe.* 2d ed. London and New York: Longman.

Ludsin, Hallie. 2003. "Cultural Denial: What South Africa's Treatment of Witchcraft Says for the Future of Its Customary Law." *Berkeley Journal of International Law* 21(1): 62–111.

Makhura, Tlou. 2002. "The Moral Economy of 'Boloyi': The Struggle between the State and Selected Eastern Transvaal Communities to Control Witchcraft in the Early 20th Century." Unpublished paper. Witwatersrand Institute for Social and Economic Research, University of the Witwatersrand, Johannesburg.

Mamdani, Mahmoud. 1996. *Citizen and Subject: Contemporary Africa and the Legacy of Late Colonialism.* Princeton, NJ: Princeton University Press.

Marneff, Guido. 1997. "Between Religion and Magic: An Analysis of Witchcraft Trials in the Spanish Netherlands, Seventeenth Century." In *Envisioning Magic,* ed. P. Schafer and H. G. Knippenberg, pp. 235–56. Leiden: Brill.

Marwick, Max. 1965. *Sorcery in Its Social Setting: A Study of the Northern Rhodesian Cewa.* Manchester: Manchester University Press.

Mavhungu, Khaukanani M. n.d. "Heroes, Villains and the State in South Africa's Witchcraft Zone." Unpublished paper, University of Stellenbosch, RSA.

Mbembe, Achille. 2002. *On the Postcolony.* Berkeley and Los Angeles: University of California Press.

Meyer, Birgit. 1999. *Translating the Devil: Religion and Modernity among the Ewe in Ghana.* Edinburgh: Edinburgh University Press (for International African Institute).

Mihalik, J., and Y. Cassim. 1992. "Ritual Murder and Witchcraft: A Political Weapon." *South African Legal Journal.*

Muchembled, Robert. 1978. *Culture populaire et cultures des élites.* Paris: Flammarion.

———. 1981. *Les derniers bûchers: Un village de Flandre et ses sorcières sous Louis XIV.* Paris: Ramsay.

Niehaus, Isak. 2001. *Witchcraft, Power and Politics: Exploring the Occult in the South African Lowveld.* With Eliazaar Mohlala and Kally Shokane. London: Pluto.

Oomen, Barbara. 2005. *Chiefs! Law, Power and Culture in Contemporary South Africa.* Oxford: Currey.

Pelgrim, Riekje. 2003. *Witchcraft and Policing: South Africa Police Service Attitudes towards Witchcraft and Witchcraft-Related Crime in the Northern Province.* Leiden: African Studies Centre.

Ralushai Commission. 1996. "Report of the Commission of Inquiry into Witchcraft Violence and Ritual Murders in the Northern Province of the Republic of South Africa." Ministry of Safety and Security, Northern Province, RSA.

Taussig, Michael. 1987. *Shamanism, Colonialism, and the Wild Man: A Study of Terror and Healing.* Chicago: University of Chicago Press.

Toulabor, Comi. 1999. "Sacrifices humains et politique: Quelques exemples contemporains en Afrique." In *Trajectoires de libération en Afrique contemporaine: Hommage à Robert Buijtenhuijs,* ed. Piet Konings, Wim van Binsbergen, and Gerti Hesseling, pp. 207–33. Paris: Karthala.

Turner, Victor W. 1954. *Schism and Continuity in an African Society: A Study of Ndembu Village Life.* Manchester: Manchester University Press.

The Ethics of Illegality in the Chad Basin

Janet Roitman

WALA MO WUJJATA SEY MO NANGAAKA: the innocent are only those who have not yet been caught. This adage is a Fulani expression often heard in the northern part of Cameroon. While it is a local dictum that often provokes smiles, smirks, and knowing laughter, this maxim does not refer to particularly local practices or to the particular habits of local people. Evidently, the logic of the expression connotes that all are guilty, but only some have been judged. The only designated subject being "the innocent," the moral critique is not necessarily directed against outlaws nor does it condemn those who preside over the law—the distinction is irrelevant, transgression being the norm. These days, this remark is often made with reference to people involved in economic exchanges that circumvent national regulatory authority. Seemingly local, these exchanges partake in regional and international economies. First, all nationals of the Chad Basin[1]—Nigerians, Cameroonians, Chadians, Sudanese, and citizens of the Central African Republic and Niger—participate in such commercial networks. Second, these networks are connected to the regional and international markets in, for instance, small arms, money and document counterfeiting, and smuggling of petrol, stolen vehicles, ivory, gold, hardware, electronics, cigarettes, and dry goods.[2]

Often, these exchanges take place with a limited amount of capital investment, involve traversing short distances, such as a mountain pass that marks an international border, and make use of a small number of social and political contacts. But just as often such exchanges involve quite significant capital investments, crossing several national borders, as in the case of small arms or American cigarettes in the trans-Sahara trade, and the support or complicity of well-placed financial and political personalities. These forms of economic exchange take advantage of, and often give rise to, frontier markets, which speckle the international borders of the nation-states of the Chad Basin (see Bennafla 1998, 2002). Although these markets sometimes appear to be poverty-stricken dust bowls, lacking tarred roads, water facilities, or electricity, they are nonetheless hubs of big business. As one former military man (who was discharged from service and imprisoned for having allegedly sold his weapon to a road bandit) put it: "Over time, I understood that even if the border zones are poor, one nonetheless makes big money there."[3]

As everywhere in the world, one can make big money in the Chad Basin by engaging in nonregulated economic exchanges. And as is often the case elsewhere, big money attracts what we habitually call "bandits." In the Chad Basin, *les coupeurs de route*—literally, "those who cut off the roads"—have been extremely active since the early 1990s. But this category of people has a very long history in the region, having confounded colonial efforts to institutionalize national borders and a fiscal base (Roitman 2005a) and being a long-standing subject of legend (Issa 2002, 2004). Historically, the activities of the *coupeurs de route* have intensified with the advent of new resources. These resources have varied over time and according to regions. They have included cattle, which have been targets of raids for centuries. These cattle *razzia* tend to intensify during drought or with rising demand in distant regions, both of which induce increased circulation. Also, colonization by the French brought the groundnut and cotton industries, which meant trucking goods and money—both simple targets of appropriation—across long distances. And the recent construction of an oil pipeline[4] from southern Chad through Cameroon has brought brand-new, four-wheel-drive vehicles, satellite phones and computers, and cash; all of which circulate on long stretches of empty, arid roads that run alongside or crisscross the borders of Chad, Cameroon, and the Central African Republic.

Today, the realms of unregulated commerce and road banditry represent two related frontiers of wealth creation in a region that has no viable industrial base and is not even an industrial periphery or a site of outsourcing for manufacturing or services. The appearance of new resources leads to much bustle in the bush, as people attempt to capture rents associated with activities that are inevitably of short duration, such as the construction of the oil pipeline, which was completed in less than two years (Tulip 2004). "Economic refugees" have migrated to the borders, where they serve as transporters, guards, guides, *passeurs,* and carriers in the domain of unregulated commerce or participate in organized road banditry. The latter are joined by "military refugees" born out of military demobilization programs and the inability of national armies to provide for their personnel. In Chad, for example, the 1992 military demobilization program, which involved approximately 27,000 men, led to the recycling of soldiers into the small-arms market, for which they have contacts and expertise.[5] Often they "enter the bush," as they say, working as mercenaries or as road bandits with organized groups of under- and unpaid soldiers as well as the unemployed from Cameroon, Nigeria, Niger, the Central African Republic, and Sudan.

Although often posited as the ultimate problem of insecurity in the Chad Basin (see Zoua 1997; Seignobos and Weber 2002), the unregulated economic activities and gang-based road banditry are crucial to the urban economy, as well as to the financing of local administrations. By allowing for certain forms of social mobility in a time of austerity and by providing rents for strapped government administrations, the relations that form these networks of exchange are also the basis for economic redistribution. However, these relationships are not merely the bases for new forms of social mobility; they are also the expressions of possibilities for thinking and enacting certain ways of accumulating as well as certain ways of thinking about and sanctioning specific forms of wealth, such as contraband. Ultimately, while viewed by most as illegal, unregulated economic activities and violent methods of extraction are also described as legitimate; most often, these alleged exceptional practices are elaborated by local people as rational or reasonable behavior. Those I spoke with in Cameroon and Chad distinguish quite explicitly between illegal activities and licit practice, as they make clear below. They also refer to a set of precepts relating to illegal status and comment upon the reasoning that leads one to engage in illegal practices—or, more distinctly, to maintain the status of illegality. More than just an instrumentalist calculation, or a strategy to maximize economic gains or personal interests, they explain this exercise in maintaining illegality in terms of licit behavior, or what they see as practices that, while not lawful (hence illegal), are nonetheless not forbidden. Illegal activities are rendered licit practice. Licit practice is in this sense understood to be what is allowed or what has become normal practice. This particular domain of illegality—that is, unregulated economic activities and gang-based highway robbery—thus creates a supplementary sense of "licit." For many people in the Chad Basin, "licit" is not simply equated with what is taken to be legal or lawful; "licit" has come to signify practices that are permissible or, to use the terms of my interlocutors, even "legitimate," given the context in which they live.

This context includes the various national states of the Chad Basin as well as the manners of governing that prevail in those states. As my interlocutors explain below, their engagement in unregulated exchanges and road banditry is not necessarily a means to critique or counter the state; it is not construed by them as an autonomous "moral economy" that etches out a space of independent economics, cultural creativity, or political resistance. Neither outlaw nor moral activity, their practices are rather a means to participate in prevailing modes of accumulation and prevailing methods of governing the economy, which are typical to most states in the world (customs fraud and granting no-bid contracts to well-connected businesses are not particularly African affairs). Indeed, the people who guarantee and direct the financing, labor recruitment, and logistical organization required by the networks constituting these activities are a heterogeneous lot. They include the urban-based merchant elite, political figures, high-ranking military personnel, local government administrators, customs officials, local chiefs, and leaders of factions or rebel groups especially active in Chad and the Central African Republic.[6] At first glance, this realm seems to be mere corruption, or the involvement of government officials and the elite business class in illegal economic activities. However, most of those with whom I spoke rejected this qualification, insisting instead on the "illegal" yet "licit" nature of these acts.

Evidently, the judgment that these acts are instances of corruption or illicit behavior is a normative position that is often not relevant to those engaged in such practices. This view assumes distinctions between the public and private realms, and between rational and irrational behavior, that are neither universal nor generalized. That seems obvious. Often less apparent in commentary on banditry, theft, and unregulated commerce, however, are the very distinctions between corruption, illegality, and illicit status made by those engaged in such practices. The connection they make between illegal and illicit, or the translation between the two, passes through military-commercial relations and the nexus of the state (see Roitman 2005b). That is, the networks of people who engage in unregulated economic activities and road banditry partake in prevailing modes of governing the economy in the Chad Basin. These networks involve relationships between agents of the state, those who straddle lucrative economic positions and government positions, and those who are simply trying to make money according to the available resources.

More than this physical or social engagement, though, these relationships and their associated activities are expressions of truths about state power, or the ways in which one governs both populations and the economy. As Veena Das and Deborah Poole have commented (2004: 4): "An anthropology of the margins offers a unique perspective to the understanding of the state, not because it captures exotic practices, but because it suggests that such margins are a necessary entailment of the state, much as the exception is a necessary component of the rule." Unregulated economic activity and road banditry are necessary entailments of the state insofar as they circumscribe new forms of economic rents and political constituencies. However, the state is also a necessary entailment to these activities insofar as they are dependent upon relations forged with customs officials, governors, mayors, and the police or gendarmerie.

Moreover, engaging in illegal yet licit economic activities involves recognition and even confirmation of certain ways of thinking about the economy and the act of governing. This engagement is said to be licit because "this is the way it's done"—this is an acceptable way of working; this is an admissible way of making money. Despite the contradiction in terms, the illegal realm is a domain of licit behavior; the practice of illegality is an ethics insofar as it is a practice of truth. In what follows, I consider the latter topic by reflecting upon not merely the ways in which these ostensibly marginal activities and spaces generate forms of livelihood but also how they substantiate specific modes of self-understanding. This reflection is a first step toward understanding certain questions about relationships between what is deemed illegal and what is deemed licit. How do local people problematize their own engagement in illegal activities? How do they construe the illegal domain as part of a licit world? How do they posit and elaborate the question of what is good in life? How do they elaborate the matters of who speaks morally and how to speak morally?[7]

Entering the Labor Market, Doing a Day's Work

In January 2002, Alhadji Yaou reminisced about the time he found himself in an armed attack while traveling in a small bus on the road between Demsa and Gashiga in Cameroon:

> They said that those who attempted to flee, well, their wives would have new husbands this year. They said that to joke, but I think they were serious. . . . At one point, a child started to cry. So one of the *coupeurs* said to make it stop. The mother said that the child was thirsty. The *coupeur* responded by saying, "There is water here, but if he drinks some he'll become a thief." An old woman spoke to the *coupeur* very politely and with a maternal tone: "Manga am, ngouyka na doum saniya na?" [My big one, isn't thievery a vocation?].[8]

One can imagine that the maternal tone invoked a certain irony. And yet road banditry is often described by both those engaged in it and by local observers as a form of work. Historically, the *zarguina* (roughly translated as "bandits," but with a connotation of a class of actors) have been associated with the local chiefdoms, some of them attaining status as *bandits-notables* (bandit-dignitaries); working under the protection of various important chiefs, they had the right to "work" the chiefdom's territory in return for a part of the spoils. This is still the case most notably in the territory of Rey Bouba in northern Cameroon, the recently deceased chief having been an important member of the reigning political party, the Rassemblement Démocratique du Peuple Camerounais (RDPC). In the traces of

these historical figures and in the extant political context today, road
banditry is often viewed as a source of employment and a means of social
mobility. This kind of work depends upon collaborations that lead to a
hierarchy of bosses and workers, who form a well-financed but somewhat-
ephemeral labor market.

A former road bandit describes this as follows:

Were you the head of a gang?
> No, no! I played various roles in the attacks I participated in. I carried the
> sack of spoils [*le sac du butin*]. I assured the gang leader's security.
> I picked up the arms after an operation. I participated in the planning of an
> attack. I never commanded. I didn't have my own group. You know, to
> have your own group, you have to have the means and the relations.

What means? What relations?
> You have to buy arms, give something to the guys before going to the
> attack, pay for their food, lodge them for days somewhere, pay informers
> who go to the marketplace to identify people who've made a lot of money,
> etc.

And the relations?
> (*sigh of aggravation*) I told you that I don't know everything. The leader
> [*le chef*] of the team, sometimes he's someone I've never even seen before.
> My prison friends would take me to him, and after an attack sometimes
> we'd never meet again, not even at the marketplace. In the Central African
> Republic, I had a chief [gang leader] who later became my neighbor in the
> [agricultural] fields! There were two guys working in his fields with whom
> we'd done operations.
>
> . . .

What relations does the chief of the gang need?
> Are you naive or are you doing this on purpose? Do you think that you
> can do this kind of work without protection? For example, the chief who
> had his fields next to mine, in one operation we got a lot of money. I don't
> know how much exactly, but between the money we found, the jewelry,
> the watches, etc., the booty [*le butin*] came to something in the millions
> [of francs de la Communauté Financière Africaine]. We were fifteen or
> twenty people, I can't remember. I got 150,000 CFA. Since we attacked
> cattle herders and cattle merchants, well, it's sure that the leader got one
> over on us since, for himself, he kept millions. But afterward, when I saw
> him in the fields cultivating, I understood that it was the man in the car
> who kept most of it.

*Wait a minute! Who is the man in the car? This is not the first time I've heard
people talk about a man who comes in a car just after an attack.*

Oh! I can't really say. In any case, we threw all the arms and the spoils into the trunk of the car. Those who had military uniforms also threw them in. We dispersed and then I got my part in the evening, at the rendezvous.

. . .

And the man in the car?

I never saw him again. But I'm certain that he went back to the city.

Because he lives in the city?

Obviously! If it was someone from one of the villages around here, I would know him! A car in a rural area, that doesn't go unnoticed.

What does the man in the car who comes from the city and makes you risk your life for a pittance represent for you?

You're the one who says that it's a pittance! Do you know what a civil servant's salary is in the Central African Republic? The 150,000 CFA that I got allowed me to spend a peaceful Ramadan and to clothe my family for the festivities. What job brings in 150,000 CFA for no more than a half-day's work?[9]

No doubt, this work is well paid, as is attested by a letter[10] written by a man who describes himself as a "military personnel–*coupeur de route.*" This letter to the prefect of the Logone and Chari Department of Cameroon, which borders Chad, is supposed to be an official complaint regarding an unpaid salary of 120,000 CFA, the equivalent of a professional, or "white-collar," salary in the region. Due to the transgression of nonpayment, the soldier–road bandit denounces his employers and warns the prefect that he himself is being sought after for his role in the deaths of nine Cameroonian soldiers.

The bush, 17-1-94

Chadian military personnel in the Cameroonian
territory aka *coupeur de routes* in the Logone
and Chari Department

To Monsieur the Prefect of the Logone and Chari

It is an element of the Chadian military who is writing this letter to you asking [explaining] but why did I do this. Because we were paid each end of the month 120,000 F by month, but they did not pay me the month of December 1993 so I resigned. Their foolishness [error] of 1st month of 1994, so I am informing you of the people who support us in the bush. They are Alhadji Mohammed Teiga aka Malham. There is Alhadji Lal Ghamat. There is Kanga Goudei. There is Alhadji Salam Collector-of-Everything-and-Nothing [*choucou choucou*], salesman of spare car parts in Koulem. There is Alhadji El Amhadou and then Christophe Pasteur, who delivers wine, "33" export [beer], Beaufort [beer], Castel [beer], and Wiskis [whiskey]. He is the owner of the Bar Gazelle in Koulem. All the members that I just cited to you are those who furnish us with everything we need. Their special envoy is also a member who goes by the name Kanto. They rented us for 29,000,000 FCFA. Why? Because the Secretary of State at the Defense [Department] brought in the military to kill the Arabs ["Arab Choa"].[11] But we killed Cameroonian military, nine soldiers. Now they are looking for the Commissaire de la sécurité; 2nd, the Commandant of the company; 3rd, the mayor of the city, 4th, the subprefect. You are being sought after in the town of Koulem at every hour.

I thank you for my information but I leave you. I am going to N'djamena. I apologize for what is happening in Cameroon. I send you my photos as a souvenir.

D. M.

It should be noted that the title "Alhadji" refers to powerful businessmen who supposedly have made the *hadj* to Mecca. Two of these businessmen mentioned in the letter are well-known commercial and political figures in the region. It is also interesting to note the participation of "Christophe Pasteur," a Frenchman living in Koulem. But the point is that Mr. D. M. would even submit such a letter to the prefect, which indicates the formalization of these activities and the idea that one has a right to claim unpaid sums of money through official channels, since they are viewed as salaries and involve officialdom.

Overall, though, the assertion that theft is work is not unique to mercenaries and road gangs. While the latter surely practice perhaps the most radical or brute form of seizure, such manners of expropriation are widespread. For instance, military personnel and customs officials find rents on fraudulent commerce more attractive than, and often a necessary complement to, their official salaries. This has led to a specific denomination for them in Chad: "*les douaniers-combattants,*" who are "customs officials–soldiers" or "fighting customs officials."[12] It has also led to the blurring of the lines denoting civil versus military status, and even civilians versus administrators. For instance, when arriving at Ngueli, the bridge that is the entry to N'djamena, the Chadian capital, and that spans the Logone River, which marks the border between Cameroon and Chad, one is accosted by numerous people asking for identification papers and vehicle documents. Often, someone in a uniform reviews these documents and then negotiates a fee for passage, which is formally presented as an official tariff. Shortly thereafter, a man in street clothes might appear, asking for the same documents. When you explain that you have just presented them to the government official, the "civilian" will brandish his official identity card, demonstrating that he is the "real" customs or security official. Who was the first man? Just some boy who had borrowed his uncle's uniform or, more likely, someone who had been given the uniform and told to go out and collect the day's pay. As one customs official said: those who cross the border "can be summoned by diverse people in civilian clothes or in uniform. These people pass themselves off as either gendarmes, customs officials, police, members of the presidential special services, etc. . . . The problem is that there is a sort of amalgam and one doesn't know who does what. The multiplicity, the incoherence, the mix of uniforms brings on confusion. It seems that we're dealing with a blurring that is voluntarily maintained because it is part of a logic of accumulation created and maintained by the security forces who round up their monthly pay in this way."[13]

But summoning, assembling, or even supplementing—all connotations of "rounding up"—one's monthly pay is an economic strategy that is not simply the ruse of unpaid or underpaid civil servants. For the general population, smuggling activities and large-scale banditry are forms of "work," which they contrast quite explicitly to "fraud" or "theft." The start of a conversation with a well-known smuggler who works the borders between Nigeria, Cameroon, and Chad highlights this point:

To start with, what does the activity of a trafficker [traffiquant] *in this region consist of?*
    To start with—as well—what do you mean by "trafficker"? Are you insinuating that we violate the law or that we take advantage of a situation, or something like that?
No, no! Not that you take advantage, but, after all, you aren't ordinary economic operators.
    What is an ordinary economic operator?
It's someone who we can identify by his activity, his address, etc. He pays taxes, he has a boutique or a store at a specific place; it's someone whose life and activities obey certain norms.
    If I didn't have a specific activity and a specific address, how did you know that I master the route to Nigeria, and how did you know that at this very hour I would be here, on the Ngueli Bridge?
I made some inquiries and Abba Maïna led me here.
    So I'm well known, or else he would have led you to someone else; there are many people who go to Nigeria, to Chad, and elsewhere.

OK. You are definitely one of the oldest, most regular, and most well known in the cross-border commerce.

Voilà! Cross-border commerce is the expression that fits.[14]

Another conversation with a former *coupeur de route,* who mysteriously escaped execution after having been arrested following the murder and "roasting" of a prominent police officer, reiterated this reasoning:

How do you want me to address you?

Why do you want, my name? They told me that you want to write history! My name is of no use for that. And what name would I give you anyway? I've had so many; I changed my name several times. Only my mother calls me by my real name. So even if I give you a name, it's inevitably a false name, a name that I used at a given time or a certain place.

Give me a name anyway. For example, a name that you used in an instance when you were robbing.

No! I wasn't robbing; I was working.

. . .

Yes, but stealing is not working!

You don't understand anything. The thief is like the liar. The liar wastes his spit for nothing; he talks to earn nothing. The thief takes by reflex; he takes everything that passes in front of him, even useless things. . . .

You seem proud to have been a different kind of thief.

Are you trying to insult me? I'm telling you for the last time that, when there is a salary at the end, you are not a thief. Me, I work the roads.[15]

The idea that theft and highway robbery constitute work is more than just a rationalization of illegal practice; it is a reflection that is grounded in particular notions about what constitutes wealth, what constitutes licit or proper manners of appropriation, and how one governs both wealth and economic relations. This is particularly influenced by the fact that the materiality of the civil link between the state and its subjects is realized through taxes and welfare services, as in many parts of the world, *as well as* through wealth produced in domains—such as private markets associated with development and public-works projects—that exceed the infrastructures of the state. Since the 1980s, structural-adjustment programs, downsizing (known locally as *dégraissage*), and privatizations have pared down—or in fact displaced[16]—the sites from which the state enacts such transfers and hence from which it governs salaries, benefits, workers, and workdays, *as well as* economic rents, benefactors, clients, and syndicates. Hence, the status of wealth, work, and state appropriations has come to the fore as a set of unstable referents.

Illegal but Licit: "Long Live the Tolerant Police!"

For many people in the Chad Basin, seizure is more than a brute means of accumulation. With the pluralization of regulatory authority (Roitman 2001, 2005a), through which the denizens of this region are subject to various—state and nonstate, or official and unofficial—figures of regulatory authority, "taxation" is potentially effected in many sites and by various people. This was affirmed by Bakaridjo (the fictitious name of the *coupeur de route* from the Central African Republic who had a decent Ramadan thanks to his "road work") in response to the following question:

I want to understand better. The man in the car allowed you to have a good Ramadan. Between him and President Ange Félix Patassé [of the Central African Republic], who is more useful to you?

Patassé is a good-for-nothing [*un vaurien*], a scared man who cries over the least gunshot. I pay my taxes to Patassé. The man in the city gives me the means to pay Patasse's tax. Patassé sabotages the state; he steals from the Central African Republic, which is already very poor, and starves the people. My employer [gang leader] both fills in and rectifies [*combler*] the theft created by Patassé.

With 150,000 CFA? [Bakaridjo's earnings]

Patassé never gave me 15 CFA! In all of Patassé's offices [state administration], you have to pay for services! In any case, I don't give a damn about what you think. I deplore the deaths, of course. I've never killed anyone. In fact, once when a companion killed a passenger in cold blood because he didn't like the sight of him, the gang leader shot him after the operation and we split his part [*son butin*] among ourselves.

So, in conclusion, you are unconditionally devoted to the man who allows you to take care of your family, whatever the provenance of the resources?

I was. I stopped now. I told you before; I paid by going to prison. Anyway, money has no color, no odor. A man should be ashamed of hunger. When one has all his limbs and all his senses intact, one must work. Me, I never attacked a poor man. What would I take from a poor man? I am sure that the merchants and others who fall into our attacks are people who earn their money illicitly.

Illicitly?

Yes.

Why?

They buy cheaply; they sell at very high prices, without respect for Islamic rules of commerce. They don't pay the charity tax. And we pray to Allah that we will fall upon such people [during attacks]. Moreover, when they

negotiate cattle all day at the market, when do they have the time to pray?
We see them at the market; they don't pray.

And you pray before going to work the road?
What do you think?

What prayers do you do? Which verses?
You also want to work the road? Allah exercises everyone's prayers. Those
who don't want to pay the *zakkat* [Islamic charity tax], we take up the
responsibility to take it from them. It's a charity payment on their fortune,
a revenue tax.

So you replace the state tax services! Is that legal? Is it legitimate?
Legal? Surely not! As for legitimacy, it is not for you or anyone else to tell
me how I should assure my survival. You, the civil servants, you have your
"benefits" on the side. Is that legitimate? When people are named to a
position of responsibility, they bring along their close relations, members
of their tribe. What happens to those who don't have relations in high
places? In any case, for me, the ends justify the means and long live the
man with the car.[17]

Although Bakaridjo refers to "Allah," "Islamic rules of commerce," and
"the charity tax," not every *coupeur de route* is Muslim; many are members of the flourishing African Independent or Pentecostal Churches, some
practice several religions, and some do not recognize monotheistic traditions. I chose to reproduce Bakaridjo's comments here because he speaks
quite directly about "tax," explaining that his appropriation of the charity
tax is effected both as a critique of the state and as a critique of the merchant elite. Critical of Patassé, Bakaridjo claims to steal from the state in
light of the state's negligence. But he is not stealing from the state itself and
does not maintain that stealing is a means to take vengeance on the state
or to resist it effectively. Bakaridjo's explicit claim is that he steals to pay
"Patassé's tax," referring thus to a transfer and a link between his levies
and the state's impositions. Furthermore, and most important, Bakaridjo
states quite frankly that his work is not legal, but that it is legitimate. This
rationale is construed in terms of the charity tax, or redistribution.

In the Chad Basin, as in many parts of the world, violent appropriation
is a modality not only of social mobility but also of social welfare, being
intrinsic to the nexus of relationships that provides and ensures economic
security. The networks that underlie and allow road bandits and smugglers
to work establish important economic transfers and economic redistribution; they found and guarantee forms of protection; and they offer socia-
bility to people who are often marginalized. Having said that, we should

exercise caution with respect to the idea that those partaking in seizure and theft are social bandits, as exemplified by Robin Hood.[18] The ultimate reference for such a thesis is, of course, Eric Hobsbawm's *Bandits,* which argues, as I do herein, that social bandits make up a professional class and that they are involved in acts and processes of economic redistribution as much as criminality. Where our depictions depart from one another is in the attribution of philanthropic qualities to these acts and their relationship to social justice and rebellion (see especially Hobsbawm 2000: 18–19, 168).

As the many critiques of Hobsbawm's work on bandits insist, one cannot conflate the myriad myths and lore about bandits and banditry, on the one hand, and the lives of bandits or the lived experience of banditry, on the other.[19] Although many *griots* have sung the praises of bandits in the history of the Chad Basin (see Issa 2002), the status of bandits, then, as now, was extremely ambivalent, being both revered and feared. Moreover, during colonization, the "brigand-chiefs" constructed for themselves positions for economic accumulation by straddling the line between officialdom, as intermediaries for the colonial administration, and non-officialdom, as leaders of well-known highway gangs (Roitman 2005a: chap. 6). This ambivalence, which characterizes both organized banditry and unregulated economic activities today, is such that one cannot clearly delineate these endeavors in terms of a counter-realm, or as instances of rebellion, resistance to the state, or acts of social justice. While Robin Hood is said to have stolen from the rich to give to the poor, bandits and those involved in unregulated commerce in the Chad Basin are financed by the rich and steal or traffic as a way of entering into the labor market and participating in a particular political economy. In that sense, rather than constituting an "antisociety" (Hobsbawm 2000: 172) composed of a contained and oppositional moral universe—or what is more frequently referred to as a distinct moral economy—bandits, smugglers, and traffickers seek a certain mode of integration by partaking in recognized modes of governing the economy.[20] While critical of state regulatory authority, the *coupeurs de route* maintain that those who govern them act in ways that are justifiable and even licit, given the world in which they live.

Thus, the ongoing cycle of theft and seizure is often construed by locals as a marginal condition that is in fact the norm, a perspective put forth by a young man who works the unregulated border trade:

> The government's latest policy is the struggle against poverty. In order to get money from the whites, Cameroon says that it is now a Highly

Indebted Poor Income Country [HIPIC], while we know that in our region
we are a great power. People of all nationalities come here every day, to
Mbaimboum. . . . Cameroon is a HIPIC by cheating, by demagogy, in
order to have the white man's money. So Cameroonians follow the
example of the state!
Meaning?
The state steals from the whites, the civil servants steal from the state, the
merchants steal from the civil servants by selling them products at prices
incompatible with their standard of living or by making them pay exorbi-
tant rents on housing, and the bandits steal from the merchants and the
civil servants, who, together, transformed the state into a criminal entity.
In fact, me, I don't condemn Cameroon for having really become a HIPIC
because, if Cameroon steals from the whites, it's due to the fact that the
whites always stole from Africa.[21]

This refers to the fact that, in the late 1980s, mechanisms for the exchange of debt, or the emergence of debt markets that dominated international financial markets during the 1980s (the Baker and Brady Plans),[22]
became a crucial element of African political economies. These debt markets engendered what Olivier Vallée (1999) calls "political economies of
debt," which involve not only the debt trade but also the displacement of
public law in favor of commercial law. In effect, the debt market is based
on various modalities for the conversion of debt into investment credits,
funds for development projects, stock options in newly privatized companies (electricity, telephone), rights to natural resources (gas and oil), and
promissory notes that become objects of speculation and exchange. Such
conversions—or the selling of debt by national states and public companies—involve value transformations, or the reformulation of distinctions
between public wealth and the private domain. These processes for transforming public debt into private wealth have allowed strapped public treasuries to access hard currency and, more typically, have ensured the
enrichment of public personalities, who have placed such currency in
off-shore accounts and bought into, via their rights constituted in debt, recently privatized companies. Public debt has been converted into private
wealth (Vallée 1999), making the state of liability a resource in itself (Roitman 2003).

Thus, the assertion that theft and violent appropriations are illegal and
yet licit—or acceptable or "legitimate" modalities (as Bakaridjo put it)—
is based on specific understandings about manners of rendering illegality
a form of licit practice, habits of straddling the fine line between criteria

that denote public versus private wealth, and ways of remaining both marginal and indispensable to productive systems. These statements extend beyond the circumscribed sphere of road banditry and smuggling insofar as they refer to a larger realm of knowledge that includes practices of government, such as the debt trade. Such practices are often dependent upon or generated out of the very ambivalence of certain statuses, such as "public," "private," "governed," "governors"—as was noted on a recent cover of a widely read African news magazine: "Cameroon: Cop or Hoodlum?" (*Jeune Afrique Économie* 2002).

Statements and interpretations about how illegality is licit practice are also widespread with regard to unregulated economic activities, such as those pursued by the motorcycle-taximen, the original clandestine operators of the Villes Mortes campaign.[23] In the late 1990s, and in an effort to quell *incivisme fiscal* and to capture this lucrative domain, motorcycle-taxis were legalized through a series of regulations. These included a new tax (*l'impôt libératoire*), a driver's license, vehicle registration, vehicle insurance, a vehicle inspection sticker, a permit to carry passengers, a parking permit, and a custom's receipt for imported motorcycles. Drivers are now supposed to paint the motorcycles yellow and wear helmets and gloves, none of which I have ever seen. Most young taximen do not pay these myriad impositions, which might be described as a host of mini-seizures. But this is not because they do not have the means, since most taxi fleets are financed by merchants, gendarmes, police, prefects, and even governors. The motorcycle-taximen—who are often called *les attaquants* (the attackers) or *les casquadeurs* (the cascaders)—simply refer to a different register of appropriations, which, ironically, often involves the very same people who are responsible for the collection of official taxes. In response to criticism for not having paid his official taxes, one young motorcycle-taximan, a member of the Association des Moto-taximen in Ngaoundéré, declared:

> We pay our taxes every day! Whether we have all the right papers for the motorcycle or not, we pay taxes to the police and gendarmes. In fact, it's become a reflex. The policemen of Ngaoundéré don't stop me anymore. I'm an old hand in the moto-taxi business. I've driven moto-taxis for people in high places, for men in uniform [who are owners of fleets of clandestine motorcyles]. Furthermore, often even when the police don't stop me, I go to them to pay the tribute [money]. . . . Since the policeman is also a chief—in fact, we call him "chief" [*le chef*]—you have to go toward him even when your papers are in order, especially when you are in order.[24]

During the same conversation, another moto-taximan added:

> The police and the moto-taximen, we're partners. We know that if we are dis-
> posed to giving them a bit of money from time to time, we can work together.
> Together—that is, the police and the moto-taximen—we exploit illegality.
> Even when you have all your papers in order, you're in illegality because the
> motorcycle is illegal. Not even 5 percent of the motorcycles are painted yel-
> low. We have imposed our vision of things on the authorities. The police
> themselves close their eyes; they can always find an infraction to ticket. That
> way, they have money for beer. . . . So that the system can continue to func-
> tion properly, it's important that there are people in violation because, if
> everyone was in line with the law, the authorities—the police—wouldn't gain
> their share and then they would suppress the motorcycles on the pretext that
> they cause accidents, that we are hoodlums, etc. Today, maybe we are hood-
> lums, but we are hoodlums who help sustain families and contribute to the
> well-being of agents of the force of law. Long live the tolerant police [*la police
> compréhensive*]![25]

The Ethics of Illegality: "Giving to Continue to Have"

When asked whether they considered their activities licit or illicit, there
was general agreement among the moto-taximen that "anything that can
move a poor man from hunger and begging is licit." But one young man
argued:

> We struggle in domains that force you to circumvent the law—with all the
> risks. For example, we sell contraband petrol and medicines, etc., which
> are officially forbidden. But what do you expect? Often those who are
> supposed to see that people respect the law are our sponsors; they give us
> our original financing. A customs official who finances a petrol smuggler
> is not going to attack him [the smuggler] or the protégés of his colleagues!
> And without us, the work of the policeman, the customs official, the tax-
> man, the head of the gendarmes, would have no interest for those who do
> it. Thanks to us, they have no financial problems.
>
> *But that's corruption![26]*
>
> That's not corruption. When you give 10,000 or 20,000 CFA to a police-
> man or a customs official to get your merchandise through, what does that
> change for the national economy? Corruption is when one sells the Régie
> Nationale des Chemins de Fer [rail company], the SNEC [water com-
> pany], the SONEL [electric company], etc. Everyone knows that that's
> negotiated; there are big commissions. One single person can earn in a
> privatization more than all of Touboro [a local town known for contra-

band] can produce, save in a decade. Us, we give with pleasure and the police receive with pleasure, just like the customs official. They've become family.[27]

An older and well-known smuggler—who, above, insisted on his status as an "ordinary economic operator"—corroborated:

> The civil servants are people who always have financial problems. They have needs that are not covered by their salaries, and so they become indebted to those who have money. In the end, needy civil servants and us, we have the same bosses [*patrons*] and this is not the government but rather the merchants. Look! Since we have been here [on the Ngueli Bridge], have you seen a single man or woman stopped by the Cameroonian customs agents or the gendarmes? All these hundreds of people who pass by here have their papers in order? The customs agents or the gendarmes who come here [to work] don't seek to be transferred elsewhere unless they have problems with the big merchants or if they've amassed enough wealth. The passport for all that you want to do here, it's the franc CFA. Instead of paying for official documents at 200,000 CFA, it's better to just give 50,000 CFA with your own hands. That way, you have papers and protection.
>
> *Corruption?*
> What do you call corruption? They say that Cameroon is the world champion of corruption. How can a poor country be the world champion of corruption? They say that in Arab countries, in France, and in the United States, there are people who have more money than the Cameroonian government. I imagine that those countries have several times over what Cameroon possesses! Giving 5,000 CFA, 10,000 CFA, or 50,000 CFA, what does that represent in the Cameroonian economy?
> *Someone else recently said the same thing to me. Explain what you mean by corruption. Giving 5,000 CFA to a gendarme or a customs official is illegal!*
> I told you that every profession, like every religion, has its codes. Giving 5,000 is not giving 15 million. It's part of the code of trafficking: giving to continue to have.[28]

The code of trafficking, or the code of the route, was explained as follows:

> The Koran governs the Islamic religion, the Bible governs Christianity, the Torah is for the Jews, the road manual is for those who drive. . . . You cannot take the Koran to adore Jesus, you can't go to church with the road manual. If you take the Torah to fix your motorcycle, you will soon end up with a car-

cass in its place. . . . I say that a trafficker who wants to respect the law of the
government cannot succeed because trafficking is not governed by the law of
the government. It is governed by the law of the roads. If, when leaving Nigeria with petrol, you go see the customs officials to give them some money so
that you can get through, they are going to arrest you. They'll say that you're
suspicious, that you're not an ordinary trafficker, you want to tempt them,
you're a spy. But if, while you're trying to evade them, they find you in the
bush, then you can negotiate because you're in the normal order of the law of
trafficking.[29]

These arguments all present the rationality of illegality, a disposition
that is both economically strategic and socially productive. While "trafficking is not governed by the law of the government," traffickers and the
police and customs officials have "become family." While outside the
realm of "the law," and hence described as obviously illegal, unregulated
commerce and gang-based banditry are nonetheless perceived as a "normal order," as licit activities insofar as they are admissible and have in
some ways come to represent certain truths about the economic, or about
ways of acting effectively in the economic realm. This is the case because,
as one of the moto-taximen said, "So that the system can continue to function properly, it's important that there are people in violation. . . . [We]
help sustain families and contribute to the well-being of agents of the force
of law." In the Chad Basin, maintaining states of illegality is a mode for establishing and authenticating the exercise of power over economic relations and forms of wealth, giving rise to political subjects who are at once
subjected to governmental relations and active subjects within their realm.
Thus, as was just explained, the code of trafficking refers to and engages
with a larger code of governmental relations. As participants in the world
of unregulated commerce and road banditry recognize, this code of trafficking may be illegal, since it departs from the codes and regulations of
official law, but it is neither illicit nor illegible. It must be understood from
within its own script, which, while circumventing government, partakes
in modes of governing the economy that are fundamental to the workings
of the various national states of the Chad Basin.

One might argue that this poses the problem of the efficacy of modes
of governing, since it would seem that the various nation-states of the
Chad Basin are not producing self-governing citizens, or people who enact
the spontaneous payment of official taxes. But the problem of efficacy
depends, of course, on the criteria upon which it is judged, or the register
to which one refers. Government law and the "law of the roads"—or the

code of officialdom and the code of trafficking—are deployed simultaneously, their conditions of emergence being mutually constituted. Their logics propagate certain forms of state power, being the very raison d'être of security forces and customs officials, as well as specific practices of governing the economy, being sources of the scripts by which forms of wealth are recognized and circumscribed as such.

As a realm in which one evaluates the nature of licit practice, as well as representations of the self and self-conduct, unregulated commerce and gang-based road banditry etch out a space of ethics. And yet this does not entail reference to a set of stable moral precepts or an absolute authority that sanctions conduct. Nor does it entail an autonomous and oppositional "moral economy" that has emerged in the margins of state failure.[30] Those we have heard from in these pages do not necessarily doubt the legitimacy of state institutions and administrations. They do not confirm legitimacy crisis readings of their situation, which maintain that the failure of state institutions to ensure law and order or to establish legality itself incites recourse to illegal activities as a mode of critique and resistance to the state—assuming, then, that a prior state of normalcy (legitimacy) has been transgressed and that the project of modernity has been compromised and is being reclaimed by social forces. To the contrary, state institutions everywhere in the world participate in and even initiate illegal economic practices (e.g., the transformation of public monies into private funds through privatizations or publicly financed, no-bid contracts), which is part of the reason that people living in the Chad Basin deem them "licit." They say that their own activities are illegal and yet licit because they are simply modes of economic accumulation and of governing the economic, or a way of participating in forms of reasoning that constitute a particular political economy.

Therefore, because evaluations of what constitutes licit practice and licit self-conduct are not derived from a set of ethical standards that are distinct from those associated with official government, the forms of resistance associated with illegal yet licit practices are necessarily generated out of states of domination. Practices of resistance are "never in a position of exteriority in relation to power" (Foucault 1990: 95, 97). In that sense, the ethics of illegality is not comparable to "a set of moral principles relating to or affirming a specific group, field, or form of conduct," as goes the classical definition of morality.[31] Morality implies a set of standards concerning the distinction between right and wrong or good and bad. This is not the distinction being made by my interlocutors in the Chad Basin. They are less concerned with whether or not their behavior is good or bad than the ways in which their actions relate to certain forms of reasoning: the law of trafficking, the raison d'être of the forces of law and order. Although they refer to a code (the code of trafficking), this is not described as a moral code, which would set forth categorical foundations regarding the nature of humanity and determine ethical versus unethical behavior. Moreover, they refer to several codes relating to state law, trafficking, governmental practices, and religious precepts, all of which inform various aspects of their practice.

This manner of referring to an ensemble of codes and precepts—and not a self-contained moral economy or a specific, a priori "morality"—contradicts the idea of morality as metaphysics, or morality as a set of values and standards that transcend time and contingency. For one, the very idea of a moral economy raises the question of the very limits of "the moral" and of the category of "morality." Its unspoken term is usually "culture" or whatever it is that is supposed to bring this economy together as a consistent form of morality. Or, to the contrary, its unspoken term is "economy," or the presupposition that there is an unspecified "economy" (coherence?) to people's moral practice. That is, this concept of the moral economy often presupposes the ontological status of morality (Roitman 2000).[32] Furthermore, reference to a moral economy or to a realm of morality as a stable and authoritative realm that can be either preordained or located as an object of knowledge must be specific about the line between "the moral" and "the nonmoral." How does one recognize or define moral considerations against human rationales that are not of the moral order?[33] And what does one make of the road bandits, smugglers, and *passeurs* of the Chad Basin, who, like us, refer to rules, codes, standards, and precepts that exhibit internal contradictions?

In some respects, the practices of the road bandits and smugglers affirm this critique of the relevance of a moral code; they do not construe their codes and what they take to be as "licit" or "legitimate" in terms of an autonomous, coherent, or preordained form of authority. While they refer to codes and laws (the law of the road, the code of trafficking), these are heterogeneous; they do not compose a "quasi-juridical form" to which the subject refers as "a law or set of laws (see Foucault 1970, 1984: 32–39). Nor are they construed as being based on a metaphysical conception of truth that transcends human desires and practices (for a critique of morality as a metaphysical conception of truth, see Nietzsche 1974, 1967). To such conceptions of morality, Foucault contrasted ethical practice, which, while involving codes and rules, consists of manners and exercises for self-understanding within a nexus of relationships. This ethics involves problematizing; it inscribes a mode of questioning about the self and the construction of the self in the world.[34] It is the manner in which I have understood the lives of those who are engaged in organized road banditry and unregulated economic activities in the Chad Basin. Less concerned with the "truth" of the principles informing their practice, the smugglers, road warriors, and *douaniers-combattants* are very much interested in their own reasoning and in how it is constructed out of and within certain power situations, which implies critical engagement with an ensemble of forms of reasoning. In that sense, they describe their relations to various truths: about the ways in which power is exercised over them; about the ways in which wealth can be procured; about violence, indebtedness, and illegality. They comment upon their reasoning or their relationships to these truths, and especially the ways in which they both question and live those truths. The ethics of illegality problematizes certain lived experiences and specific concepts, such as wealth, work, accumulation, and economic regulation that are both critical to and unstable in that experience. Conversations with them give insight into the ways in which power situations are apprehended as such according to various, specific, historical codifications of these concepts and of the very rationalities of power relations.

Notes

For their kind support I thank the SSRC-MacArthur Foundation Program on Peace and Security Fellowship; the Ciriacy-Wantrup Fellowship of the University of California, Berkeley; and the MacArthur Foundation Program on Global Security and Sustainability. I also thank Saïbou Issa, University of Ngaoundéré, who collaborated closely with me in this research; Tobias Rees, who asked me some very difficult questions; and John Comaroff, who made useful suggestions. All translations are my own. Parts of this text appear in Roitman 2005b.

1. The Chad Basin is a vague geographical concept (see Roitman 2004a). I use the term here to refer to what are today northern Nigeria, northern Cameroon, Chad, and the Central African Republic. I lived in this region during various extended periods from 1992 to 2002.

2. Scant sources include the following: on kalashnikovs, *Jeune Afrique* 1992; on the continental drug economy, Observatoire Géopolitique des Drogues 1995; on petrol smuggling, Herrera 1998. More generally, see Bennafla 1996, 1997; Grégoire 1998.

3. 17 November 2001, Ngahoui, Cameroon. The conversations reported herein generally took place in Fulani, French, and Arabic. In a few instances, interpreters assisted with translation in situ. Some conversations took place with the assistance of my colleague Professor Saibou Issa, in which case dialogue was transcribed at a later time. Conversations with those involved in unregulated commerce

or road banditry generally took place at specific sites along the borders (hamlets, trading posts, well-known border-crossing points. When contacts were needed to arrange a meeting with a specific personality, these meetings were held in drinking establishments or in secured places specified by the person involved.

4. Oil exploitation and the pipeline have been undertaken by a consortium led by Exxon (40 percent), with the participation of Chevron (25 percent) and Petronas (35 percent). In June 2000, after much contestation, the World Bank guaranteed this private oil development project to the tune of $3.7 billion. For details, see Tulip 2004.

5. See *Jeune Afrique* 1992; *Le Progrès* 1997; *N'djamena Hebdo* 1997; Teiga 1997.

6. Some of whom were recently accused by *coupeurs de route* before a military tribunal in Cameroon. See Guivanda 2002.

7. On this view of ethics and its relation to the process of self-formation (and not self-discovery), see Paul Rabinow's tremendously erudite book, *Anthropos Today* (2003), especially the introduction and chapter 1. See also Foucault 2001.

8. 20 January 2002, Touboro, Cameroon.

9. 14 November 2001, Meiganga, Cameroon.

10. Proper names have been replaced by initials, pseudonyms, or "XXX." The town of Koulem is fictitious so as to protect the anonymity of those involved. The translation erases the charm of the language and style of the French version. I also corrected the spelling and some of the grammar to facilitate reading. The original letter is as follows:

A. M.   La Brousse du 17-1ᵉʳ-94
Elément de Soldat
Militaire Tchadien dans le
teritoire Camerounais
dit Coupeur de Routes dans le
departement de Logone et Chari

A Monsieur le Préfet du logone et chari

C'est mois l'élément millitaire Tchadien qui vous est ecrit cette [illisible] Parce que on nous Paye chaque fin de mois 120 000 F Par mois . mais on ma Pas Payer le mois de Decembre 93. don j'ai demissionner leur Bettisse la le 19 1ᵉʳ mois 94. don je vous informe les Person qui nous soutins en Brousse. Sont: il ya Alhadji M. T. qui dit XXX. Il ya Alhadji L. O. il K. G. Il ya Alhadji S. choucou choucou ! Vendeur de Piece detacher à Kousseri. Il ya Alhadji E. A. Et Puis christophe Pasteur qui nous delivre le vin "33" Export les Beaufort. Les Castel. Et les Wiskis C'est le Proprietère de Bar XXX de Kousseri. Tous les membre que je vous est siter là so. Son ceux qui nous Ravitaies avec tous chosse. leur envoiyeur SePeciale. C'est aussi un mamabre qui rePon au nom de Kanto. Il nous Son louer à 29.000 000 Fca Pourquoi Parce que le Secrait . . . d'état à la défense Amadou Ali à amèner les militaire Pour tuè les arabe. Mais on a tuè les militaire camerounais 9 solda. maintenan il sont à la recherche du *commissaire de a Securutè Public Mr. XXX* 2ème le commandant de comPagie 3ème le maire de la ville XXX. 4ème le Sous Préfet vous etait recherch . . . dans la ville de Kousseri même à qu'elle Leur.

Je vous Remerci de mes informations. mais je vous quite. je Pars sur
N'Djamena je deman . . . de esquise de ma Pas de ce que fait au Cameroun. je
vous envois mes Photos comme Souvenir.
Signé: A. M.

11. "Arab Choa" refers to an ethnically and linguistically defined community
residing in Chad and western Sudan.

12. Scant references include Abba Kaka 1997 and Ngarngoune 1997 on the
military's rent-seeking activities, and Faes 1997 on the guerilla movement in
the vicinity of Lake Chad.

13. 8 December 2001, Kousseri, Cameroon.

14. December 2001, Kousseri, Cameroon.

15. 14 November 2001, Meiganga, Cameroon.

16. See Hibou 1999 on this process, which she calls the "privatization of the
state."

17. 14 November 2001, Meiganga, Cameroon.

18. This clarification stems from queries put to me by Florence Bernault,
Stephen Collier, Mirjam de Bruin, and Tobias Rees.

19. Hobsbawm recognizes this point in the preface to the revised edition of
Bandits (2000). The classic critique of Hobsbawm 2000 is Blok 1972; see also
Blok 1974: 97–102.

20. Doubtless, these people develop special forms of behavior and argots, as
Hobsbawm (2000: 172) says. But these are modes of distinction as opposed to
modalities of an antisociety.

21. 15 November 2001, Meiganga, Cameroon.

22. James Baker, the former US secretary of state, was behind the initiative that
established a list of middle-income countries of high strategic interest due to their
very high levels of debt outstanding with commercial banks. In 1989, Nicholas
Brady devised an official program for "voluntary debt reduction," which would
absorb these debts through market mechanisms. For an excellent, in-depth account of the emergence of this debt regime, read Callaghy 2001.

23. In May 1991, the National Coordination of Opposition Parties and Associations organized the Opération Villes Mortes campaign, which involved a strategy of civil disobedience implementing general strikes, work boycotts, economic
blockades, and the use of clandestine services—such as motorcycles that served as
"hidden" taxis—to deny taxation. This campaign aimed to undermine the fiscal
base of the regime in power, led by President Paul Biya. Indeed, Opération Villes
Mortes crippled the Cameroonian economy. Those who participated in the movement expressed their criticism of the regime's exactions and levies, which ultimately finance the ruling party and the political elite; the state's methods of extraction, which are often heavy-handed; and the regime's failure to provide
economic opportunities and economic security to local populations. In turn, the
regime dubbed the Opération Villes Mortes movement and the general refusal to
pay taxes *"incivisme fiscale,"* which was intended to typify the movement as "uncivil," or beyond the pale of civic behavior. For further analysis, see Roitman
2005a.

24. December 2001, Ngaoundéré, Cameroon.

25. December 2001, Ngaoundéré, Cameroon.

26. This question was asked, not as an accusation, but rather as a way to encourage further explanation.

27. 23 November 2001, Touboro, Cameroon.

28. December 2001, Kousseri, Cameroon.

29. November 2001, Mbang Mboum, Cameroon.

30. Hobsbawm's revised edition (2000) of his 1969 book, *Bandits,* supposedly takes into account the "context of politics," arguing that there are "historical conditions" for the emergence of social banditry. These include the disintegration of state power and administration as well as the failure of states to ensure law and order (2000: x). For another view of social bandits and their role in state centralization and state formation, see Barkey 1994. See also Bayart 1994.

31. *New Oxford American Dictionary.* Nor is the ethics of illegality an ethos insofar as its practices do not capture the "spirit" of a particular time period or a given "culture."

32. It should be noted that E. P. Thompson (1966, 1971), who first coined the term "moral economy" in his inquiry on the idea of working-class culture, was concerned with economic class as "an event," which he sought to describe "as a process of self-discovery and self-definition" (1966). This is a far cry from many current uses of the term in the social sciences and is in some ways in keeping with Michel Foucault's concerns regarding the practice of ethics and *le souci de soi.* See Roitman 2001 for commentary.

33. For elaboration, see Williams 1972 and 1985, which are two among many contributions to the debate over the possibility of moral philosophy.

34. As Paul Rabinow notes (1997: xxxvi) in his extremely lucid and helpful review of Foucault's work on ethics and subjectivity, "'being' is given through problematizations and practices; it is not prior to them." In an interview with Stephen Riggins (Rabinow 1997: 131), Foucault refers to the way in which ethics is not a form of morality:

> SR: Beyond the historical dimension, is there an ethical concern implied in *The History of Sexuality?* Are you not in some ways telling us how to act?
>
> MF: No. If you mean by ethics a code that would tell us how to act, then of course *The History of Sexuality* is not an ethics. But if by ethics you mean the relationship you have to yourself when you act, then I would say that it intends to be an ethics, or at least to show what could be an ethics of sexual behavior. It would be one that would not be dominated by the problem of the deep truth of the reality of our sex life. The relationship that I think we need to have with ourselves when we have sex is an ethics of pleasure, of intensification of pleasure.

References

Abba Kaka, A. 1997. "Cette fraude qui tue!" *Le Temps* (N'djamena) 69 (9–15 April): 8.
Barkey, K. 1994. *Bandits and Bureaucrats: The Ottoman Route to State Centralization.* Ithaca, NY: Cornell University Press.
Bayart, J.-F., ed. 1994. *La réinvention du capitalisme.* Paris: Karthala.
Bennafla, K. 1996. "Rapport sur les échanges transfrontaliers informels au Tchad." Unpublished manuscript, Université de Paris X—Nanterre.

————. 1997. "Entre Afrique noire et monde arabe: Nouvelles tendance des échanges 'informels' tchadiens." *Revue Tiers Monde* 38, no. 152 (October–December): 879–96.

————. 1998. "Mbaiboum: Un marché au carrefour de frontières multiples." *Autrepart* 6:53–72.

————. 2002. *Le commerce frontalier en Afrique Centrale.* Paris: Karthala.

Blok, A. 1972. "The Peasant and the Brigand: Social Banditry Reconsidered." *Comparative Studies in Society and History* 14:195–504.

————. 1974. *The Mafia of a Sicilian Village: A Study of Violent Peasant Entrepreneurs, 1860–1960.* Oxford: Oxford University Press.

Callaghy, T. 2001. "Networks and Governance in Africa: Innovation in the Debt Regime." In *Intervention and Transnationalism in Africa: Global-Local Networks of Power,* ed. T. Callaghy, R. Kassimir, and R. Latham, pp. 115–48. Cambridge: Cambridge University Press.

Das, V., and D. Poole. 2004. "State and Its Margins: Comparative Ethnographies." In *Anthropology at the Margins of the State,* ed. V. Das and D. Poole, pp. 3–33. Santa Fe, NM: School for American Research.

Faes, G. 1997. "Le dernier maquis." *L'Autre Afrique* 1 (21–27 May): 64–69.

Foucault, M. 1970. *The Order of Things: An Archaeology of the Human Sciences.* New York: Random House.

————. 1984. *Histoire de la sexualité.* Vol. 2, *L'usage des plaisirs.* Paris: Gallimard.

————. 1990. *The History of Sexuality.* Vol. 1, *An Introduction.* New York: Vintage Books. (Originally published 1978.)

————. 2001. *L'herméneutique du sujet: Cours au Collège de France, 1981–82.* Ed. Frédéric Gros. Paris: École des Hautes Études-Gallimard-Seuil.

Grégoire, E. 1998. "Sahara nigérien: Terre d'échanges." *Autrepart* 6:91–104.

Guivanda, R. 2002. "Des coupeurs de route accusent." *L'Oeil du Sahel* (Cameroon) 75 (21 February): 3.

Herrera, J. 1998. "Du 'fédéral' et des 'Koweïtiens': La fraude de l'essence nigériane au Cameroun." *Autrepart* 6:181–202.

Hibou, B., ed. 1999. *La privatisation des états.* Paris: Karthala.

Hobsbawm, E. 2000. *Bandits.* Rev. ed. New York: New Press. (Originally published 1969.)

Issa, S. 2002. "*Sonngoobe,* bandits justiciers dans la plaine du Diamaré (Nord-Cameroun) sous l'administration française." *Ngaoundéré Anthropos* (University of Ngaoundéré) 3:153–73.

————. 2004. "L'embuscade sur les routes des abords sud du lac Tchad." In "Autour du lac Tchad," ed. J. Roitman. Special issue, *Politique Africaine* 94 (June): 82–104.

Jeune Afrique. 1992. 19 November, pp. 28–30.

Jeune Afrique Économie. 2002. Vol. 337 (14 January–17 February).

Nietzsche, F. 1967. *On the Genealogy of Morals: Ecce Homo.* New York: Random House. (Originally published 1887.)

————. 1974. *The Gay Science.* New York: Random House. (Originally published 1882.)

N'djamena Hebdo. 1997. "Lorsque démobilisation rime avec développement." 281 (15 May): 6–7.

Ngarngoune, S. 1997. "Alerte au Sud." *N'djamena Hebdo* 280 (8 May): 4.

Progrès, Le (N'djamena). 1997. "Armée: Lumière sur la démobilisation et la réinsertion." 13 May, pp. 10–11.

Observatoire Géopolitique des Drogues. 1995. *Géopolitique des drogues, 1995.* Paris: La Découverte.

Rabinow, P., ed. 1997. *Essential Works of Foucault, 1954–1984*. Vol. 1, *Ethics, Subjectivity, and Truth*. New York: New Press.

———. 2003. *Anthropos Today*. Princeton, NJ: Princeton University Press.

Roitman, J. 2000. "Économie morale, subjectivité et politique." *Critique Internationale* 6:48–56.

———. 2001. "New Sovereigns? Regulatory Authority in the Chad Basin." In *Intervention and Transnationalism in Africa: Global-Local Networks of Power*, ed. T. Callaghy, R. Kassimir, and R. Latham, pp. 240–66. Cambridge: Cambridge University Press.

———. 2003. "Unsanctioned Wealth; or, The Productivity of Debt in Northern Cameroon." *Public Culture* 15(2):211–37.

———, ed. 2004a. "Autour du lac Tchad." Special issue, *Politique Africaine* 94 (June): 7–104.

———. 2004b. "Productivity in the Margins: The Reconstitution of State Power in the Chad Basin." In *Anthropology at the Margins of the State*, ed. V. Das and D. Poole, pp. 191–224. Santa Fe, NM: School for American Research.

———. 2005a. *Fiscal Disobedience: An Anthropology of Economic Regulation in Central Africa*. Princeton, NJ: Princeton University Press.

———. 2005b. "Modes of Governing in the Chad Basin: The Garrison-Entrepôt." In *Global Assemblages: Technology, Politics, and Ethics as Anthropological Problems*, ed. A. Ong and S. Collier, pp. 417–36. Malden, MA: Blackwell.

Seignobos, C., and J. Weber. 2002. *Eléments d'une stratégie de développement rural pour le Grand Nord du Cameroun*. Vol. 1, *Rapport principal*. Montpelier: CIRAD.

Teiga, M. B. 1997. "Une armée, certes, mais combien de divisions . . ." *l'Autre Afrique*, 17–23 December, pp. 14–15.

Thompson, E. P. 1966. *The Making of the English Working Class*. New York: Vintage Press.

———. 1971. "The Moral Economy of the English Crowd in the Eighteenth Century." *Past and Present*, pp. 76–136.

Tulip, S. 2004. "Le bassin tchadien à l'épreuve de l'or noir: Réflexions sur la 'nouvelle donne pétro-politique' en Afrique centrale." In "Autour du lac Tchad," ed. J. Roitman. Special issue, *Politique Africaine* 94 (June): 59–81.

Vallée, O. 1999. "La dette privée est-elle publique? Traites, traitement, traite: Modes de la dette africaine." *Politique Africaine* 73 (March): 50–67.

Williams, B. 1972. *Morality*. Cambridge: Cambridge University Press.

———. 1985. *Ethics and the Limits of Philosophy*. Cambridge, MA: Harvard University Press.

Zoua, Jean-Baptiste. 1997. *Phénomène des coupeurs de route dans le nord-Cameroun: Une épine dans la plante des pieds des responsables du maintien de l'ordre*. Unpublished manuscript, Chef d'état-major de la région militaire no. 4, Garoua.

Criminal Obsessions, after Foucault
Postcoloniality, Policing, and the Metaphysics of Disorder

Jean Comaroff and
John L. Comaroff

Perhaps it is because our lives are so chaotic, so filled with unsolved mysteries, incomplete stories, uncaught murderers that crime fiction is so popular. I believe that is why South Africans are so hooked on American TV crime series . . . because somewhere, somehow, someone is solving crimes. At least in fiction justice is served.

MICHAEL WILLIAMS, *The Eighth Man*

PEOPLE ACROSS THE PLANET HAVE, in recent years, been uncommonly preoccupied with public order, crime, and policing. From Britain to Brazil, Nigeria to the Netherlands, Slovakia to South Africa,[1] the specter of illegality appears to be captivating popular imaginations. In much of the world, to be sure, this preoccupation is far from groundless. It is true that "accurate" crime statistics may be impossibly difficult to arrive at;[2] such actuarial artifacts depend, after all, on what is seen to constitute a felony in the first place, on what counts as evidence, on how much is conceded to the truth claims of aggregate numbers. It is also true that the *perceived* threat of criminal assault is often incommensurate with the "real" risk to persons and property; as it happens, that risk remains more unevenly distributed in South Africa than it is in most places.[3] All this notwithstanding, the incidence of violent crime here, and its effects on the lives of ordinary citizens, are *not* to be trivialized. They are perfectly real. As criminologists have come to recognize, the burgeoning violence endured by segregated black communities under apartheid has, especially since the late 1980s, spilled over into once-tranquil, tightly policed "white" cities and suburbs.[4] This is an integral part of our story.

And yet, at the same time, there seems to be more to the public obsession with criminality and disorder than the mere *fact* of its reality. South Africans of all stripes are also captivated by *images* of crime and policing, whether it be in the form of avid rumor or home-grown *telenovelas*, Hollywood horror or high theater, earnest documentaries or trashy melodramas. Whatever dangers they may dodge on the streets by day, at night, behind carefully secured doors, a high proportion of them indulge in vicarious experiences of extravagant lawlessness by way of the media, both imported and local. Why should this be so?

The South African preoccupation with law and order—or, rather, with its mediated representation—is neither new nor unique. "Even though crime exists . . . in what the public chooses to think of as epidemic proportions," wrote Stuart Scheingold of the United States two decades ago, "we still feel compelled to invent it."[5] For over a century, in fact, fictional "cops and robbers" have provided a compelling topos for popular mythmaking all over the world; clearly, they offer pliant allegorical terms for exploring the nature and limits of social being almost everywhere. This taste for crime fiction is not restricted to those who consume it as mass entertainment. Nor is it of interest only to those who contemplate order in the abstract. To the contrary, theater and fantasy appear integral to the workaday routines of policing itself. As if to make the point, Scotland Yard recently hired a professional magician, using "illusions as a metaphor for real life situations" to "boost [the] confidence and . . . leadership skills" of its superintendents.[6] In like vein, as we shall see, the strained South African Police Services (SAPS), whose cadres include some successful diviner-detectives,[7] devote considerable effort to staging illusory victories over the dark forces of violence and disorder. But why all the drama? Why would august officers of the law—the very embodiment of the state at its most rational, legitimate, and forceful—feel a need to play around, to act out, in this manner? Has Foucault not convinced us that it is the panopticon, rather than the theater, that holds the key to power in its modernist form?

The Uses of Horror

Crime looms large in the post–Cold War age. Increasingly flexible in its modes of operation, it often mimics corporate business,[8] constituting an "uncivil society" that flourishes most energetically where the state withdraws: hence the implosion of ever more virtual, more vertiginous forms of fiscal fraud, ever more supple, border-busting markets in illegal substances, armaments, and mercenary violence—all facilitated by the liberalization of trade, by new kinds of financial instruments, and by cutting-edge communications media. Hence, also, the role of organized crime: of mafias, and of business-oriented "gangs" in posttotalitarian polities which, for a fee, perform services that governments no longer provide.[9] Such criminal "phantom-states," notes Derrida,[10] are a fact of our times. Often embedded in complex transnational relations, often relying on highly sophisticated technologies, they shade into the networks of terror that are rapidly replacing conventional threats to "national" security.[11] Indeed, received distinctions between crime and terror, always inchoate, are being revised as we speak, each term being deployed, ideologically, to make sense of, and to "fight," the other. Thus it is that we have "*the* war" on terror, on drugs, on gangs, on illegal aliens, on corporate corruption, and so on. Note, in this respect, that in 2002 Egged, the Israeli bus company, sued Yasser Arafat and the Palestinian Authority for damages incurred as a result of suicide bombings; in the same year, Americans bereaved on 9/11 filed a claim against Islamic charities, the Sudanese state, Saudi Arabian banks, and others for their support of Osama bin Laden—actions that would reduce the *intifada* and World Trade Center attacks to common illegalities actionable by recourse to tort law.[12] Under these conditions, abetted by such instruments as the U.S. Patriot Act, crime and terror merge in the epistemic murk of a "new" global system that both reproduces and eclipses its old international predecessor. The upshot is that social order appears ever more impossible to apprehend, violence appears ever more endemic, excessive, and transgressive, and police come, in the public imagination, to embody a nervous state under pressure. Officers of the Los Angeles Police Department, hardly known for their civility, have described themselves as "the outer membrane of civilization" in a disorderly world.[13] Similarly, the policeman protagonist in a stunning piece of postcolonial South African theater, Neil McCarthy's *The Great Outdoors,* observes that the "line between order and chaos" is like "one strand of a spider's web."[14]

The obsession with crime and lawlessness is not merely a commentary—at least, in South Africa—on social order, sui generis. It is also a reflection on the state of the nation. Take mass advertising, a genre that seeks to transform nightmare into desire. In April 2001, the *Guardian* observed that "bolted doors, patrolling dogs defending gated communities and dark figures cocking guns in the shadows appear even in ads for toilet paper and popcorn."[15] At the time, a music radio station in Johannesburg was promoting itself, on huge billboards, by means of just two words: MORE POLICE.[16] And, even more wryly: "YOU CAN TAKE THE CAR. JUST LEAVE THE RADIO. 98.7FM." This counterpoint between panacea and panic, pop and the politics of enforcement, ardent consumerism and Hobbesian anarchy, is hardly subtle. Texts like these are haunted by the specter of immanent attack, above all, attack by unruly black youths. Violent crime, here as in the United States, has become the lightning rod for an escalating range of everyday anxieties, which are fed by the insecurity of the privileged as they witness the anger and impatience of those excluded from the Promised

Land. In the banal theatrics of the mass media, crime becomes racialized and race criminalized. And both, if we may be forgiven the term, are youthenized.

Regarded in this light, South Africa appears to evince what Mark Seltzer has termed a "pathological public sphere;[17] it is increasingly at the "scene-of-the-crime," he argues, that contemporary publics are constituted. But there is more at stake in the popular obsession with scenes of violent disorder in this particular postcolony. This, after all, was, until not long ago, a racist police state; its transition from the *ancien régime,* moreover, was husbanded by a celebrated Truth and Reconciliation Commission whose deliberations were based on a model of justice that sought to address atrocities past without resort to punishment. Consequently, beyond constituting a public, the "scene-of-the-crime" in South Africa, broadly conceived, is also the source of a passionate politics on the part of government, a politics aimed at making manifest both the shape of the nation *and* a form of institutional power capable of underwriting its ordered existence. What we have here, in other words, is an *inversion* of the history laid out by Foucault in *Discipline and Punish,*[18] according to which, famously, the theatricality of premodern power gives way to ever more implicit, internalized, capillary kinds of discipline. Indeed, it is precisely this telos—which presumes the expanding capacity of the state to regulate everyday existence and routinely to enforce punishment—that is in question in South Africa. To wit, the drama that is so integral to policing the postcolony is evidence of a desire to condense dispersed power in order to make it visible, tangible, accountable, effective.[19]

These theatrics, we shall see, are anything but hidden or half-hearted. More often than not they assume the overdrawn shape of melodrama, a genre, according to Peter Brooks, that polarizes conflicting forces in such a way as to "make evident, legible, and operative" values that lack the transcendent authority of a religion, a dominant ideology, or whatever.[20] So it is with the spectacle of policing, the staging of which strives to make actual, both to its subjects and to itself, the authorized face, and force, of the state—of a state, that is, whose legitimacy is far from unequivocal. Nor is this true only in postcolonies. According to Malcolm Young, an ethnographer of British law enforcement: "police culture possesses a dramaturgical or melodramatic inflection." It mobilizes "illusion, praxis, and imagery" in "well-directed" social productions, deploying "mythical archetypes . . . in exaggerated games of 'cops' and 'robbers'";[21] melodrama in blue, so to speak. Young should know. He was himself a career police officer. His testimony returns us to one of our opening questions, now phrased more specifically: In what ways have illusion and fantasy been implicated in the work of law enforcement in recent South African history? And what might changes in the nature of police performance, in all senses of that term, tell us about the postcolonial—post-Foucauldian?—state, about its powers and its differences from its precursor?

A great deal, in answering these questions, hangs on the way in which we grasp the connection between modernist state power and popular fantasies of law and order. Gramsci, for instance, observed that judicial apparatuses are "always in discredit" with the public, a corollary of which is the enduring appeal of private and amateur sleuths.[22] Especially pertinent to our story, in this respect, is the reflection of C. L. R. James on detective fiction in America after the Great Depression.[23] There has, of course, been a long-standing infatuation with extralegal enforcement in US history; it has expressed itself not just in the popularity of such things as the dime western but also in the horror of public lynchings. James's exploration of the salience of the genre in the 1930s is to be read against this backdrop. Popular film, comics, and radio at the time, he recalls, were finely tuned to mass desire and frustration, giving allegorical shape to apprehensions about the meaning of freedom, prosperity, and nationhood in the midst of epic crisis. It was a moment of reckoning, too, for the liberal state and its moral economy; its failure to nurture a capitalist commonwealth had driven many ordinary people to desperation. Yet the avidly consumed crime drama of the period seldom spoke of economic collapse, labor struggles, or fear of war. This, James insists, was less a matter of deliberate sabotage than of a silent, "armed neutrality" among the classes.[24] In the space vacated by politics, dyspeptic private eyes sallied forth in the name of the law, sharing some of the hoodlum chic of gangsters themselves: above all, a "*scorn for the police as the representatives of official society.*"[25] As ruling institutions lost legitimacy, gumshoes—men of iron, men of irony—became purveyors of a cynical justice that acknowledged anger, appetite, fallibility, power. In so doing, they made it possible to imagine a social order wrought by heroic action in the cause of a greater moral good.

The detective fiction of post-Depression America bears some kinship with popular imaginings of law and order in South Africa after apartheid: its reference to rapidly changing social and economic conditions; to the shock effect of mass joblessness and the unfulfilled promise of a new age of prosperity; to a perceived failure of the regulatory state; to a view of the police as inefficient and easily corruptible; to the bipolarization of crime into, on the one hand, petty felonies committed by drab *misérables* driven by necessity and, on the other, the flamboyant larceny of defiant anti-heroes. If the US crisis yielded the New Deal, it remains to be seen what kind of deal the "new" South Africa fashions for itself. In the meantime, criminality has come to be represented, as it was in America during the 1920s and 1930s and would be again in the late-twentieth-century inner city, as a means of production—or, rather, of productive redistribution—for those alienated by new forms of exclusion. At the same time, there is more at work in contemporary South Africa than simple deprivation. As Jonny Steinberg points out, and mass-mediated drama affirms, the local underworld is not the sole preserve of the poor; it is peopled, as well, by the "well-healed and well-educated." This suggests that, for an ever more visible sector of the population, most of all young black men, gangster "lifestyles" have a seductive appeal.[26] It also suggests, after C. L. R. James and many popular movies and musics since his day, that the outlaw embodies, often in deeply racialized guise, a displaced discourse about desire and impossibility, one as characteristic of the neoliberal moment in South Africa as it was of the Depression era United States. Here, too, the state is regarded with ambivalence, roughly in proportion to its alleged failure to secure the well-being of its citizens. Here, too, violence speaks elegiacally of a very general angst about the anomic implosion of the established order of things.

The sheer fecundity of crime-as-*imaginaire* is no mystery. Thoroughly grounded in the experience of the real, it gives voice to a fundamental conundrum of social being in the secular liberal state, a conundrum of unsettling relevance in the United States since 9/11: How much freedom ought to be alienated, in the cause of security, to any regulatory regime, especially one whose legitimacy is open to question. This is a tension that dramas of law and order tend everywhere to resolve, in Durkheimian fashion, by making the obligatory appear desirable.[27] But fantasy is never reducible to pure functionality. Crime fiction also provides readily available tropes for addressing ironies, for ventilating desires, and, above all, for conjuring a moral commonweal, especially when radical transformation unseats existing norms and robs political language of its meaning. In these circumstances, the felon personifies an existence beyond the law, an existence at once awesome, awful, and sublime. Mogamat Benjamin, high-ranking member of a deadly gang in Cape Town's notorious Pollsmoor Maximum Security Prison, told a TV team: "I am powerful; I am partly God."[28] He was referring to his capacity to determine the lives and deaths of other inmates, even warders. Brusque iconoclasm of this kind opens a space of possibility, a space in which order is up for grabs, a space in which new modes of being are forged in the heat of unspeakably transgressive violence as the state withdraws or is rendered irrelevant. Benjamin and his brethren run a complex organization in the dark interstices of the jail by means that elude its administration, means that spill back into the tough terrain on which their gang does its usual business.[29] Shades here of another revered Benjamin, Walter Benjamin, for whom violence in its archetypal, mythic form was a "manifestation of the Gods."[30] It is awesome, he argued, *because* it threatens state monopoly over the law; note how "'great' criminal[s]," even when their ends are repellent, arouse the "secret admiration of the public."[31] But why do these figures, large and small, take on such intense salience in the here-and-now? Is this a result of the unique predicament of the postcolony? Or did it exist before?

Some clues from elsewhere may be helpful. James Siegel, for example, shows how, in an Indonesia facing political and economic dissolution, "the body of the criminal" has become the alibi against which the integrity of the nation and the law is asserted.[32] The "dangerous classes" serve a similar symbolic end in an ever more polarized, postindustrial Britain, says Malcolm Young: police invoke them to authorize "wars"—again, that term—on behalf of "the social order" against whatever is seen to imperil it.[33] Likewise, in parts of the Mediterranean and Latin America outlaws are cast as a fearsome anachronism over which modernist states must exercise authority in order to sustain the viability of the polity and its sovereign space.[34] In sum, the figure of archfelon, albeit culturally transposed, seems to be doing similar work in many places, serving as the ground on which a metaphysics of order, of the nation as a moral community guaranteed by the state, may be entertained, argued for, even demanded.

The question, then, is plainly this: To the extent that discourses of crime and enforcement, as *popular* national fantasy, are endemic to the imaginary of modern state power, how might current changes in the nature and sovereignty of states—especially postcolonial states—be tied to the criminal obsessions sweeping so many parts of the world? Why do outlaws, as mythic figures, evoke fascination in proportion to their penchant for ever more graphic, excessive, unpredictable violence? In South Africa today, Rob Marsh points out, it is *white*-collar crime that is most likely to "bring the country to its knees."[35] But it is red-blooded assault on persons and property that is of most public concern. Violence, in short, is immensely productive, sometimes horrifyingly so: quite apart from its capacity to redirect the flow of wealth, it usurps representation, reveals the limits of order, and justifies state monopolies over the means of coercion.

Self-evidently, violence is never just a matter of the circulation of images. Its exercise, legitimate or otherwise, tends to have decidedly tangible objectives—and effects. Indeed, it was the raw clarity of physical force that persuaded Fanon of its potential for liberating colonized bodies and minds.[36] This notwithstanding, its means and meanings always exceed its immediate ends, precisely because they rely on poetic techniques to inflate their impact. Could this be why brute coercion everywhere is inherently theatrical, its perpetrators upping the emotional ante via a host of self-dramatizing techniques—before, during, and after the fact? Begoñia Aretxaga, following Zulaika and Douglass, notes that brutality sets those who wield it in a "play-like" frame, one in which extraordinary feats seem achievable, in which all pretense of distinguishing fact from fabrication disappears.[37] Those who wish to command must constantly invoke violence, if not directly, then in displaced or mimetic form. It is this invocation—above all, by those entrusted with the *im*possibility of enforcing the law—with which we are concerned here: its rough play, its predilection for criminal fantasy, its response to the vicissitudes of state power. The police become visible, argues Giorgio Agamben, citing Benjamin, where the legal dominion of the state runs out; their "embarrassing" proximity to authority is manifested in perpetual displays of force, even in peaceful public places.[38] As we shall see, where governance is seriously compromised, law enforcement may provide a privileged site for staging efforts—the double entendre is crucial here—to summon the active presence of the state into being, to render it perceptible to the public eye, to produce both rulers and subjects who recognize its legitimacy. Herein, we shall argue, lies the affinity between policing, drama, and illusion. Herein, too, lies the source of popular preoccupations with the representation of law and order. Those, recall, were the two issues with which we began.

Let us move, then, onto the shifting planes of recent South African history. Scene 1 opens in the late 1980s, in what was the last act of the dying apartheid regime.

Capers with Coppers: The Closed Museum and the Spectral State

We begin with an anomaly: a public museum closed to the public, perhaps indefinitely. If this is an oxymoron, it is one that indexes the contradictory implications of radical democratization for the construction of a nation of free citizens on the vestigial ruins of a police state, the ruins of a polity founded on racial exclusion.

In 1999, when we first visited the South African Police Museum, housed in a shabby, elegant Victorian building in Pretoria, the executive capital of the country, it was shut for "renovation." The edifice, which had been the national Police Headquarters in the 1930s, was, we were told, in dangerous disrepair. This was visibly so, although it soon became clear that the wear and tear was not merely architectural. For the public exhibition space had coexisted, in the apartheid era, with something else, something clandestine, something now abhorrent: the epicenter, and an interrogation facility, of the infamous national security service. The bizarre coexistence of the two within the same walls—the museum below, the secret police above—appeared to be beyond coincidence. But more of that in a moment. It was not only the lurking traces of state terror that compromised the building. The content of the exhibits, once very popular with patrons, had themselves become inappropriate. State museums, of course, are more or less blatant statements, conjuring up the national populations, subjects, and interests for which, and to which, they speak. In times of historical change, they offer glaring indictments of denatured ideologies, of a slippage between state and nation, signifiers and signifieds. Not surprisingly, they have become prime objects of argument about the politics of representation in the "new" South Africa. Behind closed doors, in the late 1990s, the staff of the Police Museum pondered how to make their displays relevant to the postapartheid era.

We had been drawn to the place by an interest in the changing public sense of police work brought by the advent of majority rule.[39] The indefinitely closed museum called forth a historical speculation, a hypothesis if you will: that reforming the image of the old South African Police Force, jackboot of the state, into that of the South African Police *Services,* a gentler, human-rights-oriented, community-friendly agency, could well turn out to be an exercise in impossibility. By the late apartheid years, when it became increasingly difficult to contain the contradictions of the racial state, the South African Police Force operated, for the most part, as a paramilitary force. Its security branch existed above the law, torture and deadly force were routine in the treatment of political dissidents, and a dense network of informers extended its capillaries into every sphere of existence. Against this background, the state portrayed the police as heroic defenders of order against terror, treason, and savage insurrection.

The Police Museum spoke unchallenged from the heart of that state. It began life in 1968 as a haphazard collection of relics—murder weapons, graphic photographs of "ritual" mutilations, the personal effects of a famous female poisoner—all from landmark cases of the more or less distant past, these being used, early on, in the training of cadets. With the recruitment in 1982 of a museologist, Tilda Smal, herself a police officer, the collection was developed in an altogether-more-ambitious direction, combining edification with entertainment, high melodrama with low-tech installations. Central to its design was a series of tableaux that, together, composed a specifically South African history of crime and punishment. They also served as the setting for what would become the best-known feature of the institution, its Night Tours, during which staff of the museum and the Police Education Unit brought epic felonies to life by impersonating famous "criminals."

There could hardly be more literal or vivid evidence of the dramaturgy, the melodrama, of police work. But what did it all mean? What prompted otherwise-austere officers of a police state to inhabit the personae of their archenemies—indeed, to make public exhibitions of themselves in order to delight and terrify rather-ordinary patrons and their children? What might their play have had to do with the more sinister rituals that took place backstage in this extraordinary venue?

We take up the story with the help of the curator.[40] The museum, said Sergeant Smal, was allowed to display artifacts only from cases that had ended in convictions. It cataloged the triumph of law and order over enemies of the state. In the 1980s, the range of exhibits—a mixture of dioramas, documents, and objects—covered two key domains of police work. One was the apprehension of spectacular criminals; the other, the protection of "national security" against the threat of "terrorism" and, later in the decade, "dangers on the borders." Installations of the first kind featured the likes of Daisy de Melker, perhaps South Africa's most notorious serial killer: indicted for poisoning two husbands and one of her children, de Melker was a horrific inversion of the national stereotype of the genteel white female, entrusted with reproducing the moral essence of her race.[41] Such emblems of aberration *within* the nation were set off from the peril to its existence posed by those alienated from it: by Poqo, the armed wing of the radical Pan-African Congress, for instance, which, in the early 1960s had made a particular target of the police,[42] and by the "Rivonia conspiracy," uncovered with the arrest, in 1962, of several top African National Congress (ANC) leaders, most notably Nelson Mandela, who were alleged to be plotting treason. Dioramas dealing with defensive action on the borders depicted a hostile alliance of others bent on bringing down the ruling regime: exiled "terrorists," sympathetic frontline African states, and international communism. As this installation underlined, the dividing line between the military and the police was conspicuously fuzzy in the late years of minority rule.

Night Tours, in which the tableaux were animated, were started in

1990 as a onetime experiment to entertain a group of "VIPs" from the International Police Association. Word spread. Besieged by inquiries from an interested public, the staff decided to offer the tours on request. Soon the demand became overwhelming: at one point, there were three a week, all year, each for forty visitors. Performances continued until the building closed in April 1999. Initially, most visitors, both night and day, were white Afrikaans-speaking South Africans. Later, Africans, especially school groups, began to patronize the place. By that time, efforts had been made to revise the exhibits (see below). The Police Museum, in which everything was free of charge, seems to have been popular above all with the superpatriotic and the very poor. Toward the end, the Night Tours attracted some cultured critics of the regime, for whom this dark, if not wholly intended, parody—its freak-chic—became an excursion into the comic underside of the police state.

The staff look back on the tours with great fondness. These were occasions of carnivalesque camaraderie, occasions that gave license for various sorts of play, some of it decidedly ambiguous. As visitors entered the building, they came upon cops in anachronistic uniforms on antique bicycles; a somewhat heavy-handed signal, this, that they had departed real time for the domain of history-as-theater, of docudramaturgy. As we intimated earlier, the vaudeville itself turned on the willingness of the officer-players to inhabit the identities of public enemies. This willingness, almost a caricature of the mix of outrage and enjoyment that Lacan calls *jouissance,* may be read, following Aretxaga,[43] as an appropriation by state functionaries of the "seductive and fearful power" of their adversaries. But there is more at work here. The performance also recalls the repetitive enactment of paradox characteristic of African rituals under colonial conditions.[44] The Night Tours replayed the Hegelian enslavement of white rulers to the terror of the *swart gevaar,* a "black danger" largely of their own making. In the play, the pragmatics of melodrama permitted the separation of the civil from the savage, enabling the law to appear to act decisively upon forces of darkness, as if to redress the contradictions endlessly reproduced by colonial rule. The curator acknowledged that her staff presumed that patrons would be fascinated by sensational crime—and eager for vicarious terror. Consequently, they sought to provoke first horror and then deliverance, such "vicarious adventures in the illicit and the brutal," Scheingold notes, being a "prelude" to the gratification, to the "discharges of anger," promised by "society's act of retribution."[45] In dramatizing the difficulties of defending an enlightened order against uncouth odds, the police-players elevated their audience into metonymic citizens of the

nation as moral community—and, also, into a public in need of state protection from a vast mass of unruly others.

Visitors remember the tours vividly. One critical observer described the
performance as a "home-grown chamber of horrors": part amateur theater, part fairground haunted house. Thus, Daisy de Melker walked the
halls dressed in period costume, offering visitors coffee from her poison
flask. The real thing, that is, *not* a facsimile. Setting the scene was a cast of
characters who embodied less alarming threats to everyday order: a few
policewomen garbed as prostitutes; a couple who postured as addicts in
front of a light show that simulated a bad trip; a group of "authentic" *sangomas* (traditional healers), who enacted a trance to dramatize the dangers
of "black magic." Also brought to life was Panga Man, a notorious black
criminal who attacked courting white couples while they were parked in a
leafy spot in Pretoria, not far from the museum. Bearing a panga, a large
scythe, he would assault the men and rape the women—to whom, it was
said, he then gave bus fare home. There could hardly have been a more intense figuration of the dark, erotically charged menace that stalked the cities
in the white imagination, threatening civility and its social reproduction.
This nightmare gained fantastic irony when the attacker turned out to be
a mild-mannered "tea boy" at police headquarters.[46] Epitomizing the
standard colonial terrors of rapacious black sexuality and subaltern betrayal, Panga Man featured centrally in a regular museum display, which
depicted a car sawn in half to reveal a couple looking up in petrified expectation of an imminent strike. During Night Tours, a door would burst
open in the wall behind, and an African officer would leap out, brandish-
ing the eponymous weapon. "We thought of having him shout something
as he did so," the curator told us. "But the first time we tried it everybody
screamed so loudly, he could hardly be heard. People nearly fainted."

By the mid-1990s, with the dawn of the postcolony, efforts were made
to add fresh exhibits to the museum, acknowledging the possibility of
different readings of history and the presence of new sorts of citizen-
consumer. The aim, said Tilda Smal, was to document the role of the police
in the apartheid years in such a way as to capture black viewpoints on that
history. This took it on faith that it was possible, *within* the same signifying economy, to pluralize existing displays, their ideological scaffolding,
and the kind of nation they presumed. Thus, installations on terrorism
were revised to explain the rationale of the liberation movements. And
tableaux were included to document the Sharpeville massacre of 1960,
in which scores of nonviolent African protestors were shot to death by
police, and the insidious indignities of the pass system. Popular with the

public, itself now changing in social composition, was a depiction of the saber-rattling antics of the white-right Afrikaner Weerstand Beweging (Afrikaner Resistance Movement), whose assertive racist posturing was the very essence of neofascist melodrama. These changes produced some paradoxical moments—like one in which Nelson Mandela, played by a SAPS look-alike, stood inside a replica of his Robben Island cell and answered polite questions from curious visitors.

Nor were the tours uncontroversial, particularly among older white police officers. The museum, now under the jurisdiction of an ANC-administered Ministry of Safety and Security, had entered an era of postcolonial contestation, becoming a space of argument as never before. Whatever the *contingent* causes, its closure suggests that it collapsed under the weight of its own contradictions, wrought by thoroughgoing changes in the racial composition and status of the police, in the ideology of enforcement, and, most of all, in the relation of citizenry to government. But the question of what should be exhibited, how and why, pointed to something more than a shift in the way in which the nation narrates its past and future. It signaled a transformation in the social imaginary of the state itself—and the ways in which it deploys horror to make itself visible. About which more in a moment. In the meantime, the museum staff, undaunted, continue to plan future displays: on, for example, the more sensational abuses revealed by the Truth and Reconciliation Commission,[47] on the "evils" of the "witch doctor's art," and on such spectacular murderers as the so-called Norwood serial killer, who, as it happens, had been a regular police sergeant. But, as these museologists are coming to realize, it is difficult to capture, in tableau, the realities of policing the postcolony, at least not without rethinking the regime of representation required by the present moment. To be sure, in the final years, the Night Tours themselves ran up against this difficulty, finding that the line they presumed between fact and fantasy, order and chaos, safety and violence, was dissolving. In one instance, a harbinger of things to come, the police actors staged a robbery involving hostages and a fake intervention on the part of the Flying Squad, a rapid-response unit, firing blank bullets. By this time, however, violent crime had become a pervasive preoccupation, especially in the inner city, where the museum was located. As the shots went off, panic ensued. Unclear, in the midst of the mayhem, was whether or not the performance had been overtaken by a real attack from the streets outside.

It was not the first time that theater and brute reality had been confounded in this house of horrors. As we sat in the closed museum, talking to the curator about its past and its (im)probable future, Smal gestured toward the ceiling and recalled how, in the old days, the Pretoria branch of the Security Police had been housed above. "A lot of famous people were interrogated here," she said, "almost the whole current government." The edifice had been home, then, to another, more sadistic form of theater: the surreal techniques of information gathering, of violence and terror, that were the stock-in-trade of "special policing" under apartheid. Since 1994, several prominent figures have revisited the site of their incarceration and torture: the upper reaches of the building have, for former enemies of the state, become a space for revisiting the past, a space for personal and collective re-membering.[48]

During the heyday of the museum in the 1980s, its staff and visitors used an entrance on the east side of the building. The Security Police used the west side. When political prisoners were brought in, the clanking of their handcuffs and leg irons was audible in the exhibition space below. Smal said that she had found it hard to believe what she had heard and seen at the time. But, she noted, for patrons it all seemed "part of the show." In this way, the museum was the facade for state terror, and state terror the mise-en-scène for the museum.

We are confronted here with the strangeness of the real,[49] the unnerving interpenetration of force and fantasy, of policing and performance, of the interiors and exteriors of the state-as-violence. There was no simple line, in this house with two entrances, between backstage and frontstage, between actors and audience, between the producers and consumers of a phantasmagoric reality. Ordinary citizens unwittingly played along in the fabrication and reproduction of precisely the sense of apocalypse—the terrifying threats to order—that legitimized the deadly exercise of coercion in the name of governance. Despite the distinction between public display and secret interrogation, each represented an aspect of the melodrama, of manufacturing truth by evoking terror, that appears essential to enforcement everywhere, one that takes especially cavalier and destructive forms in totalitarian states, where a continuing sense of emergency exonerates the most savage of disciplinary practices. In South Africa, in the present era of "human-rights" policing, these practices have been radically transformed. But, as we shall see shortly, the reliance of the law on melodrama has not disappeared. In answer to one of our opening questions, there is both continuity, because it is in the nature of enforcement, *and* change, because of shifts in the political culture of its context.

Old horrors leave their traces. While the future of the Janus-faced edifice hangs in the balance, its uncanny past haunts those who were part of it, those who seek now to reconfigure its purpose in the present. Toward the end of our conversation, the curator remarked: "We have a few resident ghosts in the building." One, she confided, likes to play (note that verb again) with the security system when people work after hours, a phantom, perhaps, with a particularly poignant sense of irony. Museum personnel attest to strange nocturnal experiences. South Africans of all races have always been actively engaged with the supernatural, although an obsession with the occult has been especially noticeable during this time of transition.[50] One Sunday evening, when Smal was alone in the building, the alarm began to sound furiously. Unable to switch it off, she sat resignedly for two hours, waiting, as she put it, "for the spirit to play herself out." On another occasion, she reports having shouted: "Daisy," de Melker, that is, "leave the intercom alone!" The mechanism, she said, "went wild."

But other, unnamed forces also spook this building, struggling to find voice in the great re-visioning of the past occasioned by the birth of the postcolony. It is as if the specters of bygone events are unable to find embodiment—or a means of representation—in the present, notwithstanding laudable efforts to foster new cultures of recollection; as if farce and tragedy, humor and horror, must confront each other before an awful history can become a habitable present. Those who spend time on the upper floors during the small hours speak of an unquiet presence along the corridors. Some say that it is because many prisoners had "committed suicide" here, "suicide" being a secret-police euphemism for "killed in custody." More recently, a security guard shot himself on the premises. Another person came off the street to take his own life in the courtyard. Black South Africans, in particular, disliked working in the place. Many still do. Here we get to the nub of the issue. The lower floors of the building may be frequented by the ghosts of playful lady poisoners and other random spirits, but the upstairs has an altogether more sinister aura. Museum staff told us that, in the former Security Police stronghold, "there is a really strange feeling." People hear the footsteps of those long departed. No one feels comfortable in the place. This is hardly surprising: only perpetrators and victims know what unspeakable acts and agonies those walls have witnessed. Thus it is that history shadows the reluctant consciousness of those—above all, those responsible for justice, law, and order—who must find ways to reconcile their activities in the past, a past that truly *was* another country, with the radically altered moral sensibilities of the present.

No wonder the Police Museum remains shut. It does so not just because its cabinet of horrors requires drastic revision in the postcolony, but because it must find new modes of melodrama, new forms of conjuring order from terror—all the more so since, in recent times, the public preoccupation with violent crime, fed by avid electronic and print media, has made humdrum reality seem much scarier than fiction. In the event, the now-multiracial staff of the SAPS Education Unit has, over the past few years, begun experimenting with other genres of self-representation—among them, video shows, popular puppetry, and street theater—to dramatize a contemporary clutch of nightmares: domestic assault, rape, gun-related violence, drug abuse.[51] As befits the ethos of a liberalizing state, they take their shows on the road to the various provinces of the postcolony. We follow them to one such provincial outpost, there to explore the nature of police drama after apartheid. And so, on to scene 2.

Play Accidents, Choreographed Crimes: Performing the State

In November 1999, we read in the national press that Mafikeng-Mmabatho—capital of North West Province, where we were living and working at the time—was to host an exhibit on violence against women.[52] This was to be part of a countrywide campaign, Project Harmony, that sought to draw public attention to the government's newly minted Domestic Violence Act. Members of the North West Police Services, the papers announced, would stage educational performances at taxi ranks, those remarkable agoras of African postcolonies. Our inquiries about the event drew a blank, however. Nobody, neither the local police nor anyone else, knew a thing about it.

It was only after we traveled to the Secretariat for Public Safety and Liaison at its provincial headquarters, ten kilometers north of town, that we learned the whereabouts of the exhibit. It was to be held in the foyer of the North West Provincial legislature. The Secretariat, it should be noted, is a regional division of the national Department of Safety and Security, under whose aegis falls the newly reorganized SAPS;[53] although, at the time, relations between the two bodies were rather ill-defined. The new National Crime Prevention Strategy, adopted in 1996, promulgated a dispersed but "integrative" approach in which provincial governments were charged with "co-ordinating a range of . . . functions . . . to achieve more effective crime prevention."[54] Precisely how this was to be done remained opaque, however, even to those entrusted with the urgent task of promoting "community security." Here, patently, was local government faced with the demand to invent itself.

This is where Project Harmony came in. The directive from the state that provincial governments should raise public awareness of the then-imminent Domestic Violence Bill implied a clear line of action—hence the announcement of the exhibit that proved so strangely elusive. But why, we wondered, *had* it been so hard to find? And why was it being staged in the Provincial Parliament? This is hardly a *public* space: security was so tight that only members of government, their staff, and accredited visitors were admitted. Inside, in the grand lobby, two rather-flamboyant members of the Police Education Unit fussed, with professional flourish, over a single tableau. The display was small but striking. A *very* still life, its centerpiece was a bed with disheveled sheets. Across them lay a life-size model of a female, race indeterminate, clad in the shredded remnants of upmarket underwear. Her body was bruised and bloody, her throat cut. A knife lay close to her face. Yellow tape cordoned this off as a crime scene, which was framed by posters and works of art, all depicting violence against women, all urging the public—in English and Afrikaans but *not* Setswana, the local language—to "speak out against abuse."

What are we to make of this grisly spectacle, whose artful detail seemed so to exceed its function? And why was a diorama ostensibly intended to educate "the public" placed so securely beyond its gaze? The actions and anxieties of the police artistes offered a clue. The display had to be ready for viewing by the parliamentarians, political and civic dignitaries, and press people who had been invited to attend a ceremonial session marking the passage of the Domestic Violence Act. *They* were the target audience. It was they who were meant to witness that, notwithstanding mounting skepticism, local police and local government could cooperate effectively to fight crime. But the investment of those responsible for the exhibit, and the emotional power packed into it, implied that it was also a site of *self-construction*. Its authors, in the name of the SAPS, seemed intent on configuring a collective sense of moral purpose in the face of a daunting world in which violence was thought to have become endemic, ubiquitous, even unpoliceable.

What we were witnessing, in short, was the state performing for itself, performing itself. The state making statements. And drawing its charge from a violated female body that, in a shift from the older signifying economy, had come to stand for the moral citizen victimized by the new arch-enemies of the people. For the salience of the meticulous melodrama played out in this political setting was that it was a simulacrum of *governance*, a rite staged to make actual and authoritative, at least in the eyes of an executive bureaucracy, the activity of those responsible for law and order. And, by extension, to enact the very possibility of govern*ment*. For the battle against crime, epitomized in sexualized attacks on women, has become diagnostic of the efficacy of the postcolonial regime at a time when the nation's foes—its rapists and murderers, its gangsters and gunmen, its carjackers and drug dealers—are, for the most part, also its own recently liberated subjects; this, recall, being one of the contradictions faced by the Police Museum in its efforts to revamp its signifying economy. In showing visible attentiveness to the sanctity of the female body, to the specter of violence against it, and to policing those who would desecrate it, the state objectified itself—to itself.

But the institutional face of government also insists that it be recognized by its subject-citizens—which takes us to the other face of police performance, its *public* enactment. One such enactment came at us, literally, two months later. At 8:30 a.m. on a Tuesday morning in downtown Mafikeng, as children rushed to school and businesses opened their doors, we heard an oncoming cacophony of horns and sirens, obviously a motorcade. Down the street hurried a motley array of conveyances: a few lumbering Public Order Police trucks (aptly named "hippos" in the bad old days), a number of patrol cars, and several civilian sedans, about twenty vehicles in all. Each contained a few uniformed officers of different ranks and races, who waved energetically to those gathered in bewilderment on the sidewalks. On the doors and hoods of these vehicles were scrawled messages in English. One condemned the abuse of women. The other proclaimed, "Give them toys, not guns," invoking a growing concern about violent acts perpetrated by children. This, self-evidently, was yet a further nod toward crime prevention. But it was also an effort to establish a palpable police presence on the streets by playing on the nightmare of a nation consumed by brutality, a nation in which violated mothers were producing a generation of infant felons.

People along the roadside, having discerned that the motorcade was "put on by the police," paid it little heed. The once-ubiquitous, menacing presence of the law has been drastically reduced here as elsewhere in the "new" South Africa. By contrast, police *performances,* especially under the sign of mass education and public relations, have become much more common. "The streets are full of *tsotsis* [gangsters]," one old man complained to us, "and all the police can do is play." The choice of this last word will not go unnoticed.

The observation itself has some basis. Local law enforcement officers, sensitive to the ambivalence with which they are regarded, have devised various home-grown techniques through which to enact their visibility, efficacy, resolve, and responsibility before a population fearful to inhabit public space. One of their performances—a fake traffic pileup, staged without warning at a busy intersection in Mafikeng during the morning rush hour—was so authentic that it caused pandemonium. And one, all too real, accident. Ironically, the aim of the exercise had been to draw attention to a campaign for safe driving: carnage on the roads, much of it caused by alcohol and criminal negligence, is another evil besetting the province. So rapid has been the rising death toll that it seems less accidental than an index of new dangers lurking in the unrestrained pursuit of freedom, not least the freedom to consume, that has come with the end of apartheid—and with the expansive, and expensive, ethos of neoliberalism.

Unlike the rape scene but like the motorcade, the accident inserted itself into the thick of street life. It deployed the full power of the law—the right to usurp public space and time, to conjure with truth, to evoke terror by mimicking death—all to impress upon "the community" the authoritative presence of the police, whose absence from crime scenes had been subject to much local criticism. But the smash was *also* intended, as was the Rabelaisian procession, to be a functional ritual: one that would turn popular ambivalence toward the SAPS into positive affect by dint of carefully staged emotions as transformative for the actors as for their audience. For here, again, the actors *were* the audience, the audience actors. Their drama was at once opaque to the public, yet made that public part of the staging. The unmarked pileup, along with the almost-illegible signs in the motorcade[55] and the hidden-away exhibit at the Parliament, implies a form of reflexivity in which the performers sought, by aping epics of disorder, to interpellate themselves as legitimate agents of caring enforcement: agents whose role in grappling with a new catalog of national nightmares would be recognized, and respected, by the populace at large. For policing in this new era presumes a high measure of consent from citizens, a consent still very much in question.

If, as Malcolm Young says, policing everywhere relies on "well-directed social productions" to maintain the mythic divide between good and evil, is it any wonder that the new SAPS, still struggling to define itself on a reconfigured moral and political landscape, should evince a strong tendency to "act out"?[56] Or, as in the Police Museum, is it any wonder that the line between staged performances and the melodrama of everyday police work should often disappear—which it does in many theatrically staged, mass-mediated arrests. This was brought home to South Africans a few years back by a series of ostentatiously publicized raids, led with extravagant ceremony by the national chief of police, on those Johannesburg "gentleman's clubs" alleged to be trafficking in alien sex-workers.[57] While it did not lead to many arraignments, the operation dramatized a recurrent terror of the reconstituted nation: the growing mass of illegal immigrants, archetypal others, whose very being-there is thought to endanger both the borders and the interiors of the postcolony. That such performances—many of which feature police showing off their mastery in melodramas of despoiled female bodies—may be tentative and dispersed, that they lack the compelling power often attributed by anthropologists to communal rituals, is precisely the point. It is through their uncertain playing out that the "new" South African polity is taking tangible shape.

Conclusion

We have argued that, in postcolonial South Africa, dramatic enactments of crime and punishment—both those disseminated by the state and those consumed by various publics—are not merely fabrications after the event; nor are they reflections, inflections, or refractions of a simple sociological reality. To the contrary, they are a vital part of the effort to *produce* social order and to arrive at persuasive ways of representing it, thereby to construct a minimally coherent world-in-place; even more, to do so under neoliberal conditions in which technologies of governance—including technologies of detection and enforcement—are, at the very least, changing rapidly and are, in some places, under dire threat. In these times, criminal violence is taken to be diagnostic of the fragility of civil society; concomitantly, officers of the law become the prime embodiment of a state-under-pressure—thus the irony of contemporary South Africans who, in the effort to build a posttotalitarian democracy, find themselves calling for "more Police." Theirs appears to be a decidedly post-Foucauldian predicament, wherein disorder seems to exceed the capacity of the state to discipline or punish. It is a predicament in which both those who would wield power and their putative subjects find it necessary to resort to drama and fantasy to conjure up visible means of governance.

This story could, of course, be read *not* as post-Foucauldian but as a historical narrative that proves the Foucauldian point; or, rather, that reinforces a Foucauldian telos by playing it in reverse to show how, when modern power runs out, primitive spectacle returns once more. We would argue otherwise: that the distinction between politics-as-theater and biopolitics underlying this telos is too simple; that it is itself the product of a modernist ideology that would separate symbolic from instrumental coercion, melodrama from a politics of rationalization. Melodrama may be the medium of first resort where norms are in flux and the state is incapable of ensuring order. But the history of modern policing suggests that theater has *never* been absent from the counterpoint of ritual and routine, visibility and invisibility. It has always been integral to the staging of power and of law and order in authoritative, communicable form; recall, one last time, the testimony, in this respect, of Malcolm Young, the policeman-ethnographer. That counterpoint, in short, lies at the very heart of governance, be it metropolitan or colonial, European or African, past or present.

There is a more than arbitrary connection, then, between law enforcement, theater, and dramatic fiction.[58] Crime and punishment are especially salient to the reciprocal fantasy through which police and public construct each other across the thin blue line[59] that makes palpable the power of the state, the thin blue line that, imaginatively, stands between anarchy and civility, the thin blue line that underscores the fragility of order and gives focus to popular preoccupations with the threat of social meltdown. All the more so since, with the rise of global capitalism and the mutation of the old international system, new geographies of crime and terror, themselves ever more murkily interrelated, have rearticulated criminality inside nation-states with criminality across nation-states, making both harder to contain or comprehend. All the more so, too, since the world-historical conditions of this neoliberal age—among them, the weakening sovereignty of nations and their borders, the diminishing capacity of governments to control either the means of coercion or the commonweal, the challenge of cultural politics to the liberal rule of law and its grounding in universal human rights—have made policing in its modernist sense difficult, perhaps even impossible.

This may be most readily visible in postcolonial, posttotalitarian contexts, where there is a paucity of civil institutions to counter the contraction of the welfare state. It is, however, as urgently felt in, say, the post-industrial north of England[60] as in the northerly provinces of South Africa. And it expresses itself everywhere in the criminal obsessions of both rulers and subjects. Thus, while much current opinion, stretching from libertarian to Foucauldian, might minimize the importance of "the state," there is plentiful evidence in popular fantasy of a nostalgia for authoritative, even authoritarian government. This much is evident in the reflexive self-constructions of South African police, who dramatically inflate both the necessity to wrest community from chaos and their capacity to do so. Their melodramas are founded on a dialectic of production and reduction: on the productive conjuring of a world saturated with violence and moral ambiguity, the threat of which they alone are able to reduce to habitable order. Thus it is that, in their *imaginaire,* a metaphysics of *dis*order—the hyperreal conviction, rooted in everyday experience, that society hovers on the brink of dissolution—comes to legitimize a physics of social order, to be accomplished through effective law enforcement. Thus it is, reciprocally, that many ordinary South Africans are drawn to mass-mediated dramas in which men with badges confront, and typically overcome, the most heinous, most violent, most antisocial of felons. Thus it is, too, that, distilled in a fictional economy of representation, fantasies become facts, impossibilities become possible, and the law, as foundation of the nation-state, becomes visible once more.

Notes

This chapter first appeared in *Critical Inquiry* 30 (Summer 2004): 800–824.

1. In our forthcoming study *The Metaphysics of Disorder: Crime, Policing, and the State in a Brave Neo World,* we interrogate patterns of crime and their representation in South Africa, past and present—and annotate, in detail, both primary and secondary data on the topic. Given constraints of space in this context, we are compelled to offer a relatively sketchy set of references in support of our statements here and below. For further relevant evidentiary materials, and materials on evidence, see the *Nedbank ISS Crime Index* and the monographs published by the Institute of Security Studies; these are to be found on the Web at www.iss .org.za.

2. The general point has been made often, of course; it is part of the more general question of the nature of quantitative evidence: how it is constructed, by what processes of abstraction it takes on significance, how it circulates, and how it is attributed meaning. More mundanely, however, for just one example that relates specifically to South African crime figures (as everywhere, a highly controversial question), see Rob Marsh, *With Criminal Intent: The Changing Face of Crime in South Africa* (Cape Town: Ampersand Press, 1999), pp. 176–86.

3. See, e.g., Mark Shaw and Peter Gastrow, "Stealing the Show? Crime and Its Impact in Post-apartheid South Africa," *Daedelus: Journal of the American Academy of Arts and Sciences* 130, no. 1 (2001): 235–58, especially 243; Martin Schönteich, "Sleeping Soundly, Feelings of Safety: Based on Perceptions or Reality?" *Nedbank ISS Crime Index* 5, no. 2 (2001): 1–6.

4. See, e.g., Tony Emmett, "Addressing the Underlying Causes of Crime and Violence in South Africa," in *Behind the Mask: Getting to Grips with Crime and Violence in South Africa,* ed. Tony Emmett and Alex Butchart (Pretoria: Human Sciences Research Council Publishers, 2000), p. 290; John Matshikiza, introduction to *The Drum Decade: Stories from the 1950's,* ed. M. Chapman (Pietermaritzburg: University of Natal Press, 2001), p. xi; Mungo Soggot, "When Orange Farm Meets Sodwana Bay," in *From Jo'burg to Jozi: Stories about Africa's Infamous City,* ed. Heidi Holland and Adam Roberts (London: Penguin Books, 2002), p. 227.

5. Stuart A. Scheingold, *The Politics of Law and Order: Street Crime and Public Policy* (New York: Longman, 1984), p. 68.

6. See Jamie Wilson, "War on Crime Is Just an Illusion," *Guardian,* 28 April

2001, p. 11. Said one skeptic in the force: "Perhaps he could make several thousand more police officers appear on the streets of the capital to help combat the number of burglaries and robberies and help us protect the public.

7. Some of these diviner-detectives have drawn the attention of the national media: see, e.g., Sam Kiley, "SAPS Man Aims to Kill in His Role as *Sangoma*," *Star,* 7 August 1997, p. 2; see also *Search for Common Ground*, a widely watched television documentary first broadcast by SABC3 on 17 July 1997. Others, like Sergeant Moshupa of the SAPS at Itsoseng in North West Province, with whom we worked in 1999–2000, were known locally for bringing visionary powers to bear on their police work.

8. Johannes Leithäuser, "Crime Groups Become an Increasing Security Threat, Officials Assert," *Frankfurter Allgemeine Zeitung,* 22 May 2001, English edition, p. 2.

9. On Russia, see Nancy Ries, "Mafia as a Symbol of Power and Redemption in Post-Soviet Russia," paper read at workshop "Transparency and Conspiracy: Power Revealed and Concealed in the Global Village," London School of Economics, May 1999. In Cape Town, South Africa, a daily newspaper, *Cape Argus,* published a four-day series (4–7 August 2003) of headline feature articles under the title "Gangland (Pty) Ltd." "(Pty) Ltd." designates a limited company in South Africa. The series—and especially the article by Michael Morris, "Gangsterism Provides . . . but It Takes Away More," 6 August, p. 14—makes exactly this point.

10. Jacques Derrida, *Specters of Marx: The State of Debt, the Work of Mourning, and the New International,* trans. Peggy Kamuf (New York: Routledge, 1984), p. 83.

11. The director of the European police agency, Europol, noted in 2001 that transnational crime posed a growing threat to domestic security in European countries, and that governments should "examine whether the resources that had previously been spent on military defense would be better invested . . . in domestic security"; see Leithäuser, "Crime Groups Become an Increasing Security Threat," p. 2.

12. These legal actions were reported all over the world. In South Africa, news of the impending Egged suit first appeared in "Israel to Begin Pulling Out of Gaza, Bethlehem," *Cape Times,* 19 August 2001, p. 2. The story of the 9/11 suit was carried by most major U.S. newspapers in August 2002.

13. Peter J. Boyer, "Bad Cops," *New Yorker,* 21 May 2001, p. 60.

14. Neil McCarthy, *The Great Outdoors,* unpublished playscript, p. 23. The play was premiered on 30 June 2000, at the Standard Bank National Arts Festival in Grahamstown, South Africa.

15. Jacques Peretti, "Selling the Same Old Story," *Guardian* (Media), 30 April 2001, p. 8.

16. "Police," of course, is the name of an internationally famous rock group.

17. Mark Seltzer, *Serial Killers: Death and Life in America's Wound Culture* (New York: Routledge, 1998).

18. Michel Foucault, *Discipline and Punish: The Birth of the Prison* (New York: Vintage Press, 1995).

19. Here, and in general, we acknowledge with gratitude the extraordinarily insightful reading given to this argument by the editors of *Critical Inquiry* and, in particular, by Bill Brown.

20. Peter Brooks, *The Melodramatic Imagination: Balzac, Henry James, Melodrama, and the Mode of Excess* (1976; New Haven: Yale University Press, 1995), p. viii.

21. Malcolm Young, *An Inside Job: Policing and Police Culture in Britain* (Oxford: Clarendon Press, 1991), pp. 3–4.

22. Antonio Gramsci, "The Detective Novel," in *Selections from Cultural Writings,* ed. David Forgacs and Geoffrey Nowell-Smith, trans. William Boelhower (Cambridge, MA: Harvard University Press, 1985), pp. 369–70.

23. C. L. R. James, *American Civilization,* ed. Anna Grimshaw and Keith Hart (Cambridge and Oxford: Blackwell, 1993), pp. 118–19. On the relevance of James's work to the current South African scene, see Leola Johnson, "The Social Bandit after Apartheid," *Macalester International* 9 (2000): 260–68, especially 260.

24. James, *American Civilization,* p. 123.

25. Ibid., p. 124, emphasis in original.

26. Jonny Steinberg, "Introduction: Behind the Crime Wave," in *Crime Wave: The South African Underworld and Its Foes,* ed. Jonny Steinberg (Johannesburg: Witwatersrand University Press, 2001), p. 4.

27. See, e.g., Victor W. Turner, *The Forest of Symbols: Aspects of Ndembu Ritual* (Ithaca, NY: Cornell University Press, 1967).

28. Mogamat Benjamin quoted in Allan Little, "Miracles in Maximum Security," *Guardian* (Saturday Review), 28 April 2001, p. 3.

29. See Kelly Gillespie, "Bloodied Inscriptions: Institutionality, Productivity, and the Question of Authorship" (MA thesis, University of Chicago, 2002).

30. Walter Benjamin, *Reflections: Essays, Aphorisms, Autobiographical Writings,* ed. Peter Demetz (New York: Schocken Books, 1978), p. 294. Cf. Michael Taussig, *The Nervous System* (London: Routledge, 1992), p. 116.

31. Benjamin, *Reflections,* p. 281; cf. Gramsci, "Detective Novel," pp. 69–70.

32. James T. Siegel, *A New Criminal Type in Jakarta* (Durham, NC: Duke University Press, 1998).

33. Young, *Inside Job,* 3.

34. Paul Sant Cassia, "Better Occasional Murders Than Frequent Adulteries: Banditry, Violence and Sacrifice in the Mediterranean," *History and Anthropology* 12 no. 1 (2000): 65–99, especially 66–67.

35. Marsh, *With Criminal Intent,* p. 178.

36. Frantz Fanon, *The Wretched of the Earth,* trans. Constance Farrington (New York: Grove Press, 1968), p. 86.

37. Begoña Aretxaga, "A Fictional Reality: Paramilitary Death Squads and the Construction of State Terror in Spain," in *The Ethnography of Political Violence: The Anthropology of State Terror,* ed. Jeffery A. Sluka (Philadelphia: University of Pennsylvania Press, 2000), p. 64; Joseba Zulaika and William Douglass, *Terror and Taboo: The Follies, Fables, and Faces of Terrorism* (New York: Routledge, 1996), p. 135.

38. Giorgio Agamben, *Means without End: Notes on Politics,* trans. Vincenzo Binetti and Cesare Casarino (Minneapolis: University of Minnesota Press, 2000), pp. 104–5; Walter Benjamin, p. 287.

39. We thank Hillel Braude, Claudia Braude, and Mark Gevisser, whose ac-

counts of visits to the museum in the early 1990s are reflected in our description here.

40. Interview with Sergeant Tilda Smal, South African Police Museum, Pretoria, 10 August 2000.

41. Daisy de Melker was hanged in 1932 for the murder of her son Rhodes. The court also believed that she had killed her two husbands—in order to inherit their money—but could not establish conclusive evidence to this effect. De Melker was widely rumored to have put five of her other children to death as well, but she was never charged with these homicides. See, e.g., Rob Marsh, *Famous South African Crimes* (Cape Town: Struik, 1991), chap. 6.

42. Poqo (which, in Xhosa, means "for ourselves alone") patterned itself on the Kenyan Mau Mau liberation movement. Its cadres staged attacks on police and other whites in Cape Province, often using pangas. In 1963, acting on a tip-off from the authorities in Basutoland, where the organization's leadership was in exile, the South African Police arrested some two thousand suspected members; see, e.g., Tom Lodge, *Black Politics in South Africa since 1945* (London: Longman, 1983), p. 247.

43. Aretxaga, "A Fictional Reality," p. 64.

44. Max Gluckman, "Rites of Rebellion in South-East Africa," in *Order and Rebellion in Tribal Africa: Collected Essays* (London: Cohen and West, 1963); Turner, *Forest of Symbols;* Jean Comaroff, *Body of Power, Spirit of Resistance* (Chicago: University of Chicago Press, 1985).

45. Stuart A. Scheingold, *The Politics of Street Crime: Criminal Process and Cultural Obsession* (Philadelphia: Temple University Press, 1991), p. 175.

46. Inside knowledge enabled the culprit to evade the police for four years. Eventually convicted on multiple counts of rape, he was sentenced to death and hung.

47. Plans center on such sites as Vlakplaas, notorious for the training of terror troops to counter "enemies" of the apartheid state.

48. According to Smal, Tokyo Sexwale, former premier of Gauteng Province (which includes Pretoria), recalled, on a recent visit, the last time he had been inside the building. It was when he was brought there "at 4 a.m. on a cold morning in July, directly from prison"; he was detained for several days of interrogation. Interview with Tilda Smal, 10 August 2000.

49. E. J. Clery, *The Rise of Supernatural Fiction, 1762–1800* (Cambridge: Cambridge University Press, 1995), p. 174.

50. See Jean Comaroff and John L. Comaroff, "Occult Economies and the Violence of Abstraction: Notes from the South African Postcolony," *American Ethnologist* 26, no. 3 (1999): 279–301; Jean Comaroff and John L. Comaroff, "Alien-Nation: Zombies, Immigrants, and Millennial Capitalism," *Codesria Bulletin* 3/4 (1999): 17–28, reprinted in "Enduring Enchantments," ed. S. Dube, special edition, *South Atlantic Quarterly* 101, no. 4 (2002): 779–805.

51. To date, the Education Unit has not dealt with witch killings and other occult activities, largely because officers of the Occult Related Crime Unit have suggested that doing so might draw the wrath of Satanists. Museum staff told us that "satanic graffiti" have, in fact, been painted in the vicinity of the building.

52. *Citizen,* 20 November 1999, p. 6. Mafikeng-Mmabatho designates a com-

posite town with a complex history. Mafikeng, the Place of Stones, was, from the late nineteenth century, the capital of the Tshidi-Rolong, a large Tswana chiefdom. With the coming of European settlers and colonial overrule, a segregated white town, (mis)named Mafeking—made famous by the siege of 1899–1900, during the South African War—grew up across the railway line from the African village. When the ethnic "homeland" of Bophuthatswana was created by the apartheid regime in the 1970s, its center, Mmabatho, was built alongside Mafikeng/Mafeking. Thus it was that the conurbation came to be referred to, rather awkwardly, as Mafikeng-Mmabatho. The old Mafeking, as exclusive white enclave and as a spelling for the place, has disappeared since 1994. We refer to either Mafikeng or Mmabatho below, depending on where in the town the events in question occurred.

53. The national Secretariat for Safety and Security was established by the Police Service Act of 1995, which emphasized three key policy areas: democratic control, police accountability, and community participation in issues of safety and security. See Department of Safety and Security, Republic of South Africa, *In Safety and Security*, White Paper on Safety and Security, 1999–2004 (Pretoria: Department of Safety and Security, 1998).

54. Ibid., p. 31.

55. It is noteworthy that, when we mentioned the procession to police at the Lomanyaneng station, one of the largest community police centers on the outskirts of Mafikeng, none of them knew anything about it.

56. Young, *Inside Job*, p. 4.

57. "Brothel Raided," *Pretoria News*, 3 March 2000, p. 1; P. Molwedi, "Brothel Owner Granted Bail of R10 000," *Star*, 7 March 2000, p. 2.

58. Echoes, here, of D. A. Miller's claim that there is a "radical *entanglement* between the nature of the novel and practice of the police." D. A. Miller, *The Novel and the Police* (Berkeley and Los Angeles: University of California Press, 1988), p. 2 et passim.

59. For a comparative insight into the difficulties, under contemporary conditions, of holding the "thin blue line," see Boyer, "Bad Cops," p. 60. Boyer notes that the phrase "the thin blue line" was coined by William H. Parker, a revered police chief during the Eisenhower era.

60. Again, this paradox readily takes theatrical form. Recall that in the climactic scene of one of the most acute cinematic explorations of postindustrial Britain, *The Full Monty* (directed by Peter Cattaneo, 1997), the male strippers come onstage dressed as policemen.

On Politics as a Form of Expenditure

Achille Mbembe

THE FOLLOWING STUDY seeks to analyze modes of imagining politics in contemporary Africa that confer a central place to thoughts and practices of power as thoughts and practices of war. The notion of "war," as it is used here, does not refer merely to those specific moments in a conflict's dramatization which express themselves through hostile confrontations of forces, intensifications of combat, and subsequent acts of destruction involving human losses on battlefields. This sort of adversity, whose outcome hangs from start to finish on the decisions of armies, was well studied by Clausewitz in his time. In the case of Africa, this feature has been the object of increasing—and increasingly sophisticated—accounts over the past decade.[1]

Intent on describing particular events, these accounts have, however, underestimated the centrality that war has come to acquire in the contemporary African subject's representations of life, of the political realm, and—in particular—of the relationship to death. In fact, for more or less protracted periods in the recent history of several countries, *the giving of death* has become *a prime means of creating* the world (Mbembe 2003). War, in other words, has become one of the main sources of emergency, with the consequence that death has been assigned a central place both in the process of constituting reality and in the general psychic economy. As such, African wars have set in motion at least two *logics of expenditure,* neither of which, unfortunately, has been the object of systematic study.[2]

The first type of expenditure has to do with the capacity of combatants completely to invest in—and intensely sublimate—objects, resources, and even human persons; then to release an extraordinary amount of energy which functions to ensure their repetitive destruction—a destruction that results in a relative pleasure. From this perspective one could affirm, following Bataille's discussion of the exclusionary act, that the warlike act in contemporary Africa contains an erotic dimension. It is an aspect of anal eroticism, "just as sovereignty is . . . one particular form of sadism" (Bataille 1970, 220). This *work of destruction* has two aspects. The first concerns the extraction/consumption/excretion of natural resources (gold, diamonds, and other products of the subsoil).[3] The second logic essentially consists in "giving death" (Brinkman 2000). It is a spectacular manifestation of absolute and sovereign power, which expresses itself at the level of intention, action, or fantasy.

In the first type of expenditure, what specifies the death drive and the passion to destroy is the dynamic of *radical predation* (extraction/consumption/excretion), whereas the second form of expenditure participates in a logic of cruelty and excess (the power to do anything in the immediate moment), which is intimately linked to the status of human flesh and the gradual process of ossification (B. Diop 2000). Moreover, this latter form of predation opens up the possibility of risking death and having oneself killed in the name of that for which one is ready to live (*a process of politics as sacrificial act*). With this risk, more or less fully assumed, the principle of loss goes hand in hand with the will to exercise power over the unknown force that death represents—a primal scene if ever there was one.[4]

Now, as Castoriadis (2002: 26) conveniently points out, that for which a society, a community, indeed individuals, are prepared to live and die, "is usually neither material nor 'real.'" Very often, the politics of life and death take shape around "significations of the social imaginary." These significations are embodied and instrumentalized in institutions by and through which, in times of so-called civil peace, the double relationship of force and violence constitutes, organizes, and instrumentalizes itself in spaces of struggle "about power, with power, for power" (Foucault 1997, 16–17).

In this way, "wartime" is not so different from "political time," to the point where Clausewitz himself could declare that war was politics continued by other means. Reversing that proposition, and formulating the thesis according to which it is politics that is war continued by other means, Foucault was able to show how, in large part, the role of political power was "perpetually to use a sort of silent war to reinscribe that relationship of force, and to reinscribe it in institutions, economic inequalities, language, and even the bodies of individuals" through an assortment of technologies and apparatuses (2003, 16 [1997, 17]).

But if the true terms of power rest, finally, in its capacity to prosecute war in other forms, what sorts of fractious confrontations are signified, in the last instance, by politics in Africa? Is it possible to interpret the persistence of authoritarian forms of power, or even the experiences of peace and reconciliation, as episodes of, or radical displacements occasioned by, war? On the other hand, given that war is as much a means of obtaining sovereignty as a method of exercising the right to kill, what place do contemporary forms of political imagination—as thoughts on war—assign to life, death, and the body, and under what forms do they envision the inclusion of these entities in the order of power?[5]

To respond to these questions, I will first identify some of the structuring elements—or contexts of production—of the material conditions of life in Africa in the last quarter of the twentieth century. Next, I will examine three formations of the imaginary, each specific in many ways, yet also entangled with and continually implicating each other in a myriad images of political struggle and war as they implicate bodies, things, and life.

In the first configuration, politics is imagined as a deliberate and conscious rejection of war and a process of sublimating conflict and violence: politics as *gift*. In the second, politics is conceived as a process of preserving individual life, owing to the very presupposition of its sacrificeability. The third opens a space to the possibility that anybody can kill (or be killed by) anybody else. Throughout this exercise, I will be indicating certain key points around which conceptualizations of conflict crystallize and through which the convertibility of the idea of politics takes place in confrontation with death.

Diffraction and Dispersion

In the course of the last quarter of the twentieth century, three major occurrences profoundly affected the material conditions of the production of life in Africa: (1) the tightening of monetary constraint and the resulting resurgence of imaginaries of long distances and far-away vistas; (2) the concomitance of democratization and informalization of the economy and of state structures; (3) the dispersion of state power and the fragmentation of society.

Having come about simultaneously, these three conditions have at times potentiated each other; sometimes, too, their effects have canceled each other out, or, inversely, they have served to incite each other, to the point of provoking an enfolding of individual and social experience. These processes constitute, in their simultaneity, an emerging framework of political imaginings, a framework that assigns a preponderant place to struggles for or against power, confrontations whose goal is the triple hold on resources and objects, on the body, and, ultimately, on life itself.

Let us take the tightening of monetary constraint and its effect of reviving imaginaries of long distances and far-away locales.[6] This tightening is partly linked to changes that occurred, barely a decade after the era of formal decolonization, in the manner in which Africa was integrated into the international economy. Commencing in the early 1970s, these shifts have extended over roughly a quarter century and are still far from reaching their end point. Structural-adjustment programs of the 1980s and 1990s have constituted one of the most memorable turning points in this process, even though they might not have played the role, in themselves, that their critics generally assign to them. These programs have had scant impact on African countries in relation to international specialization structures. But they have aided the development of new economic configurations that can no longer be adequately described, and explained, by either the old structuralist schemes of "center-periphery" or dependency theories—still less those of "marginalization."

In effect, between the 1980s and 2000 in Africa, an atomized capitalism developed upon the debris of a rentier economy, without the creation of either agglomeration or enormous poles of growth. The latter had in the past been dominated by state companies controlled by their clients and by monopolies operating on a captive market that dates, for the most part, from the colonial era. The dichotomy of urban-rural economies—or of formal and informal sectors—characteristic of the immediate postcolonial period fell to pieces. It has been replaced by a patchwork, a mosaic of spheres—in short, by a diffracted economy composed of several intermeshing centers which maintain changing and extremely volatile links with both the surrounding environment and international pathways. From this radical fragmentation a multiplicity of economic territorialities can emerge, often within the same country, sometimes nested within each other, sometimes disjointed. It is in this context that mining, petroleum, and commercial-fishing enclaves have come to play a decisive role.

Whether sea or land based, these enclave economies are by nature extractive. They are, in practice, disconnected from the rest of the national territory or are connected only by tenuous, even underground networks. This is notably the case with maritime petroleum exploitation. Yet, at the same time, these economies articulate directly with the pathways of international commerce. When they do not give rise to logics of war or conflict, the enclaves themselves tend to be disputed spaces. At times they are controlled by multinationals to which the central state extends—or practically delegates—sovereignty; at times, in collusion with rebel armed formations, the enclave economy typifies the osmosis between extractive activity, warfare, and mercantile activity.

Another aspect of the transnationalization of African economies in the last quarter of the twentieth century has been the emergence of free zones and corridors, whose objective is to create a friendly business environment within delimited spaces that are granted a privileged place in fiscal planning. This is notably the case in southern Africa. As with the enclave economy, that of the corridors is completely oriented toward export and is, from this standpoint, particularly sensitive to the shocks of global demand and the volatility of circumstance. Next comes a combination of zones in flux, territories in disinheritance or capitation, and parks and natural reserves—veritable extraterritories administered under various indirect regimes and exploited by mining, tourist, or forest companies.

Of all the consequences resulting from this process of the atomization of Africa's market economy, two in particular have played a key role in forming imaginaries of the political as a combative relationship, a game of chance, and a confrontation with death. On the one hand, two types of violence that had been relatively separate in the past are now combining and enhancing each other: the violence of the market, set in motion by struggles for access to resources and by the latter's privatization; and social violence, rendered uncontrollable due to the loss of the state's monopoly on it. On the other hand, the actors in this social struggle and the forms taken by the struggle itself have both diversified. The refusal of a common sharing of civilian life has manifested itself in a generalized exchange of violence. In this exchange, not only do enemies tend to become indispensable figures in the constitution of one's own identity, but they are also the objects of an obligatory predation (de Heusch 2002). More and more, the culminating point of this predation is the *massacre*.

By way of example, let us take the violence of the market (via privatization) and the tightening of monetary constraint.[7] These two factors have weighed on African societies in palpable ways. A key role has been played by processes that either institutionalize various currencies or render them obsolete: in most countries, monetary relationships have been characterized by structural incompleteness, expressed not only in the fact that ostensibly national currencies have been in permanent competition with other currencies within their own economic space (*the multiplicity of currencies*) but, more fundamentally, through the absence of correspondence (at least in certain periods in the history of certain countries) between currency and sovereignty (see Mubarak 2002). To this flight of the national currency must be added the flight of forms of capital. Both of these departures are explainable, in a general sense, by the emergence of dollar-based networks of transactions.

These dollar-based networks are vertically integrated into the international economy. Locally, transactions in various domains (tourism, hotels, banks, even illegal enterprises) are partially or totally rendered and sold in foreign currencies. Thus, in the former Zaire, for example, there were cases of monetary secession in which entire populations rejected the use of the official currency in one or more provinces of the national territory.[8] In most cases the monetary relationship in African economies has always been a relationship in process, never assured either of its legitimacy or of its sovereignty. Alongside cases of the supplanting of former currencies by new ones must be added the capriciousness of monetary value—a capriciousness exacerbated by dizzying rises in prices, sudden and successive devaluations, and stagflation.[9] Finally, the growing volatility of money has combined with the speed of its circulation and its local scarcity (see, e.g., Marie 1995; Brydon 1999).

The widespread drying up of liquidities, followed by their progressive concentration along certain pathways whose conditions of access have become ever more draconian, has resulted in a brutal contraction of the number of people capable of passing debts on to others—capable, that is, of submitting others to obligations which they are compelled to pay off in an appropriate manner.[10] The nature of debt itself has changed, with the "protection debt" becoming the ultimate signifier of kin relations, be they real or fictive.[11]

More than had previously been the case, money has become a force of separation between individuals and an object of intense conflict between the insatiable need for wealth for some and the frantic pursuit of liquidity for others, like a protective but utterly fragile shell. Thus has a new *economy of persons* appeared, based on purely market and object-like relationships. Bonds established through things have solidified, as has the primacy accorded to such things, even though the division between utility and morality has grown deeper. It is this cleavage that now governs the value of persons and the measure of their utility and, in circumstances where this value and utility are not in evidence, that condemns these persons to relations of capture, or destruction pure and simple (Bales 1999).

Moreover, the controlled influx and fixing of money's movement around specific resource extraction zones—the latter functioning in the manner of former trading posts—have permitted the formation of *enclaves* within devastated economies (enclaves of petroleum, diamonds, tourism, etc.). As explained above, the concentration of valuable resource extraction activities around these "reserves" has, in turn, transformed them into privileged spaces of conflict and war. War conditions are fed by the increasing commercialization of extractive products. As a result of this ensemble of activities, new possibilities of linkage to the global economy have opened up. They are mediated by various dynamics, from the hemorrhaging of capital to the basic criminal economy, such as in arms trafficking.

By thus contributing to the emergence of a new geography of conflict and the appearance of new territorial forms and economies of scale, money movements have accelerated the fragmentation of national and regional economic spaces. While certain spaces have exhibited an advanced state of demonetarization, indeed, a return to barter or subsistence practices, others have undergone processes of dollarization with unforeseen effects (De Boek 1998). In general, this double movement of the omniaccessibility of money on the one hand and its extreme scarcity on the other has only reinforced a situation in which everyone's rights and value are being increasingly based on the principle of purchase and sale.

Even more important to this discussion are the cultural imaginaries set in motion by this double movement. In light of the constraints resulting from the drastic decline of fiduciary circulation, a central feature of these imaginaries has been the incessant imperative to travel far away to earn money (Bryceson 2002; de Haan 1999; Hart 1988). The new drive to acquire earnings has provoked an unprecedented resurgence of *imaginaries of the far off and "long distance"* (Simone 2001; Diouf 2000). In part, this resurgence has manifested itself in a novel growth in the capacities of private actors for extensive mobility. Yet it has also manifested itself in violent attempts to immobilize and spatially "fix" entire categories of the population, resulting in the appearance of numerous "gray zones," where direct forces proceed to organize "death en masse," notably by means of wars (Edkins 2000).

In the context of the diffractions evoked above, a new form of governmentality has thus arisen. The new governmentality consists in managing the mobility of individuals, indeed multitudes, largely by extrastate jurisdictions or armed formations. This management has become inseparable from the control of bodies whose opportunities for movement have been restricted: bodies that are driven to mass exodus, then immobilized in exceptional spaces such as "camps" and other "security zones"; or physically incapacitated by means of various mutilations; or collectively destroyed, on the model of old human sacrifices, by means of massacres. A more tragic, more extreme alternative is systematically being substituted for the policing and disciplinary techniques used during the authoritarian period to ensure control of individuals; the choice between obedience and disobedience that characterized the model of the colonial *"commandement"* and postcolonial authority is being replaced by the choice between survival and death.

What is now at stake in the exercise of this power that is more fragmentary and capillary than ever before is similar, in large part, to what is at stake in war itself: the possibility of the production and reproduction of life itself. This new form of governmentality is founded on the multiplication of extreme situations and the *capture and assault* of the body and life, only to better control the flux of resources, objects, and goods that have been freed up by the process of informalization or by means of capitation and other forms of private, indirect government. But as life increasingly becomes a colony of immediate powers, its terms are not just economic. It is important, accordingly, to dwell for a moment on the meaning of this work of destruction, a major portion of which consists in the expenditure of countless human lives.

Bataille (1967) noted in his time that this form of expenditure calls into question the classic principle of utility. Drawing in particular on the sacrifices and wars of the Aztecs, he analyzed what he called "the cost of life" in its relationship to "consumption." At the same time he confirmed the existence of a power formation where the preoccupation with sacrificing and immolating the greatest possible numbers constituted, in itself, a form of "production." Here, human sacrifice was understood according to the belief that the sun needed to consume the hearts and blood of the greatest number of people, especially prisoners.

This being the case, war was the answer to a necessity—namely, the reproduction of the solar cycle. It was not primarily linked to some general will to conquest. Its central concern was to make the act of consumption possible. By this act, the risk of seeing the sun grow dark—and thus of life extinguishing itself—was averted (Bataille 1967: 67 and passim). The human sacrifices, for their part, enabled restitution to the sacred world of that which servile usage had degraded and rendered profane. This form of destruction—of violent and profitless consumption—constituted, according to Bataille, the best means of negating the utilitarian relationship between persons and things.

In the contemporary African case that concerns us here, massacres and destruction of human lives participate, in many ways, in a more or less similar principle of negation. It is not clear, however, that such bloody squanderings contribute to the production of sacred things—the function that Bataille assigns to sacrifice in general. At its source lies, rather, the idea of an enemy, a "foreign body," that must be expelled or eradicated. Insofar as the relationship to the enemy expresses itself in the mode of a struggle between different kinds of being, it is possible to assert that such a logic of enmity constitutes a form of "total politics."

The war complex in this present case nonetheless contains the ensemble of activities that Bataille described as participating in "expenditure." It is concerned with all of these ostensibly unproductive forms which, following from this fact, seem not to contribute at all to production in either the short or middle term: luxury, mourning, worship, spectacles, perverse sexual activities, displays of sorrows and cruelty, partial torture, orgiastic dances, lurid scenes, dazzling pleasures, the excision of bones, the violent satisfaction of coitus—in short, the pursuit of an exaltation that facilitates excretion.

As a "foreign body" or "poison," the enemy is thus submitted to the excremental impulse: it must be "expelled" like some despicable thing from which it is necessary to brutally break off. Under these conditions, violence is capable of taking on aspects of "defecation." But the logic of "defecation" does not exclude other dynamics. Such is the case with that other form of violence that seeks to ingurgitate and incorporate the slain enemy. This logic of mastication has as its goal the capture of the victim's virile condition and reproductive power. The logics of both defecation and mastication require the violation of prohibitions and taboos.

Because they rest in very large part on the values of itinerancy rather than those of sedentary life, the new dynamics of earnings acquisition has contributed to a deep shift in forms of belonging. Social violence tends to crystallize around new and crucial questions concerning the constitution of identities, the modalities of citizenship, the management of people's mobility, the circulation of goods, and the conditions of capturing floating resources. In these new forms of social and political struggle, three themes are given priority: community of origin (region and autochthony), "race," and religion.

At least two conceptions of citizenship have come to oppose each other in the public mind. The first is the official idea that a citizen of a country is someone recognized as such by the state. The second is the conception that citizenship flows principally from bloodlines (real or presumed), that is, birth and genealogy. Bonds through bloodlines in fact authorize the distinction between "autochthonous people" and "outsiders," the "natives" (original inhabitants) and "foreigners." This identity production has enabled the present-day continuation of former kingdoms and chiefdoms, as well as the birth of new ethnic groups—either by separation from the older ones or by amalgamation. It has also fostered violent conflicts unleashed by numerous population movements. Finally, it has fed irredentisms, notably in countries where minorities feel themselves excluded from the material fruits of power (see Vlassenroot 2002; Eyoh 1998; Pérouse de Montclos 1999).

Two sorts of polis and two sorts of civic spaces have thus appeared in complex, interlacing forms: the *intramuros* polis (place of origins and custom, whose signs one carries along in case of need as one travels to distant places) and the *extramuros* polis (that which is made possible by dispersion and immersion in the larger world).[12] From the fact that each polis henceforth has its "double" at its disposal, an emblematic role is established, which is now played by migrants and diasporas (Kupferberg 1998). For the remaining populations, the double process of *transnationalization of African societies* and of folding back on origins has had the effect of reviving conflicts around the relationship between "community" and property.

The dispersion and scattering imposed by the need to acquire earnings from afar have certainly not abolished older characterizations of "community." In many cases, the latter remains the territory of origin, concrete and geographically situated: that which one appropriates, which one defends and tries to protect against those who are not part of it (Geschiere 2004), and in the name of which one kills and—if necessary—is killed. Considerable inflections have nevertheless appeared in the relation between "that which belongs to more than one, many, or all" (and whose sharing stems from a system of reciprocal obligations that flow from belonging to the same "community of origin") and that which, being strictly "private," answers to a strictly individual enjoyment.

A further effect of this scattering is that mastery over the consequences of transnationalization has come to imply not merely the control and domination of distances but also the art of multiplying appurtenances, this leading to an overvaluing of the status of a chain of "intermediaries," those who weave connections with the external world, brokers, and specialists in the business of objects, narratives, and identities. The overvaluing of these statuses has benefited from the growing gap between official borders and actual borders (Mbembe 2000). The consequence has been not only a higher velocity of migration but also the constitution of pathways and networks that, exceeding the territorial framework of postcolonial states, have become specialized elements in long-distance resource mobilization (Babu 2002; Sumata 2002; Fall 1998).

In another register, monetary possession (or its impossibility) has profoundly altered the frameworks shaping individuality and regimes of subjectivity. Where scarcity dominates, the intensity of needs and the impossibility of their satisfaction have been so acute that a rupture has come about in the way that social subjects experience desire, longing, and satisfaction. The perception that money, power, and life are all governed by *the law of chance* has become ever more dominant. Vast fortunes are built overnight without the factors that contributed to them being in the least bit apparent. But fortunes also vanish to the same rhythm, without visible cause. With nothing certain and everything possible, risks are taken with money as they are taken with the body, power, and life. Time, as well as life—and death—come down to an enormous game of chance. In contrast, among social groups capable of easily amassing fortunes, it is the connection between desire and its objects that has changed, giving rise to a sensual and hedonistic preoccupation with consumption, such that idolatrous possession and the ostentatious enjoyment of material goods become the site for staging new lifestyles (Warnier 1993).

In either case, the cultural contents of the process of differentiation have been the same: an acute awareness of the volatility and frivolity of money and fortune that goes along with an instantaneous conception of time and value—of the shortness of life. Although the strategies followed by individual actors may vary from one situation to another, the conception of time and value as contained and exhausted in the moment, and of money as volatile and frivolous, has contributed significantly to the transformation of imaginaries, as much of wealth as of destitution and power. Power, and fortune, enjoyment, misery, and death itself, have first and foremost been experienced in terms of materialist criteria—hence the emergence of subjectivities at whose center lies the need for tangibility, palpability, and tactility. Ultimately, these characteristics can be found in forms of action expressing violence as much as pleasure.[13]

Let us now examine the effects of *the concomitance of democratization and the informalization of the economy and state structures*.[14] Throughout the last quarter of the twentieth century, the informalization of the economy and the dispersion of state power in Africa have been superimposed. In certain cases, these two phenomena have intersected. In still others, they have canceled each other out. Very often they have reinforced each other. For instance, by the beginning of the 1980s the cultural and institutional mechanisms that made subjugation possible, and through which subordination took place, had reached their limits. Beneath the facade of law and order and the theater of the state, an underground process of gradual dispersion was under way (Bayart, Mbembe, and Toulabor 1993). To be sure, in spaces where the state had consolidated itself over the preceding decades, the administration still had a large portion of its coercive resources at its disposal. But the material conditions of the exercise of power and sovereignty had deteriorated bit by bit, due to the disruptive impact of constraints linked to debt repayment and the application of structural-adjustment policies. The unraveling continued throughout the 1990s with no end to the economic crisis in sight, the crumbling of state structures occasionally taking on novel forms.

At the heart of the process of informalizing state structures lies the threat of *general insolvency,* which, during the last quarter of the twentieth century, characterized economic and material life as a whole. Because the drying up of liquidities affected both state and society, it served to substantially alter the systems of equilibrium and exchange that had been the underpinnings of state socialization during the authoritarian period (Mbembe 2001). As the default on budgetary payments at the state level became ever more the rule, the chain of outstanding payments extended to the level of society at large. Social actors reacted by intensifying practices of avoidance and embezzlement, by recourse to various forms of fiscal disobedience, or by increasing practices of falsification and desertion. At the same time, far from giving rise to a popular capitalism, the distribution of state assets through privatization entailed a ceding of a large part of the public patrimony to private operators, some of whom were already holders of political power. The simultaneity of these two processes—general insolvency and changes in regimes of appropriation of what, until then, had been the object of a co-possession, however fictive—deepened the crisis of ownership.

   The processes surveyed above have cumulatively shifted the parameters of the struggle for subsistence. In fact, the distinction between struggles for subsistence proper and utter *struggles for survival* has dissolved (Lugalla 1995; Harts-Broekhuis 1997). In both cases, everyday life has come to be defined by the paradigm of threat, danger, and uncertainty. A social world has gradually taken form where general distrust and suspicion go hand in hand with the need for protection against increasingly invisible enemies (Geschiere 1995; Niehaus 2001; Ashforth 2005). In many places this social sensibility has been reinforced by the preachings of the new Pentecostal churches, whose core message centers on the generalized battle against demons (Meyer 1999). With the production of life now occurring in a general context of insecurity—and, in extreme cases, in proximity to death—social struggles have become increasingly linked to actual war activity (Jackson 2002). In return, war, as a major signifier of daily life conduct, has by extension become the central signifier of political struggle, where the struggle for power asserts itself at first glance as *power to give death,* and resistance to power now is vested in the living person as its object and point of anchorage (Kistner 2002).

   Starting from the central impact that monetary constraint would prove to exercise throughout the 1980s, I have just shown how the concurrent informalization of economic and state structures, while accelerating the transnationalization of African societies, also favored the emergence of a political imaginary whose central signifier is war, that is to say, the capacity to take away the life of the enemy. It is now necessary for me to focus on a simultaneous process, whose amplifying effect on this imaginary is unquestionable: *the dispersion of state power and the diffraction of society.*

This dispersion will take paradoxical forms that, reciprocally reinforcing each other, will stamp a singular face on African processes of democratization. In one respect, the weakening of the state's administrative capacities will go hand in hand with the privatization of some of its distributive functions (Mbembe 2001; Hibou 1999). In another respect, the premium granted to deregulation will manifest itself on the ground as a movement of *deinstitutionalization,* itself conducive to the spread of informal practices. This informality will be found not only in economic domains but at the very center of the state and administration and in all aspects of social and cultural life having any sort of connection with the struggle for survival.

The generalization of informal practices gives rise to a proliferation of social authorities over production of norms (with none of these authorities being able to completely impose norms of its own). It also leads to an unprecedented and exponential increase in opportunities to avoid rules and laws, at the very moment when the punitive capacities of public powers and other social authorities will be most weakened (Mbembe and Roitman 1995). Hereafter, among both public and private actors, the schemes that will prevail will be those aimed at modifying norms for the purpose of increasing revenues and drawing maximum profit from the weakening of formal institutions (Niger-Thomas 2001).

More consequentially, democratization is occurring at a moment when, because of the brutality of monetary constraints, the process of the *diffraction* of society has reached unprecedented depths. In the context of the struggle for survival that characterizes the last quarter of the African twentieth century, this diffraction of society has taken diverse forms. In addition to the extreme images and limit situations of wars, territorial recompositions, forced displacements of populations, and massacres, it reveals itself in the recourse by social subjects to multiple registers of action and to a similar proliferation of codes of legitimation (Roitman 2003a).

All of this—a multiplicity of identities, allegiances, authorities, and jurisdictions, an emphasis on mobility and differentiation, a volatile sense of time and duration, a growing exchangeability of objects and convertibility of things into their opposite, and the rising utility of improvisational practices—will be pressed into service as everything becomes an object of negotiation and commerce (Berry 1989) To the fragmentation of public power there will respond, like an echo, the constitution, multiplication, and dissemination of nodes of conflict within society. New arenas of power will gradually emerge as survival imperatives come to emphasize the increasing autonomy of the spheres of social and individual life. More than ever, practices of informalization will no longer limit themselves solely to mere economic aspects and strategies of survival. They will become, bit by bit, *privileged forms of the cultural and political imagination.*

This new cultural state will have considerable effects on psychic life, the constitution of social movements, and the forming of alliances and coalitions. On the one hand, improvisation, informal "arrangements," and the imperative to capture power immediately and hold on to it at all costs will all be privileged to the detriment of long-term "projects." The result will be cultural instability of a structural nature. Alliances will continually be forged and dissolved. The provisional and constantly renegotiable character of contracts and agreements will foreground the fundamental reversibility of these processes. On the other hand, opposition will have a relatively weak presence. It will act on the whim of circumstances, continually zigzagging between principles, trade-offs, and compromises, in a context of abrupt reversals and overall fluidity. The entanglement of segmentary and hierarchical logics (profane dynamics and invisible ones, the occult and the sacred, divergent interests and multiplying allegiances and relations of authority) will prevent the coalescence or lasting crystallization of social movements—hence the interminable portioning out of conflicts, the void of legitimation, and the fragmentary, fissiparous, and mutually destructive nature of organized struggles.

The structuring factors examined above have not only weighed heavily on the effects of democratization in Africa. They have also set limits to the transformation of political imaginaries and political models. In the remainder of this essay I will examine three cultural configurations, at times distinct, at times mutually entangled, at times superimposed, that all indicate, in different ways, the extent to which struggles for physical survival and the reproduction of life itself are now the principal stakes in the exercise of power and in the imaginaries of war and democracy in Africa.

On Politics as Domestication of Violence

The first cultural configuration is one in which politics is expressly imagined as a gift and as a means of rejecting war and sublimating conflict and violence. The sublimation of conflict does not imply that conflict does not manifest itself publicly or that it is nipped in the bud. Nor does it have as its goal the cessation of discord—quite the contrary. It involves putting in place an ensemble of institutions responsible for deliberation

and negotiation, a series of languages and signs—in short, the invention
of a culture of public life that incorporates change as a value. Thus, the automatic resorting to a test of strength, which would signal the beginning
of a society's general march to self-destruction, is rendered superfluous.
Accordingly, conditions are created such that partisan struggles, however
severe they may be, do not have as their elemental goal the physical anni-
hilation of the adversary. Nor do they have sedition or violent dissent as
their only outlet. Instead, they draw legitimacy from their contribution to
the making of a civic body that, by domesticating violence, gives birth to
and consolidates the possibility of "political coexistence" and, ipso facto,
creates conditions that allow everyone to lead the "good life" that they
please.

One of the most dramatic moments in this sublimating process is the
electoral moment. In the dramaturgy of democracy, the election combines
the three qualities of rite, liturgy, and magic. As with any rite or liturgy,
this requires a certain performativity. Like religion and magic, it constitutes its own authorizing language while remaining fundamentally poly-
semic; it involves a certain symbolic efficacy. In short, the electoral moment constitutes the most incontestable, collectively validated procedure
to vie for power: a form that thereafter averts the imperative to kill. It is
here that, in the dramaturgy of democracy, the electoral act assumes a civi-
lizational dimension: it renders obsolete the primordial relationship between political struggle and the sacrificial act. In other words, the election
authorizes the elimination of the apparent need to resort to transgression
in the struggle for power. Thereafter, the debt thus established between
those who govern and those who are governed is no longer a blood debt.
It is of a different order.

The electoral moment constitutes, moreover, a fragment of time that
combines figures, letters, insignia, images, and numbers; it partakes of the
oracle and divination as well as prophesy, since it compels power's aspi-
rants to publicly evoke past things (taking stock) and to summon future
things (promises and illusions). This fragment of time brings about an exchange, at the conclusion of which the possibility of a political coexistence
is reconfirmed and reconsecrated. It is, therefore, a pagan ritual, and also
a vast semiotic field, but of a markedly sacramental nature. Now, as we
will see shortly, the status of the election in democratization movements in
Africa is defined not only by its ambivalence but also by the aleatory and
uncertain quality of the process itself: its degree of contingency and inde-
terminacy.[15] The liturgy meant to symbolize the overtaking of conflict and
violence turns out to be the specter that, paradoxically, continues to haunt

society, bringing dissension to the heart of the "community," in the form
of threat of impending war or of fraud or of division and discord. Because
it bears directly on the "capture of power" and its distribution, the election is the characteristic moment of the straining of the bond. Having
power as its prize, it generates disputes that threaten to destroy all possibility of political coexistence. The election presents, therefore, a sinister
quality. It can transform itself into a race toward death.

There is no better illustration of the foregoing than an ensemble of relatively stable political regimes that enjoy a seeming legitimacy (South
Africa, Botswana, Mauritius, Benin, Senegal, Mali). Most of these regimes
are the product of compromises negotiated over relatively long periods. As
a result of these compromises, new constitutions have been adopted. The
principal institutions of formal democracy have been put in place—even
if, at times, disagreements remain regarding their functioning operation.
Elections are held regularly, and competition for power among the elites
takes place according to generally accepted rules. The press is free. Opposition parties carry out their activities with minimal obstruction. The care-
fulness of deliberation, the search for compromise, and the resolve to allay
conflicts all underlie the demeanor of the principal actors of public life and
become, with each passing day, a structuring aspect of political culture.
These advances are not, however, irreversible, and the possibilities for a
change in power structures remain.

The Senegalese example suggests, in this respect, that the ousting of
long-established powers by electoral means is more likely to occur in countries where traditions of openness to the outside and practices of appropriating symbols coming from distant places are relatively old; where,
while drawing upon multiple sources, cultural networks and intellectual
influences are elastic enough to produce hybrid and syncretic forms; and
where, despite the relative force of regional identities and the entrench-
ment of sometimes-severe conflicts, religious identities and indigenous
forms of social stratification outweigh ethnic affiliations alone (C. Diop
1994). In such contexts a period of association—prolonged or intermittent—between opposition parties and the government is essential. This association can come about as part of coalition or national-unity governments, where the opposition parties nonetheless preserve their autonomy,
notably during electoral consultations. Participation in the management
of public affairs allows these parties to equip themselves with the means
to wider institutionalization. Although such an occurrence hardly pre-
cludes disagreements and, sometimes, serious conflicts that can lead to
riots or imprisonments, it encourages the reciprocal assimilation of elites

and the gradual emergence of a culture of compromise between diverse political forces; the compromise concerns the definition of constitutional rules and electoral reforms—in short, the organization of the state.

However, for the electoral act to function as a means of domesticating violence and to bring about change at the head of the state, a number of conditions would have to be met. First, cleavages within the party in power must lead to the marginalization and exclusion of those currents that could then gather enough resources and adherents and garner enough support from African and international networks to succeed in constituting themselves into an opposition equipped with an autonomous capacity to mobilize. Next, a coalescence of traditional opposition forces and new dissident formations would need to form around a charismatic leader and a minimum plan. Finally, in situations where the strength of unions allows it, they could turn themselves into a political lever for change.

To succeed, a mobilization with a view to bringing about regime change would need to take at least two forms, one external and the other internal. First, a successful challenge to the legitimacy of the regime in power would need to extend beyond national borders. Besides the usual denunciation of human rights abuses in the media and international enclaves, such denunciation would aim, if not to ostracize the regime, at least to discredit it. Through adroit use and instrumentalizing of the new international lexicon (struggle against corruption, transparency, state of law, good governance, etc.), the opposition forces would need to convince the international community of the bankruptcy of the regime in power and of the risk of destabilization that its hold on power poses to the region as a whole. They would need to present the necessity of constitutional reforms and free, transparent elections as an urgent issue and as a security concern shared not only within the country but beyond its borders as well. In thus transforming elections in one country into a major risk for the security of a subregion as a whole, the stakes could be repositioned: the costs could be considerably raised for the regime in power were it tempted to launch a show of force. Moreover, intervention would be facilitated for third-party states, emissaries, and regional and multilateral organizations anxious to prevent war and contain conflict.

Second, the "multilateralization" of elections (and thus the call for intervention) can come about only if they are supported by an internal mobilization. The latter would target the collaboration of two strata in particular: women and youth (children, students, and the unemployed). The rallying of these social groups would need to manifest itself not just in registrations on election lists. It would also need to provide the opposition

with effective forms of pressure. With children, students, and the unemployed, a real *power of the street* could take root, capable of unsettling the
established regime by presenting the specter of an urban insurrection. Internal mobilization could culminate in effective access to domestic units
(owing to the influence of the mothers of families) and female communication networks woven into the social fabric. No victorious electoral strategy is possible, however, without participation from the rural zones—that
captive reservoir of postcolonial African power (Boone 1992).

Since the beginning of the seventies local political arenas, especially
those in rural settings, have been affected by a number of profound transformations. Organizations of natives from the same village have multiplied, at the same time that various changes have occurred in the nature
and patterns of the state's presence. The proliferation of village associations can be understood, in large part, by the desire of professionals and
city-dwellers to gain respectability and support in their native regions as
they seek to advance their integration into the national political game.
Control of the rural zones is also crucial in most countries immersed in
war, whether in mobilizations aimed at capturing power or in efforts on
the part of established regimes to confront rebellions and armed dissidents
(McGregor 1998).

The social base of most ruling African regimes is not currently in the
cities, as is often claimed, but in the villages (Bates 1981). Even though, in
certain cases, the significance of migrant networks has increased and their
role in the material survival of rural populations has consolidated, a certain cultural primacy nevertheless continues to be accorded to the values
of sedentary life. Despite the importance taken on by cities as the purveyors of modernity's resources, the symbolic valuing of statuses and the acquisition of legitimizing resources are still consolidated by way of a return
to the village (Vidal 1991; Le Pape 1997). The prevalence of kinship, origins, and genealogy as dynamic cultural metaphors and tropes of languages of legitimation has only reinforced this leverage. As a result, the
village has remained, along with religious associations and various broth-
erhoods, a strategic site of political confrontation, notably during election
times and in the context of decentralization policies (Bierschenk and
Olivier de Sardan 1998).

These decentralizing processes have occurred together with profound
territorial boundary changes that have generated multiple social, political,
and cultural stakes. Such redistricting has generally manifested itself in al-
locations of services and employment. Still more importantly, in the larger
context of the transnationalization of African societies, control of local
resources has proven to be a powerful factor in gaining access to interna-

tional ones. In many countries, the redistricting of territories has allowed local elites to shore up their intermediary positions between a locality, the state, and international connections. Since the mobilization of local symbolic and cultural resources is indispensable to negotiations with international actors, it is abundantly clear that the logics of locality and the logics of globalization, far from being opposed, mutually reinforce each other.

Moreover, since control of local resources takes place through administrative, political, and symbolic means, many social actors have tried to mobilize customary solidarities in order to come out on top in competition with elites from the same locality. This is one reason that processes of decentralization and democratization have so clearly contributed to the resurgence of conflicts over autochthony and to heightened tensions between a locality's autochthonous peoples and migrants and outsiders (Geschiere and Nyamnjoh 2000). Solidarities based on genealogico-territoriality are everywhere being reinterpreted, and rivalries and conflicts internal to local communities relaunched. Production of locality and production of autochthony thus constitute two faces of the same movement, carried out by diverse actors: customary chiefs, notables, marabouts, professional elites, various associations, political parties, brokers, local government officials, civil servants, networks of mutual assistance, and urban elites. By means of both formal and covert procedures and at the whim of relations of force, loyalty, or tacit agreements that are ever changing and often difficult to disentangle, all these actors contribute to the crystallization of local arenas.

The loosening of the incumbent party's clamp on the rural vote takes place in two ways. The first is by the mediation of new generations of unofficial institutions whose function, over the last quarter of the twentieth century, has been to manage social and spatial mobility. Whether taking the form of women's associations, traders' associations, prayer groups, mutual-assistance societies, or cultural or development societies, many institutions now serve as communication channels between urban elites and their villages and communities of origin (Trager 1998). They are distinct from customary institutions properly speaking (chiefdoms, royalties), though they also serve as organic sites for the negotiation of identities and local interests between newer and older elites (Fisiy and Goheen 1998). The loosening then takes place through the relative neutralization of customary and religious authorities and marabout networks. In the absence of such neutralization, the cultural conditions of society will often have reached a point where the religious allegiance of followers no longer hinders individual political choices when, if need be, they contradict the instructions of customary and clerical authorities.

But the unseating of a long-established power is also the outcome of a vast cultural fermentation. The latter has come to pass through the emergence of new forms of artistic, musical, theatrical, and religious writings. It is also seen in the emergence of new intellectual figures in the public field who are able to articulate the concerns of the times through the mediation of texts that are disseminated in various ways. All of this is facilitated by a weaving together of territories by means of modern communication media such as the radio and portable telephone and by continuous movement between the towns and countryside. It is also facilitated by the formation of a veritable public sphere that has crystallized around daily newspapers and private radio stations. However, a successful change of power requires that the military opt for neutrality; that a relative duplicity on the part of local and foreign business elements pushes them to diversify their risks by secretly backing the opposition while at the same time financing the regime in power; and that pressure for relatively transparent elections is exerted upstream. This pressure would need to touch upon all aspects of the electoral code, from the establishment of an independent organization and delineation of voting districts to the counting of votes, the dispatching of ballot boxes, and the proclamation of results.

As can be seen, the electoral moment is hardly devoid of conflict. Quite the contrary, it carries a strong potential for violence; rather than leading to appeasement and a civilization of political mores, it could lead to an intensification of combative relations—as has been demonstrated in the postelectoral turmoil, indeed warfare, in various countries (Makumbe and Compagnon 2000). Furthermore, the Senegalese example demonstrates that the sublimation of violence by means of elections can occur at the same time that, in the same country, an open war is taking place, as is the case in Casamance. The electoral moment remains, in this sense, a central moment in the struggle for power. In the case we have been examining, this struggle is no longer necessarily carried out from body to body and is not measured by the depth of physical wounds inflicted by the adversary. It is displaced onto another symbolic economy, within which war as such, even if it remains latent, is nonetheless mimicked—all the more so as it is not actually set in motion. At the limit of these mimicries of an undeniably dramatic nature, willful murder is avoided, duty and debt are cemented together, and power is not released from responsibility.

On Politics as Fear of Death and Will to Survive

As a counterpoint to political imaginaries that make the project of domesticating violence their central object are cultural configurations where politics consists in conserving individual life by virtue of the presupposition of its sacrifice. In other words, the production of political imaginaries hinges on two parameters: the fear of death and the will to survive. During the authoritarian period, many political regimes had cultivated the notion that, in societies marked by cultural differences and ethnic diversity, the foundation of political community must rest, first and foremost, upon the direct or indirect threat to their subjects' individual integrity. Thus, the latter needed to immunize themselves against this threat, not by contesting its foundations, but by measuring, at each step, the risk that such contestation would entail for the conservation of life itself. For individual subjects, immunizing themselves against death involved continually calculating the risk to which their words and actions could expose them—and contriving, at any price, the means of avoiding such a situation or extracting themselves from it (Esposito 2000, 25–30).

In such circumstances, the angle of refraction from which the subject considered life and gauged the political environment was the desire to avoid death at all costs. And it is this desire that the state instrumentalized, not to release subjects from the anxiety that was its corollary, but to build uncertainty. Instability and the unexpected became, from this vantage point, resources for the exercise of power.

But the concern to avoid death at any cost also produces new political imaginaries in those regimes where elites in power since independence have successfully resisted pressure from oppositional forces, where they have been able to impose, unilaterally, the rules of the political process. These rules conform to the most elementary procedural aspects of competition. But they nonetheless allow the elites to maintain their hold on the principal levers of the state and economy and guarantee their continuity of power. Fundamental disagreements between the government and the opposition persist in these countries, and a conflict situation endures in which latent periods alternate with periods of acute violence. In most of these cases, the unilateral imposition of the rules of the political game involved two phases. In the first phase it was a matter of containing the surge of protest, which required a repression that was sometimes cunning, sometimes expedient, brutal, and uncompromising (imprisonments, shootings, imposition of emergency measures, press censorship, diverse forms of economic coercion). Regimes in power also looked for ways to depoliticize social protest, to give an ethnic face to the confrontation, and to characterize street movements as simple riots. During this repressive phase, these regimes expanded the army's role to the overall maintenance and control of people's movements. In certain cases, entire regions were placed under a double military-civilian administration.

Where the established regimes felt the most threatened, they pushed the logic of radicalization to its extreme by inciting or supporting the emergence of gangs or militias, which were controlled either by accomplices operating in the shadows or by military or political officials holding positions of power within formal and visible structures (Anderson 2002). In some cases, the existence of the militias was limited to the period of conflict. In others, the militias gradually acquired autonomy and transformed themselves into veritable armed formations within command structures distinct from those of the regular armed forces (Gore and Pratten 2003). In still other cases, formal military structures served as a cover for outlaw activities, where the multiplication of traffickings went hand in hand with the pillaging of natural resources and private property and outright political repression (McGregor 2002).

Three consequences followed from the fragmentation of the monopoly of force and the inequitable distribution of the means of terror in these societies: first, the dynamics of deinstitutionalization and informalization accelerated; second, a new social division emerged, separating those who are protected from those who are not. Finally, more than ever, political struggles tended to be settled by force, with arms circulation becoming one of the principal elements of social division and a central element in the dynamics of insecurity, preservation of life, and access to property.

In a second phase of the imposition of political rules by elites, it was necessary to divide the opposition by aggravating ethnic tensions and playing internal rivalries off against each other. At times, in regions where the opposition had strong support, local conflicts were stirred up (between natives and outsiders, sedentary groups and nomads, fishers and farmers) to better justify repression. The governing powers then counted on the continuation of these conflicts to weaken protest, dry up internal resources, and foster conditions that would exhaust the masses. This process of exacerbating ethnic conflict and cultural difference also ensured the division of the intelligentsia by reducing its members to defending the interests of their regions and communities of origin. Once this emasculation came about, it was necessary to make concessions, notably by setting in place secondary reforms that left the structure of domination intact. In general, this phase of violence went along with a large-scale thrust toward privatization of the economy. By and large, these regimes managed to radically transform the economic foundations of their domination. The latter would henceforth rest on other material bases.[16]

Thus, no peaceful change of power took place in these countries. Some segments of the opposition rejoined the governing power. The forms of violence and methods of its management took on completely new dimensions. Both urban criminality and rural plundering intensified (Mburu 1999). New forms of carving up territory appeared, where entire zones (rural or urban) escaped the control of the central government (Mitullah and Kibwana 1998), and land conflicts became bitter. But the forms of violent resource appropriation also became more complex, and linkages appeared between the armed forces, police, justice system, and criminal elements. Fixed points of conflict allowed permanent involvement of portions of the military in internal tasks of repression (notably in the cities), in border wars, or in pacification campaigns in rebel regions situated within the confines of the national territory. Significant portions of the police and justice system have used the pairing of war and trafficking to their private advantage.

When changes at the head of the state have not been the result of coups, they have been the result of rebellions sustained from outside. Whether by natural means (sickness) or criminal means (murder, assassination), the death of the autocrat, his disappearance, or his escape—in short, his eviction from power by violence—remains a fundamental part of the political imaginary in the cultural configurations examined above. This *desire to murder* is profoundly linked to the postulate of duration that underlies the experience of power. Given the slim possibility of reversing power by electoral means, only assassination can contradict the principle of uninterrupted continuation of power. In such political cultures, one lives in permanent anticipation of an outcome whose form, contours, actors, and moment seem to elude everybody.[17]

On Politics as a Work of Death

The final cultural configuration is that which defines politics in terms of the possibility that anybody can be killed by anybody else. This possibility is perceived, if not as legitimate, then at least as constituting a general rule or commonly accepted practice. Though it has continuities with the preceding configuration, this one presents characteristics of its own.

First, this configuration rests on a pyramid of modes of destroying life, whereas the former dwelled on the conditions of life's conservation and the price paid to that end. Second, in establishing a relationship of relative equality through the capacity to kill and be killed—a relative equality that hinges on the possession or the nonpossession of weapons—this configuration allows politics to express itself, fundamentally, as a work of death. Third, in elevating violence to sometimes convulsive, sometimes parodic forms, this cultural configuration foregrounds the functional character of terror, fright, and panic and makes possible the destruction of all social bonds—other than the bond of hostility. It is this bond of hostility that explains the relationship of active disassociation, of which war is but one violent expression. It is equally this bond of hostility that allows the idea to be instituted and normalized according to which power can be acquired and exercised only at the cost of the lives of others, and where, essentially, one can only "politically live together" at the cost of the death of the other.[18]

Three processes have played a determining role in this regard. The first concerns *the forms of differentiation within military institutions* over the last quarter of the twentieth century. The second involves changes in the law of distribution of weapons within African societies during the period considered. The last concerns the emergence of militarism as a political culture founded on the use of force and the emergence of an ethic of masculinity that rests on the public and violent expression of acts of virility.

Concerning the first process, it is important to note that military institutions underwent significant transformation in the closing years of the twentieth century. Those years coincided with the end of armed anticolonial struggles and the appearance, then spread, of a new generation of wars that have introduced several key characteristics. For a start, their principal targets are not so much hostile armed formations as civilian populations (Le Pape and Solignan 2001). In addition, their central stake is the control of resources, whose modes of extraction and forms of commercialization feed, in turn, the murderous conflicts and practices of predation (Samset 2002). And, in order to legitimize their exploits, actors in these wars no longer resort to anti-imperialist rhetoric or to any project of emancipation or social revolutionary transformation, as was the case in the 1960s and 1970s. They draw instead upon moral categories whose uniqueness lies in combining imaginaries of modern utilitarianism with residues of autochthonous philosophies of *being*—on life and governance of oneself (*self-craft*)—hence the preponderance of tropes and dichotomies that draw upon ontology, degeneracy, and theologies of health: death and corruption, evil and sorcery, wealth and devouring, illness and madness, conversion and redemption, judgment and damnation, and the like.

This new cycle of war has come about at the same time that armies have undergone increasing internal differentiation. First, a growing internal inequality developed within military institutions; complicated by economic crisis, life conditions in the barracks deteriorated. In several countries this accelerated pauperization of the troops (often accompanied by the non-payment of wages) was the source of violence and public disorder. Next, racketeering became standard practice, the soldiery not hesitating to establish roadside barriers or even to organize open raids against the civilian population for the purpose of acquiring or confiscating belongings. The technologies of political control became ever more tactile—indeed, anatomical—as the armed forces ranged more freely across societies and intruded ever more violently into the various spheres of everyday life. In contexts where, as we have seen, struggles for survival increasingly focused on opportunities for mobility, the exercise of control took the form of a frenetic multiplication of "permits" whose possession was a precondition for movement. Under these conditions, the highest echelons of the army were able to create their own customs and contraband networks—when they were not investing in arms and mineral trafficking and other lucrative operations.

The second process that has played a direct role in the generalization of combative relations is the overturning of the law of weapons distribution within the societies under consideration. In this context, "law of weapons distribution" must be understood simply as the quality of power relations that develops whenever political disagreement and other forms of dispute can be settled by recourse to the force of arms. As already indicated, the last quarter of the twentieth century was characterized by the progressive loss of the state's monopoly on violence as this monopoly gradual devolved to a multiplicity of authorities that operated with relative autonomy, either outside the state or within. The breakdown of this monopoly also sanctioned the appearance of private operators and entrepreneurs of violence, some of whom have gradually acquired the ability to organize and mobilize human and material resources with warfare in mind. More than merely access to arms, or the speed of their circulation, it is this capacity to capture and remobilize the resources of violence that makes a critical difference and that follows from radical change in the law of distribution of arms in society.

There thus emerges *a new form of governmentality*. Both the exercise and object of power have fundamentally altered. It is no longer so much a matter of "suppressing" or "disciplining" as "killing en masse." Where formerly a great rupture existed between the state and society, another power economy has emerged, which is characterized by multiple and capillary relations of force at the level of both state and society and in the relation between the two. There is no more telling site of this shattering of the distinction between state and society than in the techniques of war. As has already been indicated, war no long necessarily sets armies against each other or sovereign states against each other. War increasingly sets armed formations acting under state cover against stateless armies that nonetheless control well-defined territories; both sides in these conflicts have civilian populations, whether unarmed or constituted in militias, as their targets.

The regulation of the population thus takes place in very large part through war, which itself increasingly involves a process of selecting and appropriating resources necessary for the reproduction of life. The forces that shape life—that order and manage it—are essentially forces that are armed or that act through the mediation of arms, whether in combat situations or in the banal circumstances of everyday life. Under these conditions, power is infinitely more brutal than it was during the authoritarian period. Its intent is no longer to discipline as such. If it still maintains its tight grid of bodies (or their agglomeration within camps or so-called security zones), this is not so much to inscribe them in disciplinary apparatuses as to better inscribe them, when the time comes, within the order of that maximal economy that has become the "massacre"—a more or less updated form of age-old human sacrifices (Law 1985). The widespread experience of insecurity has, in turn, sharpened the social distinction between those who carry weapons (both creators of insecurity and purveyors of protection) and those who, because they lack them, perpetually run the risk of seeing their lives and property forfeited.

When contemporary wars have led to the military victory of one of the parties in conflict, they have not necessarily been followed by liberalization of the regimes thus put in place by force. To the contrary, what have emerged are social formations and political entities that combine traits of military principalities, predisposed to combative relations; tyrannies, formed by an armed nucleus and cliques that exercise quasi-absolute control over long-distance trade and natural resources; and, in certain cases, authoritarian regimes attired in "developmentalist" guise. In cases where armed dissidents have not vanquished state power in its entirety, they have provoked territorial divisions and succeeded in controlling entire regions that they administer on the model of colonial concessioner societies (Coquery-Vidrovitch 1972), especially where mining deposits are found (e.g., diamonds in Sierra Leone and Angola). In some cases, no military or state administration exists as such. The administration of public affairs is carried out by means of family clans, while the amassing of wealth is left in the hands of private operators (Prunier 2000).

Territorial fragmentation thus takes various forms: emerging regional fiefdoms controlled by independent forces, each receiving marketable resources from and backed by neighboring states (as with Congo-Kinshasa, Sierra Leone, and Somalia); war zones on the borders of neighboring states

(Uganda, Eritrea, Ethiopia, Sudan, and Rwanda); breakaway provinces or regions within national boundaries (Angola, Uganda, and Casamance); security belts around capitals and adjacent regions (Congo-Brazzaville); internment camps of civilian populations deemed close to the rebels (Burundi and Rwanda); economic predation with the support of mercenaries from distant places (like Ukraine, Romania, Bulgaria, and South Africa); and general practices of dehumanization in war zones (Liberia, Congo-Kinshasa, Angola, Sierra Leone, and Sudan).

War as a new form of governmentality draws on the debris of *bodies of knowledge* or, at the very least, *fragments of discourse* meant to legitimate it. These bodies of knowledge and discourse no longer rest on a single "archive," such as the "anticolonial archive" and its various vulgates (national liberation, anti-imperialism, revolution, and so forth). They rarely refer, as in former times, to a collective emancipation project or to revolutionary social transformation. To be sure, the rhetoric on eradication of corruption, protection of the environment, or minority rights—integral parts of the international lexicon—still supplies connotations of a fundamental moral conflict to some of these disagreements. But these miscellaneous relics of knowledge and fragments of discourse are drawn from quite diverse sources.

Some of these discursive fragments are founded on the violent manipulation of utopias. They blend together the desire for sacrifice, the will to eliminate existing tyrannies, and ideologies aiming at dissolving differences linked to race or the survival of ethnic groups who perceive themselves as threatened. Others draw their central categories from indigenous interpretations of the social world in terms of illness, misfortune, and healing (Janzen 1982). War, under these conditions, appears as an immense therapeutic liturgy. Still others rely on kernels of meaning extracted from monotheistic religions or messianic eschatologies of a religious sort, when they are not borrowing their normative models from autochthonous imaginaries of the occult. Others claim to inscribe themselves on the horizon of a modernity whose materialist, utilitarianist, and hedonistic dimensions they seek to commandeer.[19]

But whatever their discursive underpinnings, their political manifestations are achieved through grueling wars, in the course of which thousands—indeed, hundreds of thousands—are massacred, and hundreds of thousands are either displaced or confined in camps (Hyndman 1999). As a result, the dominant political culture distinguishes itself from all others by the high degree of articulation between the production of political utopias and death en masse. The "styles of killing" themselves hold little variation; neither do the aftermaths of death. In the case of massacres, especially, bodies divested of being are quickly returned to the state of skeletons. The morphology of these skeletons is now inscribed in the register of an *undifferentiated generality:* simple remains of an unburied pain, emptied and meaningless corporealities, strange repositories submerged in a cruel stupor. In the case of the Rwandan genocide, where a large number of skeletons were, if not exhumed, at least conserved in a visible state, a tension remains between the *petrification of bones,* with their strange coldness, and their obstinate desire to signify something meaningful. There does not seem to be, in these fragments marked with impassivity, any ataraxia: nothing but the illusory defiance of a death already come to pass.[20]

In other cases, where physical amputation replaces immediate death, the removal of limbs opens the way to the deployment of incision techniques, of removals and excisions, which here, too, have the osseous phenomenon as their object. The vestiges of this demiurgic surgery remain long after the event, in the form of human figures undoubtedly alive but in whom the corporeal totality has been replaced by pieces, fragments, folds, indeed massive wounds difficult to close again; wounds that serve constantly to place under the gaze of the victim the morbid spectacle of his or her transition from the realm of flesh.

The Relationship of Reciprocal Negation

The third process directly linked to the escalation of combative relations is *the emergence of a culture of militarism,* which, as I have already indicated, rests on an ethic of masculinity that assigns a large place to the violent and public expression of acts of virility. The successive crises of the last quarter of the twentieth century have variously affected relations between men and women and between men and children. In some cases, they have played a role in deepening already-existing inequalities between the sexes. In others, they have entailed a deep modification of the general terms in and through which both masculine domination and femininity were expressed.[21]

Among the most diminished categories of social relationship is the status of "head of family," generally held by men, which has declined especially starkly in places where the power to provide can no longer be exercised. In short, the new cycle of subsistence struggles generated by crisis has opened possibilities of "movement" for relatively small numbers, and women have played a disproportionately influential role in the process, particularly in spheres of material life that depend on informal or illegal activity (see Niger-Thomas 2001). These increased opportunities for mobility have accompanied a renewed contestation of masculine prerogatives and an intensification of violent relations between the sexes (Oyekani 2000; Posel 2003)—a development that has led, in turn, to two major consequences, generally passed over in silence by analysts. First, one of the pillars of masculine domination, namely, the notion of *family debt,* has been strongly undermined and has become an object of acute contestation. This notion had, until recently, been constituted in terms of the asymmetrical relations within the family between men and women and between men and children. One of the cornerstones of African phallocratic systems was, in fact, the idea of the debt of sons with regard to fathers and that of the *complementarity of inequality* between men and women. The view that, because he comes from the father and is supposed to be engendered by him, the child—and notably the son—is like a *possession* came close to being a dominant ideology in African forms of patriarchy.

The relationship between the man and woman within the family proceeded from a logic with two levers: that of *appropriation* and that of *reciprocal instrumentality between unequals.* With regard to the woman, as with the child, the masculine prerogative involved feeding, protecting, and guiding, in return for which a form of domination was exercised, founded on the narcissistic constitution of the masculine self (ideologies of seduction and virility) and the discriminations of patrimony. It so happens that the culture of militarism rests in large part on these same frameworks, which it reproduces in the domestic sphere and, above all, which it extends to the civil and political sphere. Here armed men perform, with regard to those who are nothing to them, the same functions as those of the father in the family unit and have at their disposal some of the same attributes. Under these conditions, the military prerogative becomes the masculine prerogative par excellence. An active process of demasculinization thus strikes the whole of civil society as the pleasure of male domination becomes exclusively the privilege of "military" society.

Another modality of domination could be called *domination of the phallic variety.* This form of domination is all the more strategic in the crystallization of power relations not only because it rests on a mobilization of the subjective underpinnings of masculinity and femininity but also because it has direct and intimate links to the general sexual economy. From this perspective, it refers to the psychic life of power as such (Butler 1997). Indeed, at the center of certain African constructions of masculinity and power has been the phallus (Mbembe 2001). Masculine domination derives a large part of its power and drama less from putting life in danger during wartime than from the capacity of the male individual to prove his manliness at the expense of the woman, to gain masculine validation through the very one who is subjugated.[22]

But far from leading to a subsiding of battles between the sexes, the crisis over the functions of masculinization and power has led to increasing manifestations of brutality in everyday relations. Bit by bit, there are scarcely any acts of violence that do not leave imprints on the victims' bodies, as if there is no longer any pleasure, however brief, that does not express itself through a hardening of the dichotomy of the sexes. Also emerging, if not in the public sphere then at least in the collective unconscious, are previously repressed forms of sexuality such as homosexuality and lesbianism.[23] Faced with the impression—widespread among men—of threatening feminization, *rites of affirmation of manhood,* homophobia among them, are multiplying. Reinforced by the context of war, a tension is foregrounded between that which is threatened with abolition and that which has already been eliminated—this consolidating the relation of substitutability between the phallus and the gun.

In one respect (at least for many of the child-soldiers who now form the main body of troops) the affirmation of manhood itself takes place by way of the gun. The possession of a gun acts as an equivalent to the acquisition of a phallus at the end of the virginal age. But the mediations between the gun and the phallus are not just imaginary. Giving death by means of a gun takes place almost simultaneously with being put to the test by the sexual act—in this case, generally, by means of collective rape. In another respect, to own a gun is to enjoy a position of almost unlimited access to sexual goods; above all, it is to gain access in a very tactile way to a particular form of abundance in which the woman is constituted as the surplus—that which can be spent without worry of replenishment.

Finally, the sexual act itself succeeds in becoming not just an element of rape but of violence as well: rape, insofar as access to the woman's interiority takes place by forced entry; violence, insofar as force is used to possess and dominate an alien will, as it would be used in battle. Thus are pleasure by means of the gun and pleasure by means of the phallus fused. In the first case, pleasure is consummated through the production of an inert body emptied of all life. In the second case, it is consummated by a release as violent as it is brief: the orgasmic abatement by means of which the power to take pleasure is converted into the power of radical objectification of the other, whose body one torments, hollows, and drains in the very act of rape.

Conclusion

All of these developments indicate that, far from being linear, the trajectories of political transformation in Africa are quite varied. Moreover, they are hardly irreversible. Although the routes followed by different countries certainly present significant differences, they also bear witness to deep convergences. Or rather, in each country a concatenation and entanglement of configurations is increasingly found. The forms of the political imagination are diverse as well. They rely on paradoxical logics that, for this very fact, challenge the dichotomies generally accepted in traditional analyses of politics and cultural production in Africa. As for the rest, the material conditions of life's production have been profoundly transformed during the last quarter of the twentieth century. These transformations were accompanied by a decisive shift in paradigms and imaginaries of power, politics, and conflict. At the same time a range of new operations have appeared, whose articulation and dissemination, and whose interlacing with heterogeneous forces, have gradually altered the routine connections that had been established between life, power, and death.

Notes

1. See the recent special issues of the journal *Politique Africaine,* for example, on Côte d'Ivoire (2003), Liberia, Sierra Leone, and Guinea (2002), and the Democratic Republic of Congo (2001). See also Cilliers and Dietrich 2000; Ellis 1999; Richards 1996; Allen 1991; Wilson 1992; Geffray 1990.
2. On the notion of "expenditure," see Bataille 1967.
3. Bataille treats "excretion" as one of the two polarized human impulses, the other being "appropriation," the elementary form of which is oral consumption. Excretion, he affirms, appears as a consequence of a heterogeneity. It releases various impulses, that of ambivalence being particularly well known. See Bataille 1970, 58–60.
4. For a fictional rendition of this power, see Kourouma 2000.
5. On the connections between life and power and the possibility of defining politics through its relation to life, see Foucault's analyses of "biopower" and "governmentality" (1994) and Agamben 1998. See *Multitudes* 2000 for a critique of the notion of "biopolitics."
6. On historical aspects of imaginaries on long distance, see, e.g., Boahen 1962; Johnson 1976; Stewart 1976.
7. If economic analyses of this period's monetary policies are often taken into account, such is not the case for the relations between currency and the social imagination in general. However, see Stiansen and Guyer 2000; Guyer 1994; Vallée 1989.
8. On this issue, see the general discussions in the special issue of *Economies et Sociétés* (1996).
9. For an orthodox reading of these phenomena, see Holmes 2002.
10. On problems brought about, in particular, by inflationary pressures, and on the manner in which these pressures have in turn structured the struggles for money and survival in urban areas, see Guyer, Denzer, and Agbaje 2002.

11. On other approaches to "debt," see Roitman 2003b.

12. For this sort of "city," see the contributions gathered in *Hommes et Migrations* 2000, as well as Faist 1998.

13. On the topic of this hedonism, see Monga 2005.

14. Countless studies have appeared on "informalization" practices in Africa. Unfortunately, most limit themselves to economic aspects or to those concerning strategies for material survival, either accumulation strategies or relationships between the "informal" sector and the state. Very few have dwelled upon informalization practices as contemporary forms of the cultural and political imagination. They have been even less concerned with identifying and analyzing the relations between these processes and the constitution of new arenas of power. It is these last two aspects that I refer to when using the term "informalization" in the present study.

15. On this subject, see the compilation assembled in Nohlen, Krennerich, and Thibaut 1999.

16. This calls to mind various situations in Eastern Europe. See especially Windolf 1998; Misztal 1996.

17. If, during the 1970s, coups were carried out in the name of the "revolution" or under the pretext of safeguarding national unity or to put an end to the waste and corruption of civil regimes, the democratization movement has, from the beginning of the 1990s, dealt the military regimes a different hand, obliging them to find new forms of legitimation. Some of them have become "civilianized" in the process, often at the conclusion of controversial elections (e.g., Ghana, Burkina Faso). The failure of multipartyism in several countries has, however, privileged the emergence of new forms of praetorianisms, whose main justification has now become to break the impasses to which the failed democratizing process has led (e.g., Niger, Côte d'Ivoire). On the international level, however, the military regimes have had less and less room to maneuver. And many of them hold power for relatively short periods and on the condition of indicating a timeline for the return to civil government. A new cycle of coups has thus opened up. In fact, it is no longer uncommon to see civilian opposition parties themselves calling upon the army. In most cases, this shortcut allows them to sidestep the electoral path and to share power within transitional governments.

18. This categorization has been aided by Roberto Esposito's study (2000).

19. On various readings and critiques of these dimensions, see Bataille 1991; Bennett 1999; Comaroff and Comaroff 1999.

20. For a rendering of these conditions in contemporary African fiction, see B. Diop 2000.

21. On these transformations, see, e.g., Ashforth 1999; Sindjoun 2000.

22. On the idea of "natural death" and its relations to forms of glorification of manhood, see Rauch 2000, chap. 2.

23. On homosexuality, see McLean and Ngcobo 1995; Murray and Roscoe 1998; Epprecht 1998; Donham 1998.

References

Agamben, Giorgio. 1998. *Homo Sacer: Sovereign Power and Bare Life.* Trans. Daniel Heller-Roazen. Stanford, CA: Stanford University Press.

Allen, T. 1991. "Understanding Alice: Uganda's Holy Spirit Movement in Context." *Africa* 61:370–99.

Anderson, David M. 2002. "Vigilantes, Violence and the Politics of Public Order in Kenya." *African Affairs* 101:531–55.

Ashforth, Adam. 1999. "Weighing Manhood in Soweto." *CODESRIA Bulletin* 3/4:51–58.

———. 2005. *Witchcraft, Violence, and Democracy in Post-apartheid South Africa.* Chicago: University of Chicago Press.

Babu, Cheikh Anta. 2002. "Brotherhood Solidarity, Education and Migration: The Role of the *Dahiras* among the Murid Muslim Community of New York." *African Affairs* 101:151–70.

Bales, Kevin. 1999. *Disposable People: New Slavery in the Global Economy.* Berkeley and Los Angeles: University of California Press.

Bataille, Georges. 1967. *La part maudite, précédé de la notion de dépense.* Paris: Minuit. Translated by Robert Hurley as *The Accursed Share: An Essay on General Economy,* 3 vols. in 2 (New York: Zone Books, 1988–91).

———. 1970. *Oeuvres complètes.* Vol. 2, *Ecrits posthumes, 1922–40.* Paris: Gallimard.

Bates, Robert H. 1981. *Markets and States in Tropical Africa: The Political Basis of Agricultural Policies.* Berkeley and Los Angeles: University of California Press.

Bayart, Jean-François, Achille Mbembe, and Comi M. Toulabor. 1993. *Le politique par le bas: Contribution à une problématique de la démocratie en Afrique noire.* Paris: Karthala.

Bennett, David. 1999. "Burghers, Burglars, and Masturbators: The Sovereign Spender in the Age of Consumerism." *New Literary History* 30:269–94.

Berry, Sara. 1989. "Social Institutions and Access to Resources." *Africa* 59(1):41–55.

Bierschenk, Thomas, and Jean-Pierre Olivier de Sardan. 1998. *Les pouvoirs au village: Le Bénin rural entre democratization et decentralization.* Paris: Karthala.

Boahen, A. Adu. 1962. "The Caravan Trade in the Nineteenth Century." *Journal of African History* 3(2):349–57.

Boone, Catherine. 1992. *Merchant Capital and the Roots of State Power in Senegal, 1930–1985.* Cambridge: Cambridge University Press.

Brinkman, I. 2000. "Ways of Death: Accounts of Terror from Angolan Refugees in Namibia." *Africa* 70:1–24.

Bryceson, Deborah F. 2002. "Multiplex Livelihoods in Rural Africa." *Journal of Modern African Studies* 40(1):1–28.

Brydon, Lynne. 1999. "'With a Little Bit of Luck . . .': Coping with Adjustment in Urban Ghana, 1975–90." *Africa* 69(3):366–85.

Butler, Judith. 1997. *The Psychic Life of Power.* Stanford, CA: Stanford University Press.

———. 1999. "Revisiting Bodies and Pleasures." *Theory, Culture, and Society* 16(2):11–20.

Castoriadis, Cornelius. 2002. *Sujet et vérité dans le monde social-historique, séminaires, 1986–1987: La création humaine I.* Paris: Seuil.

Cilliers, Jakkie, and Christian Dietrich, eds. 2000. *Angola's War Economy: The Role of Oil and Diamonds.* Pretoria, RSA: Institute of Security Studies.

Comaroff, Jean, and John L. Comaroff. 1999. "Alien-Nation: Zombies, Immigrants, and Millenial Capitalism." *CODESRIA Bulletin* 3/4:17–28.

Coquery-Vidrovitch, Catherine. 1972. *Le Congo au temps des companies concessionaires, 1898–1930.* Paris: Mouton.

De Boek, Filip. 1998. "Domesticating Diamonds and Dollars: Identity, Expenditure and Sharing in Southwestern Zaire (1984–1997)." *Development and Change* 29:777–810.

de Haan, Arjan. 1999. "Livelihoods and Poverty: The Role of Migration; A Critical Review of the Migration Literature." *Journal of Development Studies* 36(2):1–47.

de Heusch, Luc. 2002. "L'ennemi 'ethnique.'" *Raisons Politiques* 5:53–67.

Diop, Boubacar Boris. 2000. *Murambi: Le livre des ossements*. Paris: Stock.

Diop, Coumba, ed. 1994. *Senegal: Essays in Statecraft*. Also published in French as *Sénégal: Trajectoires d'un état* (Dakar, Senegal: CODESRIA, 1992).

Diouf, Mamadou. 2000. "The Murid Trade Diaspora and the Making of a Vernacular Cosmopolitism." *Public Culture* 12:679–702.

Donham, Donald. 1998. "Freeing South Africa: The 'Modernization' of Male-Male Sexuality in Soweto." *Cultural Anthropology* 13(1):3–21.

Economies et Sociétés. 1996. Special issue, "Change, compétition et répartition des rôles entre monnaies." Vol. 33.

Edkins, Jenny. 2000. "Sovereign Power, Zones of Indistinction, and the Camp." *Alternatives* 25:3–25.

Ellis, Stephen. 1999. *The Mask of Anarchy: The Destruction of Liberia and the Religious Dimension of an African War*. New York: New York University Press.

Epprecht, Marc. 1998. "The 'Unsaying' of Indigenous Homosexualities in Zimbabwe: Mapping a Blindspot in an African Masculinity." *Journal of Southern African Studies* 24(4):631–51.

Esposito, Roberto. 2000. *Communitas: Origine et destin de la communauté*. Paris: Presses Universitaires de France.

Eyoh, Dickson. 1998. "Conflicting Narratives of Anglophone Protest and the Politics of Identity in Cameroon." *Journal of Contemporary African Studies* 16(2):249–76.

Faist, Thomas. 1998. "Transnational Social Spaces out of International Migration: Evolution, Significance and Future Prospects." *Archives Européennes de Sociologie* 39(2): 213–47.

Fall, A. S. 1998. "Migrants' Long Distance Relationships and Social Networks in Dakar." *Environment and Urbanization* 10(1):135–45.

Fisiy, Cyprian, and Miriam Goheen. 1998. "Power and the Quest for Recognition: Neotraditional Titles among the New Elite in Nso, Cameroon." *Africa* 68(3):383–481.

Foucault, Michel. 1994. *Dits et écrits*. Vol. 3. Paris: Gallimard.

———. 1997. "Il faut défendre la sociéte." In *Cours au Collège de France de 1976*. Paris: Gallimard/Seuil.

———. 2003. *Society Must Be Defended: Lectures at the College de France, 1975–1976*. Ed. Mauro Bertani and Alessandro Fontana. Trans. David Macey. New York: Pidacor.

Geffray, Christian. 1990. *La cause des armes au Mozambique: Anthropologie d'une guerre civile*. Paris: Karthala.

Geschiere, Peter. 1995. *État et sorcellerie au Cameroun*. Paris: Karthala.

———. 2004. "Ecology, Belonging and Xenophobia: The 1994 Forest Law in Cameroon and the Issue of 'Community.'" In *Rights and the Politics of Recognition in Africa*, ed. Harri Englund and Francis Nyamnjoh. London: Zed Books.

Geschiere, Peter, and Francis Nyamnjoh. 2000. "Capitalism and Autochthony: The Seesaw of Mobility and Belonging." *Public Culture* 12(2):423–52.

Gore, Charles, and David Pratten. 2003. "The Politics of Plunder: The Rhetorics of Order and Disorder in Southern Nigeria." *African Affairs* 102:211–40.

Guyer, Jane I., ed. 1994. *Money Matters: Instability, Values and Social Payments in the Modern History of West African Communities*. Portsmouth, NH: Heinemann.

Guyer, Jane I., LaRay Denzer, and Adiqun Agbaje, eds. 2002. *Money Struggles and City Life: Devaluation in the Popular Economy in Nigeria, 1986–96*. Portsmouth, NH: Heinemann.

Hart, Keith. 1988. "Kinship, Contract and Trust: The Economic Organization of Migrants in an African City Slum." In *Trust: The Making and Breaking of Cooperative Relations*, ed. Diego Gambetta. London: Basil Blackwell.

Harts-Broekhuis, A. 1997. "How to Sustain a Living: Urban Households and Poverty in a Sahelian Town of Mopti, Africa." *Africa* 67(1):106–31.

Hibou, Béatrice. 1999. *La privatisation des états*. Paris: Karthala.

Holmes, Mark J. 2002."The Inflationary Effects of Effective Exchange Rate Depreciation in Selected African Countries." *Journal of African Economies* 11(2):201–18.

Hommes et Migrations. 2000. Special issue, "Marseille, carrefour d'Afrique." No. 1224.

Hyndman, Jennifer. 1999. "A Post–Cold War Geography of Forced Migration in Kenya and Somalia." *Professional Geographer* 51(1):104–14.

Jackson, Stephen. 2002. "Making a Killing: Criminality and Coping in the Kivu War Economy." *Review of African Political Economy* 29(93):517–36.

Janzen, John M. 1982. *Lemba, 1650–1930: A Drum of Affliction in Africa and the New World*. New York: Garland Publishing.

Johnson, Marion. 1976. "Calico Caravans: The Tripoli-Kano Trade after 1880." *Journal of African History* 17(1):73–93.

Kistner, Ulrike. 2002. "Sovereign Power and Bare Life with HIV/AIDS: Biopolitics South African Style." Unpublished manuscript.

Kourouma, Ahmadou. 2000. *Allah n'est pas obligé*. Paris: Seuil.

Kupferberg, Feiwel. 1998. "Models of Creativity Abroad: Migrants, Strangers and Travellers." *Archives Européennes de Sociologie* 39(1):179–206.

Law, Robin. 1985. "Human Sacrifice in Pre-colonial West Africa." *African Affairs* 84:53–87.

Le Pape, Marc. 1997. *L'énergie sociale à Abidjan*. Paris: Karthala.

Le Pape, Marc, and Pierre Solignan. 2001. *Une guerre contre les civils: Réflexions sur les pratiques humanitaires au Congo Brazzaville (1998–2000)*. Paris: Karthala.

Lugalla, Joe L. P. 1995. *Crisis, Urbanization, and Urban Poverty in Tanzania: A Study of Urban Poverty and Survival Politics*. Lanham, MD: University Presses of America.

Makumbe, John, and Daniel Compagnon, eds. 2000. *Behind the Smokescreen: The Politics of Zimbabwe's 1995 General Elections*. Harare: University of Zimbabwe Publications.

Marie, A. 1995. "'Y a pas l'argent': L'endetté insolvable et le créancier floué, deux figures complémentaires de la pauvreté abidjanaise. *Revue Tiers Monde* 36:1301–24.

Mbembe, Achille. 1997. "The 'Thing' and Its Double in Cameroonian Cartoons." In *Readings in African Popular Culture*, ed. Karen Barber. Bloomington: Indiana University Press.

———. 2000. "At the Edge of the World: Boundaries, Territoriality, and Sovereignty in Africa." *Public Culture* 12(1):259–84.

———. 2001. *On the Postcolony*. Berkeley and Los Angeles: University of California Press.

———. 2003. "Necropolitics." *Public Culture* 15(1):11–40.

Mbembe, Achille, and Janet Roitman. 1995. "Figures of the Subject in Times of Crisis." *Public Culture* 7(2):323–52.

Mburu, Nene. 1999. "Contemporary Banditry in the Horn of Africa: Causes, History and Political Implications." *Nordic Journal of African Studies* 8(2):89–107.

McGregor, JoAnn. 1998. "Violence and Social Change in a Border Economy: War in the Maputo Hinterland, 1984–1992." *Journal of Southern African Studies* 24(1):37–60.

————. 2002. "The Politics of Disruption: War Veterans and the Local State in Zimbabwe." *African Affairs* 101:9–37.

McLean, Hugh, and Linda Ngcobo. 1995. "'*Abangibhamayo Bathi Ngimnandi*' (Those Who Fuck Me Say I'm Tasty): Gay Sexuality in Reef Townships." In *Defiant Desire,* ed. Mark Gevisser and Edwin Cameron. New York: Routledge.

Meyer, Birgit. 1999. *Translating the Devil.* Edinburgh: Edinburgh University Press.

Misztal, B. A. 1996. "Postcommunist Ambivalence: Becoming of a New Formation?" *Archives Européenes de Sociologie* 37(1):104–40.

Mitullah, Winnie V., and Kivutha Kibwana. 1998. "A Tale of Two Cities: Policy, Law and Illegal Settlements in Kenya." In *Illegal Cities: Law and Urban Change in Developing Countries,* ed. Edésio Fernandes and Ann Varley. London: ZedBooks.

Monga, Célestin. 2005. "Let's Eat." In *Beautiful-Ugly: African and Diasporic Ethics,* ed. Sarah Nuttall. Cape Town, RSA: Kwela Books.

Mubarak, Jamil A. 2002. "A Case of Private Supply of Money in Stateless Somalia." *Journal of African Economies* 11(3):309–25.

Multitudes. 2000. "Biopolitique et biopouvoir." Theme issue, no. 1 (March).

Murray, Stephen, and Will Roscoe, eds. 1998. *Boy-Wives and Female Husbands: Studies in African Homosexualities.* New York: St. Martin's Press.

Niehaus, Isak A. 2001. *Witchcraft, Power, and Politics: Exploring the Occult in the South African Lowveld.* London: Pluto Press.

Niger-Thomas, Margaret. 2001. "Women and the Arts of Smuggling in Western Cameroon." *African Studies Review* 44(2):43–70.

Nohlen, Dieter, Michael Krennerich, and Bernhard Thibaut, eds. 1999. *Elections in Africa: A Data Handbook.* Oxford: Oxford University Press.

Oyekani, Felicia, ed. 2000. *Men, Women and Violence.* Dakar, Senegal: CODESRIA.

Pérouse de Montclos, Marc Antoine. 1999. "Pétrole et conflits communautaires au Nigeria: Perspectives historiques." *Afrique Contemporaine* 190:20–38.

Politique Africaine. 2001. "RDC: la guerre vue d'en-bas." Vol. 84.

————. 2002. "Liberia, Sierra Leone, Guinée: La regionalization de la guerre." Vol. 88.

————. 2003. "La Côte d'Ivoire en guerre: Dynamiques du dedans et du dehors." Vol. 89.

Posel, Deborah. 2003. "The Scandal of Manhood: Unmaking Secrets of Sexual Violence in Post-apartheid South Africa." Paper presented at the "Sex and Secrecy" conference, University of the Witwatersrand, June.

Prunier, Gérard. 2000. "Recomposition de la nation somalienne." *Le monde diplomatique* 553:23.

Rauch, André. 2000. *Le premier sexe: Mutations et crise de l'identité masculine.* Paris: Hachette.

Richards, Paul. 1996. *Fighting for the Rain Forest: War, Youth, and Resources in Sierra Leone.* Portsmouth, NH: Heinemann.

Roitman, Janet. 2003a. "The Ethics of Illegality in the Chad Basin." Paper presented at the African Studies Association annual conference, Boston, November.

————. 2003b. "Unsanctioned Wealth; or, The Productivity of Debt in Northern Cameroon." *Public Culture* 15(2):211–37.

Samset, Ingrid. 2002. "Conflict of Interests or Interests in Conflict? Diamonds and War in DRC." *Review of African Political Economy* 29(93):463–80.

Simone, Abdou M. 2001. "On the Worlding of Cities in Africa." *African Studies Review* 44(2):15–41.

Sindjoun, Luc, ed. 2000. *La biographie sociale du sexe: Genre, société et changement au Cameroun*. Paris: Karthala.

Stewart, Charles C. 1976. "Southern Saharan Scholarship and the *Bilad Al-Sudan*." *Journal of African History* 17(1):73–93.

Stiansen, Endre, and Jane Guyer, eds. 2000. *Credit, Currencies and Culture: African Financial Institutions in Historical Perspective*. Uppsala: Nordic Africa Institute.

Sumata, Claude. 2002. "Migradollars and Poverty Alleviation Strategy Issues in Congo." *Review of African Political Economy* 29(3):619–28.

Trager, Lillian. 1998. "Home-Town Linkages and Local Development in South-western Nigeria: Whose Agenda? What Impact?" *Africa* 68(3):360–82.

Vallée, Olivier. 1989. *Le prix de l'argent CFA: Heurs et malheurs de la zone franc*. Paris: Karthala.

Vidal, Claudine. 1991. *Sociologie des passions*. Paris: Karthala.

Vlassenroot, Koen. 2002. "Citizenship, Identity Formation and Conflict in South Kivu." *Review of African Political Economy* 29(3):499–515.

Warnier, Jean-Pierre. 1993. *L'esprit d'entreprise au Cameroun*. Paris: Karthala.

Wilson, Ken. 1992. "Cults of Violence and Counterviolence in Mozambique." *Journal of Southern African Studies* 18:527–82.

Windolf, Paul. 1998. "Privatization and Elite Reproduction in Eastern Europe." *Archives Européenes de Sociologie* 39(2):335–76.

Contributors

Teresa P. R. Caldeira is Associate Professor of Anthropology at the University of California, Irvine. Her research has focused on the interconnections among urban violence, spatial segregation, and democratization. Currently, she is studying changing gender and generational roles among São Paulo youth under neoliberal conditions. Her book *City of Walls: Crime, Segregation, and Citizenship in São Paulo* won the 2001 Senior Book Award of the American Ethnological Society.

Jean Comaroff is the Bernard E. and Ellen C. Sunny Distinguished Service Professor, University of Chicago. John L. Comaroff is the Harold H. Swift Distinguished Service Professor, University of Chicago, and a Senior Research Fellow at the American Bar Foundation. Both are Honorary Professors at the University of Cape Town. Jean is the author of *Body of Power, Spirit of Resistance;* together they have coauthored *Of Revelation and Revolution* and *Ethnography and the Historical Imagination.* They have also coedited, among other books, *Modernity and Its Malcontents, Civil Society and the Political Imagination in Africa,* and *Millennial Capitalism and the Culture of Neoliberalism.* They are currently completing *The Metaphysics of Disorder: Crime, Policing, and the State in a Brave Neo World.*

Peter Geschiere is Professor of African Anthropology at the University of Amsterdam and a former professor at Leiden University. His publications include *The Modernity of Witchcraft: Politics and the Occult in Postcolonial Africa.* He has coedited *Globalization and Identity: Dialectics of Flow and Closure* (with Birgit Meyer) and *The Forging of Nationhood* (with Gyan Pandey). He has also written on various aspects of political economy and culture in West Africa. At present he is working on *Autochthony and Citizenship: New Modes in the Politics of Belonging in Africa and Elsewhere.*

Achille Mbembe is Research Professor in History and Politics at the University of the Witwatersrand; his primary scholarly affiliation there is with WISER, the Wits Institute for Social and Economic Research. A former Executive Director of the Council for the Development of Social Science Research in Africa (CODESRIA) in

Dakar, Senegal, he has written extensively on African history, government, and politics and is presently conducting research on the city of Johannesburg in the post-apartheid period. His books include *La naissance du maquis dans le Sud-Cameroun (1920–1960): Histoire des usages de la raison en colonie* and, most recently, *On the Postcolony*, published in both French and English. He is currently completing a book on the political life of sovereignty.

ROSALIND C. MORRIS is Professor of Anthropology at Columbia University, where she is also Associate Director of the Center for Comparative Literature and Society and a former Director of the Institute for Research on Women and Gender. She is the author of *In the Place of Origins: Modernity and Its Mediums in Northern Thailand*, as well as numerous essays on the mass media and visual culture, gender, and the theorization of representation. Presently, she is working on an ethnography of a gold-mining community in South Africa.

JANET ROITMAN is a Research Fellow with the Centre National de la Recherche Scientifique (CNRS). She is a member of the Groupe de Sociologie Politique et Morale (GSPM) and an Associate of the research laboratory Mutations Africaines dans la Longue Durée (MALD) in Paris. She is also an instructor at the Fondation Nationale des Sciences Politiques de Paris. Her recent publications include *Fiscal Disobedience: An Anthropology of Economic Regulation in Central Africa*, "Productivity in the Margins: The Reconstitution of State Power in the Chad Basin," in *Anthropology at the Margins of the State*, edited by Veena Das and Deborah Poole, and "Modes of Governing in the Chad Basin: The Garrison-Entrepôt," in *Global Assemblages: Technology, Politics, and Ethics as Anthropological Problems*, edited by Aiwha Ong and Stephen Collier.

NANCY SCHEPER-HUGHES is Professor of Medical Anthropology at the University of California, Berkeley. She is best known for her ethnographies *Saints, Scholars, and Schizophrenics: Mental Illness in Rural Ireland* and *Death without Weeping: The Violence of Everyday Life in Brazil*. She has also published several edited volumes, including, most recently, *Commodifying Bodies* (with Loic Wacquant) and *Violence in War and Peace* (with Philippe Bourgois). Her contribution to this volume is the product of continuing research and political engagement in the plantation market town of Timbaúba/Bom Jesus da Mata. Her next book will be *Parts Unknown: The Global Traffic in Human Organs*.

PATRICIA SPYER is Professor of Anthropology at Leiden University. She is the author of *The Memory of Trade: Modernity's Entanglements on an Eastern Indo-*

nesian Island, editor of *Border Fetishisms: Material Objects in Unstable Spaces,* and coeditor of the *Handbook of Material Culture.* She has published on, among other topics, violence, media and photography, historical consciousness, and religion. Her current research focuses on the mediations of violence and postviolence in the Moluccas, Indonesia.

Index